Printing Arab Modernity

# Arts and Archaeology of the Islamic World

*Edited by*

Marcus Milwright (*University of Victoria*)
Mariam Rosser-Owen (*Victoria and Albert Museum*)
Lorenz Korn (*University of Bamberg*)

VOLUME 7

The titles published in this series are listed at *brill.com/aaiw*

# Printing Arab Modernity

*Book Culture and The American Press in Nineteenth-Century Beirut*

*By*

Hala Auji

TUTA SUB AEGIDE PALLAS 1683

BRILL

LEIDEN | BOSTON

Cover illustration: People working at the American Press, Beirut, ca. 1856–1910. Source: YDS/RG117/010/0055/0004-Jessup Papers. Courtesy of Special Collections, Yale Divinity School Library.

Want or need Open Access? Brill Open offers you the choice to make your research freely accessible online in exchange for a publication charge. Review your various options on brill.com/brill-open.

Typeface for the Latin, Greek, and Cyrillic scripts: "Brill". See and download: brill.com/brill-typeface.

ISSN 2213-3844
ISBN 978-90-04-30999-9 (hardback)
ISBN 978-90-04-31435-1 (e-book)



This book is printed on acid-free paper and produced in a sustainable manner.

*For Mira, Ramzi, and my parents*

# Contents

Acknowledgements IX
Notes on Transliteration XI
List of Figures XII
List of Abbreviations XV

1 Introduction 1

2 The American Press and Its Legacy 18

3 Evangelizing between Script and Print (1834–1840) 35

4 Print for Shifting Alliances and Readers (1841–1851) 64

5 Protestant Ideals and Arab Intellectual Ambitions (1852–1867) 92

Epilogue 131

*Appendices*

Appendix 1: Annual Number of Arabic Publications from the American Press, 1836–1867 135
Appendix 2: List of Arabic Publications Produced at the American Press, 1836–1867 136

Bibliography 139
Index 150

# Acknowledgements

This book would not have been possible without the help and support of numerous individuals and institutions. I must first extend my deepest gratitude to Nancy Um, my mentor-turned-dear friend, for her unwavering guidance and inspiration throughout the years. Her insightful, detailed, and generous feedback on this project in its various stages was truly exceptional. As any of her former students can attest, her commitment to her advisees is unequaled and extends well into our professional journeys as educators and researchers. I would also like to acknowledge Harvard University's Houghton Library, which allowed me to complete research on this project through a Houghton Mifflin Visiting Fellowship in Publishing History. My sincerest appreciation also goes to Catherine Hansen, who graciously took on the task of reading and editing this book at a very busy and eventful time for her during the last year. I owe a special debt to my friend and fellow historian, Rana Issa, who enthusiastically read and provided astute comments on this book's chapters. Producing this book's index would not have been possible without the dedicated assistance of Rim Assi. In order to get this book through its final stages of production, Patrick McGreevy, Dean of the Faculty of Arts and Sciences at the American University of Beirut, generously offered the necessary support, for which I am thankful. The editors at Brill, particularly Teddi Dols, exhibited great patience and encouragement as I reworked parts of this book, at times extending beyond agreed-upon deadlines. Many more individuals helped by providing comments on various aspects of this study. Although I do not name them all here, I do indicate their helpful contributions in the footnotes of relevant chapters. I must also thank the two anonymous reviewers for their discerning observations and thorough feedback.

Research for this project was possible thanks to the assistance of staff members and directors at numerous institutions and libraries in Lebanon and the United States. Dr. Kaoukab Chebaro and Ms. Samar Mikati Kaissi of the American University of Beirut's Archives and Special Collections went out of their way to assist me with my research requests and graciously provided me with images for this book. Personnel at Harvard University's Houghton Library kindly made countless boxes from their archives readily available for me and assisted with detailed image orders from across the Atlantic. When I was unable to visit their collections, special collections staff at Yale University Library and the Presbyterian Historical Society, on several occasions, kindly took time from their busy schedules, to locate, copy, and send requested materials my way. The Bayerische Staatsbibliothek München (Bavarian State Library, Munich), Universitäts- und Landesbibliothek, Bonn (Bonn University and Library), the Harvard University's Widener Library, and Harvard Divinity School's Andover-Harvard Theological Library graciously allowed me to reproduce digitized images from their collections.

Colleagues at the American University of Beirut (AUB) and fellow members of professional institutions offered significant support and inspiration. My gratitude goes out to the faculty members of the Department of Fine Arts and Art History at AUB whose friendship and support made this journey an enjoyable one. I benefitted from inspiring questions and comments from attendees at public lectures, conferences, and symposia where I presented different phases of this project. These forums included the "Majalis" of the AUB Islamic Studies Program at the Center for Arab and Middle Eastern Studies, the annual meetings of the Middle East Studies Association, the Historians of Islamic Art Association "Majlis," the annual conference of the Society for the History of Authorship, Reading, and Publishing, the annual meeting of the American Printing History Association, and the NYU Institute of Fine Arts-Frick Collection Symposium on the History of Art.

More people than can be named here offered thoughtful comments, words of reassurance, and much-needed company for breaks from writing. To all these individuals: thank you. I hope I will be able to repay my many debts to you one day. Finally, the unconditional and enthusiastic support of my family, Atika, Hassan, Mona, and Hosni, made this study a possibility. In the end, this project would never have been completed were it not for the excitement, critical feedback, patience, love, and sense of humor of Ramzi and Mira, who endured my late-nights, tight schedule, and work-filled weekends as I wrote the following chapters. You have been my rays of light.

# Notes on Transliteration

The transliteration of most Arabic words and names appearing in this book follows the format outlined in the *International Journal of Middle East Studies* (*IJMES*) general transliteration guidelines.

This includes:

- The use of accepted spellings in English of certain words (e.g. sultan and emir) and names of places (e.g. Beirut, Istanbul, Cairo, and Tabriz).
- The use of English equivalents for Arabic terms found in Merriam-Webster's Collegiate Dictionary, in which such terms appear without diacritics. For some exceptions, the *ʿayn* and *hamza* are preserved (e.g. Qur'an and ʿulamaʾ).
- Names of certain authors who opt for English or French spellings of their Arabic names in their publications appear according to these preferences.
- When the Arabic surname of an individual appears on its own, the definite article "al-" is used (e.g. al-Bustānī not Bustānī).

Exceptions are the following:

- Ottoman Turkish words (e.g. *sanjak*) are not transliterated, unless they are also prominently used in Arabic.
- When needed, an "s" is applied at the end of singular versions of Arabic words instead of using their conventional plural forms in Arabic.
- The only exception to the above is the use of the term *milal* (as the plural form of *milla*)
- In accordance with common usage, the initials of transliterated names of people and places are capitalized.
- Arabic book, periodical, and newspaper titles are fully transliterated with only the first major term in the title capitalized.

# List of Figures


1 Map of key provinces, cities, and villages in Ottoman Syria, ca. 1830 22

2 Introduction from Nāṣīf al-Yāzijī, *Kitāb faṣl al-khiṭāb fī uṣūl lughat al-iʿrāb* (Beirut, 1836). Courtesy of the Widener Library, Harvard University, Cambridge, MA (OL 25470.230) 39

3 Opening pages of Chapter Two from Nāṣīf al-Yāzijī, *Kitāb faṣl al-khiṭāb fī uṣūl lughat al-iʿrāb* (Beirut, 1836). Courtesy of the Widener Library, Harvard University, Cambridge, MA (OL 25470.230) 40

4 Detail of *basmala* in the form of a *tughrā'* from Nāṣīf al-Yāzijī, *Kitāb faṣl al-khiṭāb fī uṣūl lughat al-iʿrāb* (Beirut, 1836). Courtesy of the Widener Library, Harvard University, Cambridge, MA (OL 25470.230) 41

5 Introduction from George B. Whiting, *Kitāb fī al-imtināʿ ʿan shurb al-muskirāt* [sic] (Beirut, 1838). Courtesy of the Houghton Library, Harvard University, Cambridge, MA (*98Miss168) 43

6 First chapter from George B. Whiting, *Kitāb fī al-imtināʿ ʿan shurb al-muskirāt* [sic] (Beirut, 1838). Courtesy of the Houghton Library, Harvard University, Cambridge, MA (*98Miss168) 44

7 Introduction from *Qaṭf maqālāt al-qiddīs yūḥannā fam al-dhahab ʿan muṭālaʿat al-kutub al-muqaddasa* (Beirut, 1836). Accessed from Hathitrust.org, public domain, Google-digitized 45

8 Opening pages from *ʿIlāj mufīd li-l-hawā' al-aṣfar al-mubīd* (Beirut: American Press, 1837). Courtesy of the Houghton Library, Harvard University, Cambridge, MA (*98Miss168) 46

9 Title page from Nāṣīf al-Yāzijī, *Kitāb faṣl al-khiṭāb fī uṣūl lughat al-iʿrāb* (Beirut, 1836). Courtesy of the Widener Library, Harvard University, Cambridge, MA (OL 25470.230) 47

10 Frontispiece and title page from John Johnson, *An Abridgment of Johnson's Typographia, or the Printers' Instructor: With an Appendix* (Boston: C.L. Adams, 1828). Courtesy of the Houghton Library, Harvard University, Cambridge, MA (B 4488.116*) 48

11 Title page from George B. Whiting, *Kitāb irshād al-masīḥī fī imtiḥān al-nafs* (Beirut, 1837). Courtesy of the Houghton Library, Harvard University, Cambridge, MA (*98Miss168) 50

12 Title page from *ʿIlāj mufīd li-l-hawā' al-aṣfar al-mubīd* (Beirut: American Press, 1837). Courtesy of the Houghton Library, Harvard University, Cambridge, MA (*98Miss168) 50

13 Colophon with finis motif from *Kitāb al-zabūr al-ilāhī li-dāūd al-nabī* (Beirut: American Press, 1838). Courtesy of the Andover-Harvard Theological Library, Harvard Divinity School, Cambridge, MA (816.9 Arabic 1838) 51

14 Title page from *Kitāb al-majmaʿ al-anṭākī* (Beirut: Maṭbaʿat Dayr Mār Yūḥānna al-Mullaqab bi-l-Shuwayr, 1810). Courtesy of the Universitäts- und Landesbibliotek Bonn, Germany (Goussen 4' 2163, urn:nbn:de:hbz:5:1-13954) 53

15 *Right*, title page showing the word *kitāb* from George B. Whiting, *Kitāb fī al-imtināʿ ʿan shurb al-muskirāt* [sic] (Beirut, 1838). Courtesy of the Houghton Library, Harvard University, Cambridge, MA (*98Miss168) 54

16 *Right*, title page; *left*, first page from *Kitāb al-tawārīkh al-ma'khūdha min al-kitāb al-muqaddas* (Malta, 1832). Courtesy of the Bayerische Staatsbibliothek München, Germany (A. or.1260) 56

17 Introduction from Buṭrus al-Bustānī and Eli Smith, *Kitāb al-bāb al-maftūḥ fī aʿmāl al-rūḥ* (Beirut, 1843). Courtesy of the Widener Library, Harvard University, Cambridge, MA (KD 56851) 65

18 *Right*, title page; *left*, first page from Nāṣīf al-Yāzijī, *Kitāb faṣl al-khiṭāb fī uṣūl lughat al-iʿrāb* (Beirut, 1854). Accessed from Hathitrust.org, public domain, Google-digitized 66

19 Problems with the Watts typeface indicated in red seen in Nāṣīf al-Yāzijī, *Kitāb faṣl al-khiṭāb fī uṣūl lughat al-iʿrāb* (Beirut, 1836). Courtesy of the Widener Library, Harvard University, Cambridge, MA (OL 25470.230) 70

20 Example showing the new "American Arabic" typeface used in *Kitāb al-ājurrūmiyya* (Beirut, 1841). Courtesy of the Houghton Library, Harvard University, Cambridge, MA (*98Miss168) 72

21 Title page from Buṭrus al-Bustānī and Eli Smith, *Kitāb al-bāb al-maftūḥ fī aʿmāl al-rūḥ* (Beirut, 1843). Courtesy of the Widener Library, Harvard University, Cambridge, MA (KD 56851) 76

22 Title page from *Injīl rabbinā yasūʿ al-masīḥ* (Beirut: l'Imprimerie Catholique, 1877). Courtesy of the Universitäts- und Landesbibliotek Bonn, Germany (Goussen 4' 2074, urn:nbn:de:hbz:5:1-13622) 82

23 Title page from *Kitāb al-ifkhūlūjiyyūn al-kabīr: istiʿmāl kahnat al-rūm al-kātūlīk* (Jerusalem: The Franciscan Mission Press, 1865). Courtesy of the Universitäts- und Landesbibliotek Bonn, Germany (Goussen 4' 2099, urn:nbn:de:hbz:5:1-8256) 83

24 *Right*, title page; *left*, first page from *Al-īḍāḥ al-qawwīm fī ḥaqq al-thābitīn ʿalā al-ḥisāb al-qadīm* (Beirut: l'Imprimerie Catholique, 1859). Courtesy of the Universitäts- und Landesbibliotek Bonn, Germany (Goussen 2252, urn:nbn:de:hbz:5:1-14518) 84

25 Opening pages of Chapter One from Nāṣīf al-Yāzijī, *Kitāb majmaʿ al-baḥrayn* (Beirut, 1856). Courtesy of the Archives and Special Collections, Jafet Library, American University of Beirut, Lebanon (CA 892.78:Y359mA:1856:c.1) 100

26 First page from Nāṣīf al-Yāzijī, *Nabdha min dīwān al-shaykh nāṣīf al-yāzijī* (Beirut, 1853). Courtesy of the Houghton Library, Harvard University, Cambridge, MA (Miss 480.38) 101

27 Opening pages from Buṭrus al-Bustānī, *Kitāb misbāḥ al-tālib fī baḥth al-maṭālib* (Beirut, 1854). Courtesy of the Widener Library, Harvard University, Cambridge, MA (OL 21632.2) 102

28 Opening pages from Buṭrus al-Bustānī, *Khuṭba fī ādāb al-ʿarab* (Beirut, 1859). Courtesy of the Houghton Library, Harvard University, Cambridge, MA (*98Miss168) 103

29 Title page from Buṭrus al-Bustānī, *Khuṭba fī ādāb al-ʿarab* (Beirut, 1859). Courtesy of the Houghton Library, Harvard University, Cambridge, MA (*98Miss168) 104

30 Title page from Nāṣīf al-Yāzijī, *Nabdha min dīwān al-shaykh nāṣīf al-yāzijī* (Beirut, 1853). Courtesy of the Houghton Library, Harvard University, Cambridge, MA (Miss 480.38) 105

31 Title page from Buṭrus al-Bustānī, *Kitāb misbāḥ al-tālib fī baḥth al-maṭālib* (Beirut, 1854). Courtesy of the Widener Library, Harvard University, Cambridge, MA (OL 21632.2) 106

32 Title page from Ibrāhīm ibn Khalīl al-Najjār, *Kitāb miṣbāḥ al-sārī wa nuzhat al-qārī* (Beirut, 1855). Courtesy of the Archives and Special Collections, Jafet Library, American University of Beirut, Lebanon (CA 956 N16A vol.1: c.1) 107

33 *Right*, title page; *left*, first page from *Maqāmāt al-ḥarīrī fī al-lughah al-ʿarabiyya wa-l-funūn al-adabiyya* (Cairo: Dār al-Ṭibāʿa, 1856). Accessed from Hathitrust.org, public domain, Google-digitized 108

34 *Right*, title page; *left*, first page from *Maqāmāt al-ḥarīrī [maʿa] sharḥ ... muẓhir al-dīn al-shīrāzī* (Tabriz, 1856/7). Accessed from Hathitrust.org, public domain, Google-digitized 109

35 Erroneous gaps between letterforms (circled) from the introduction of Buṭrus al-Bustānī, *Kitāb misbāḥ al-tālib fī baḥth al-maṭālib* (Beirut, 1854) 115

36 Opening pages from Buṭrus al-Bustānī, *Dīwān abu al-ṭayyib aḥmad ibn al-ḥusayn al-mutanabbī* (Beirut: al-Maṭbaʿa al-Sūriyya, 1860). Accessed from Hathitrust.org, public domain, Google-digitized 116

37 Opening pages from *Sharḥ al-tibyān li-l-ʿukbarī ʿala dīwān abī al-tayyib aḥmad ibn ḥusayn al-mutanabbī* (Cairo: Dār al-Ṭibāʿa, 1870). Courtesy of the Bayerische Staatsbibliothek München, Germany (2 A.or.148 m-12) 118

38 Title page from Buṭrus al-Bustānī, *Dīwān abu al-ṭayyib aḥmad ibn al-ḥusayn al-mutanabbī* (Beirut: al-Maṭbaʿa al-Sūriyya, 1860). Accessed from Hathitrust.org, public domain, Google-digitized 119

39 Opening pages from Buṭrus Karāmī, Khalīl Sarkīs, and Amīn Sarkīs, *Al-darārī al-sabʿ: ay*

# List of Abbreviations

| | |
|---|---|
| ABCFM | American Board of Commissioners for Foreign Missions |
| ABS | American Bible Society |
| ATS | American Tract Society |
| AUB | American University of Beirut |
| BFBS | British and Foreign Bible Society |
| *BRISMES* | *British Journal of Middle Eastern Studies* |
| *CSSAAME* | *Comparative Studies of South Asia, Africa and The Middle East* |
| CMS | Church Missionary Society |
| *IJMES* | *International Journal of Middle East Studies* |
| PHS | Presbyterian Historical Society |
| SPC | Syrian Protestant College |
| YDSL | Yale Divinity School Library |

CHAPTER 1

# Introduction

In the 1830s the merchant-city of Beirut, located along the Ottoman Syrian coast, was on the road to becoming a dynamic site of multi-confessional convergence and contention. Between the Egyptian occupation in 1831 and the constitution of the minority-dominated Mount Lebanon region as an official, semi-autonomous, *mutaṣarrifiyya* (protectorate) in 1862, the city experienced mass migrations from rural areas and subsequent urban growth and development. Beirut's urbanization throughout the mid-nineteenth century coincided with this port city's growing importance as a center for global maritime trade. During this period, Beirut's position as a regional Arabic publishing hub was also taking shape. By the mid-nineteenth century, this cosmopolitan urban center (in addition to others, including nearby Cairo and Alexandria) saw a burgeoning of presses, type foundries, and binderies – funded by foreign missionaries as well as Christian, Muslim, and Jewish members of its growing urban class – which altered the face of local book production. Although printed Arabic books, many of which can be traced to "oriental" presses in Europe, had long been in circulation amongst Ottoman elites, scholars, and clergy members, it was not until the late nineteenth century that local publishing (traditionally a marginal practice) overtook customary Islamic and Christian scribal practices as the dominant mode of book manufacture. This technological shift, which both standardized production and expanded circulation, played a central role in spreading radical, intellectual, and political thought via historical, scientific, and literary publications in the Ottoman Empire and its hinterlands. Known as *al-nahḍa al-ʿarabiyya* (the Arab renaissance), this period between the last quarter of the nineteenth century and the eve of the First World War was characterized by momentous economic and socio-political changes in Arab regions, including reforms in urbanization, industrialization, commercialization, and the growing popularity of ideas about nationhood.

Studies on the history of the Arab press in the eastern Mediterranean emphasize the press's importance to fin de siècle movements, particularly those rooted in secular thought, such as nationalism. Although the regional significance of the Arab press during the late 1800s is well recognized, the press's earlier history was also a transformative moment in book production, one where nascent printing practices interfaced with centuries-old scribal ones. While a handful of regional presses operated in short spurts from the 1700s, the Arab press only emerged as a viable enterprise after the establishment of Cairo's Government Press in Būlāq (*al-Maṭbaʿa al-Amiriyya bi-Būlāq*) in 1820, and did not become a popular mode of book production until the 1870s, with the increasing prevalence of local private presses. Throughout its nascent period, the press persisted in an economy still largely dominated by well-established monastery and mosque scribal workshops. The concurrence of scribal and printing practices led to a dynamic moment in book manufacture that saw the interface between these two modes of production impact their conventions and significances. During this earlier moment in book manufacture, printed books circulated amongst local (Christian, Muslim, and Jewish) ecclesiastical and elite members of society who formed a coterie of manuscript readers. Such publications, many of which were distributed by regional missionary organizations, also found readers in school pupils and seminary students, forming a nascent print readership.

While acknowledging the regional significance of the Arab press during the late 1800s, this book shifts the terms of the current debate by exploring the Arab press's earlier period at mid-century, at the time when the rise of printing continued to overlap

 | DOI 10.1163/9789004314351_002

with dominant scribal traditions. This experimental moment, from roughly the 1820s to the 1860s, resulted in dynamic approaches to the content, layout, organization, and visual conventions of Arabic print culture that varied in their responses to scribal customs and methods, and shifting notions of what books and texts should look like. The transitional nature of this phase in the history of local publishing is exemplified by the products of the Presbyterian American Board of Commissioners for Foreign Missions' (ABCFM) press in Beirut.

Established in 1834, this missionary press, commonly known as *al-Maṭbaʿa al-Amrikāniyya* (the American Press),[1] published works that covered secular and religious subject matter. These publications, which ranged from small booklets to multi-volume books, were printed for the multi-confessional, Arabic-speaking residents of Ottoman Syria and the surrounding region. What is particularly interesting about this missionary press is that its products were funded by the Presbyterian American Syria Mission,[2] as an extension of its evangelical work, as well as local Arab intellectuals.[3] These latter included Nāṣīf al-Yāzijī (d. 1871) and Buṭrus al-Bustānī (d. 1883), who printed their own works (which would take front and center during the later *nahḍa* period) as well as those of their contemporaries. The early publications of these authors and their contemporaries, in both their content and visual programs, are important indicators of their views on popular intellectual debates. In particular, these debates related to conceptions of a Syrian identity[4] as well as emergent attitudes towards nationalism. Thus this nascent period in the history of Arabic printing in the eastern Mediterranean in general, and of the American Press in particular, constituted a crucial locus for the production of literary, political, and scientific works that would become the forebears of the late-nineteenth-century *nahḍa*.

The publications examined in this book were printed during the Press's early years, mostly from 1834 to 1867, and include various editions of religious narrative fiction, secular works on Arabic grammar, science, and arithmetic (frequently written by local Arab scholars), controversial anti-Catholic literature, and Protestant renditions of the Bible and extracts from it. This book engages in a detailed visual analysis of these overlooked printed works, specifically their manuscript format, typography, and ornamentation, through a combination of design and Islamic art historical methods. This examination extends to a consideration of the printed artifacts' importance as material objects whose physical dimensions – including size, binding, design layout, and typography – can reveal print's early regional uses and meanings, particularly in comparison to contemporaneous manuscripts and publications in circulation. Concurrently, by exploring the multiple religious and political dimensions of the American Press's important publications, this study also considers how changes in the design and content of these works throughout the years reflect shifts in the mission's evangelical goals, and responses to local religious and communal concerns. In doing so, this book also covers the early history of the American Press, based upon a rich body of primary source material from missionary archives at Harvard, Yale, the Presbyterian Historical Society, and the American University of Beirut. The methodology employed also includes a close reading of contemporary literary, historical, and critical studies on nineteenth-century Lebanon, as well as an assessment of global studies on book history and print

1 In this book, I refer to this press as the American Press and the Press.

2 I interchangeably refer to this mission as the Syria Mission, the Protestant mission, and the American mission.

3 By Arab Christian intellectuals (*muthaqqaf*), I am referring to the educated and scholarly members of non-Muslim Ottoman communities who identified as Arab and were affiliated with local Christian religious groups. At times, if they were involved in the emergent printing industry as authors, producers, and/or readers, I also refer to such individuals as print literati or print intellectuals.

4 In this book, I use the term Syrian as it relates to the emergent notion of a non-Ottoman national identity that became central to discourses on social reform and change in the Ottoman provinces during the mid-nineteenth century. This is further discussed in Chapter 5.

production. In considering the various challenges and adaptations involved in early Arabic print production, this study questions prominent theories regarding the large-scale, uniform impact of the Arab press in the nineteenth century and the notion of the printed book as a fixed, stable object. Ultimately, the book demonstrates how the publications struck off the American Press represented visual and textual negotiations of diverse local religious values, and societal interests in secular thought and education, during a formative period when these concepts and conventions were in flux.

### Arabic Printing and the *nahḍa*

Many twentieth and twenty-first century scholars have attributed the importance of the Arab press during the late nineteenth century to its role in disseminating intellectual and political thought in the Ottoman Empire and its surroundings. In addition to its association with the growing importance of Arab journalism and publishing, this *nahḍa* period was also characterized by widespread local economic and socio-political shifts, most of which were negotiated within the "political public sphere."[5] Similar developments were also taking place globally, and these Ottoman reforms impacted urbanization, industrialization, and commercialization, and included the growing popularity of nationalism.[6] Thus the dual functions, or threads, of the *nahḍa* (the cultural and the political) frequently intersected.[7]

Traditional scholars of Middle Eastern studies have, to varying degrees, embraced this period as a quintessential moment of Westernization, one in which local Arab elites adopted the cultural perspectives, technologies, and political views of the Ottoman region's European and American entities.[8] For instance, historians such as Philip K. Hitti, George Antonius, and Albert Hourani describe the *nahḍa* as the moment that saw the reemergence and/or advancement of Middle Eastern cultural movements, the modernization/secularization of education, and the birth of pan-Arab nationalist ideas.[9] The latter of these, pan-Arabism, was particularly popular after the Second World War, notably during the period in which these historians were writing. This worldview aimed to bridge ethnic and religious differences via common language and

5 Nadir Özbek, "Defining the Public Sphere During the Late Ottoman Empire: War, Mass Mobilization and the Young Turk Regime (1908–18)," *Middle Eastern Studies* 43, no. 5 (2007): 795–809.

6 For a view of Ottoman education reforms, notions of Westernization, and the rise of the urban class during this period, see Fatma Müge Göçek, *Rise of the Bourgeoisie, Demise of Empire: Ottoman Westernization and Social Change* (Oxford: Oxford University Press, 1996). See also Göçek, "Decline of the Ottoman Empire and the Emergence of Greek, Armenian, Turkish, and Arab Nationalisms," in *Social Constructions of Nationalism in the Middle East*, ed. Fatma M. Göçek (Albany: State University of New York Press, 2002), 15–84. For non-Western social histories of the widespread social, political, and cultural changes at the dawn of the "modern" period, see Peter Gran, *Beyond Eurocentrism: A New View of Modern World History* (Syracuse: Syracuse University Press, 1996). For Ottoman industrialization, see Donald Quataert, *Ottoman Manufacturing in the Age of the Industrial Revolution* (Cambridge: Cambridge University Press, 1993).

7 The dual facets of this period are described well in Fruma Zachs and Sharon Halevi, "From difāʿ al-nisāʾ to masʾalat al-nisāʾ in Greater Syria: Readers and Writers Debate Women and their Rights, 1858–1900," *International Journal of Middle East Studies* (hereafter cited as *IJMES*) 41, no. 4 (2009): 615.

8 Keith Watenpaugh explains that historians espousing these views "assert the existence of a dialectical relationship between the commitment to modernization," such as Western technologies and institutions, "and a conservative reaction against modernity, in this context the ideation of the post-Enlightenment social and intellectual processes that led to the 'rise of the West.'" Watenpaugh, *Being Modern in the Middle East: Revolution, Nationalism, Colonialism, and the Arab Middle Class* (Princeton: Princeton University Press, 2006), 5.

9 See Hitti, *History of the Arabs* (London: Macmillan, 1937); Antonius, *The Arab Awakening*, 2nd ed. (London: Hamish Hamilton, 1945); Hourani, *Arabic Thought in the Liberal Age*, 2nd ed. (Cambridge: Cambridge University Press, 1983).

secular thought as part of a nationalist political program. It emerged mostly in response to political developments in the region, specifically the germination of the project of the Israeli nation-state. These scholars largely attribute such developments to the predominance of privately run presses (as Western introductions to the region via missionaries and colonial entities), as well as missionary-run schools and universities. Even those who contend that the missionary presses (with their largely religious output) played no significant role in initiating secular and nationalist developments in the Arab world[10] accept the general significance of the printing press in prompting regional change.

In studies of Arabic printing, customary narratives of the *nahḍa* as a harbinger of nationalism, secular thought, and modernization, often attribute a central role for printed books and journals in the late nineteenth century. Although recent studies have pointed to fractures and dissonances in the period's narratives,[11] this pivotal movement is sometimes positioned as a direct consequence of the "printing revolution" in the Middle East. Such scholars continue to view the adoption of print technologies, in place of more customary scribal methods of manuscript copying, as the linchpin for the rapid transmission of ideas via the mass production and wide circulation of books.[12] Even those historians and literary scholars who seek to avoid having the development of Arabic printing in the region overshadow important social and political developments on the ground still emphasize the *nahḍa*'s late nineteenth-century importance in the emergence of modernizing reforms and nationalist ideologies.[13]

This *nahḍa* period, traditionally understood to encompass the years from the last quarter of the nineteenth century to the first decades of the 1900s, was certainly informed by an earlier period, most notably between the beginning of the eighteenth century and the dawn of the nineteenth. Recently, a number of scholars have revisited popular and widespread understandings of the *nahḍa*, an effort which has a bearing on this study and its framing. Recent scholarship in historical and literary disciplines has questioned the almost exclusive focus

10 A.L. Tibawi, *American Interests in Syria 1800–1901: A Study of Educational, Literary and Religious Work* (Oxford: Oxford University Press, 1966), 306–08.

11 For instance, see Nadia Bou Ali, "Collecting the Nation: Lexicography and National Pedagogy in al-nahda al-ʿarabiyya," in *Archives, Museums and Collecting Practices in the Modern Arab World*, eds. Sonja Mejcher-Atassi and John P. Schwartz (Farnham: Ashgate Publishing, 2012), 33–56. Ilham Khuri-Makdisi discusses the complex web of external impulses at the heart of this period in her pivotal *The Eastern Mediterranean and the Making of Global Radicalism, 1860–1914* (Berkeley: University of California Press, 2010).

12 This includes a wide array of both pre- and post-twentieth century sources (mostly from within the discipline of bibliography) on the history of the Arab press. Examples of pre-twentieth century sources include: Wahid Gdoura, *Bidāyat al-ṭibāʿa al-ʿarabiyya fī isṭānbūl wa-bilād al-shām: taṭawwur al-muḥīt al-thaqāfī, 1706–1787* (Riyadh: Maktabat al-Malik Fahd al-Waṭaniyya, 1993); Khalīl Ṣabbāt, *Tārīkh al-ṭibāʿa fī al-sharq al-ʿarabī* (Cairo: Dār al-Maʿārif, 1958); Lūwīs Shaykhū, *Tārīkh fan al-ṭibāʿa fī al-mashriq*, 2nd ed. (Beirut: Dār al-Mashriq, 1994). Recent sources embracing views of the Arab press's revolutionary impact include: Eva Hanebutt-Benz et al. eds., *Middle Eastern Languages and the Print Revolution: A Cross-Cultural Encounter* (Mainz: Gutenberg-Museum, 2002); Dagmar Glass, "Die *nahḍa* und ihre Technik im 19. Jahrhundert: Ärabische Druckereien in Agypten und Syrien," in *Das gedruckte Buch im Vorderen Orient*, ed. Ulrich Marzolph (Dortmund: Verlag für Orientkunde, 2002), 50–84; Geoffrey Roper, "Fāris al-Shidyāq and the Transition from Scribal to Print Culture in the Middle East," in *The Book in the Islamic World: The Written Word and Communication in the Middle East*, ed. George N. Atiyeh (Albany: State University of New York, 1995), 209–31.

13 Recent studies include: Abdulrazzak Patel, *The Arab Nahdah: The Making of the Intellectual and Humanist Movement* (Oxford: Oxford University Press, 2013); Carol Hakim, *The Origins of the Lebanese National Idea, 1840–1920* (Berkeley: The University of California Press, 2013); Jens Hanssen, *Fin de Siècle Beirut: The Making of an Ottoman Provincial Capital* (Oxford: Clarendon Press, 2005).

placed on the late nineteenth-century in the study of the *nahḍa*, as in the example of research on early Arab debates on women's social roles and political rights in studies of prominent publications of the period.[14] While these themes have been frequently addressed in scholarship dealing with the late nineteenth- and early twentieth-century periods of the *nahḍa*, these authors argue that not enough attention is paid to similar discussions and precedents that took shape in intellectual spheres during the earlier decades of the 1800s.[15] Similarly, Nadia al-Bagdadi and Dana Sajdi, in their respective publications,[16] argue for a shift in focus from the late 1800s to the early 1800s (in al-Bagdadi's case) and even the eighteenth century (according to Sajdi). Additionally, both problematize the earlier scholarship's enthusiastic propagation of the narrative of the Arab "printing revolution" at the expense of important and prevalent manuscript traditions.

For instance, while al-Bagdadi states that she does not deny the widespread impact of printing practices within the realms of literary knowledge, she argues that scholars need to be "careful not to overrate the effects of the technical innovation itself."[17] She calls for a closer examination of "the politics and strategies underlying the coexistence of print and manuscript in the realm of intellectual and artistic production" during the 1850s.[18] Also emphasizing the centrality of manuscript practices to the transmission and production of knowledge, Sajdi argues for a departure from a "technologically-determined" narrative of Arab modernity. Instead she provides an alternative reading, which proposes "a connected and ongoing history of practices and genres into which print was habilitated and which print, in turn, transformed." Thus, she views journal publishing, "which is so emblematic of both the Arab nahḍa … and of the impact of print, as a continuation" of manuscript practices, particularly historical chronicles written during the eighteenth century.[19]

Informed by these recent studies, especially those of al-Bagdadi and Sajdi, this book shifts the focus from the much-discussed importance of the press during the late nineteenth century to an exploration of the printed Arabic book's earlier history, at a time when it co-existed with dominant scribal traditions. As will be shown in the following chapters, the nascent period in the regional history of Arabic printing saw an overlap of different bookmaking practices, where print was adapted to emulate scribal conventions and methods that suited local readers' perceptions of the book at the time. As cultural and socio-political changes took hold in the region, the emergent print intelligentsia's views of the book and its forms, meanings, and uses as a medium for transmitting, producing, and organizing knowledge shifted as well. This resulted in the emergence of alternate visual and intellectual practices in the realm of print production.

Contemporaneously, the Arab press during the early to mid-nineteenth century saw the production of literary, political, and scientific works that became the forebears of late nineteenth-century intellectual movements. Arab Christian intellectuals like al-Bustānī and al-Yāzijī printed their first books at the American mission's press in Beirut between 1837 and the 1860s. In their content, organizational methods, physical dimensions, and visual conventions, these publications are important indicators of how these individuals grappled with emergent views on preserving an Arab heritage while also contributing to popular intellectual debates. Concurrently, such intellectuals also explored new forms of the book and the ways in which the

14 Zachs and Halevi, "From difāʿ al-nisāʾ to masʾalat al-nisāʾ."

15 Ibid., 615–16.

16 Al-Bagdadi, "Print, Script and the Limits of Free-thinking in Arabic Letters of the 19th Century: The Case of al-Shidyaq," *Al-Abhath* 48–49 (2000–01): 99–122; Sajdi, "Print and its Discontents: A Case for Pre-Print Journalism and Other Sundry Print Matters," *The Translator* 15, no. 1 (2009): 105–38.

17 Al-Bagdadi, 101.

18 Ibid.

19 Sajdi, "Print and its Discontents," 107.

characteristics of print could be adapted to their particular interests and socio-political concerns, such as those related to emergent concepts of a Syrian national identity.

### Studying the Printed Arabic Book

While rooted in art and design history's intrinsically visual analytical methods, this book approaches Arabic manuscript and print production through a multifaceted lens by combining the methods of bibliography, literary studies, and history. This interdisciplinary approach may, at times, risk appearing unwieldy; indeed, such a multidimensional method appears to be part and parcel of any study that takes up the book in its countless manifestations, uses, and meanings. Past scholarship has critiqued book studies and publishing history as unhinged, unbound, or unruly precisely because of this lack of disciplinary allegiance and this methodological elasticity.[20] However, as Leslie Howsam argues in her *Old Books & New Histories: An Orientation to Studies in Book and Print Culture*, book history scholars must be more aware of the "boundaries [studies of books] negotiate" if the field is to be taken seriously as a "rigorous practice."[21] She does this by charting out the three disciplines in the humanities that traditionally deal with the study of books and/or print culture – bibliography, literary studies, and history – and demonstrates how these fields tend to converge, overlap, and diverge in scholarship on the book from the "Western" perspective. While informed primarily by the study of European or North American products, Howsam's description of these disciplinary boundaries and the interdisciplinary crossings associated with them can be applied to studies of publishing, books, and print culture in the Middle East as well.[22]

In the realm of Arabic and Islamic printing and publishing, studies also follows various approaches, mostly along literary,[23] historical,[24]

20 Cyndia S. Clegg, "History of the Book: An Undisciplined Discipline?," *Renaissance Quarterly* 54, no. 1 (2001): 221–45; Michele Moylan and Lane Stiles, eds., *Reading Books: Essays on the Material Text and Literature in America* (Amherst: University of Massachusetts Press, 1996); John A. Sutherland, "Publishing History: A Hole at the Center of Literary Sociology," *Critical Inquiry* 14 (Spring 1988): 574–89; Robert Darton, "What is the History of Books?" *Daedalus* 111, no. 3 (1982): 65–83.

21 Howsam, *Old Books & New Histories: An Orientation to Studies in Book and Print Culture* (Toronto: University of Toronto Press, 2006), 9.

22 For a historiography of writing on Arabic printing see Roper, "The Printing Press and Change in the Arab World," in *Agent of Change: Print Culture Studies after Elizabeth L. Einstein*, eds. Sabrina A. Baron et al. (Amherst: University of Massachusetts Press, 2007), 251–67.

23 Zachs and Halevi, "From difāʿ al-nisāʾ to masʾalat al-nisāʾ"; Basilius Bawardi, "*Hadiqat al-Akhbar* Newspaper and Its Pioneering Role in the Arabic Narrative Fiction," *Die Welt der Islam* 48 (2008): 170–95; Halevi and Zachs, "Asma (1873): The Early Arabic Novel as a Social Compass," *Studies in the Novel* 39, no. 4 (2007): 416–30; Ami Ayalon, "The Syrian Educated Elite and the Literary *nahḍa*," in *Ottoman Reform and Islamic Regeneration*, eds. Fruma Zachs and Itzchak Weismann (London: I.B. Tauris, 2005), 127–66; Stephen Sheehi, "Arabic Literary-Scientific Journals: Precedence for Globalization and the Creation of Modernity," *Comparative Studies of South Asia, Africa and The Middle East* (hereafter cited as *CSSAAME*) 25, no. 2 (2005): 438–48; Ayalon, *Reading Palestine, Printing and Literacy: 1900–1948* (Austin: University of Texas Press, 2004); Johann Strauss, "Who Read What in the Ottoman Empire (19th–20th Centuries)?" *Middle Eastern Literatures* 6, no. 1 (2003): 40; Zachs, "Mīkhaʾīl Mishāqa: The First Historian of Modern Syria," *British Journal of Middle Eastern Studies* (hereafter cited as *BRISMES*) 28, no. 1 (2001): 67–87; Sheehi, "Inscribing the Arab Self: Buṭrus al-Bustānī and Paradigms of Subjective Reform," *BRISMES* 27, no. 1 (2000); Sasson Somekh, "Biblical Echoes in Modern Arabic Literature," *Journal of Arabic Literature* 26, no. 1/2 (1995): 186–200; Sabry Hafiz, *The Genesis of Arabic Narrative Discourse: A Study in the Sociology of Modern Arabic Literature* (London: Saqi, 1993).

24 Nile Green, "Persian Print and the Stanhope Revolution: Industrialization, Evangelicalism, and the Birth of Printing in Early Qajar Iran," *CSSAAME* 30, no. 3 (2012): 413–90; Green, "Journeymen, Middlemen: Travel,

and bibliographic lines, and most of which deal with the *nahḍa* and its broader cultural and socio-political implications. Of these disciplines, bibliographical contributions are not only the most broad and varied, but also the most useful to this present study. For one, scholarship from this field constitutes the greatest (numerical) contribution to studies of Arabic printing. Additionally, bibliographic studies (in their varied emphases and methods) engage the history of the book as object, an approach not often pursued by literary and historical scholarship. Taken up by bibliographers, librarians, conservators, and historians who have extensive experience handling physical copies of these tomes, bibliographic studies are the only ones to provide a material analysis of printed Arabic books, in addition to examinations of output numbers, types of books produced, and the impact of their circulation on readers. Challenging disciplinary boundaries, this field attempts to incorporate various perspectives, including publishing history, production methods, book design, consumption, economic trade, sociology, and authorship, into its studies of the book.

Nevertheless, it is important to identify a generational rift apparent in these bibliographic studies. Traditional bibliographies of printing in the Arab world published before 1960 in Arabic and French are less interdisciplinary than their successors. These works also tend to emphasize issues of chronology, and underscore the importance of European entities and traditions in establishing regional Arabic presses.[25] The most prominent of these studies situate the history of Arabic printing within a teleological framework that highlights its development in the Arab world as a struggle between knowledge and ignorance, freedom and oppression, and advancement and regression.[26] In presenting a purpose-driven narrative of the printing press in the Middle East, with its origins in Western technology and concepts, this scholarship chiefly situates the Arab press as a vehicle for modernization and advancement, one that breaks away from "regressive" manuscript practices.

More recent scholarship on the Arab press, particularly from the 1990s onward, provides further detail by focusing on particular books, individual presses, and/or presenting a localized narrative of Arabic printing practices. Some of these bibliographic studies are informed by the work of Elizabeth Eisenstein, a bibliographer who in 1979 defined the direction of European printing history.[27] Like Eisenstein, these sources on Arabic printing emphasize issues of output, standardization in production, and textual preservation in their focus on

Transculture, and Technology in the Origins of Muslim Printing," *IJMES* 41, no. 2 (2009): 203–24; Maurits van den Boogert, "The Sultan's Answer to the Medici Press? Ibrahim Muteferrika's Printing House in Istanbul," in *The Republic of Letters and the Levant*, eds. Van den Boogert et al. (Leiden: Brill, 2005), 265–91; Juan R.I. Cole, "Printing and Urban Islam in the Mediterranean World, 1890–1920," in *Modernity and Culture: From the Mediterranean to the Indian Ocean*, eds. Leila Tarazi Fawaz and C.A. Bayly (New York: Columbia University Press, 2002), 344–64; Reinhard Schulze, "The Birth of Tradition and Modernity in 18th and 19th Century Islamic Culture: The Case of Printing," *Culture & History* 16 (January 1997): 29–72; Adeeb Khalid, "Printing, Publishing, and Reform in Tsarist Central Asia," *IJMES* 26, no. 2 (1994): 187–200; Francis Robinson, "Technology and Religious Change: Islam and the Impact of Print," *Modern Asian Art* 27, no. 1 (1993): 229–51.

25 These surveys emphasize aspects of progress and development and aim to credit certain regions, communities, and/or individuals with the advancement of printing in the Arab world. Examples include: Abū al-Futūḥ Riḍwān, *Tārīkh maṭbaʿat būlāq: wa-lamḥa fī tārīkh al-ṭibāʿa fī buldān al-sharq al-awsaṭ* (Cairo: al-Maṭbaʿa al-Amīriyya, 1953); Ṣabbāt, *Tārīkh al-ṭibāʿa*; Joseph Nasrallah, *L'imprimerie au Liban* (Beirut: l'Imprimerie de Saint-Paul, 1948); Fīlīb dī Tarrāzī (Philippe de Tarrazi), *Tārīkh al-ṣiḥāfa al-ʿarabiyya*, 4 vols., 2nd ed. (Beirut: al-Maṭbaʿa al-Adabiyya, 1914); Shaykhū, *Tārīkh fan al-ṭibāʿa*.

26 Ṣabbāt, 5.

27 Eisenstein, *The Printing Press as an Agent of Change: Communications and Cultural Transformations in Early Modern Europe*, 2 vols. (Cambridge: Cambridge University Press, 1979).

the technology of print.[28] Writing within a postcolonial framework, a number of these works also question the emphasis placed on colonial and missionary presses in the region by singling out the importance and success of local Arab Christian and Muslim presses.[29] These historical or analytical bibliographic studies demonstrate more sensitivity to the broader debates in the secondary literature than earlier studies, and place an emphasis on local Arab protagonists in their accounts. Some of this scholarship, however, tends to repeat narratives of a "rupture" between print and scribal traditions and of print's uniform global impact, albeit from the perspective of the Arab world.

Unlike earlier scholarship, twenty-first-century bibliographic studies of Arabic printing move beyond the technologically centered approach to one that engages issues of materiality, social history, and cultural specificity. This scholarship draws on the important work of books scholars such as Roger Chartier,[30] D.F. MacKenzie,[31] and Adrian Johns.[32] These and other scholars[33] transformed the field of bibliography by calling for an understanding of books as objects, by emphasizing the ways in which a book's materiality relates to broader socio-political currents, and by considering culturally specific studies of print's forms, uses, and significance.[34] Geoffrey Roper is one of few bibliographic historians to consider the technological and cognitive overlaps in the shift from scribal to printing practices in the region, particularly through the work of the well-known nineteenth-century author Fāris al-Shidyāq (d. 1887).[35]

In work on Arabic and Islamic printing in particular, later scholars deal with the tangible materiality of books (and of the artifacts of print culture) as physical objects much more concretely than their predecessors did. In her analyses of early printed books from Egypt and other Arab

28 Abdelkader Ben Cheikh, *Communication et société: pouvoir lire et développement culturel* (Tunis: Publications du centre de recherches en bibliothéconomie et sciences de l'information, 1986); Ben Cheikh, *Book Production and Reading in the Arab World* (Paris: UNESCO, 1982).

29 A few of these include: Khālid Muḥammad ʿAzab and Aḥmad Manṣūr, *Al-kitāb al-ʿarabī al-maṭbūʿ: min al-judhūr ila maṭbaʿat būlāq* (Cairo: Dār al-Miṣriyya al-Lubnāniyya, 2008); Joseph Kahale, *ʿAbd-allāh zākhir, mubtakir al-maṭbaʿa al-ʿarabiyya* (Aleppo: Markaz al-Inmāʾ al-Ḥaḍārī, 2002); Maḥmūd M. al-Ṭanāḥī, *Al-kitāb al-maṭbūʿ bi-misr fī al-qarn al-tāsiʿ ʿashir: tārīkh wa taḥlīl* (Cairo: Dār al-Hilāl, 1996); Gdoura, *Bidāyat al-ṭibāʿa al-ʿarabiyya*; Fawzi M. Tadrus, *Printing in the Arab World with Emphasis on the Būlāq Press in Egypt* (Doha: University of Qatar, 1982).

30 Chartier, "The Printing Revolution: A Reappraisal," in Baron, *Agent of Change*, 397–408; *The Order of Books: Readers, Authors, and Libraries in Europe between the Fourteenth and Eighteenth Centuries* (Cambridge: Polity Press, 1994); "Texts, Printing, Readings," in *The New Cultural History*, ed. Lynn Hunt (Berkeley: University of California Press, 1989), 154–75; *Cultural History: Between Practices and Representations*, trans., Lydia G. Cochrane (Ithaca: Cornell University Press, 1988).

31 McKenzie, *Bibliography and the Sociology of Texts* (London: The British Library, 1986); "Printers of the Mind: Some Notes on Bibliographical Theories and Printing-House Practices," *Studies in Bibliography* 22 (1969): 1–75.

32 Johns, *The Nature of the Book: Print and Knowledge in the Making* (Chicago: University of Chicago Press, 1998).

33 Such works develop issues initially brought forth by Henri-Jean Martin and Lucien Febvre in their seminal text *L'apparition du livre* (Paris: Albin Michel, 1958) that calls for a study of the uses of print and an understanding the technical aspects of production. This was later translated into English as *The Coming of the Book: The Impact of Printing, 1450–1800*, trans. David Gerard, eds. Geoffrey Nowell-Smith and David Wooton (London: N.L.B, 1976).

34 Similar studies have been taken up in the realm of non-Western traditions. Examples from Asian and Native American studies include: Phillip Round, *Removable Type: Histories of the Book in Indian Country, 1663–1880* (Chapel Hill: The University of North Carolina Press, 2010); Miles Ogborn, *Indian Ink: Script and Print in the Making of the English East India Company* (Chicago: University of Chicago Press, 2007); Anindita Ghosh, *Power in Print: Popular Publishing and the Politics of Language and Culture in Colonial Society, 1778–1905* (Oxford: Oxford University Press, 2006).

35 Roper, "An Autograph Manuscript of Ahmad Faris As-Sidyaq: Prepared by him for the Press," in *Writings and Writing from Another World and Another Era*, eds. Robert M. Kerr and Thomas Milo (Cambridge: Archetype, 2013), 341–56; "Fāris al-Shidyāq."

societies, Jihān al-Sayyid, for instance, provides a detailed description of colophons, title pages, and watermarks among other visual elements relating to the printed page.[36] Similarly, in his work on the still greatly overlooked lithographed books of Qajar Iran from the early 1800s, Ulrich Marzolph examines images from these illustrated works by focusing on issues of chronology and sources of influence for the figurative drawings.[37] In a published lecture on the American Press in Beirut, Dagmar Glass studies the typeface produced at the Press and its broader significance to Arab notions of modernization by considering the development of this metal type and which Ottoman-region presses utilized it.[38] In sifting through, cataloging, and categorizing examples of print (a taxonomy extending to typefaces and illustrations), such scholarship provides a much needed basis from which these works and their visual conventions can be explored for their broader social and intellectual implications.

Also notable is the fact that visual literacy has not been adequately addressed compared to the much-privileged textual aspects of books and print culture.[39] In the realm of visual history, a number of scholars challenge the centrality of textual analysis to historical studies of the book in particular, and material culture in general. Johanna Drucker is one noteworthy scholar who uses design and art historical methodologies in her work on book history and visual literacy. In her recent study on visual epistemology,[40] Drucker points out that although experiences of everyday life are "mediated by visual formats and images, the bias against visual forms of knowledge production is longstanding in our culture."[41] She explores the links between "knowledge and visuality"[42] by considering the cultural and historical dimensions of graphics (which she applies to print, manuscripts, and digital media). In an earlier work on twentieth-century experimental texts by the Futurists and their contemporaries, Drucker investigates the materiality of type-based works through a consideration of the uses and limits of structuralist and poststructuralist linguistic methods. Examining "the status of writing [as] the visual form of language,"[43] the author reconsiders the "oppositional definition" of literary and visual disciplines within mid-twentieth-century literary and art criticism, in which "visuality was defined in part by its exclusion of literary or linguistic activity."[44] Bringing her printing and design knowledge to bear on studies of such works, which had been previously sidelined

36 Al-Sayyid, *Al-biblīyūghrāfiyya al-taḥlīliyya: dirāsa fī awāʾil al-maṭbūʿāt al-ʿarabiyya* (Alexandria: Dār al-Thaqāfa al-ʿIlmiyya, 2000).

37 Marzolph, "Illustrated Persian Lithographic Editions of the Shahname," *Edebiyat* 13, no. 2 (2003): 177–98. See also his *Narrative Illustration in Persian Lithographed Books Handbook of Oriental Studies/Handbuch Der Orientalistik* (Leiden: Brill, 2001).

38 Glass, *Malta, Beirut, Leipzig, and Beirut Again: Eli Smith, the American Syria Mission and the Spread of Arabic Typography in 19th Century Lebanon*, ed. Angelika Neuwirth (Beirut: Orient-Institut der Deutschen Morganländischen Gesellschaft, 1997). Roper also takes up a similar study of the materiality of early Arabic printing by considering issues of typeface and layouts seen in the books published by the Church Missionary Society in Malta. See Roper, "Arabic Books Printed in Malta 1826–42: Some Physical Characteristics," *History of Printing and Publishing in the Languages and Countries of the Middle East*, ed. Philip Sadgrove (Oxford: Oxford University Press, 2005), 111–29; "The Beginnings of Arabic Printing by the ABCFM, 1822–1841," *Harvard Library Bulletin* 9, no. 1 (1998): 50–68.

39 For instance, in Howsam's appraisal of the "comprehensive logic and the indiscriminate inclusiveness of bibliographical scholarship," she seems to overlook visually oriented disciplines such as art and design history. However, these particular disciplines are equipped with the necessary tools for a comprehensive study of visual materiality, an important component of books and print culture. Howsam, *Old Books and New Histories*, 15.

40 Drucker, *Graphesis: Visual Forms of Knowledge Production* (Cambridge, Mass.: Harvard University Press, 2014).

41 Ibid., 16.

42 Ibid., 19.

43 Drucker, *The Visible Word: Experimental Typography and Modern Art, 1909–1923* (Chicago: The University of Chicago Press, 1994), 4.

44 Ibid., 6.

as "aberration[s]" by "high modernist criticism," Drucker takes up a critical interpretation of typography's signification in its visual form and poetic effect.[45] Similarly, though for a different purpose, Finbarr B. Flood adopts a linguistic approach in his study of the visual and textual dimensions of fourteenth-century South Asian material culture. Arguing that the "dominance of a textual paradigm has obscured the semiotic potential of materials and materiality even as they relate to textual sources," Flood contends that texts (while valuable historical sources) should not be prioritized over material culture as objects of inquiry in relation to South Asian history.[46]

Informed by both Drucker and Flood's approaches, this book considers the importance of visual conventions in conjunction with literary/textual ones, while extending this material examination to other aspects of the printed book. The present study applies the interdisciplinary approaches of recent historical bibliographies to the social history of the Arab press. In doing so, it locates the "visuality" of the book in its graphic and material dimensions as a form of knowledge production within a historical inquiry into the socio-political and cultural significance of Arabic printing. In this approach, the physical components of books – typography, layout design, binding, and dimensions – are read as important markers of visual literacy within contemporaneous artistic, intellectual, and reading realms. In the case of the Arabic book, Islamic art, via its long history inextricable from that of codicology and the study of manuscripts,[47] provides the methods needed for a close examination of printed books as visual objects worthy of close inspection.

45 Drucker, *The Visible Word*, 6–8.

46 Flood, *Objects of Translation: Material Culture and the Medieval "Hindu-Muslim" Encounter* (Princeton: Princeton University Press, 2009), 9–11.

47 Such as David Roxburgh, *The Persian Album, 1400–1600: From Dispersal to Collection* (New Haven: Yale University Press, 2005).

## Islamic Manuscript Traditions and Arabic Printing

In light of its mechanized production and circulation, the printed Arabic book was generally regarded as an object that, while replicating certain elements from scribal practices, was not necessarily worthy of a close visual reading. Although a number of prominent scholars in the field have turned their attention to the significance of the introduction of printing in the realm of Islamic book production, careful visual analyses tend to be limited to manuscripts that are characterized by manual skill and the physical marks of the artist's presence.[48] One may argue that the present tangential interest in the printed Arabic book reflects the field of Islamic art history's general ambivalence towards nineteenth-century productions.

Although the field is by no means conclusively defined in its scope and realm of inquiry, some subjects have gained more traction than others. Until very recently, the attitude towards nineteenth-century art and architecture in the field of Islamic art history has oscillated between a sense of discomfort and outright avoidance. A number of scholars address the lacuna of nineteenth-century subject matter in prominent surveys and studies.[49] For instance, Margaret Graves suggests

48 Key examples include: Sheila Blair, *Islamic Calligraphy* (Edinburgh: Edinburgh University Press, 2006); Jonathan Bloom, *Paper before Print: The History and Impact of Paper in the Islamic World* (New Haven: Yale University Press, 2001); Brinkley Messick, *The Calligraphic State: Textual Domination and History in a Muslim Society* (Berkeley: University of California Press, 1993); Johannes Pedersen, *The Arabic Book*, trans. Geoffrey French, ed. Robert Hillenbrand (Princeton: Princeton University Press, 1984).

49 Flood, "From the Prophet to Postmodernism? New World Orders and the End of Islamic Art," in *Making Art History: A Changing Discipline and its Institutions*, ed. Elizabeth Mansfield (London: Routledge, 2007), 31–53; Margaret Graves, "Feeling Uncomfortable in the Nineteenth Century," *Journal of Art Historiography* 6 (June 2012): 1–27; Doris Behrens-Abouseif and Stephen Vernoit, eds., *Islamic Art in the 19th Century: Tradition,*

various reasons for the occlusion of nineteenth-century visual productions in the traditional field of Islamic art. In particular, she draws attention to the deep-rooted nineteenth-century European fantasy of "medieval" Islamic societies and culture that continued to proscribe modernity from studies involving Islamic art and architecture well into the twentieth century.[50] A complementary argument can be made for the study of print culture in the Islamic world. The customary, though inaccurate, belief that products of the Arab press are merely expressions of nineteenth-century social changes that created an instantaneous "rupture" with past book-making traditions and values complicated any analysis of such products as important material artifacts. Thus, earlier scholarship on the Islamic book, similar to other subspecialties in the field, either covered periods before the late 1700s or, in studies of nineteenth-century manuscripts, conspicuously circumnavigated the emergence of printing traditions.

In the past decade, however, attitudes towards nineteenth-century productions have shifted amongst Islamic art historians with the emergence of new scholarship.[51] A good amount of work on this era also exists in the form of theses and dissertations in progress, which will certainly alter the field drastically in the coming years. Additionally, the subject of printing in the Muslim world is beginning to garner interest amongst a new generation of scholars concerned with the material dimensions of book production and writing.[52] Recent contributions to the field include those that analyze publications by İbrahim Müteferrika at his press in Istanbul during the 1700s. They locate these publications on a parallel plane with dominant scribal practices in order to understand their political, intellectual, and artistic significance.[53]

While this recent scholarship[54] is indicative of a shifting landscape in art historical studies of the

*Innovation and Eclecticism* (Leiden: Brill, 2006); Vernoit, *Occidentalism: Islamic Art in the Nineteenth Century* (London: Nour Foundation in association with Azimuth Editions and Oxford University, 1997).

50 Graves, 21–23.

51 Recent works include: Ahmet Ersoy, *Architecture and the Late Ottoman Historical Imaginary: Reconfiguring the Architectural Past in a Modernizing Empire* (Farnham: Ashgate Publishing, 2015); Wendy Shaw, *Ottoman Painting: Reflections of Western Art from the Ottoman Empire to the Turkish Republic* (London: I.B. Tauris, 2011); Paula Sanders, *Creating Medieval Cairo: Empire, Religion, and Architectural Preservation in Nineteenth-Century Egypt* (Cairo: The American University in Cairo Press, 2008); Mary Roberts, *Intimate Outsiders: The Harem in Ottoman and Orientalist Art and Travel Literature* (Durham: Duke University Press, 2007).

52 Kathryn Schwartz, "Meaningful Mediums: A Material and Intellectual History of Manuscript and Print Production in Nineteenth Century Ottoman Cairo" (PhD Diss., Harvard University, 2015); Natalia Kasprzak, "Quranic Matters: Media and Materiality" (PhD Diss., University of North Carolina at Chapel Hill, 2014); J.R (Wayne) Osborn, "The Type of Calligraphy: Writing, Print, and Technologies of the Arabic Alphabet" (PhD Diss., UC San Diego, 2008).

53 Yasmin Gencer, "İbrahim Müteferrika and the Age of the Printed Manuscript," in *The Islamic Manuscript Tradition: Ten Centuries of Book Arts in Indiana University Collections*, ed. Christiane Gruber (Bloomington: Indiana University Press, 2010), 155–93; Emily Zoss, "An Ottoman View of the World: The *Kitab Cihannūma* and Its Cartographic Contexts," in Gruber, *Islamic Manuscript Tradition*, 195–219. Such essays differ from previous writing on this topic, which focused on issues of bibliography; see Van den Boogert, "The Sultan's Answer"; Christoph K. Neumann, "Book and Newspaper Printing in Turkish, 18th–20th Century," in Hanebutt-Benz, *Middle Eastern Languages*, 227–48; William J. Watson, "İbrahim Müteferriḳa and Turkish Incunabula," *Journal of the American Oriental Society* 88, no. 3 (1968): 435–41.

54 Some other works include: Thomas Milo, "Towards Arabic Historical Script Grammar: Through Contrastive Analysis of Qur'an Manuscripts," in *Writings and Writing from Another World and Another Era: Investigations in Islamic Text and Script in Honour of Dr Januarius Justus Witkam Professor of Codicology and Paleography of the Islamic World at Leiden University*, eds. Robert Kerr and Thomas Milo (Cambridge: Archetype, 2013), 248–92; O.P. Scheglova, "Lithograph Versions of Persian Manuscripts of Indian Manufacture

Islamic and Arabic book, there is still much ground to cover. For starters, although bibliographic, literary, and historical accounts abound, there is a lacuna in art historical scholarship when it comes to Arabic and/or Islamic printing practices and the book in Pakistan, parts of India (Calcutta, Lucknow, and Delhi), and Indonesia. Additionally, from the few art historical studies of pre-twentieth-century Arabic/Islamic printing available, most seem exclusively focused on lithographic practices, probably because this tradition was closely associated visually and technically with those of scribal works. Despite the mechanical nature of lithography, this particular printing technology (at least during the earlier decades of the nineteenth century) entailed a direct transfer of a handwritten/hand-illustrated artwork onto the lithographic stone. In sharp contrast, letterpress products almost exclusively rely on the mechanical imprint of precast/pre-carved metal/wood typefaces, ornaments, and rules. One could argue that the evidence of the artist, scribe, calligrapher, illuminator, or illustrator's hand is more readily apparent in lithographic works than in those produced via letterpress. Does this mean that lithograph productions, given their close emulation of the calligraphy, illuminations, and illustrations found in Islamic manuscripts, preserve the "aura"[55] of the original artwork/artist (arguably) intact?

In contrast, letter-pressed Arabic books with simple, unadorned, text-emphasizing layouts receive little visual analysis of their typographic compositions. Is this oversight simply due to the fact that art historians are better equipped to read image as text than to analyze text as image? Thus far, the visual analysis of Arabic print culture (from the premodern to the contemporary moment) is mostly undertaken by design practitioners, particularly those interested in typeface design and present-day debates on the place of Arabic typography. A number of design practitioners and scholars also explore the importance of Arabic typefaces in the digital realm in recent publications.[56] Yet, there remains an unexploited opportunity for visual, social, and historical examinations of past and current trends in Arabic printing.

By turning a spotlight on letter-pressed Arabic publications, with features ranging from the decorative to the solely typographic, this book endeavors to craft a language for examining the materiality of such objects that brings together tools of visual analysis from Islamic manuscript studies and design history. This study employs a codicological analysis (traditionally limited to manuscript studies) of Arabic publications that includes a study of binding, production methods, calligraphic techniques, and illuminations/ornamental elements, while also considering issues specific to design and printing practices, such as typeface designs and typographic compositions. By not limiting its examination of printed works to those that clearly emulate or refer back to scribal practices, this book strives to contribute a useful set of analytical tools to the study of the emergent field of Arabic printing history.

In so doing, this study of the printed Arabic book during the nineteenth century contributes to discussions of modernity as it relates to the mechanization and standardization of book production through the emergent printing industry. The scholarship on modernity is one that is both extensive

in the Nineteenth Century," *Manuscripta Orientalia* 5, no. 1 (1999): 12–22. An older study that first set up the printed book as a continuation of manuscript traditions was George Atiyeh's edited volume, *The Book in the Islamic World*.

55 Walter Benjamin, "The Work of Art in the Age of Mechanical Reproduction," in *Illuminations* (London: Pimlico, 1999), 211–44.

56 Rana Abou Rjeily, *Cultural Connectives* (London: Mark Batty Publisher, 2011); Thomas Milo, "Arabic Script and Typography: A Brief Historical Overview," in *Language Culture Type: International Type Design in the Age of Unicode*, ed. John D. Berry (Zurich: Graphis Press, 2002), 112–27; Huda Smitshuijzen-Abifares, *Arabic Typography: A Comprehensive Sourcebook* (London: Saqi, 2001); Yassin H. Safadi, "Printing in Arabic," *The Monotype Recorder* 2 (September 1980): 2–7.

and heavily contested.[57] Indeed, as argued by Alev Çinar, the term "modernity" itself is "one of the most controversial terms in scholarly literature, and to it is ascribed many, sometimes contradictory, meanings."[58] Its myriad interpretations are historical, cultural, and social, relating to industrialization, secularism, and capitalism.[59] Additionally, the use of this term[60] is "more challenging for scholars of non-European contexts due to the complexity of the experience of modernity in these places."[61] Recent scholarship on the subject contests the Eurocentric perspective (or ruling metanarrative[62]) by considering "multiple,"[63] "alternative,"[64] "attitudinal,"[65] or "convergent"[66] modernities. As argued by Kirsten Scheid in her research on early twentieth-century artists working in Mandate Lebanon:

"Whether there truly was a singular source for modernity, as the 'Eurocentric' model would have it, or multiple sources, as an 'alternative modernities' model would hold, it is the strategies these actors [in her case, Arab artists] chose for defining and enrolling others in their projects of modernizing that remain to be explained.... Artist-intellectuals sought to embody a modernity that is best understood as convergent.... [M] ost proclaimed the self-evident universality of art."[67]

My interest in this book is to contribute an art historical dimension to the cultural understanding of that moment. This is informed by similar investigations into aesthetic dimensions in studies of emergent modernities during the nineteenth and twentieth centuries.

57 A few key examples include: Tarek El-Ariss, *Trials of Arab Modernity: Literary Affects and the New Political* (The Bronx: Fordham University Press, 2013); Kirsten Scheid, "Necessary Nudes: *ḥadātha* and *mu'āṣira* in the Lives of Modern Lebanese," *IJMES* 42 (2010): 203–30; "The Agency of Art and the Study of Arab Modernity," *MIT-Electronic Journal of Middle East Studies* 7 (Spring 2007): 6–23; Lara Deeb, *An Enchanted Modern: Gender and Public Piety in Shi'i Lebanon* (Princeton: Princeton University Press, 2006); Jonathan Holt Shannon, *Among the Jasmine Trees: Music and Modernity in Contemporary Syria* (Middletown, Conn.: Wesleyan University Press, 2006); Keith D. Watenpaugh, *Being Modern in the Middle East: Revolution, Nationalism, Colonialism, and the Arab Middle Class* (Princeton: Princeton University Press, 2006); Alev Çinar, *Modernity, Islam, and Secularism in Turkey: Bodies, Places, and Time* (Minneapolis: University of Minnesota Press, 2005); Dilip Parameshwar Gaonkar, ed., *Alternative Modernities* (Durham: Duke University Press, 2001); S.N. Eisenstadt, "Multiple Modernities," *Daedalus* 129, no. 1, Multiple Modernities (2000): 1–29; Timothy Mitchell, ed., *Questions of Modernity* (Minneapolis: University of Minnesota Press, 2000).

58 Çinar, 1.

59 Ibid.

60 To avoid the fraught nature of this term, some scholars opt for their own variations on the concept. Lara Deeb, for instance, uses the term "modern-ness" to denote "the state of being modern as 'modern' is understood in a particular context." Deeb, *An Enchanted Modern*, 4, 4n9.

61 Ibid.

62 Çinar, 7.

63 See Eisenstadt, "Multiple Modernities," 1–29. All the essays in this special issue of *Daedalus* explore the possibility of "multiple modernities" as a varied, universal construct and concern that provides an alternative to the essentialized view of a single, Eurocentric, or "Western" notion of modernity.

64 See essays in Gaonkar, *Alternative Modernities*.

65 For instance, Çinar argues that modernity needs to be studied as a "specific attitude toward society ... that constructs the present as deficient and in need of remedial intervention that will transform it toward the future." Çinar, 7.

66 Scheid proposes that the concepts of modernity (in early twentieth-century Beirut) related to the notion of "change as not merely improving and imposing social order but also rupturing its temporal flow and overflowing its spatial boundaries. This is the essence of *convergent* modernity." Scheid, "Necessary Nudes," 215.

67 Ibid.

## Debates about Missionary-Arab Encounters

This book's analysis of the broader social, political, and religious issues negotiated upon the pages of publications printed at the American Press is predicated upon an understanding of American missionary-Arab engagements during the nineteenth century that moves beyond the polarizing views adopted in the traditional and post-colonial scholarship dealing with such encounters. Traditional sources on nineteenth-century missions in Ottoman Syria have disputed whether missionary activity amounted to a series of "altruistic" acts driven by religious zeal, or were disguised vehicles of imperial expansion[68] that paved the way for twentieth-century political involvements, such as contemporary American imperialism.[69] This binary debate is prevalent in post-colonial missionary-local studies, particularly the "cultural imperialism" model centered on a dichotomy between colonialists/imperialists and the "subaltern" communities upon which they act. As in other fields, such perspectives in missionary studies stem from Edward Said's paradigm-shifting views on the Western consumption and classification of the "orient" in literary texts.[70] While these studies take on the all-important task of disrupting the colonial narrative by discrediting imperial histories and structures, they also dismantle histories of "native" agency. As Arif Dirlik argues, the post-colonialist project "revers[es] historical narratives" by "replacing memories of colonization, victimization" according to "the identity needs of the present."[71]

Reconsidering the post-colonial model,[72] some contemporary scholars of missionary institutions call for alternate readings of the relationship between missionaries and local residents.[73] Ussama Makdisi, for instance, argues that dismissing individual missionaries wholesale as "cultural imperialists" risks "ignor[ing] the polyvalent registers

68 See William Hutchinson, *Errand to the World: American Protestant Thought and Foreign Missions* (Chicago: University of Chicago Press, 1987); Stephen Neill, *A History of Christian Missions*, 2nd ed. (Westminster: Penguin Books, 1987).

69 Most recently, sociologist Samir Khalaf makes the plausible point that Lebanon's current political history and the United States' regional involvement is sufficient evidence of missionary imperialist agendas (even if inadvertent). Khalaf, *Protestant Missionaries in the Levant: Ungodly Puritans, 1820–1860* (Oxford: Taylor and Francis, 2012), Kindle edition, prologue.

70 Edward Said, *Orientalism* (New York: Vintage Books, 1978); *Culture and Imperialism* (New York: Vintage Books, 1993).

71 Arif Dirlik, "Whither History? Encounters with Historicism, Postmodernism, Postcolonialism," in *History After the Three Worlds: Post-Eurocentric Historiographies*, eds. Arif Dirlik et al. (Latham: Rowman and Littlefield Publishers, 2000), 249–50.

72 Many are informed by historian Ryan Dunch's work on missionary activity in late Qing China in which he argues that dismissing foreign missionaries as cultural imperialists creates an essentialized discourse. See Dunch, "Beyond Cultural Imperialism: Cultural Theory, Christian Missions, and Global Modernity," *History and Theory* 41, no. 3 (2002): 301–25. See also Peter Golding and Phil Harris, eds., *Beyond Cultural Imperialism: Globalization, Communication and the New International Order* (London: Sage, 1996), 302.

73 Recent scholarship includes: Barbara Reeves-Ellington, *Domestic Frontiers: Gender, Reform, and American Interventions in the Ottoman Balkans and the Near East* (Boston: University of Massachusetts Press, 2013); Heather Sharkey, ed., *Cultural Conversions: Unexpected Consequences of Christian Missionary Encounters in the Middle East, Africa and South Asia* (Syracuse: Syracuse University Press, 2013); Ussama Makdisi, *Artillery of Heaven: American Missionaries and the Failed Conversion of the Middle East* (Ithaca: Cornell University Press, 2008); Habib Badr, "American Protestant Missionary Beginnings in Beirut and Istanbul: Policy, Politics, Practice and Response," in *New Faith in Ancient Lands: Western Missions in the Middle East in the Nineteenth and Early Twentieth Centuries*, ed. Heleen Murre-van den Berg (Leiden: Brill, 2006), 211–40; Ellen Fleischmann, "Evangelization or Education: American Protestant Missionaries, the American Board, and the Girls and Women of Syria (1830–1910)," in Murre-van den Berg, *New Faith in Ancient Lands*, 263–80.

of native worlds and the deliberate choice made by many individuals … to associate with foreign missionaries."[74] Others, such as Jeffrey Cox, emphasize the need for the inclusion of "master narratives" (those which the post-colonial perspective repudiates) in order to both understand and acknowledge the "mixed messages" created when Christian missions encounter non-Western Christians and other belief systems.[75]

Informed by some of these perspectives, the chapters that follow strive to present a history of early Arabic printing via the complex interactions between American missionaries and members of Syrian communities. Terms to describe such encounters that have been popular in recent post-colonial studies, like "hot zones," "contact zones," or "zones of hybridity,"[76] are intentionally avoided. While they attempt to address the problems of the bipolar approach of traditional studies, these labels and their uses still tend to stress the meeting of two divergent cultures/entities in which the primary role of the missionary/colonialist is inescapable.[77] Instead, this book underscores the juxtaposition of varying and dynamic worldviews to demonstrate not only how local residents reacted to and pushed against the mission's framework, but also how the Protestants themselves had to change their views as a result, thus revising their proselytizing practices and perceptions of local groups. However, given the limited availability of primary sources, for example the personal journals and records of local Arab Christian and Muslim individuals involved in the earlier stages of the print industry, this study relies almost exclusively on missionary records in addition to the printed books themselves. Such a dependence on missionary accounts (even if out of necessity) presents a host of challenges for the writing of a history that moves beyond a simple focus on the missionary perspective. Related anxieties continue to plague missionary historians who work beyond the cultural imperialist framework, yet still must rely almost exclusively upon imperial, colonial, or missionary archives.[78]

Working within these limitations, this book endeavors to highlight the nuances and complications of missionary-local relational dynamics in a number of ways. One is by reading the missionary sources as constructed narratives, which all archives, whether state-sanctioned or elite-sponsored, indeed are. In the case of foreign missions that had to contend with pressure to succeed from a board of trustees and patrons at "home," the inconsistencies, discrepancies, and variations in these accounts are made evident. When reporting to the Board or patrons in Boston and the US, for instance, missionaries in Beirut frequently over-sold or fabricated stories of local encounters, political events, and perceptions of local concerns and events. Such discrepancies, and the ways in which missionaries were forced by local circumstances and interactions to alter their views and approaches, become clear when considering more "private" accounts such as personal letters and journal entries. Another approach is reading missionaries' perceptions (particularly the "shortcomings") of certain local employees alongside realities on the ground, mostly through letters between

74 Makdisi, *Artillery of Heaven*, 10.

75 Cox, "Master Narratives of Imperial Missions," in *Mixed Messages: Materiality, Textuality, Missions*, eds. Jamie S. Scott and Gareth Griffiths (Hampshire: Palgrave Macmillan, 2005), 9–10.

76 As espoused by the works of Homi Bhabha in his seminal *The Location of Culture* (London: Routledge, 1994), and Mary L. Pratt in her widely-referenced *Imperial Eyes: Travel Writing and Transculturation* (London: Routledge, 1992); "Arts of the Contact Zone," *Profession* 91 (1991): 33–40.

77 Cox provides a similar criticism, see *Imperial Fault Lines: Christianity and Colonial Power in India, 1818–1940* (Stanford: Stanford University Press, 2002), 15.

78 "If only we could tell both sides of the story, [scholars] ask […] from the point of view of both colonizer and colonized, and weave the two points of view into a unified story based on a thorough knowledge of the history and culture of both sides of the binary." Cox, *The British Missionary Enterprise since 1700* (London: Routledge, 2008), 6.

missionaries and locals. Since materials from the perspective of Arab Christian residents in the mission's records are sparse, the niceties, requests, and complaints found in such correspondences are read closely for their subtleties and subtext. Finally, including Press books and pamphlets – which were produced, either with the support of the mission or by local scholars and elites – as primary sources provides an additional layer for understanding the complexities of missionary-local relations. These publications (as well as those of the American Press) provide an important common ground upon which the coevality[79] of complex missionary and local perspectives is negotiated. The development of the art of the book, for instance, shows how the mission's evangelical ideals and views of Protestantism were formulated in response to religious values upheld by the local multi-confessional milieu and competing Catholic missions. This also accounts for the role that local Arab scholars and residents played in both altering this mission's views and tactics, and charting out their own intellectual and social trajectories. In this vein, books and pamphlets (in their content, dimensions, visual conventions, and production methods) help move the discussion of such encounters beyond a reading of binary oppositions by presenting the at once divergent, complementary, and contradictory ideas adopted in various ways by both the missionaries and local participants.

Writing on the historical developments of encounters between Arabs and Americans must avoid reiterating the binary cultural opposition allegedly manifest in meetings between "East" and "West," which continue to pervade discourses on such relations today. This study avoids the "clash of civilizations"[80] model by exploring the complexity associated with the simultaneous, and fragmentary, presence of differing worldviews, religious values, and cultural norms, and how this dynamism led to various degrees of assimilation and change. Relying on a breadth of archival and secondary sources, this book reframes the narrative of interactions between American and local Arab ideals – as they related to missionary printing – to incorporate a broader discussion of complex concerns within local society as a whole. In this way, this project contributes an art historical angle to recent scholarly analyses of early contacts between American interlocutors and the Arab world that aim to provide a better understanding of such encounters.

### The American Press and Its Publications

This book is not organized as an exhaustive history of Arabic printing practices in the Arab world. Instead, its chapters are devoted to exploring the visual dimensions of nascent printing in Ottoman Beirut via developments at the American Press as they related to broader religious and socio-political developments in the region during the nineteenth century. While the present chapter established the broader debates in the field of study and the overarching methodological approach, the next section expounds on the nature of the American Press, as a missionary establishment, and its broader regional legacy, as one of few Arabic publishers in the Ottoman realms during the mid-1800s. It begins by laying the historical groundwork of the American Board of Commissioners for Foreign Missions' (ABCFM) Syria Mission in order to elucidate the intended role of the American Press, which was established as an extension of the missionary apparatus. This section considers the broader significance of the press within the regional context of Arab and Islamic print and manuscript production, with a special discussion of the local workforce employed at the Press.

After these first two, the chapters are organized chronologically, from 1834 to 1867. This choice stems from the changes in the visual and organizational nature of the American Press's

79 Makdisi uses a similar term in his work, see his "Reclaiming the Land of the Bible: Missionaries, Secularism, and Evangelical Modernity," *The American Historical Review* 102, no. 3 (1997): 681–82.

80 As promoted by Samuel P. Huntington, *The Clash of Civilizations and the Remaking of World Order* (New York: Touchstone, 1997).

publications that are evident from one decade to the other, and appear to negotiate specific political, social and economic developments taking place within the mission, as well as in Beirut and the Ottoman world as a whole. Structuring the book in this way also provides an opportunity to carefully trace the changing materiality of Arabic works produced at other regional presses, and the varying ways in which such presses responded to local socio-political developments through their publications. Chapter 3 considers the production methods, subject matter, and design conventions of the Press's earliest productions alongside an analysis of missionary records. The section underscores the significance of these early publications in negotiating the mission's own approach to interactions with members of local communities. Additionally, this chapter demonstrates how the printed pages of the Press's inaugural works – largely supervised local Arab employees – also speak to the dynamic nature of early printed books as sites of artistic innovation and experimentation where various local and external aesthetic impulses overlapped.

The fourth and fifth chapters explore the significances of changes to the material conventions and textual content of Press publications from 1841 onwards. Chapter 4 examines how visual shifts evident in these books and pamphlets, which may easily be dismissed as following a plain "Presbyterian aesthetic," were in fact responses to various local and external impulses. The main catalysts for such alterations included developments in the Press's typographic and production standards, pressure from the ABCFM board in Boston for a decreased emphasis on printing and education in favor of mass conversion preaching tactics, a changing local religious landscape, and a growing regional interest in secular education (resulting in a need for suitable textbooks). This chapter demonstrates how each of these various motivators led to (repeatedly divergent) practices in the mission's book production, and also how these views differed from those adopted by the Press when it was first established.

Chapter 5 considers the shifting role of the Press as a publisher of secular books edited, written, and/or funded by local Arab Christian scholars for use beyond the missionary apparatus. Works from the mid-1800s adopted various aspects of the American Press's aesthetics and production standards. This section examines the ways in which such practices likely related to changing perceptions amongst emergent print literati of what books should look like and how they should be read. In particular, this chapter interrogates the ways in which the Press's aesthetic and organizational practices served varied purposes for local scholars who were utilizing the nascent print medium to further their own political, social, and intellectual projects.

CHAPTER 2

# The American Press and Its Legacy

The history of the American Press in Ottoman Syria dates to 1810, when Protestant clergymen in Boston founded one of the first American missionary organizations with a foreign agenda. The American Board of Commissioners for Foreign Missions (ABCFM) followed in the steps of earlier British evangelical missions, specifically the British Church Missionary Society (CMS, founded in 1799) that had been active in communities throughout Asia. Following the establishment of its first foreign mission in Bombay by 1819,[1] the ABCFM formally announced its plans to send delegates to Palestine,[2] in the interest of securing Jerusalem as the heart of their mission to "Western Asia."[3] The first delegates assigned to this mission were Pliny Fisk and Levi Parsons, the latter of whom died in 1822, shortly after the two began work in the region. Jonas King later accompanied Fisk on his mission, and the two toured parts of Syria (they were also joined by Isaac Bird and William Goodell).[4]

The initial aim of the ABCFM's mission to Palestine was to convert Jewish populations, as well as Muslims, "Pagans," and those "who bear the Christian in name."[5] Missionary reports heralded this project as the way through which Jews, as a people who "long have been an awful monument to the world of the sovereignty of God," would finally, "through the benevolent prayers, and sacrifices and labors of Christians for their restoration," attain "mercy."[6] Certainly, this was rooted in a growing, millennial enthusiasm at this time for converting Jews.[7] However, the American mission's interests in Jerusalem also stemmed from both a romantic desire to establish an American post in the "Holy Land" (the cradle of early Christianity), as well as a proactive response to the burgeoning European (English, French, and Italian) presence in the Ottoman provinces along the Mediterranean.[8]

The establishment of a regional printing press, in addition to schools, parishes, and local churches, was seen as critical to the success of missionaries in "Western Asia." Indeed, early missionary reports from this region demonstrate the centrality of Bibles and religious literature to the missionary apparatus. An annual report of the ABCFM from 1820, for instance, details the number of tracts and books distributed by the first missionaries in Palestine, with one account boasting: "[Bibles] were gladly received by those who obtained them … tracts were distributed to children and others eager to possess them, with the hearty concurrence of bishops, schoolmasters, and principle inhabitants."[9] This purportedly warm reception of Protestant literature by locals tempted the ABCFM to take things further by instituting a "printing establishment in Western Asia," which was billed as most critical to the missionary's success: "they who can hear [the missionary's] voice, may be, comparatively, few.

1 *Report of the American Board of Commissioners for Foreign Missions* 10 (1819): 210–11.

2 Ibid., 229–31.

3 Western Asia, according to the ABCFM, included Syria, the Provinces of Asia Minor, Armenia, Georgia, and Persia.

4 For more on these early missionaries, see Gerald H. Anderson, ed., *Biographical Dictionary of Christian Missions* (Grand Rapids: William B. Eerdmas, 1998).

5 *Report of the American Board* 10 (1819): 230.

6 Ibid.

7 See Clifton J. Phillips, *Protestant America and the Pagan World: The First Half-Century of the American Board of Commissioners for Foreign Missions, 1810–1860* (Cambridge, MA: Harvard University Press, 1969).

8 For more on these issues, see Habib Badr, "American Protestant Missionary Beginnings in Beirut and Istanbul: Policy, Politics, Practice and Response," in *New Faith in Ancient Lands: Western Missions in the Middle East in the Nineteenth and Early Twentieth Centuries*, ed. Heleen Murre-van den Berg (Leiden: Brill, 2006), 211–40.

9 *Report of the American Board* 11 (1820): 92–93.

 | DOI 10.1163/9789004314351_003

But tracts and books reach the thousands."[10] However, even as the ABCFM was seeking funds from its subscribers for this costly venture, the missionaries to Palestine were still having trouble securing a permanent station from which to operate, let alone furnishing it with a press.

When the first American missionaries arrived in the region in 1819, they realized the difficulty of establishing a mission amongst Jewish communities in Jerusalem. For instance, half of Jerusalem's population was Muslim at the time and since, under Ottoman rule, the city was considered a holy Islamic site, there were clear restrictions on Europeans, Americans, and other "foreign" individuals taking up residence within the city's walls.[11] Additionally, the insular nature of local Jewish and Christian communities, and the established presence of fellow protestant British missionaries in that area (among other reasons)[12] led the Americans to shift their evangelizing focus from Jews in the "Holy Land" to other denominations in the Syrian provinces. These groups mostly consisted of Ottoman Syria's religious minorities, which in addition to Jewish communities included Maronite, Melkite Greek Catholic (*al-rūm al-malakiyyīn al-kāthūlīk*), Greek Orthodox (*al-rūm al-urthūdhuks*), and Armenian Orthodox Christians.[13]

In the eyes of the Ottoman state, these communities were not distinguished from each other and were collectively regarded as inferior to Muslim communities. In accordance with the seventh-century "Pact of 'Umar," non-Muslim residents from Jewish and Christian communities were tolerated as *ahl al-kitāb* (people of the book)[14] and thus were protected by the Ottoman state as *ahl al-dhimma* (people of the contract).[15] In exchange for this protection and the freedom to own property, partake in commerce, and practice their religions, such groups had to abide by various contractual obligations to the Islamic state. These included paying a *jizya* (head-tax), not preaching amongst or attempting to convert resident Muslims, and refraining from causing major local disturbances (e.g. by siding with enemies of Islam or of the Ottoman state).[16] Any inter-communal conversions, and not just efforts directed towards Muslims, were also discouraged. For the most part, the Ottoman state was apathetic with regard to conversions within these non-Muslim communities, since it was essentially able to control the Orthodox Church from Constantinople. A.L. Tibawi, to this effect, cites an eighteenth-century manuscript by the Mount Lebanon emir Ḥaydar Aḥmad al-Shihābī (d. 1835), which stipulates that by Islamic law all non-Muslims are infidels in the eyes of the state. This legal opinion was declared in 1762, seemingly in response to inter-communal violence as a result of Greek Orthodox Christians converting to Catholicism. Tibawi argues that the ruling was intended to ensure that the position and recognition of the religious communities, or

10 *Report of the American Board* 12 (1821–1825): 201.

11 See A.L. Tibawi, *American Interests in Syria: 1800–1901: A Study of Educational, Literary and Religious Work* (Oxford: Oxford University Press, 1966), 17.

12 Tibawi cites consular protection as the main cause; see his "The Genesis and Early History of the Syrian Protestant College," in *American University of Beirut Festival Book*, eds. Fouad Sarruf and Suha Tamim (Beirut: American University of Beirut Press, 1967), 258–59.

13 To avoid any unnecessary confusion, in this book these denominations are referred to as Maronite, Greek Catholic, and Greek Orthodox.

14 Defined as: "possessors of the Scripture ... denotes the Jews and the Christians, repositories of the earlier revealed books." Georges Vajda, "Ahl al-Kitāb," in *Encyclopedia of Islam, Second Edition,* ed. Peri Bearman et al. (Brill Online, 2015), http://referenceworks.brillonline.com/entries/encyclopaedia-of-islam-2/ahl-al-kitab-SIM_0383.

15 Bruce Masters, *Christians and Jews in the Ottoman Arab World: The Roots of Sectarianism* (Cambridge: Cambridge University Press, 2001), 18–19. See also, Mark R. Cohen, *Under Crescent and Cross: The Jews in the Middle Ages* (Princeton: Princeton University Press, 1994), 54–65; Ussama Makdisi, *Artillery of Heaven: American Missionaries and the Failed Conversion of the Middle East* (Ithaca: Cornell University Press, 2008), 33–37.

16 Makdisi, *Artillery of Heaven*, 33–35.

*milal,* particularly their respective Patriarchs' authority, would not be compromised in the eyes of the state.[17] However, Charbel Dagher describes the situation in more nuanced terms, explaining that the Ottoman indifference towards the competition between resident Christian communities allowed for inter-communal conversions. These were fueled by geopolitical tensions between Rome and the Eastern Church, such as the increase in Catholic missionary activity in the region, resulting in the ruling of 1762.[18] In any case, inter-communal conversions were seen as resulting in disruption, which non-Muslim communities were to refrain from causing.

The enforcement of such conditions varied across time periods and locations. By the 1860s, after numerous inter-communal conflicts, with the Ottoman government's growing interest in modernization reforms (Tanzimat or "orderings") and the emergence of the Islamic Salafi movement,[19] rulings like the Pact of ʿUmar were called into question by Muslim clerics and rulers.[20] In general, non-Muslim minorities in Ottoman Syria had frequently preferred the region's mountainous villages, which since the sixteenth century had been governed by ethnically and religiously diverse local elite families (not Ottoman officials), to the Muslim-dominant coastal cities. The two prominent ruling families during the Ottoman period (until the 1860s) were the Druze Maʿan dynasty, in power from twelfth to the seventeenth centuries, and the (mostly) Sunni Muslim Shihāb dynasty,[21] reigning from the seventeenth to the nineteenth centuries.[22] Consequently, the Mount Lebanon region, under Ottoman rule, had long become a refuge for non-Muslim minorities.[23] Seeking an alternative to their failed plan for Jerusalem, the Americans turned to the Christian villages of Mount Lebanon.

It is important to clarify that while this region's boundaries are commonly seen as the precursor to modern-day Lebanon, under Ottoman rule Mount Lebanon only became a semi-autonomous protectorate in the 1860s, after a series of inter-communal, class-related conflicts. The mountain villages saw significantly violent clashes in 1860, referred to as the Maronite-Druze War or Civil War. This violence, which had its roots in the 1840s in Mount Lebanon broke out near the modern border between Syria and Lebanon, and then extended into other parts of the region such as Damascus. The conflicts were essentially the result of class struggle, and a culmination of the peasants of Mount Lebanon revolting against their elite feudal leaders in 1858.[24] Thus,

17 Al-Shihābī's manuscript was cited in Tibawi as *Al-ghurar al-ḥisān fī akhbār abnāʾ az-zamān* [sic], from an edition published in 1933 by Asad Rustum and Fouad Bustani. See Tibawi, *American Interests*, 109–10.

18 Charbel Dagher, *Al-ʿarabiyya wa-l-tamaddun* (Beirut: Dār al-Nahār, 2008), 47–48.

19 For more on Salafism and modernity in the Ottoman world, see Itzchak Weismann, *Taste of Modernity: Sufism, Salafiyya, and Arabism in Late Ottoman Damascus* (Leiden: Brill, 2001).

20 See Masters, *Christians and Jews,* 170–78.

21 Bashīr Shihāb II (d. 1850) had converted to Christianity.

22 For a concise breakdown of elite rulers in Mount Lebanon and the region during this period, see Leila Tarazi Fawaz, *An Occasion for War: Civil Conflict in Lebanon and Damascus in 1860* (Berkeley: University of California Press, 1994), 15–18.

23 Donald Quataert provides a brief overview of interactions between the Ottoman state, its resident Muslims, and non-Muslim minorities: see *The Ottoman Empire: 1700–1922* (Cambridge: Cambridge University Press, 2005), 174–94. See also Dominique Chevallier, "Non-Muslim Communities in Arab Cities," in *Christians and Jews in the Ottoman Empire: The Functioning of a Plural Society*, eds. Benjamin Braude and Bernard Lewis (London: Holmes and Meier Publishers, 1982), 159–65.

24 Many sources exist on the subject of these battles. See, for example, Fawwaz Traboulsi, *A History of Modern Lebanon* (London: Pluto Press, 2007); Eugene L. Rogan, "Sectarianism and Social Conflict in Damascus: The 1860 Events Reconsidered," *Arabica* 54, no. 4 (2004): 493–511; Makdisi, *The Culture of Sectarianism: Community, History, and Violence in Nineteenth-Century Ottoman Lebanon* (Berkeley: University of California Press, 2000); Marwan R. Buheiry, "The Peasant Revolt of 1858 in Mount Lebanon: Rising Expectations, Economic Malaise, and the Incentive to Arm," in *Land Tenure and Social*

during most of the timeframe covered in this book, Mount Lebanon was still a loosely defined grouping of mountain villages spread across the area's administrative *wilāyas* (provinces) (Fig. 1). Each *wilāya* was subdivided into different *sanjaks*, or districts, with one serving as the provincial capital. The borders of these *wilāyas* and *sanjaks* shifted frequently from 1820–1888. During the 1830s there were three provinces encompassing the Mount Lebanon region: the *wilāya* of Tripoli, the *wilāya* of Damascus, and the *wilāya* of Sidon. The *wilāya* of Aleppo, also part of the Syrian provinces, lay further to the north. By the early nineteenth century, the ruling dynasty in Mount Lebanon, the Shihāb family, presided over numerous villages that consisted of predominantly Maronite Christian and Druze communities, with smaller groups of Jews, Shiʿa and Sunni Muslims, and Greek Orthodox, Armenian Orthodox, and Greek Catholic Christians.

In 1823 the American mission had established a temporary outpost, initially functioning as a rest house, in the Mount Lebanon village of ʿAynṭūra. The mission even managed to establish some schools and parishes. For instance, the first school was opened in 1824, under the tutelage of a local Arab Christian teacher, Tānnus al-Ḥaddād (a Greek Orthodox Christian who converted to Protestantism). This school initially had a number of children from the Greek Orthodox community in attendance.[25] However, it was not long before the Protestants,[26] with their distribution of Bibles and religious literature and vocal critique of "papal" practices, became a growing issue for local Maronite clerics and their patriarch. This led to an expanding chasm between the Syria mission and the Maronite Patriarch. What followed was a Maronite denunciation of the Americans and their establishments, and a state-sanctioned edict against the local distribution of foreign-produced ("Frankish") Bibles.[27] Furthermore, their choice of residence, a former Jesuit school,[28] may have been perceived by local Maronites (who were in communion with Rome) as an attempt to lay claim to this Catholic mission's past efforts.[29] In various efforts at curtailing any potential local disturbance, Mount Lebanon's ruling Bashīr Shihāb II called for the Protestants to depart their residence in ʿAynṭūra. Also contributing to the growing animosity between the Protestants and local Christian communities during the 1820s was the occasional conversion of local scholars and elites to Protestantism. Perhaps the most singular case was the conversion, excommunication, and subsequent death of a young Maronite, Asʿad al-Shidyāq (d. 1830), whose story served as an early example of persecution of Protestants in

*Transformation in the Middle East,* ed. Tarif Khalidi (Beirut: American University of Beirut, 1984), 291–302; Samir Khalaf, "Communal Conflict in 19th-Century Lebanon," in Braude and Lewis, *Christians and Jews,* 107–34; Antoine J. Abraham, *Lebanon at Mid-Century, Maronite-Druze Relations in Lebanon 1840–1860: A Prelude to Arab Nationalism* (Washington, D.C.: University Press of America, 1981).

25 Discussed in Tibawi, *American Interests,* 33. However, Tibawi does not mention where he retrieved this information.

26 Although the terms Protestants and Americans are used interchangeably throughout this book in reference to the Syria Mission, these individuals were not frequently distinguished as "Americans" by local residents. Due to their protection under the imperial British Consul from the 1820s until the 1840s, American members of the Syria Mission were often categorized as English. Until the 1840s, local residents saw Protestant groups as indistinguishable from each other, thus labeling European nationals simply as *ajānib* (Franks). See Makdisi, *The Culture of Sectarianism,* 90–91.

27 Discussed further in Chapter 3.

28 The Syria mission rented this space for five years. See Tibawi, *American Interests,* 23.

29 Jesuit presence in the region dated to the mid 1700s. However, towards the end of the 18th century, Rome recalled all its foreign missions due to growing anti-clerical sentiment in Europe; see Bertrand M. Roehner, "Jesuits and the State: A Comparative Study of Their Expulsions," *Religion* (*London Academic Press*) 27, no. 2 (1997): 165–82.

FIGURE 1 *Map of key provinces, cities, and villages in Ottoman Syria, ca. 1830.*

the region.[30] The rapidly widening chasm between the Americans and the Maronite communities brought much to bear upon any future interactions between these two groups and their perceptions of each other.

Following their eviction from Mount Lebanon, the Americans turned to the burgeoning and more religiously and ethnically diverse maritime town of Beirut for their headquarters.[31] Early nineteenth-century Beirut was a merchant-city[32] on the rise, one which had long set itself apart from other regional urban settings as "an asylum for immigrants from embattled regions" in the Ottoman eastern Mediterranean (*Bilād al-Shām*), growing "against the odds of the regional urban hierarchy."[33] During the late 1700s an influx of immigrants from other regional centers, many of whom were seeking protection from Ottoman urban hierarchies, found a safe haven behind Beirut's protective walls, and helped to shape the rise of Beirut as an Ottoman merchant city. Throughout this earlier period, "Beirut became not only a cherished prize [to migrant and resident elites who challenged Sulaymān Pasha's regional control of urban centers and market prices] but also an uncomfortably autonomous entity in the struggle for regional hegemony."[34] Thus, the rising stature of Beirut as an urban center essentially lay in large immigration numbers.[35] Consequently, from the 1830s onwards, Beirut began asserting itself as a cosmopolitan (though overpopulated) city. Its location beyond the administrative jurisdiction of the mountain rulers/elites and as a "maritime town with the least imperial [Ottoman] authority within its walls"[36] also allowed Beirut a certain level of distance from the central government.

By 1831 Beirut came under the temporary rule of Egyptian powers when military forces led by the general Ibrāhīm Pasha, acting at the behest of his father the Egyptian ruler Muhammad ʿAli, took control of most of the Ottomans' Syrian provinces (including the cities of Beirut and Damascus). This was in retribution for the Ottoman sultan reneging on promises made to the Egyptian Viceroy after he provided military aid during conflicts in the empire's Greek territories in the 1820s, commonly known as the War of Greek Independence. Egypt's rule over Syria ended in 1841 after a series of drawn-out battles with Ottoman military and global powers.[37] However, during this period, Beirut became an important regional port-city that saw increased maritime trade, and its position within the nineteenth-century global economy was furthered. In particular, this coastal town became the nexus between European (namely French) textile merchants and the silk industry of Mount Lebanon.[38] It also achieved more influence as an administrative and political hub when the Egyptian Viceroy designated it as the capital of the *wilāya* of Sidon in 1841.[39] Further establishing Beirut's identity as a key regional site was the implementation of Egyptian-imposed administrative and urban modernization reforms.[40]

30 Discussed further in Chapter 5. See also Makdisi, *Culture of Sectarianism*, 90–91; *Artillery of Heaven*.

31 Tibawi, *American Interests*, 23–26.

32 It became colloquially known from this period onwards as a "merchant republic," an idea still popular in the Lebanese mindset today; see Jens Hanssen, *Fin de siècle Beirut: The Making of an Ottoman Provincial Capital* (Oxford: Clarendon Press, 2005), 29.

33 Ibid.

34 Ibid.

35 See Leila Tarazi Fawaz, *Merchants and Migrants in Nineteenth-Century Beirut* (Cambridge, Mass.: Harvard University Press, 1983), 1–7.

36 Hanssen, *Fin de siècle Beirut*, 29.

37 For more on these conflicts, see Virginia Aksan, *Ottoman Wars: An Empire Besieged* (Harlow: Pearson, 2007), 363–422.

38 Hanssen, *Fin de siècle Beirut*, 31. For more on Mount Lebanon's silk industry, see Fawaz, *Merchants and Migrants*, 61–67; Akram Fouad Khater, "She Married Silk: A Rewriting of Peasant History in 19th Century Mount Lebanon" (PhD Diss., University of California Berkeley, 1993).

39 Samir Kassir, *Beirut*, trans. Malcolm B. Debevoise (Berkeley: University of California Press, 2010), 89.

40 Hanssen, *Fin de siècle Beirut*, 29–35; Kassir, *Beirut*, 96–108.

While this urban setting played an important role in providing the Syria Mission with a more adaptable environment than that of the mountain villages, the mission's Beirut station experienced its own share of instability, particularly in its intermittent closures and relocations due to local and regional conflicts, which frequently spilled into the city. The mid-1820s to the early 1830s, for instance, witnessed the Greek revolt (1821–1827), the Russian-Ottoman conflict (1828–1829), and Egypt's occupation of portions of the Syrian provinces (1830–1833).[41] During these periods, the American missionaries in Beirut were removed to Malta, a British colony that was seen as a safer option at the time, and remained under the protection of the English consul in the Ottoman Mediterranean.[42] After the mission's station was reestablished in Beirut, however, the Americans typically sought refuge in neighboring villages (like their summer residence in ʿAbay) when conflicts – like the second war between Ottoman forces and Egypt from 1839–1841[43] – impacted the city. Despite these occasional interruptions, the Americans' outpost in Beirut remained their main station and, more importantly, Beirut was cemented as the location of the ABCFM's regional Arabic press until the dissolution of the Syria Mission in the mid-twentieth century.[44]

## Regional Presses and Book-making Customs

The importance of the ABCFM's press in Beirut (the American Press) can be ascertained on a number of levels. For one, it was the Board's first foreign missionary press devoted exclusively to publishing books in Arabic. Although the British Church Missionary Society (CMS) in Malta had been publishing Arabic books for missionary use since the 1820s, their works were not limited to Arabic but included Greek and Syriac.[45] Additionally, while the ABCFM operated other regional presses in Malta (from 1822–1833) and Izmir (1833–1853) for their Ottoman outreach, both were short-lived. The former specialized in Greek and Armeno-Turkish prints (although it had an Arabic typeface which was not used), while the latter was an extension of the Protestant's mission to Armenians, and thus its publications were primarily in Armeno-Turkish and Armenian.[46]

41 For more on these conflicts and others in the Ottoman Empire, see Aksan, *Ottoman Wars*. See also Makdisi, *Culture of Sectarianism*.

42 For instance, in an 1827 letter by the American missionary Eli Smith addressed to his sister in Connecticut he informs her of the mission in Beirut's evacuation plans: "We have rumors of an approaching war … the mountains are within an hour's ride of this place [Beirut] … besides, we have united with the others here under English protection to send to Smyrna [Izmir] for a man of war to come and take us away in case of emergency [to Malta]." Records of the Syria Mission, of the American Board of Commissioners of Foreign Missions, deposited at Jafet Memorial Library Archives and Special Collections, American University of Beirut, Lebanon, American Missionaries, AA: 7.5, Box 1, File 6 (hereafter cited as AUB Archives AA7.5-1-6), Eli Smith to Hannah Smith, Beirut, 23 Jun 1827.

43 For details on this and the earlier battle with Egypt, see Aksan, *Ottoman Wars*, 363–407.

44 After the American Civil War and the reunion of divergent Presbyterian Church bodies in the US, the Syria Mission was transferred from the ABCFM to the Presbyterian Church in the USA Board of Foreign Missions (BFM) in 1870. It remained operational in the region under the BFM's direction until the early 1960s. For more on this transfer, see Records of the American Board of Commissioners for Foreign Missions deposited at Houghton Library, Harvard University, Cambridge, Mass. (hereafter cited as ABC), 16.8.1 Syria Mission (1823–1871), vol. 8, "Meeting in ʿAbay," 17 Aug 1870.

45 For more on the CMS press in Malta, see Roper, "Arabic Books Printed in Malta 1826–42: Some Physical Characteristics," in *History of Printing and Publishing in the Languages and Countries of the Middle East*, ed. Philip Sadgrove (Oxford: Oxford University Press, 2005), 111–29.

46 For more on the ABCFM press in Malta and Izmir, see J.F. Coakley, "Printing Offices of the American Board of Commissioners for Foreign Missions, 1817–1900: A

The American Press was also regionally significant as an early Arabic printing enterprise. At the time of its establishment, most books (for devotional and educational purposes) were still written by hand. Mosques, madrasas, and imperial workshops produced Qur'ans and other Islamic texts, while Christian seminaries and monasteries engaged in the manufacture of Bibles and other liturgical works. Also at the time of its establishment, this Beirut-based American Press also found itself at the nexus between age-old scribal traditions and emergent printing traditions. Not only was the press operating as a foreign body within the realm of Ottoman power, it was also one of few printing establishments within a market dominated by scribal practices. However, monastic communities did engage in printing practices from time to time. One of the more prolific of these was the monastic Greek Catholic press of al-Shuwayr, or *Maṭbaʿat Dayr Mār Yūḥānna al-Mullaqab bi-l-Shuwayr,* in Khinshāra (Mount Lebanon) from the eighteenth century on.[47]

Until the 1860s the economy of book manufacture in the Islamic world was still largely dominated by scribal workshops, with the small number of print shops coexisting with scribal workshops. Reasons for this minimal adoption of (or presumed "resistance towards") printing practices in the Ottoman realms prior to the mid-1800s have been much debated. Seeking explanations for this "delay," some scholars describe an aversion amongst Ottoman rulers and religious scholars, or ʿulama',[48] to a "Western" technology, and others reference a seemingly inherent discord between printing practices and Islamic scribal ones, among other issues.[49] Still others convincingly argue that global technological changes, such as the development of the more efficient and easier to ship Stanhope iron hand press, led to the wider adaptation of printing practices in the

Synopsis," *Harvard Library Bulletin* 9, no. 1 (1998): 11 14; "Homan Hallock, Punchcutter," *Printing History* 45, no. 1 (2003): 18–41.

47 During the 1700s, for instance, this press produced numerous editions of the Psalter (in varying sizes and formats) and other religious texts, such as catechisms for children. A number of these are currently held at the British Library; see Alexander G. Ellis, *Catalogue of Arabic Books in the British Museum*, 3 vols. (London: The British Museum, 1894–1901). The early book manufacture practices of the monastery in al-Shuwayr are elaborated upon in Carsten Walbiner, "Monastic Reading and Learning in 18th-Century Bilād Al-Šām: Some Evidence from the Monastery of Al-Šuwayr," *Arabica* 51, no. 4 (2004): 462–77. A short entry on this monastery's print activities can be found in Geoffrey Roper and Dagmar Glass, "The Printing of Arabic Books in the Arab World," in *Middle Eastern Languages and the Print Revolution: A Cross-Cultural Encounter*, eds. Eva Hanebutt-Benz et al. (Mainz: Gutenberg-Museum, 2002), 179–81. Information on one of the key printers at this location, ʿAbdallāh Zākhir, is covered extensively in Joseph Kahale, *ʿAbd-allāh zākhir, mubtakir al-maṭbaʿa al-ʿarabiyya* (Aleppo: Markaz al-Inmā' al-Ḥaḍārī, 2002).

48 For more on this class of Islamic scholars, see Amit Bein, *Ottoman Ulema, Turkish Republic: Agents of Change and Guardians of Tradition* (Stanford: Stanford University Press, 2011).

49 For a few of these sources, see M. Brett Wilson, *Translating the Qur'an in an Age of Nationalism: Print Culture and Modern Islam in Turkey* (London: Institute of Ismaili Studies, 2014); Orlin Sabev, "Waiting for Godot: the formation of Ottoman print culture," in *Historical Aspects of Printing and Publishing in Languages of the Middle East*, ed. Geoffrey Roper (Leiden: Brill, 2014), 101–20; Ami Ayalon, *Reading Palestine: Printing and Literacy*, 1900–1948 (Austin: University of Texas Press, 2004); Muhsin Mahdi, "From the Manuscript Age to the Age of Printed Books," in *The Book in the Islamic World: The Written Word and Communication in the Middle East,* ed. George N. Atiyeh (Albany: State University of New York, 1995), 1–16; Lutz Berger, "Zur Problematik der späten Einfuhrung des Buchdrucks in der islamischen Welt," in *Das gedruckte Buch im Vorderen Orient*, ed. Ulrich Marzolph (Dortmund: Verlag für Orientkunde, 2002), 15–28; Ayalon, *The Press in the Arab Middle East; a History* (Oxford: Oxford University Press, 1995); Fatma Müge Göçek, *East Encounters West: France and the Ottoman Empire in the Eighteenth Century* (Oxford: Oxford University Press, 1987), 108–15.

Islamic realms.[50] Recent scholarship, however, suggests that the need to explain the delayed adoption of printing within Islamic circles of knowledge production in the Ottoman regions actually stems from the persistence of a Eurocentric historiography on the subject of Islamic book manufacture amongst bibliographers and print historians.[51]

The perceived hesitation with regard to the print medium, specifically amongst a certain class of readers and producers of manuscripts, is certainly not limited to the Islamic world. A preference for manuscript over print within certain fields of inquiry in seventeenth-century Europe is well described by David McKitterick:

"For everyone, print was not just to share; it was to share in an uncontrolled way with an audience whose extent and nature could never be known, and whose suitability to participate in knowledge was untested by social or intellectual criteria. Hence, manuscripts offered some protection, within a coterie readership. Such issues … were inherent in many aspects of the cautiously restrictive decisions to entrust publication … to manuscript rather than to print."[52]

Print's potential for an undifferentiated and uncontrolled distribution of knowledge was viewed with caution in early European contexts. The same could certainly be argued for book production in the Islamic world, specifically in the case of Islamic texts like the Qur'an, where there is a fear of heresy or religious innovation (*bid'a*).[53] Nevertheless, prior to the nineteenth century, the Sublime Porte did not explicitly discourage the import and circulation of European copies of texts. In fact, printed Arabic books, many of which came from European presses, had long been in circulation amongst Ottoman elites, scholars, and clergy members. It is also known that copies of the Qur'an that were printed at these "foreign" presses, while not considered legal or official by the Porte or 'ulama', were circulated in the region.[54] By the mid- to late nineteenth century, local Muslim presses also began printing copies of the Qur'an, such as those produced by Osman Zeki Bey (d. 1888) under the patronage of Sultan 'Abdul Ḥamīd II (d. 1918).[55]

An important point to be noted regarding early Arabic printing is the overall quality of print production prior to the late 1800s. Technically, the equipment used for printing in Arabic at the time did not allow for a seamless translation of calligraphy's refined scripts into letterpress technology. While a few type foundries existed in parts of the Ottoman Empire, such as in Egypt and Turkey, the majority of Arabic typefaces and letterpress materials were produced in Europe and the United States well into the mid-1800s. Given the unfamiliarity with Islamic calligraphic traditions, the Arabic typefaces of European and American foundries

50 Nile Green, "Persian Print and the Stanhope Revolution: Industrialization, Evangelicalism, and the Birth of Printing in Early Qajar Iran," *Comparative Studies of South Asia, Africa and The Middle East* (hereafter cited as *CSSAAME*) 30, no. 3 (2012): 413–90.

51 For instance, Kathryn Schwartz discusses this argument in her dissertation: see "Meaningful Mediums: A Material and Intellectual History of Manuscript and Print Production in Nineteenth Century Ottoman Cairo" (PhD Diss., Harvard University, 2015), 13, 18–26. See also Dana Sajdi, "Print and its Discontents: A Case for Pre-Print Journalism and Other Sundry Print Matters," *The Translator* 15, no. 1 (2009): 105–38.

52 McKitterick, *Print, Manuscript and the Search for Order 1450–1830* (Cambridge: Cambridge University Press, 2003), 206.

53 Reinhard Schulze, "The Birth of Tradition and Modernity in 18th and 19th Century Islamic Culture: The Case of Printing," *Culture & History* 16 (January 1997): 29–72; Mahdi, "From the Manuscript Age."

54 For a thorough discussion of the circulation of European-produced Qur'ans in the Ottoman realms (as well as the printing of the Qur'an in the Ottoman world), see Wilson, 29–83.

55 Nedret Kuran-Burçoğlu, "Osman Zeki Bey and His Printing Office the *Matbaa-i Osmaniye*," in Sadgrove, *History of Printing and Publishing*, 35–57. See also, Wilson, 55–83.

were unable to accurately capture the cursive nature of Arabic calligraphy and the overall quality attributed to the calligrapher's hand. For instance, incongruous gaps between letterforms frequently appear in early examples of Arabic printing. At the same time, consistency in the shapes, proportions, and stroke weights of letterforms was lacking, particularly given the nature of Arabic writing, which required up to four variations per letter according to where it appeared in the word/sentence. The use of vocalization marks, while not imperative in the overall legibility of an Arabic text, did not conform to the appearance of such vowels in handwritten works. For instance, at times the location of a vocalization mark made it difficult to discern which letterform it belonged to in a text block. This host of factors, in addition to others, often compromised the overall legibility and aesthetic quality of printed Arabic texts that were produced with typefaces cast prior to the mid-1800s. Nevertheless, the quality of printed books at the time did not necessarily deter the production or circulation of such works.

Although the question of why printing practices in the Islamic world only became prominent in the nineteenth century continues to be debated today, what remains is that in the Ottoman realms at the time, book manufacture via print technologies was limited in comparison to manuscript production. Instead of seeking answers as to why printing practices were not as popular as scribal ones, what should be asked is how early printing conventions subsisted within the predominantly scribal economy. In order to understand the context within which nineteenth-century presses were operating, it is more beneficial (for the purposes of this study) to briefly examine aspects of regional manuscript production at the time, and what they meant for emergent printing traditions. There was also the issue of the rules and hierarchy governing the Ottoman calligraphic tradition. Arabic calligraphy had its roots in the process of reproducing the Qur'an in writing. From its early emergence in the seventh century, the tradition of bookmaking in the Islamic world underwent many changes. By the nineteenth century, a system (amongst a certain group of established scholars and ʿulamaʾ) that included the preservation of past customs and a master-student training process remained intact. Inherent to this system was the regulation of authenticity and authority within the realm of calligraphic and manuscript production. Apprentices would undergo years of intensive training with a master, who himself was trained in a similar manner and belonged to a lineage of scribal authorities that spanned several centuries. Once their training was completed to the satisfaction of the master, they would be granted a license (thus, authority) to practice the art and sign their names to their works.[56] For a specific coterie of manuscript producers and readers, which included ʿulamaʾ (whose roles hinged upon the book-production economy), an important component of scribal traditions was the author-to-copyist textual authentication system. This copying process entailed dictating the manuscript text to scribes, who would then read out loud what they wrote for the "author" (or head scribe) in order for the text to be authenticated.[57] The genealogy of scribal masters was thus well documented, with "authentic" and "legitimate" copies of manuscripts that included the signatures and/or seals of calligraphers differentiated from other productions.

However, it is also important not to overstate the rigidity of this system. In particular, the production of books was by no means limited to the strata of ʿulamaʾ and ruling elites. Unrestrained by the rules and hierarchy governing calligraphic

56 Sheila Blair, *Islamic Calligraphy* (Edinburgh: Edinburgh University Press, 2006), 476–79; Wilson, 39–40.

57 Francis Robinson, "Technology and Religious Change: Islam and the Impact of Print," *Modern Asian Art* 27, no. 1 (1993): 229–51. The roles of copyists and scribes in traditional manuscript production are described in D. Fairchild Ruggles, *Islamic Art and Visual Culture: An Anthology of Sources* (West Sussex: Wiley-Blackwell Publishing, 2011), 31–49; Adam Gacek, *Arabic Manuscripts: A Vademecum for Readers* (Leiden: Brill, 2009), 234–43.

production was an extensive lower-level copying industry of less scholarly, mass-produced texts that utilized informal, spoken variants of Arabic (e.g. not the standard *fuṣḥa*). In her work on the pre-nineteenth-century culture of Islamic book production and circulation, Nelly Hanna explains how a large number of manuscripts produced in Cairo from the sixteenth to eighteenth century were not products of the ruling class or high-level religious ʿulamaʾ. Instead, educated members of the urban (or middle) class made up of merchants, artisans, and tradesmen copied these books.[58] Similarly, Dana Sajdi brings to light the work of eighteenth-century non-ʿulamaʾ Levantine craftsmen writers who authored literary texts and historical chronicles fashioned from distinct literary traditions and genres that were popular at the time.[59] Thus, while the ʿulamaʾ in Ottoman societies certainly exerted control over the production of religious knowledge, there were other spheres of knowledge production and transmission which were not regulated by the ruling or religious elites.[60] There existed a complex multi-faceted network of manuscript manufacture at the time that was not limited to a single social strata or set of professions. Printed books produced in the Ottoman realms, while not as popular as their handwritten counterparts, subsisted within this network of manuscript production.

The earliest presses to operate in the region were mostly those of religious denominations (most of which were non-Muslim) and a few government establishments.[61] For instance, Jewish communities of European origin established printing presses in Istanbul as early as the late fifteenth century.[62] The same went for Armenian presses, which were first set up in the city during the mid-sixteenth century.[63] Muslim-operated presses in the Ottoman realms before the 1800s could be found in Istanbul, such as state-sanctioned press belonging to İbrahim Müteferrika (limited to printing non-religious works),[64] as well as the Ottoman presses established in Istanbul under Sultan Selīm III (d. 1807). One was set up in 1795/6 at the *Mühendishane* (School of Engineering and Artillery) in the Hasköy quarter. The other was launched in Üsküdar in 1803/4.[65] Both of these presses printed Arabic books from around the 1790s onwards.[66] By 1822 the State Press of the Egyptian Viceroy Muhammad ʿAli (d. 1848) in Cairo's suburb Būlāq began publishing books in Arabic on a press purchased from Italy.[67] Other early Muslim-run presses included those in Qajar Iran, which were operational from

58 Hanna, *In Praise of Books: A Cultural History of Cairo's Middle Class, Sixteenth to the Eighteenth Century* (Syracuse: Syracuse University Press, 2003), 1–12.

59 Sajdi, *The Barber of Damascus: Nouveau Literacy in the Eighteenth-Century Ottoman Levant* (Stanford: Stanford University Press, 2013). See also her "Print and its Discontents."

60 Hanna, 14.

61 For a comprehensive list of presses and their operational periods, see Schwartz, 30–35.

62 See Orit Bashkin, "Why did Baghdadi Jews Stop Writing to their Brethren in Mainz? – Some Comments about the Reading Practices of Iraqi Jews in the Nineteenth Century," in Sadgrove, *History of Printing and Publishing*, 95–110; Gad Nassi, ed., *Jewish Journalism and Printing Houses in the Ottoman Empire and Modern Turkey* (Istanbul, 2001); Ittai J. Tamari, "Jewish Printing and Publishing Activities in the Ottoman Cities of Constantinople and Saloniki at the Dawn of Early Modern Europe," in *The Beginnings of Printing in the Near and Middle East: Jews, Christians and Muslims*, ed. Klaus Kreiser (Weisbaden: Harrassowitz Verlag, 2001), 9–10.

63 Meliné Pehlivanaian, "Mesrop's Heirs: The Early Armenian Book Printers," in Hanebutt-Benz, *Middle Eastern Languages*, 53–92.

64 Maurits van den Boogert, "The Sultan's Answer to the Medici Press? Ibrahim Muteferrika's Printing House in Istanbul," in *The Republic of Letters and the Levant*, eds. van den Boogert et al. (Leiden: Brill, 2005), 265–91.

65 Clifford E. Bosworth, ed., s.v. "Matbaʿa," *Encyclopedia of Islam*, vol. 6 (Leiden: Brill, 1989): 801.

66 Abū al-Futūḥ Riḍwān, *Tārīkh maṭbaʿat būlāq: wa-lamḥa fī tārīkh al-ṭibāʿa fī buldān al-sharq al-awsaṭ* (Cairo: al-Maṭbaʿa al-Amīriyya, 1953), 24.

67 For more on this press, see Riḍwān, *Tārīkh maṭbaʿat būlāq*; Khālid ʿAzab and Aḥmad Manṣūr, *Al-kitāb al-ʿarabī al-maṭbūʿ: min al-judhūr ila maṭbaʿat būlāq* (Cairo: Dār al-Miṣriyya al-Lubnāniyya, 2008); Fawzi M. Tadrus,

the early 1800s, yet mostly produced works in Persian.[68] Presses to emerge in the Ottoman Syrian Provinces (during the 1600s–1700s) were mostly monastic print shops funded by local Christian patrons who were able to acquire their presses from European benefactors. For instance, the first known example of printing in the Syrian province comes from the monastery of Mār Anṭūniyyūs in Quzḥāyya, which printed a bilingual, Syriac, and *karshūnī* (Arabic in Syriac script) Psalter in 1610.[69] Other presses included the short-lived press of the Greek Orthodox Patriarch Athanasius III al-Dabbās in Aleppo, which lasted from 1706–1711.[70] A common aspect of these presses was the fact that few lasted long. Given the marginal nature of pre-nineteenth-century printing establishments in the Ottoman Empire, these early presses suffered from high running costs, a shortage of fonts and skilled labor, and a lack of consistent funding. As a result, some of these establishments only produced a small number of books (often in limited print runs). An exception was the previously mentioned al-Shuwayr press, where the earliest publication dated to 1734, and which continued to print books until 1899.[71]

By the mid-1800s the emergence of Arabic missionary presses like the American Press, followed by a Jesuit press in Beirut, and a Franciscan press in Jerusalem, in addition to state-sanctioned presses like Būlāq, led to the wide-spread development of a local Arab print culture. While all of these presses operated with their own religious or political agendas, they each also contributed to the growing involvement of local scholars and elites in the realms of print that led to the formation of an urban print intelligentsia made up of Muslim and Arab Christian scholars. It is through these earlier encounters between the worlds of script and print that the intellectual movements of the late nineteenth century found expression.

## The American Press and Its Workforce

In discussing the broader significance of the American Press, it is critical to underscore the fact that it did not achieve instant success as a publisher of missionary or other texts. In fact, the struggles and failures of the Press during its first three decades of operation are chronicled in detail in the three following chapters.[72] At this point it should be noted that during its early history, the Press did not control an extensive amount of equipment, thus its output numbers and dissemination cannot be compared to those of similar establishments in the US, Europe, or even other

*Printing in the Arab World with Emphasis on the Būlāq Press in Egypt* (Doha: University of Qatar, 1982).

68 For Qajar presses, see Nile Green, "Persian Print and the Stanhope Revolution: Industrialization, Evangelicalism, and the Birth of Printing in Early Qajar Iran," *CSSAAME* 30, no. 3 (2012): 413–90; Ulrich Marzolph and Anja Pistor-Hatam, "Early Printing History in Iran (1817–ca. 1900)," in Hanebutt-Benz, *Middle Eastern Languages*, 249–69; Michael Albin, "The Iranian Publishing Industry: A Preliminary Appraisal," *Libri* 36, no. 1 (1986): 1–23; B.W. Robinson, "The Teheran Nizami of 1848 and Other Qajar Lithographed Books," in *Islam in the Balkans: Persian Art and Culture of the 18th and 19th Centuries*, ed. Jennifer M. Scarce (Edinburgh: Royal Scottish Museum, 1979), 61–65.

69 Carsten Walbiner, "Ktobō d-mazmūrē d-Dawīd malkō wa-nbīyō," in Kreiser, *The Beginnings of Printing*, 22. See also ʿAzab and Manṣūr, 85.

70 Geoffrey Roper, "History of the Book in the Muslim World," in *The Book: A Global History*, eds. Michael F. Suarez, S.J. and H.R. Wooudhuysen (Oxford: Oxford University Press, 2013), 542.

71 Roper, "History of the Book," 543. For more on these early monastic presses see Walbiner, "Monastic Reading and Learning"; Kahale, *Abdallāh al-zākhir* Wahid Gdoura, *Bidāyat al-ṭibāʿa al-ʿarabiyya fī isṭānbūl wa-bilād al-shām: taṭawwur al-muḥīt al-thaqāfī, 1706–1787* (Riyadh: Maktabat al-Malik Fahd al-Waṭaniyya, 1993); Khalīl Ṣabbāt, *Tārīkh al-ṭibāʿa fī al-sharq al-ʿarabī* (Cairo: Dār al-Maʿārif, 1958).

72 See Appendix One for the annual number of publications produced at the American Press from 1836 to 1867.

missionary stations. Equipment in its print shop essentially comprised two lithographic presses and two hand presses: a "Demy" press, sometimes referred to as a "common press" in records, and a "Super Royal" press, which was a "patent Well's" press.[73] The former was in bad shape at the time and could only be used for proofs. The latter was one of the iron toggle-joint patent lever iron presses patented in 1819 by John Wells of Hartford, Connecticut.[74] This press's production rate was approximately forty-one to forty-two impressions per hour (or "two thousand impressions … in two days").[75] In addition to the letterpress, the American Press's print shop also had at least one functioning lithography press at their disposal. There was a second one on site that appears to have been damaged beyond repair (since it was not used). The mission's functioning lithographic press was mainly used to print larger sheets, such as cartographic prints, and smaller jobs, like spelling cards and alphabet sheets for schools. Based on press records from 1836, it does not seem that the missionaries viewed this method as one for printing complete books.[76] This technological preference is worth noting, since other regional presses, like those in Qajar Iran, preferred the use of lithography (as a printing process) for books, even though letterpresses were used in Qajar publishing houses.[77]

It took a few decades, until at least the 1870s, for the Press's output to increase substantially, on par with the production numbers at contemporaneous European enterprises. Technically speaking, this became feasible once the Press acquired more advanced machinery in 1855 with the purchase of a single-horse-powered steam press "capable of throwing off eight hundred impressions per hour."[78] However, the Press's importance during its earlier decades cannot be understated. In particular, its significance lay not only in its regional role as an early Arabic printing enterprise, but also the ways in which it helped negotiate the interplay of multivalent religious views and social concerns. This was an establishment from which individuals like Nāṣīf al-Yāzijī and Buṭrus al-Bustānī essentially launched their publishing careers as regionally significant scholars. It was also a significant employer and training center for apprentice printers, compositors, and type casters.

During its first thirty years of operation, the American Press relied heavily on local Armenian, Greek Catholic, Greek Orthodox, Maronite, and (sometimes) Muslim men (and in later decades, women) as printers, binders, type compositors, copyists, translators, authors, and correctors.[79] Throughout the 1830s and 1840s these individuals, in addition to al-Yāzijī and al-Bustānī, included the previously mentioned Tānnūs al-Ḥaddād, and Antūniyyū al-Khayyāṭ (possibly a Greek Orthodox

73 "Report of the Superintendent of the Press," 30 Sep 1835, United Presbyterian Church in the U.S.A. Syria Mission Records, 1808–1967, RG 115, box 1, folder 25, Presbyterian Historical Society, Philadelphia, PA (hereafter cited as PHS, RG 115-1-25).

74 For a description and illustration, see James Moran, *Printing Presses: History and Development from the Fifteenth Century to Modern Times* (Berkeley: University of California Press, 1973), 75, 79, 84, 179. One of five extant Wells presses today belongs to the Smithsonian. See Elizabeth M. Harris, *Printing Presses in the Graphic Arts Collection* (Washington, D.C.: The National Museum of American History, Smithsonian Institution, 1996), 27–28.

75 ABC 16.8.1, vol. 4, "Syria Mission to Anderson," 27 Jul 1852.

76 "Quarterly Report on the State of the Press," 30 Sep 1836; "Report on the Press," 31 Dec 1836, PHS, RG 115-1-25.

77 This issue with technology is further explored in Chapter 5.

78 The mission's request for this press was first made in 1852. See "Report on the Printing Establishment," ʿAbay, 1 Oct 1855, PHS, RG 115-1-25.

79 The division of labor at the Press between 1834 and 1855 is detailed in two key missionary records. See "Quarterly Report of the Superintendent of the Press," 30 Sep 1835; "Report on the Printing Establishment," ʿAbay, 1 Oct 1855, PHS, RG 115-1-25.

Christian).[80] In the 1850s this list included, among others, Ibrāhīm Sarkīs (d. 1885), who was an Armenian Christian hired in 1851 as a workman, but who eventually composed numerous texts for the press in the 1850s and became an important *nahḍa* author.[81] In later years this coterie of Arab print literati also involved Muslim members, such as the Sunni Yūsuf al-Asīr al-Husaynī (a graduate of the famed al-Azhar university, d. 1890) who worked on the translation of the Arabic Protestant Bible, but also served as the mission's Press corrector on numerous occasions.[82]

The Arab print literati also included those who served as Arabic teachers for the missionaries and/or mission catechists. Al-Yāzijī, a Greek Catholic whom the mission never managed to convert, was a poet from Kfarshīmā[83] who originally garnered his experience (and social status) while being employed in the Shihābī court in Mount Lebanon before he migrated to Beirut.[84] He was assigned as press corrector in 1835 shortly after being invited to teach Arabic to the missionaries in Beirut.[85] Interestingly, as press and missionary records attest, Eli Smith (d. 1857), American missionary and Press editor at the time, originally intended to hire Fāris al-Shidyāq as a key translator in 1835. Al-Shidyāq was one of the earliest regional converts to Protestantism, who subsequently converted to Islam in the 1860s. In addition to having attended the prestigious Maronite school in ʿAyn Warqa, he also worked in the field of Arabic book production with the British in Malta.[86] While he would certainly have been a more appealing choice for Smith than al-Yāzijī, al-Shidyāq declined the missionary's offer.[87] At this time, al-Ḥaddād served as an Arabic instructor at missionary schools and as a catechist, in addition to occasionally being tasked with press-related translation work. By the early 1840s al-Bustānī, also a Protestant convert who had attended the Maronite seminary in ʿAbay, moved to Beirut where he initially worked as an interpreter for the British before taking on a position with the American missionaries as an Arabic instructor.[88] It was around this time that he converted to Protestantism, and eventually began working as a copyist, translator, and unordained preacher with the mission.[89] These individuals' press-related responsibilities essentially included supervising

80 To my knowledge, no records exist on him. *Annual Report of the Press and Magazine*, 1851, PHS, RG 115-1-25.

81 "Quarterly Report of the Superintendent of the Press," 30 Sep 1835; *Annual Report of the Press and Magazine*, 1851, PHS, RG 115-1-25.

82 He was hired in 1860 to assist the missionary, and then Press editor, Cornelius Van Dyck (d. 1895) with the Arabic Bible translation. See missionary papers and records deposited at Manuscripts and Special Collections, Yale Divinity School Library, Eli Smith Family Papers, Record Group 124 (hereafter cited as YDSL, RG 124) Box 3/5, Series II. Writings, Writings of Others, Data Furnished by Dr. C.V.A. Van Dyck with Reference to the Translation of the Scriptures into the Arabic Language under the Auspices of the American Mission in Syria and the American Bible Society, 1885. See also Eli Smith and Cornelius van Allen van Dyck, *A Brief Documentary History of the Translation of the Scriptures into the Arabic Language* (Beirut: American Presbyterian Mission Press, 1900), 29. For more on this poet and scholar, see John A. Thompson, *The Major Arabic Bibles: Their Origin and Nature* (New York: American Bible Society, 1956), 23–4.

83 Matti Moosa, *Origins of Modern Arabic Fiction* (Boulder: Lynne Rienner Publishers, 1997), 124.

84 Ibid. Moosa states that al-Yāzijī migrated to Beirut in 1840, following the forced exile of Bashīr Shihāb II. However, al-Yāzijī is mentioned in press records from 1835 and he published his first book by 1836.

85 "Quarterly Report of the Superintendent of the Press," 30 Sep 1835; "Report on the Press," 31 Dec 1836, PHS, RG 115-1-25.

86 For more on al-Shidyāq, particularly his attitudes towards and experiences with the British and Americans, see Rasheed El-Enany, *Arab Representations of the Occident: East-West Encounters in Arab Fiction* (London: Routledge, 2006), 19–23.

87 "Quarterly Report of the Superintendent of the Press," 30 Sep 1835, PHS, RG 115-1-25.

88 Butrus Abu-Manneh, "The Christians between Ottomanism and Syrian Nationalism: The Ideas of Butrus Al-Bustani," *International Journal of Middle East Studies* 11, no. 3 (1980): 289.

89 ABC 16.8.1, vol. 1, "Report on Native Helpers," 1844. See also, Makdisi, *Artillery of Heaven*, 193–213.

and correcting presswork, translating English and/or Greek texts into Arabic, and producing original copy for the Press.[90]

Relying on these employees, with some versed in traditional scribal practices, certainly worked to the benefit of the mission. For one, during the earlier years of the mission and its Press the Americans grappled with language barriers and Arabic printing. Smith was probably the only member of the mission fluent enough in Arabic to compose books, essays, or tracts for the Press.[91] Between the 1820s and mid-1840s only two or three members of the mission were capable of writing and translating Arabic texts for print.[92] In addition to Smith (who published an arithmetic textbook in 1837),[93] there was George B. Whiting (who produced a tract on self-examination in 1837 and one on temperance in 1838), and William Thomson (who composed a treatise on the confession of the Christian faith in 1838).[94] With the involvement of native Arabic speakers, the texts coming off the American Press for the most part conformed to the rigorous grammatical rules and stylistic structures of written Arabic, to a degree that not all Arabic publications at the time, even those printed in London or Malta, could boast of.[95] For instance, al-Yāzijī composed a number of the mission's earliest publications, including *Baʿḍ mazāmīr li-l-tarannum,* a collection of "Psalms for Singing" printed in 1836,[96] and *Kitāb faṣl al-khiṭāb fī uṣūl lughat al-iʿrāb*, a "Discourse on the Rules of Arabic Grammar" printed in 1837.[97] During the 1840s al-Yāzijī and al-Bustānī also worked with Smith on key publications for the mission, including a new Arabic translation of the Protestant Bible from 1848-1857.[98] Although the relationships between missionaries and locals in their employ were not without their complications, for the most part minor interpersonal tensions did not negatively impact contractual arrangements. In the case of al-Yāzijī, for instance, a missionary committee set up in 1845 to discuss the terms of his "permanent salary" chafed at his inflexibility when it came to Press-related corrections, and deemed his refusal to send one of his sons to the

90 "Quarterly Report of the Superintendent of the Press," 30 Sep 1835; "Report on the Press," 31 Dec 1836, PHS, RG 115-1-25. The role of local hires, including al-Ḥaddād and al-Bustānī, as evangelists in the mid-1840s is elaborated on in ABC 16.8.1, vol. 1, "Report on Native Helpers," 1844. For more on al-Bustānī, see Makdisi, *Artillery of Heaven*, 193–213.

91 Roper, "The Beginnings of Arabic Printing," 57–59. See also A.L. Tibawi, *American Interests in Syria 1800–1901: A Study of Educational, Literary and Religious Work* (Oxford: Oxford University Press, 1966), 82; Miroslav Krek, "Some Observations on Printing Arabic in America and by Americans Abroad," *Manuscripts of the Middle East* 6, no. 8 (1992), 85.

92 See a discussion of this dearth of Arabic fluency in ABC 16.8.1, vol. 8, "Meeting at Whiting's," 27 Apr 1838.

93 *Kitāb dalīl al-ṣawāb fī uṣūl al-ḥisāb.*

94 The books and authors are listed in ABC 16.8.1, vol. 1, "Books printed at the Mission Press in Beirut, Mar 1844 [?]."

95 While these other presses hired native Arabic speakers at various points in their history, a quick study of the title pages and some content of books printed by the Church Missionary Society (CMS) in Malta and by the British and Foreign Bible Society (BFBS) in London reveals obvious linguistic and grammatical errors in their content and typographic compositions (including the BFBS's bible that the American missionaries were also circulating at the time).

96 Printed in 1836 and revised from earlier Malta editions; see ABC 16.8.1, vol. 1, "Books printed at the Mission Press in Beirut, Mar 1844 [?]."

97 Ibid.

98 In addition to the Arabic Bible, al-Bustānī worked closely with Smith on various translations in the 1840s. These included: Smith's "The Office and Work of the Holy Spirit" translated into *Kitāb al-bāb al-maftūḥ fī aʿmāl al-rūḥ* (Beirut, 1843), John Bunyan's *The Pilgrim's Progress* translated as *Kitāb siyāḥat al-masīḥī* (Beirut, 1844), and *Kitāb kashf al-ḥijāb fī ʿilm al-ḥisāb* (Beirut, 1848), which included material from Smith's earlier publication on the subject in 1837. See, ABC 16.8.1, vol. 8, "Meeting at Native Chapel," 21 Apr 1842; "Meeting at Native Chapel," 21 Apr 1842; "Meeting at Native Chapel," 10 Mar 1843; ABC 16.8.1, vol. 1, "Books printed at the Mission Press in Beirut, Mar 1844 [?]." See also "Quarterly Report of the Press," Apr–Jun 1844, PHS, RG 115-1-25.

mission's Sunday school as an "influence" on the mission's other "native assistants" that was "exceedingly pernicious."[99] Yet, despite some missionaries' negative views of al-Yāzijī, they maintained a contractual agreement with him for at least twenty-five years. More significantly, al-Yāzijī, like others on the mission's payroll, managed to thrive in association with the Syria mission by publishing many of his first works, and essentially leveraged the mission's ideals to launch an independent career in Arabic publications (a legacy furthered by his children[100]). Without the involvement of such educated Syrian employees (who were not the ones manning the presses themselves),[101] it is unlikely that the press could have produced any Arabic books in its first three decades. Press records indicate that, as late as the 1850s, many missionaries were still hesitant about taking on the trying task of Arabic textual compositions.[102]

At the same time, while they never became authors in their own right, al-Ḥaddād and al-Khayyāṭ copied and translated most of the first books printed at the American Press. Although press records do not list all the books these two individuals worked on from 1835 until the 1840s, most probably no book went to press without the involvement of either al-Ḥaddād or al-Khayyāṭ. For instance, records show that al-Ḥaddād worked on the translation and revision of *The Dairyman's Daughter* (or *Qiṣṣat ilīṣābāt ibnat al-labbān al-saʿīda*, printed at the American Press in 1836) with John Nicolayson of Jerusalem, a member of the London Society for Promoting Christianity Amongst the Jews (the London Jews Society).[103] Some books that al-Khayyāṭ worked on included *Kitāb dalīl al-ṣawāb fī uṣul al-ḥisāb* (printed at the American Press in 1837), which he translated with Smith in 1836; the translations of Thomas Hopkins Gallaudet's *Child's Book on the Soul*[104] into Arabic as *Taʿlīm al-awlād ʿan al-nafs* (printed in 1838) and *Taʿlīm al-awlād ʿan al-nafs, al-qism al-thānī* (printed in 1839).[105] Although records do not clearly state this, it is likely that al-Khayyāt wound up with the lion's share of Press-related translation and copying work[106] since al-Yāzijī was preoccupied with his own texts and teaching, while al-Ḥaddād had gone on to become a catechist and preacher.[107]

99 On this subject, the report by committee members George Backus Whiting (d. 1855) and Thomas Laurie (d. 1897) explicitly states that al-Yāzijī "is not friendly to the Evangelical Religion, has regularly absented himself from our Sabbath services and forbidden his son to attend the Sabbath school." ABC 16.8.1, vol. 8, "Meeting at Mission House," 30 Jul 1845.

100 His son Ibrahīm (d. 1906), for instance, was employed at the Jesuit missionary press in Beirut (which, incidentally, was the American Press's main missionary rival from the mid-1800s onwards). In 1898, Ibrāhīm also founded his own literary journal, *al-Ḍiyāʾ* (Illumination), which was printed in Cairo. His older sister, Warda (d. 1924), who was educated at the American Mission School for Girls in Beirut then later moved to Alexandria, also became an important poet and writer during the *nahḍa* period, publishing numerous works on women's roles in the age of modernization. For more on Ibrāhīm, see Kamal Salibi, *A House of Many Mansions: The History of Lebanon Reconsidered* (London: I.B. Tauris, 1988). For more on Warda, see Margot Badran, "The Origins of Feminism in Egypt," in *Current Issues in Women's History*, eds. Arina Angerman et al. (London: Routledge, 2012), 153–70. See also Radwa Ashur et al., eds., *Arab Women Writers: A Critical Reference Guide, 1873–1999* (Cairo: The American University of Cairo Press, 2008), 513.

101 "Quarterly Report on the Press," Dec 1836, PHS, RG 115-1-25.

102 "Report on the Printing Establishment," 1 Oct 1855, PHS, RG 115-1-25.

103 "Quarterly Report on the State of the Press," 30 Sep 1836, PHS, RG 115-1-25. See also Tibawi, *American Interests*, 73.

104 This was book was printed in two parts by the American Tract Society in 1836. Part one was printed in 1831 by Cooke and Co. in Hartford, CT.

105 "Report of the Operation of the Press," 6 Apr 1836; "Report on the Press," 31 Dec 1836, PHS, RG 115-1-25.

106 For instance, he was involved in translating Eli Smith's tract on arithmetic, *Kitāb dalīl al-ṣawāb fī uṣūl al-ḥisāb* (Beirut, 1837). "Report of the Operation of the Press," 6 Apr 1836, PHS, RG 115-1-25.

107 *Annual Report of the Press and Magazine*, 1851, PHS, RG 115-1-25.

It should be noted here that methods of copying and correcting texts at the American Press during this period clearly nodded to local scribal traditions. Many aspects of the latter were integrated at a structural level in professional print production. For instance, Press records show that, like transmission methods in manuscript production that called for dictating, copying, reading, editing, and then recopying texts until they were authenticated by the author or head scribe, texts translated at the American Press were worked over several times before getting the final approval from the press corrector and press editor.[108] In fact, the roles of the *muṣaḥḥiḥ* (corrector) and the *nassākh* (copyist) that were incorporated into the Americans' print shop, as well as other local nineteenth-century presses, had their origins in the scribal author-copyist authentication system. The fact that the American Press's employees were trained as scribes/copyists certainly helped with this Press's integration of manuscript traditions into the publishing process. However, the press corrector and copyist's jobs were not necessarily limited to fact-checking content or ensuring textual authenticity but also encompassed ensuring that printed texts upheld the standard grammatical rules and styles of formal Arabic writing, *al-fuṣḥa*. According to a record from 1836, for instance, English works were translated into "vulgar [sic]" (colloquial) Arabic by al-Khayyāṭ and then handed to al-Yāzijī, who "improved upon" them before giving them back to al-Khayyāṭ for final copying.[109]

The mission's inclusion of local Arab Christian scholars as textual supervisors and correctors, particularly those versed in scribal conventions, showed its interest in presenting and disseminating publications endorsed by members of this urban class's literati (to which local personages like al-Bustānī and al-Yāzijī belonged). The mission's desire to gain favor amongst these local Christian communities is also illustrated in the mission's production of numerous secular texts by these scholars during the late 1800s. Although the aim of the missionaries was to "articulate a sense of Christian citizenship" with local Arabic-speaking members of society, these populations were more interested in technology, education and other secular matters than the Protestant message.[110] The mission's methods, and their views of the locals, changed over the years according to the resistance and conflicts that they encountered amongst them. Consequently, the texts published by the American Press did at times reflect the interests and concerns of their local audience.

The Press not only employed individuals from diverse religious and ethnic backgrounds representative of the local communities, but also served, somewhat inadvertently, as a secular publisher of works by Arab Christian intellectuals. For example, although the Press's religious and educational publications were funded by missionary enterprises (including the ABCFM, the American Bible Society, and the American Tract Society), many of the secular publications printed at the Press, particularly in later years, were actually independent productions sponsored by Arab Christian intellectuals.[111] The American Press, while pervasively voicing missionary goals, was (through its publications) also the site where these very goals were challenged, disguised, and altered during the process of print production. Most importantly, the negotiation of Protestant millenarist views and an Arab socio-political worldview, as well as the negotiation of scribal customs and printing practices (which predated the *nahḍa*) played out in complexly nuanced and overlapping ways in the design and content of the American Press's publications.

108 "Report on the Press," 31 Dec 1836, PHS, RG 115-1-25.

109 Muhsin Mahdi, "From the Manuscript Age to the Age of Printed Books," in Atiyeh, *The Book in the Islamic World*, 10–11.

110 Munir A. Bashshur, "Higher Education and Political Development in Syria and Lebanon," *Comparative Education Review* 10, no. 3 (1966): 694.

111 These developments are discussed in Chapters 4 and 5.

CHAPTER 3

# Evangelizing between Script and Print (1834–1840)

When it was established in 1834, more than a decade after the first American missionaries arrived in the region from Boston, the American Press found itself at the nexus between age-old scribal traditions and emergent printing traditions. Not only was the Press operating as a foreign enterprise within the realm of Ottoman power, it was also one of few printing establishments within a sector dominated by scribal practices. As discussed in the previous chapter, the economy of book manufacture was still largely dominated by well-established monastery and mosque scribal workshops, which often kept the transmission and dissemination of knowledge within their respective communities and institutions. Books in their handwritten and printed forms thus circulated amongst exclusive groups of readers associated with the various local religious factions.

Despite worries about operating a press in a scribal realm, and local prejudices against their work, the missionaries appeared rather confident that their press in Beirut would be welcome given that "Arabic, Greek, and Turkish tracts and books are very much needed." The missionaries even referenced the presence of a Jewish press at Safed, stating that "if Jews, who are of all people on earth the most liable to molestation and unrighteous exaction, if *they* can thus publicly maintain a printing-press, what reason can be assigned why we cannot?"[1] However, the missionaries seemed surprised when local readers exhibited a general disinterest in the mission's first imprints. As cited in book depository records, the Americans perceived that the Ottoman Syrian population did not value intellectual pursuits. In an annual report from 1836, for instance, one missionary explains that "there has never been a great demand [for books], and there never can be, until a greater interest in education is worked up, and a larger number of intelligent readers be found in the country."[2] A similar frustration is voiced in an 1837 report from the book depository: "The sale of books is almost nothing. There is an utter unwillingness to purchase books and so small is the value that the people place upon knowledge that … they will not give even a piaster for a book which costs 20."[3] Surely this was not simply a case of widespread ignorance.

Scholars frequently cite lower literacy numbers, issues with education, and the importance of oral, group-based reading practices[4] as factors behind a marginal interest in printed books before the late 1800s. For instance, Ottoman education during this period, while inclusive of Western-style methods, was comprised of Islamic programs and military

1 *The Missionary Herald* 30 (1834): 127.

2 Records of the American Board of Commissioners for Foreign Missions deposited at Houghton Library, Harvard University, Cambridge, Mass. (hereafter cited as ABC), 16.8.1, Syria Mission (1823–1871), vol. 1, Syria Mission to Board, 31 Dec 1836.

3 "Report on the Book Depository for the Quarter ending," 27 Dec 1837, United Presbyterian Church in the U.S.A. Syria Mission Records, 1808–1967, Record Group 115, box 1, folder 25, Presbyterian Historical Society, Philadelphia, PA (hereafter cited as PHS, RG 115-1-25).

4 Konrad Hirschler, in his book on premodern reading practices and societies in various Arab cities, discusses prominent scholarly views on issues of literacy, aurality, and orality during this period. See *The Written Word in the Medieval Arabic Lands: A Social and Cultural History of Reading Practices* (Edinburgh: Edinburgh University Press, 2012), 11–31. After the implementation of education reforms, widespread changes in reading practices became evident during the 1870s, particularly in changes in the public sphere, the proliferation of reading salons and religious centers, and the continued importance of cafes as points of dissemination of information. Nadir Özbek, "Defining the Public Sphere During the Late Ottoman Empire: War, Mass Mobilization and the Young Turk Regime (1908–18)," *Middle Eastern Studies* 43, no. 5 (2007): 795–809.

 | DOI 10.1163/9789004314351_004

schools, and as such limited to educating Muslim subjects. Non-Muslim minorities interested in schooling had the option of attending local foreign missionary schools or Christian seminaries, but these remained out of the reach of non-elites. Furthermore, local Christian communities often pressured their members to withdraw their children from certain missionary establishments. It was not until the mid-nineteenth century that state education was made available to non-Muslim Ottoman minorities, thus providing local residents with state alternatives to the available missionary schools.[5]

Also, the "smallness of any middle class with a disposable income"[6] for book purchases was certainly a factor when considering how expensive printed books were at the time for non-elites, even for individuals employed at the American Press as printers, binders, and text compositors. For instance, in 1844 Fāris al-Tūwaynī (a senior Press workman) was earning approximately 228 *kuruş* (piastres) a month. Purchasing one of the mission's more expensive books selling for 20 *kuruş* would mean spending almost 9% of his monthly salary for a single publication.[7] Furthermore, one cannot disregard the low opinion local clergy and patriarchs, including Greek Orthodox, Maronite, and Greek Catholic Christians, had of these missionaries; particularly when it came to the controversial and "blasphemous" Protestant literature, printed by the British in London and Malta, which the Americans circulated during the 1820s. For instance, the British Church Missionary Society (CMS) in Malta and the British and Foreign Bible Society (BFBS) in London, printed many such books.[8] Finally, as elaborated in the previous chapter, the effective systems of knowledge transmission and production via scribal workshops already in place at the time probably obviated the need, or rather the desire, for print shop methods.

However, in order to delve further into these questions of readership and audience, the printed books themselves need to be examined more closely.[9] In addition to considering local systems of writing, knowledge production, literacy rates, and economic factors, the material and visual features of books also allow for an added understanding of the complexities involved in cultivating a local readership in Ottoman Syria. Regardless of whether or not the Protestant missionaries in Beirut clearly understood the complex dynamics of the local elite and ecclesiastic readership at the time, the Americans were well aware that scribal practices were not limited to a particular religious community or to just the elite circles. Indeed, the expansive collections of Christian, Muslim, and popular literary manuscripts amongst many of the missionaries' personal libraries speak to this point. Many of these texts are presently held in the rare books reading room at the Near East School of Theology in Beirut.[10] Consequently, and perhaps in an effort at casting a wide net, the American Press's earliest publications make clear from their

5 For more on these changes in local education, see Ussama Makdisi, *The Culture of Sectarianism: Community, History, and Violence in Nineteenth-Century Ottoman Lebanon* (Berkeley: University of California Press, 2000); Ellen Fleischmann, "Evangelization or Education: American Protestant Missionaries, the American Board, and the Girls and Women of Syria (1830–1910)," in *New Faith in Ancient Lands: Western Missions in the Middle East in the Nineteenth and Early Twentieth Centuries*, ed. Heleen Murre-van den Berg (Leiden: Brill, 2006), 263–80; Fatma Müge Göçek, "Ethnic Segmentation, Western Education, and Political Outcomes: Nineteenth-Century Ottoman Society," *Poetics Today* 14, no. 3 (1993): 507–38.

6 Juan R.I. Cole, "Printing and Urban Islam in the Mediterranean World, 1890–1920," in *Modernity and Culture: From the Mediterranean to the Indian Ocean*, eds. Leila Tarazi Fawaz and C.A. Bayly (New York: Columbia University Press, 2002), 348.

7 "Quarterly Report of the Press," Apr-Jun 1844, PHS, RG 115-1-25.

8 These publications, and the problems they posed for local readers, will be discussed further in this chapter.

9 See Appendix Two for a list of titles printed during this period.

10 This was originally the Syria Mission's seminary in Beirut, where much of the mission's possessions were later deposited.

writing style, content, and visual conventions that these publications were meant to speak to a diversity of readers, from emirs and clerical students to an emergent readership of newly educated and literate members of Beirut's urban class. These early works also demonstrate a diverse array of innovations, within the realm of Arabic printing, that were responses to local attitudes towards books and their visual dimensions during this time.

What is important to consider, however, is how the production methods, subject matter, and design of the few books produced by the Press in its early years illustrate the mission's responses to the religious attitudes and scribal practices common to local readers at the time. In fact, the mission's attempt at attracting a broad scribal readership via its publications included emulating visual conventions similar to those associated with manuscripts, tempering (at times avoiding) any evangelical tone in their textual content, and adopting local preferences in writing style. The American Press's inaugural works also speak to the dynamic nature of early printed books as sites of artistic innovation and experimentation where various local and external aesthetic impulses overlapped.

## The Experimental Conventions of Arabic Printing

### *Visual Practices*

The visual conventions of the earliest books printed at the American Press perhaps present the most illustrative example of the juxtaposition of scribal and print traditions, with the varying aesthetic modes utilized reflecting the rather experimental and dynamic approaches to the technology characteristic of this period in nineteenth-century Arabic printing history. An important example is *Kitāb faṣl al-khiṭāb fī uṣūl lughat al-iʿrāb* (A Discourse on the Rules of [Arabic] Grammar) written by Nāṣīf al-Yāzijī, the American Press corrector at the time, and published in 1836. While it was not the earliest of the mission's publications, this 168-page pocket-sized book may have been the first full-fledged production to come off the press. Two other productions, *Baʿḍ mazāmīr li-l-tarannum* (Some Psalms for Singing) and *Kitāb taʿlīm mukhtaṣar li-l-aṭfāl fī qawāʿid al-dīyāna wa-l-īmān*, an Arabic translation of Isaac Watt's *Catechism for Children*, were printed in early 1836. However, at twenty-six and sixteen pages respectively, these earlier works were not as substantial as al-Yāzijī's grammar and may be better classified as tracts or booklets, a distinction that will be elaborated upon later in this chapter.[11]

According to Press records, this work was printed for use as an Arabic textbook at the Protestant's seminary in ʿAbay.[12] However, the text's multitude of copies and editions (the first run was 1000),[13] as well as al-Yāzijī's very close involvement throughout its numerous production stages, raises questions regarding the book's producer, intended audience, and, in turn, its layout and visual conventions. For instance, a Press report from April 1836 indicates that while the mission was in the process of publishing an "Arabic Grammar," the book was al-Yāzijī's "own production."[14] It appears that the printing of al-Yāzijī's book was begun in June 1836 and initially completed by September of that year. However, according to another internal report "the author [al-Yāzijī] insisted on making great alterations on the first part of it."[15] A report from December 1836 indicates that the entire book was then reprinted with said corrections, but it was "laid aside to await future decision…[because] errors have been

11 "Report of the Operation of the Press," 6 Apr 1836, PHS, RG 115-1-25.

12 ABC 16.8.1, vol. 1, "Books printed at the Mission Press in Beirut, Mar 1844 [?]."

13 From early sales records and the fact that the book saw four reprints before the 1900s (in 1844, 1854, 1866, and 1887), it is clear that this was a popular text. ABC 16.8.1, vol. 1, "Books printed at the Mission Press in Beirut, Mar 1844 [?]."

14 "Quarterly Report on the State of the Press," 6 Apr 1836, PHS, RG 115-1-25.

15 "Quarterly Report on the State of the Press," 30 Sep 1836, PHS, RG 115-1-25.

discovered by the author."[16] Throughout these records, it is clear that the pushback and delay was entirely on al-Yāzijī's side. Surprisingly, the mission accommodated the author's requests and pressed on in resetting and reprinting the text until both parties were satisfied. This back-and-forth between al-Yāzijī and the Press editors calls into question whether this book was exclusively a missionary production or whether it was partially (or fully) funded by al-Yāzijī himself. This uncertainty mirrors that of the book's audience, since the book went on to become an important one of al-Yāzijī's texts during the *nahḍa*, evidence that the final readers came from local multi-confessional communities and were not limited to those enrolled at the mission's seminary.

The fact that this publication and its producer(s) were targeting multi-confessional scribal readers is perceptible in the book's layout and composition, which recall multiple aspects of illuminated manuscripts. The book's introductory two-page spread brings to mind the incipit *ʿunwān*[17] pages of local devotional books, which featured illuminated introductions and dedications (Fig. 2). For instance, the upper section of the printed page on the right shows an ornamental headpiece or head-plate (*sarlawḥ*), a visual trope frequently used in manuscripts to indicate the start of a chapter, which crowns an embellished cartouche for section headings.[18] Within the headpiece, a large rectangular cartouche is surmounted by an architecturally inspired design. The tapering elements capping the uppermost cartouche are made up of one square piece in the center, flanked by two triangular pieces near the corner of the cartouche, each of which is topped by a spire-like formulation. Composed of different generic fleurons (stylized floral glyphs) and punctuation marks, the overall headpiece composition clearly echoes the "w" shaped designs popular in some illuminated manuscripts.[19] A floral and a vegetal square-shaped sort punctuate each gap between the dome-like spire formations, lending the composition the grandeur of the monumental architectural entrances prominent in the region. Bands of rosettes, palmettes, and flora, which make up the spread's double-page, text-framing borders, recall the visual language of the hand-drawn geometric patterns and interlaced decorations of manuscript borders and text dividers. Variations along the same ornamental theme appear throughout the book's chapter headings, often displaying a playful use of vegetal sorts and symbols to recreate the ornate nature of print's hand-drawn counterparts (Fig. 3).

It should be noted that the use of fleurons and other ornamental printers' metal sorts in this manner was not unique to American Press publications. In fact, this innovative use of letterpress-specific elements can be seen in books printed at the CMS Press in Malta and at Būlāq Press. Although the interest in such ornamentation derived from an aim to emulate scribal traditions, the rigidity and repetition of the patterns and compositions produced via letterpress methods differed greatly from the hand-painted illuminations of regional

16 "Quarterly Report on the Press," Dec 1836, PHS, RG 115-1-25.

17 I use the term *ʿunwān* (address) based on B.W. Robinson, quoted in Adam Gacek's book, to refer to "an illuminated one- or double-page opening." Gacek describes the term's use in codices as related to the page showing the chapter heading or composition's title. See Gacek, *Arabic Manuscripts: A Vademecum for Readers* (Leiden: Brill, 2009), 119–20.

18 Scholars sometimes use the Arabic term *sarlawḥ* (*sarloh* in Persian, and *serlevha* in Turkish) interchangeably with *ʿunwān* to denote various illuminated sections of manuscript folios, specifically the manuscript frontispiece. At times, *ʿunwān* is used to refer to headpieces, while *sarlawḥ* is used in reference to decorated frontispieces. However, there does not appear to be a real consensus on the use of either term: see Christiane Gruber, ed., *The Islamic Manuscript Tradition: Ten Centuries of Book Arts in Indiana University Collections* (Bloomington: Indiana University Press, 2010), 47–48, 48n61. The present study follows Gacek's designations for the *sarlawḥ*, as the illuminated head title or headpiece surmounting the upper part of a page. See Gacek, 120–22.

19 Gacek, 122.

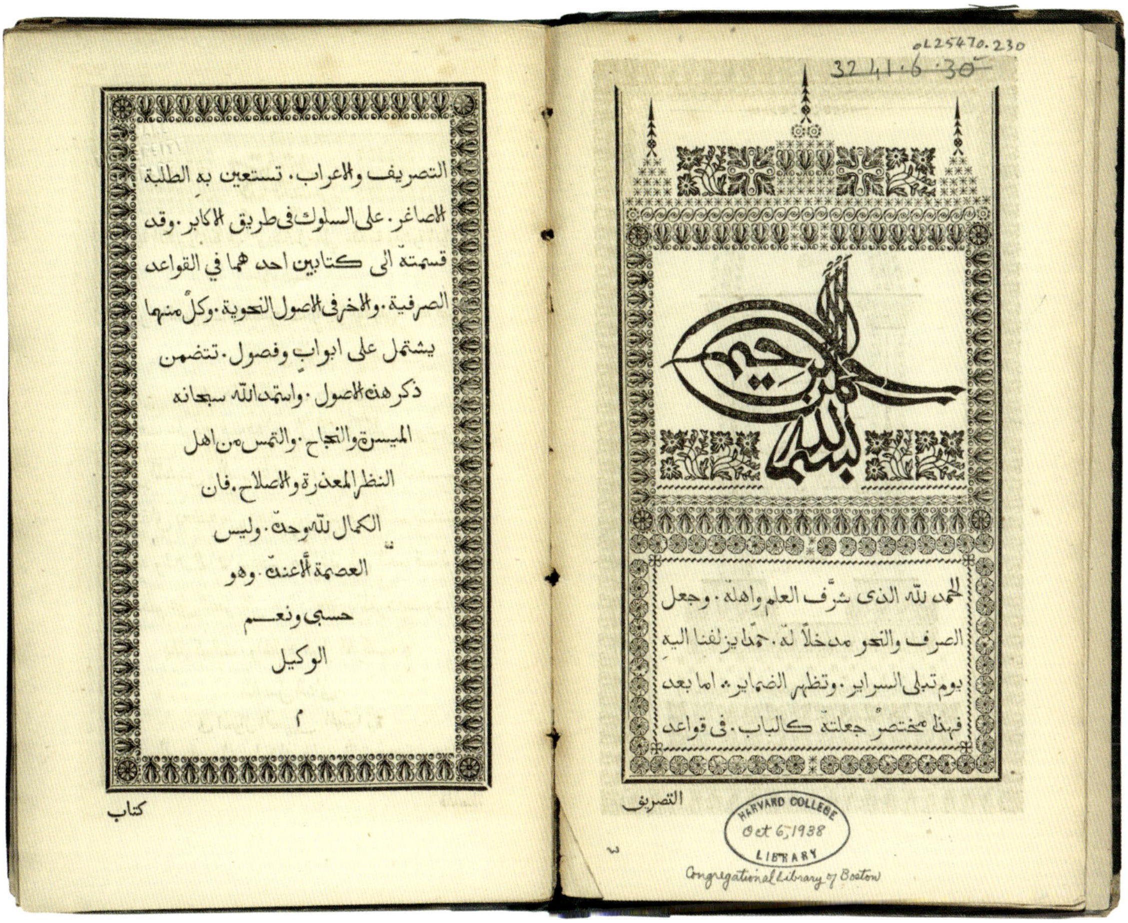


FIGURE 2 *Introduction from Nāṣīf al-Yāzijī,* Kitāb faṣl al-khiṭāb fī uṣūl lughat al-iʿrāb. BEIRUT, 1836

manuscripts from the nineteenth century. Essentially, such emergent printing conventions become characteristic of local printing during this period. As David McKitterick explains of fifteenth-century European prints (or incunabula) that also emulated that region's manuscript practices, "decoration…was not added in order to make a printed book look like a manuscript; it was added because that was expected of some kinds of books, for some audiences, markets or individuals."[20]

The most eye-catching visual feature in al-Yāzijī's book is the Muslim incantation found within the headpiece of the first page (Fig. 4). Following the textual formulae of most Islamic and Christian manuscripts, this book opens with an Arabic doxological incantation, or *basmala.* In this case, the phrase is *bismallāh al-raḥmān al-raḥīm* (In the Name of God, most Gracious, Most Merciful), which was popular in (and frequently attributed solely to) the Qurʾan and other Islamic manuscripts. Certainly, the use of this *basmala* instead of a Christian version is unusual for a Protestant mission's publications. Indeed, most of the mission's other books chiefly featured some variation of the Christian *bism-l-ab wa-l-ibn wa-l-rūḥ al-qudus* (In the Name of the Father, the Son, and the Holy Spirit). However, it was not uncommon for local manuscripts of poetry or historical chronicles copied by Christian

20 McKitterick, *Print, Manuscript and the Search for Order 1450–1830* (Cambridge: Cambridge University Press, 2003), 37.

FIGURE 3 *Opening pages of Chapter 2 from Nāṣīf al-Yāzijī,* Kitāb faṣl al-khiṭāb fī uṣūl lughat al-iʿrāb. BEIRUT, 1836

scribes, in seminaries or monasteries, to open with the Muslim incantation. Christian manuscripts produced in the region also relied heavily on calligraphic and ornamentation techniques found in Islamic productions. In fact, aside from their Biblical content, some of the books produced at local monasteries – such as those held at the Couvent Saint-Sauveur in Sidon – are almost indistinguishable from locally-produced Qurʾans in their quality of design, gilding, and illumination.[21]

Adding further intrigue to this example from al-Yāzijī's book is its appearance in the self-contained form of a calligraphic *tughrā*ʾ. This curvilinear motif, often composed with either the flexible *thuluth* or *diwānī* script, had its origins in the Mamluk period and became popular within the realm of Islamic imperial rule (including the Ottoman and Mughal empires) in which it was initially reserved for the use of emirs or sultans. In the Ottoman Empire, the emblem was used for displaying the Sultan's name and titles on official documents, coinage, and objects belonging to royal members.[22] Although many versions of the *tughrā*ʾ were used within the Ottoman period in the early nineteenth century, this calligraphic format was reformed and standardized by the calligrapher Musṭafa Rāqim

21 For examples, see Philippe Roisse, *Al-makhṭūṭat al-ʿarabiyya fī lubnān: iltiqāʾ al-thaqāfāt wa-l-adyān wa-l-maʿārif* (Beirut: CEDRAC, 2010).

22 For a detailed exploration of its many uses, see Sheila Blair, *Islamic Calligraphy* (Edinburgh: Edinburgh University Press, 2006), 336–37, 379–80, 508–13.

FIGURE 4 *Detail of* basmala *in the form of a* tughrāʾ *from Nāṣīf al-Yāzijī,* Kitāb faṣl al-khiṭāb fī uṣūl lughat al-iʿrāb. BEIRUT, 1836

(d. 1826) at the request of Sultan Maḥmūd II (d. 1839).[23] Rāqim's redesign became the standard used by the Ottoman court until the 1920s, and was frequently reproduced by contemporary calligraphers to display large-scale compositions of Qurʾanic verses and benedictions on materials from wall-mounted panel paintings (*lawḥas*) to paper-based illustrations.[24]

It is not entirely clear what material was used, how it was produced and by whom. However, based on similar components produced at other regional presses, the *tughrāʾ* in al-Yāzijī's book was probably printed from a hand-carved lead block.[25] Traditionally, local presses, such as that of al-Shuwayr, used pieces of lead to carve out intricate calligraphic formations. Additionally, the use of wood may also have been common at the time. Since the missionaries lacked the calligraphic skill needed, they possibly outsourced the production of this *tughrāʾ*, or purchased it from another local press. Most importantly, despite the rigidity of this

23 Blair, 512.

24 Ibid., 513.

25 While this specific block is yet to be located, at least two similar *tughrās* used for local presses at the time exist in a private collection in Beirut, as part of the El-Nimer Art Collection (ENAC). I am grateful to Alya Karame and Mr. Nimer for granting me access to view these blocks.

material, whoever crafted this piece successfully captured the basic proportions, stroke weight and letterforms of the *thuluth* script, thus rendering in metal the fluidity and visual complexity of the object's hand-drawn counterparts. In the printed *tughrā'* (much like similar designs from this period) three centered *alifs* span the length of the monogram. These straight shafts end with tapering terminals from which three *lām* letterforms twist into the curvilinear portion of the calligraphic form. The words are stacked from the bottom to the top, with *bismallah* at the base, followed by *al-raḥmān* at the center, within which *al-raḥīm* is nested. These attributes attest to the likelihood that this *tughrā'* was a local production by someone well versed in scribal traditions and the popularity of this contemporary calligraphic practice. From the productions of the American Press examined thus far, this is the only evident example of such an engraving. It is apparent that this engraved block was valued for both its visual elements and its content since an imprint of it reappears on a number of American Press-related publications produced in Beirut in the mid- to late 1800s (discussed in Chapter 5). Certainly this element's appearance in al-Yāzijī's *Kitāb faṣl al-khitāb* is a nod towards local calligraphic trends, which were familiar to local scribal scholars, but also appealing to Muslim and Arab Christian readers alike.

The practice of borrowing elements from scribal conventions in the early publications of the Press was limited neither to al-Yāzijī's book nor to secular productions. Rather, such aspects appear in the front matter of books from the Press that both implicitly and explicitly dealt with Protestant Christian subject matter. *Kitāb irshād al-masīḥī fī imtiḥān al-nafs* (listed as "A Christian Guide Book on Self Examination," printed in 1837) and *Kitāb fī al-imtinā' 'an shurb al-muskirāt* [sic] (listed as "A Tract on Temperance," from 1838),[26] two works written by the American missionary George B. Whiting who was stationed in Beirut at the time, dealt with religious issues via lessons on morality and behavior, and exhibited conventions similar to those found in al-Yāzijī's Arabic grammar. In the publication from 1837 (Fig. 5), the work recalls incipit manuscript pages in its employment of a self-contained *'unwān,* within which a *sarlawḥ* caps the first part of the introduction. Similarly, the tract from 1838 (Fig. 6) shows the use of decorative headpieces, which in this case crown the first page of each chapter. The designs themselves vary between these books, as does their reliance on calligraphic engravings. In the later publication for example, the headpiece frames the calligraphic subheading *al-bab al-'awal* (Chapter 1) clearly printed from an engraved block (and not movable type as seen in the body text and the subheading in Figure 5). In both instances, however, these decorated head titles were formulated (like in al-Yāzijī's book) from ornamental metal sorts in an attempt at emulating the generally accepted configurations of their hand-drawn counterparts.

A similar practice is found in religious works, such as the mission's Arabic translation of selections from St. John Chrysostom's "Homilies on the Reading of the Scriptures"[27] (Fig. 7). Here, the opening spread is made up of a dedication/title page (on the right) and the first page of the introduction (on the left). The former displays the book's title, translator and date ('Īsā Bītrū in 1833) and dedication (citations from the Bible), all of which are headlined by the Christian *basmala* and set off in an embellished cartouche. The entire text block is then enclosed in a frame of single-row palmette elements. The latter, the opening of the book's introduction, shows the use of a decorative headpiece that was similar in composition to the one used for the *'unwān* of al-Yāzijī's *Kitāb faṣl al-khitāb* (see Fig. 3).

Interestingly, a similar visual program appears in the Press's seemingly less significant ephemeral works from the 1830s. One of the earliest such productions, which was not explicitly related to the Protestants' proselytizing efforts, was a pamphlet

26 ABC 16.8.1, vol.1, "Books printed at the Mission Press in Beirut, Mar 1844 [?]."

27 *Qatf maqālāt al-qiddīs yūḥannā fam al-dhahab 'an muṭāla'at al-kutub al-muqaddasa* (Beirut, 1836).

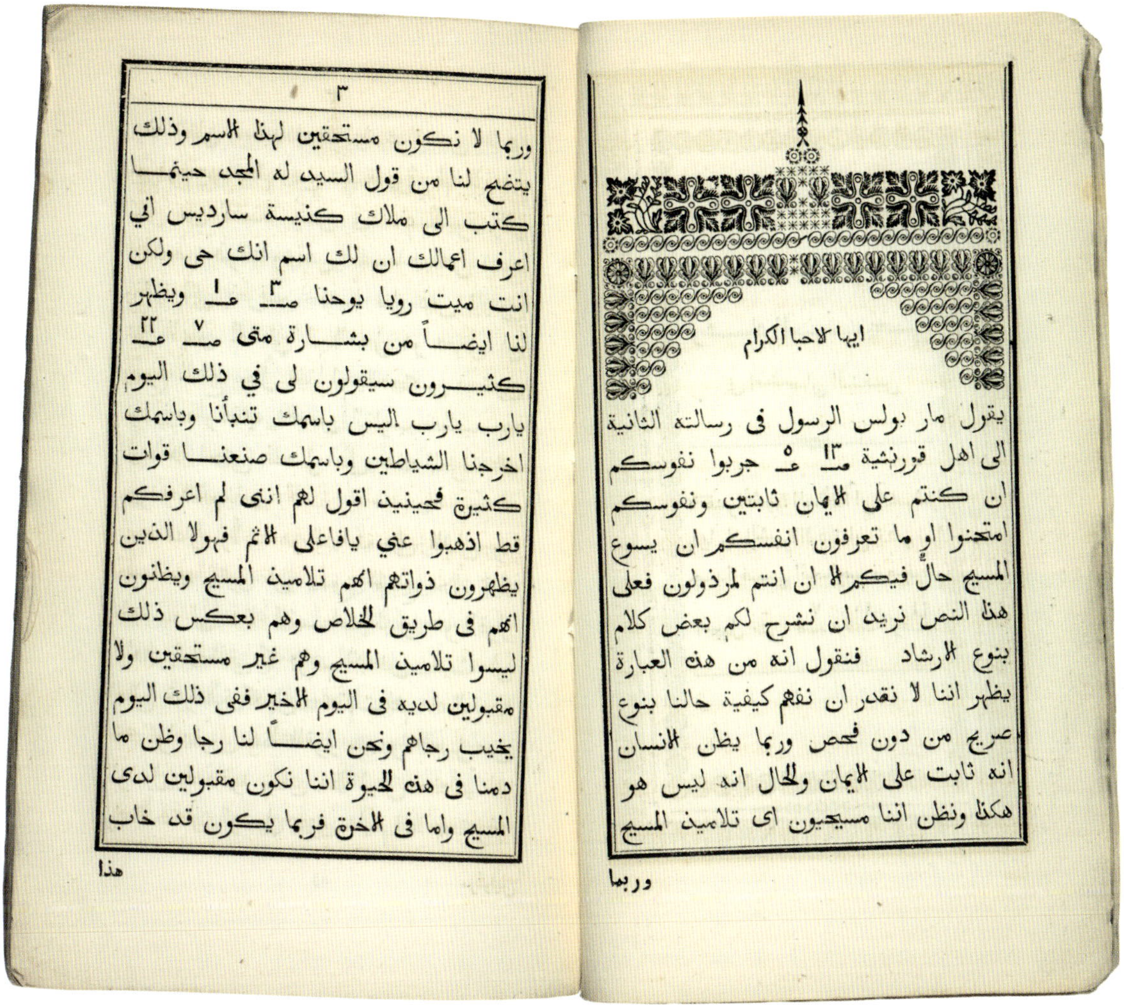
ايها الاحبا الكرام
يقول مار بولس الرسول في رسالته الثانية
الى اهل قورنثية ص ١٣ ع ٥ جربوا نفوسكم
ان كنتم على الايمان ثابتين ونفوسكم
امتحنوا او ما تعرفون انفسكم ان يسوع
المسيح حال فيكم الا ان انتم لمرذولون فعلى
هذا النص نريد ان نشرح لكم بعض كلام
بنوع الارشاد فنقول انه من هذه العبارة
يظهر اننا لا نقدر ان نفهم كيفية حالنا بنوع
صريح من دون فحص وربما يظن الانسان
انه ثابت على الايمان والحال انه ليس هو
هكذا ونظن اننا مسيحيون اي تلاميذ المسيح
وربما

٣
وربما لا نكون مستحقين لهذا الاسم وذلك
يتضح لنا من قول السيد له المجد حينما
كتب الى ملاك كنيسة ساردس اني
اعرف اعمالك ان لك اسم انك حي ولكن
انت ميت رويا يوحنا ص ٣ ع ١ ويظهر
لنا ايضاً من بشارة متى ص ٧ ع ٢٢
كثيرون سيقولون لي في ذلك اليوم
يارب يارب اليس باسمك تنبأنا وباسمك
اخرجنا الشياطين وباسمك صنعنا قوات
كثيرة فحينئذ اقول لهم انني لم اعرفكم
قط اذهبوا عني يا فاعلي الاثم فهولا الذين
يظهرون ذواتهم انهم تلاميذ المسيح ويظنون
انهم في طريق الخلاص وهم بعكس ذلك
ليسوا تلاميذ المسيح وهم غير مستحقين ولا
مقبولين لديه في اليوم الاخير ففي ذلك اليوم
يخيب رجاهم ونحن ايضاً لنا رجا وظن ما
دمنا في هذه الحيوة اننا نكون مقبولين لدى
المسيح واما في الاخرة فربما يكون قد خاب
هذا

FIGURE 5 *Introduction from George B. Whiting,* Kitāb fī al-imtināʿ ʿan shurb al-muskirāt [*sic*].
BEIRUT, 1838

on the treatment and prevention of cholera, *ʿIlāj mufīd li-l-hawāʾ al-aṣfar al-mubīd*, printed in 1837 for free distribution[28] (Fig. 8). This booklet's visual conventions clearly emulated those of scribal traditions in the employment of the ornamental frames on the cover (which, incidentally, doubles as a title page in this example). These incipit pages rely on a decorative headpiece similar to those of manuscript *ʿunwān* pages. This simply bound, twelve-page document might be easily dismissed as an insignificant ephemeral product. In studies on print culture (in both Western and non-Western realms) it is frequently the case that smaller booklets are overlooked since they are presumably more cost effective and less labor intensive than their more expensive counterparts.[29] However,

28 Henry A. Homes, *ʿIlāj mufīd li-l-hawāʾ al-aṣfar al-mubīd* (Beirut: American Press, 1837). Homes left for the Syria Mission in March 1837; see *Report of the American Board of Commissioners for Foreign Missions* 28 (1838): 68. ABC 16.8.1, vol. 1. "Books printed at the Mission Press in Beirut, Mar 1844 [?]."

29 Traditionally, in book and print studies, pamphlets are often given a subordinate classification as lesser forms, transient works. Recent scholarship, however, rather than calling for the inclusion of such products within

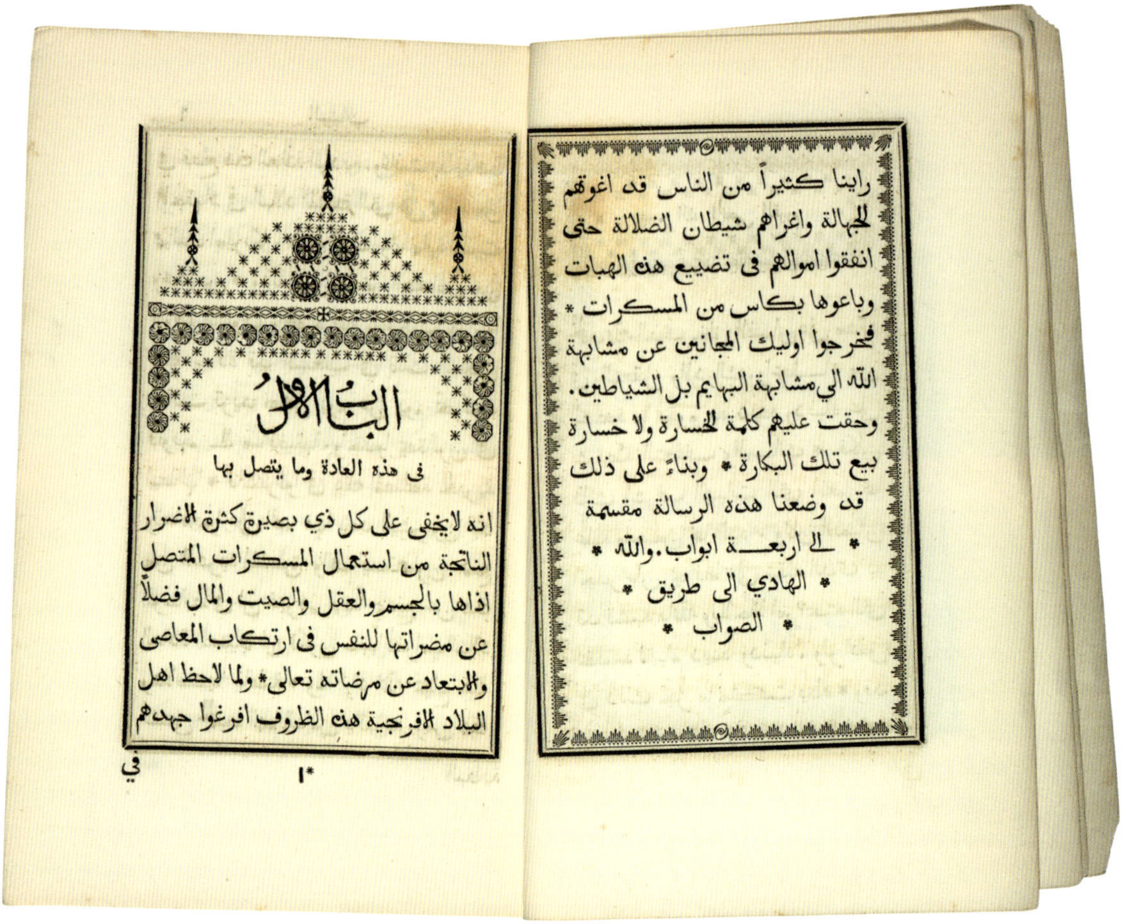

راينا كثيراً من الناس قد اغوتهم
الجهالة واغراهم شيطان الضلالة حتى
انفقوا اموالهم في تضييع هذه الهبات
وباعوها بكاس من المسكرات *
فخرجوا اوليك المجانين عن مشابهة
الله الى مشابهة البهايم بل الشياطين.
وحقت عليهم كلمة الخسارة ولا خسارة
بيع تلك البكارة * وبناءً على ذلك
قد وضعنا هذه الرسالة مقسمة
* الى اربعة ابواب. والله *
* الهادي الى طريق *
* الصواب *

الباب الاول
في هذه العادة وما يتصل بها
انه لا يخفى على كل ذي بصيرة كثرة الاضرار
الناتجة من استعمال المسكرات المتصل
اذاها بالجسم والعقل والصيت والمال فضلاً
عن مضراتها للنفس في ارتكاب المعاصي
والابتعاد عن مرضاته تعالى * ولما لاحظ اهل
البلاد الافرنجية هذه الظروف افرغوا جهدهم
في ١*

FIGURE 6 *First chapter from George B. Whiting,* Kitāb fī al-imtināʿ ʿan shurb al-muskirāt [*sic*]. BEIRUT, 1838

from this Press's publications, one can see that ephemeral products (while more cost effective, production-wise) were not necessarily differentiated from larger printed volumes, or even manuscripts. In fact, it is clear that pamphlets were approached in a manner similar to other modes of textual transmission when it came to issues of design and production. Such pamphlets were also at times listed as "books" on lists of the American Mission's publications.[30] In the case of the American Press, it appears that almost all publications from the

the broader book history narrative or canon, urge the "ephemeralizing" of books themselves by questioning the indelibility of print. Such studies argue that distinguishing between books and ephemera perpetuates the myth of singular, printed volumes as stable cultural artifacts. See for example Kevin Murphy and Sally O'Driscoll, eds., *Studies in Ephemera: Text and Image in Eighteenth-Century Print* (Lanham: Bucknell University Press, 2013). See also Joshua B. Fisher and Rebecca Steinberger, eds., *Encountering Ephemera 1500–1800: Scholarship, Performance, Classroom* (Cambridge: Cambridge Scholars Publishing, 2012).

30 For instance, the cholera pamphlet was included on the list of "Books printed at the Mission Press in Beirut," with this description: "On the Cholera. Composed by Mr. Homes. Printed 1837. 12 mo. Pp. 12, edition 4000, issued 2460." ABC 16.8.1, vol. 1. "Books printed at the Mission Press in Beirut, Mar 1844 [?]."

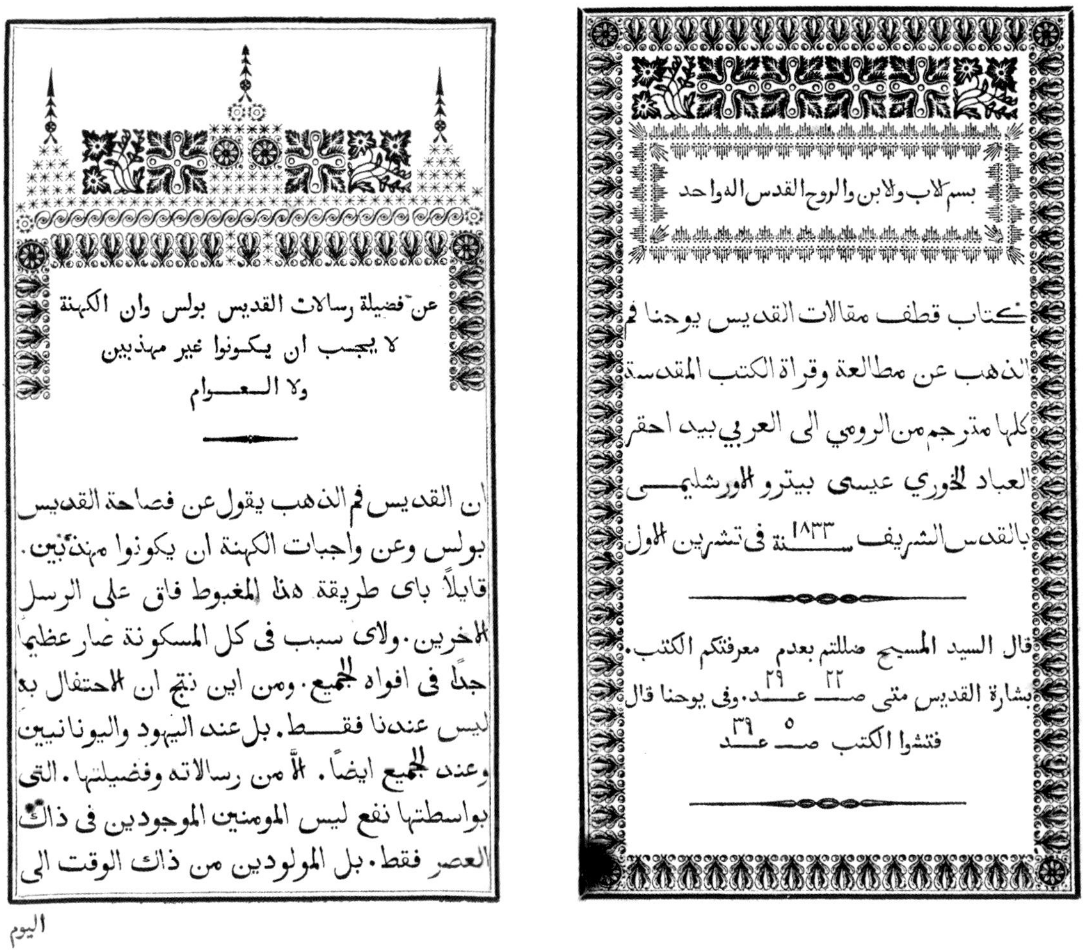

عن فضيلة رسالات القديس بولس وان الكهنة
لا يجب ان يكونوا غير مهذبين
ولا العوام

ان القديس فم الذهب يقول عن فصاحة القديس
بولس وعن واجبات الكهنة ان يكونوا مهذبين.
قايلاً باي طريقة هذا المغبوط فاق على الرسل
الاخرين. ولاي سبب في كل المسكونة صار عظيماً
جداً في افواه الجميع. ومن اين نتج ان الاحتفال به
ليس عندنا فقط. بل عند اليهود واليونانيين
وعند الجميع ايضاً. الا من رسالاته وفضيلتها. التي
بواسطتها نفع ليس المومنين الموجودين في ذاك
العصر فقط. بل المولودين من ذاك الوقت الى
اليوم

بسم الاب والابن والروح القدس الاله الواحد

كتاب قطف مقالات القديس يوحنا فم
الذهب عن مطالعة وقراة الكتب المقدسة
كلها مترجم من الرومي الى العربي بيد احقر
العباد الخوري عيسى بيترو الاورشليمي
بالقدس الشريف سنة ١٨٣٣ في تشرين الاول

قال السيد المسيح ضللتم بعدم معرفتكم الكتب.
بشارة القديس متى صـ ٢٢ عـ ٢٩. وفي يوحنا قال
فتشوا الكتب صـ ٥ عـ ٣٩

FIGURE 7 *Introduction from* Qaṭf maqālāt al-qiddīs yūḥannā fam al-dhahab ʿan muṭālaʿat al-kutub al-muqaddasa. BEIRUT, 1836

1830s relied upon the visual practices of manuscript traditions, particularly those that may have been most recognizable for the local readership.

The emulation of some scribal visual and organizational conventions in these publications (discussed in the following section on formatting) was not simply a matter of coopting such practices in an exclusive manner. Specifically, what is evident when studying the layouts characteristic of early print culture in the region, and what speaks to the truly experimental nature of printing at this time, is the fact that inspirations were culled from myriad sources, both local and global. Consider, for example, the missionary books' title pages. Title pages, in Arabic manuscripts, did not traditionally include information like a work's title, author, or date. The content of such a page often varied and was frequently added to by owners after the book was commissioned.[31] Book titles could be found in the headpiece of a manuscript's incipit *ʿunwān* page(s) or a "titlepiece" ("a decorative panel or page carrying the title of a work, or a label on a binding"[32]). Often, information related to the book's title, authorship, city of production, date, and other aspects related to the manuscript's

31 Gacek, 277.

32 Michelle Brown, *Understanding Illuminated Manuscripts: A Guide to Technical Terms* (Malibu: J. Paul Getty Museum, 1994), 121, quoted in Gacek, 278.

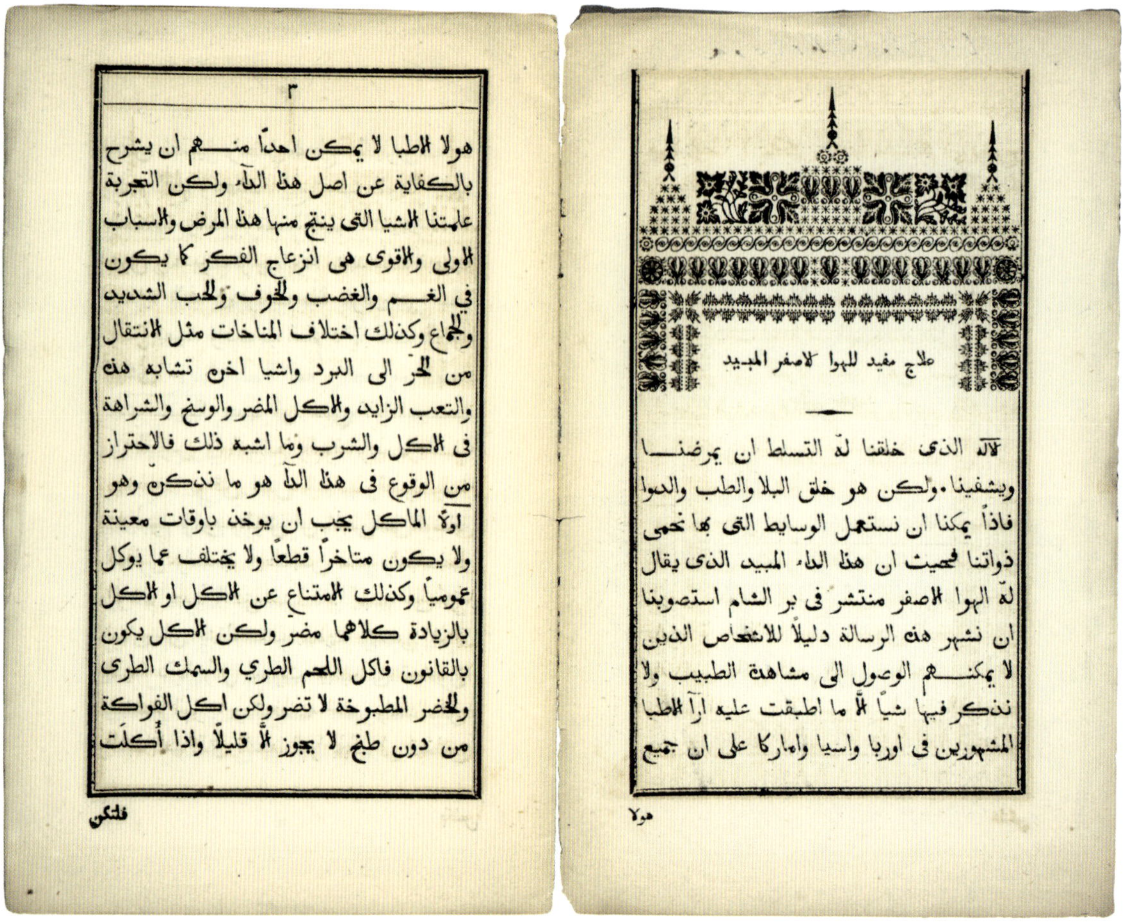


FIGURE 8 *Opening pages from* ʿIlāj mufīd li-l-hawāʾ al-aṣfar al-mubīd.
BEIRUT: AMERICAN PRESS, 1837

production could be found as scribal "signing off notes" or colophons.[33] This was not unique to printing practices in the Middle East. In fifteenth-century Europe, for instance, although manuscripts had occasionally featured an incipit folio with the book's title, the regular use of title pages, and the inclusion of information previously restricted to the colophon, was mostly a development associated with emergent printing traditions.[34] Title pages negotiated a shifting relationship between authors and the reading public, with the commodification of print being a driving force behind such developments. The publishers of early European printed books (or incunabula) began including title pages to help with cataloging

33 Gacek, 71–76.

34 Elizabeth Eisenstein argues that pages containing book titles occasionally appeared in quattrocento humanist manuscripts. However, these pages only become regular features as part of the development of printing practices. See Eisenstein, *The Printing Press as an Agent of Change*, 2 vols. (Cambridge: Cambridge University Press, 1980), 52, 52n35. Geoffrey Roper discusses a similar development seen in the initial imprints of the CMS press in Malta. See "Arabic Books Printed in Malta 1826–42: Some Physical Characteristics," in Sadgrove, *History of Printing and Publishing*, 118.

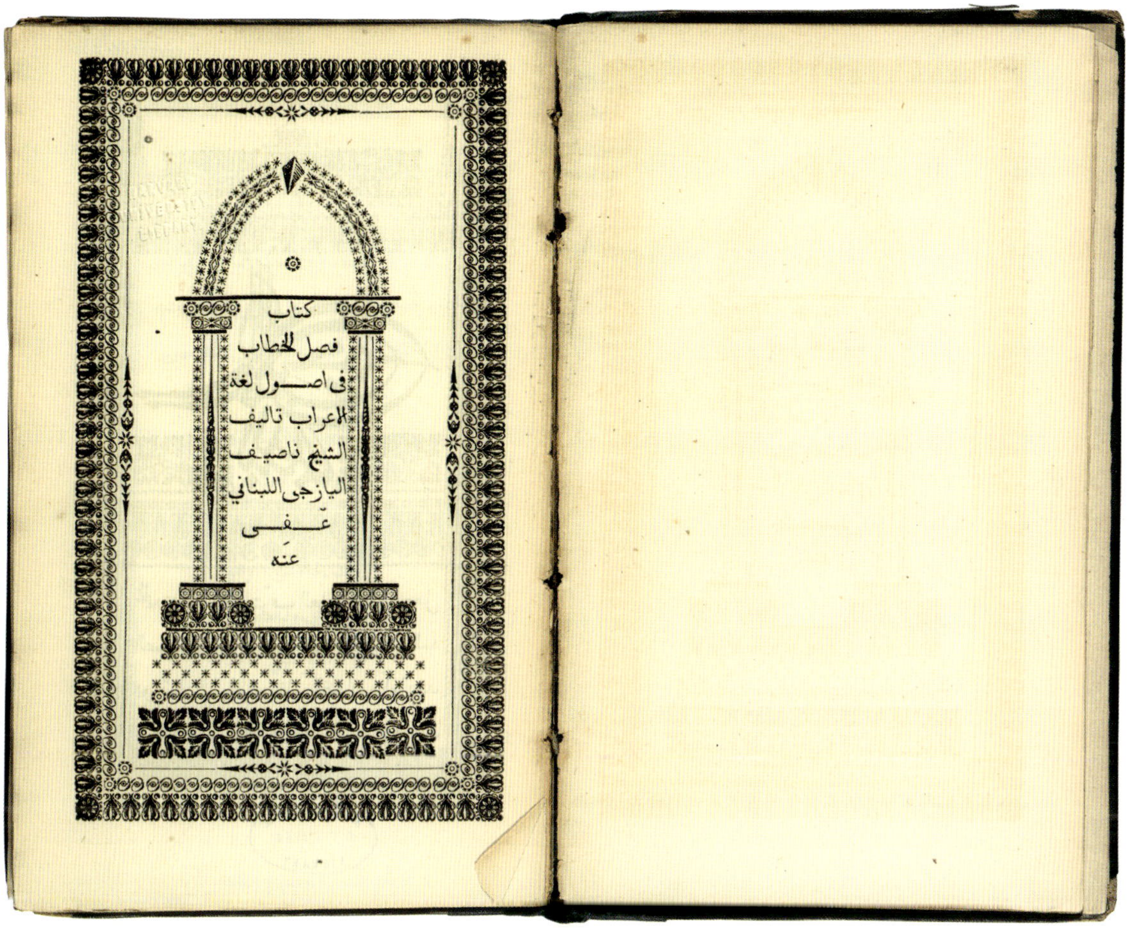


FIGURE 9 *Title page from Nāṣif al-Yāzijī.* Kitāb faṣl al-khiṭāb fī uṣūl lughat al-iʿrāb. BEIRUT, 1836

books, creating book lists for libraries, and advertising their press and the content of the printed tome.[35]

Although title pages were a part of most of the American mission's publications, including (at times) leaflets and shorter pamphlets, their designs and content varied during the 1830s. In particular, some of these pages experimented with a plethora of visual attributes from a variety of sources including European and American. This can be seen in the title page from al-Yāzijī's *Kitāb faṣl al-khitāb*. Fashioned from an assortment of ornamental types, the design compositions covering this Arabic title page (Fig. 9) mirror similar graphic arrangements found in the opening folio of *An Abridgment of Johnson's Typographia*, published in 1828 by the printer John Johnson (d. 1848)[36] (Fig. 10). Both examples illustrate a pointed arch, flanked by Ionic-style columns mounted on embellished pedestals that enclose each respective book's title and author. The graphics from Johnson's popular work on printing may have mirrored a popular interest in neoclassical aesthetics in American and British art and architecture at the

35 Eisenstein, *Agent of Change*, 59, 106, 106n203.

36 John Johnson, *An Abridgment of Johnson's Typographia, or the Printers' Instructor: With an Appendix* (Boston: C.L. Adams, 1828).

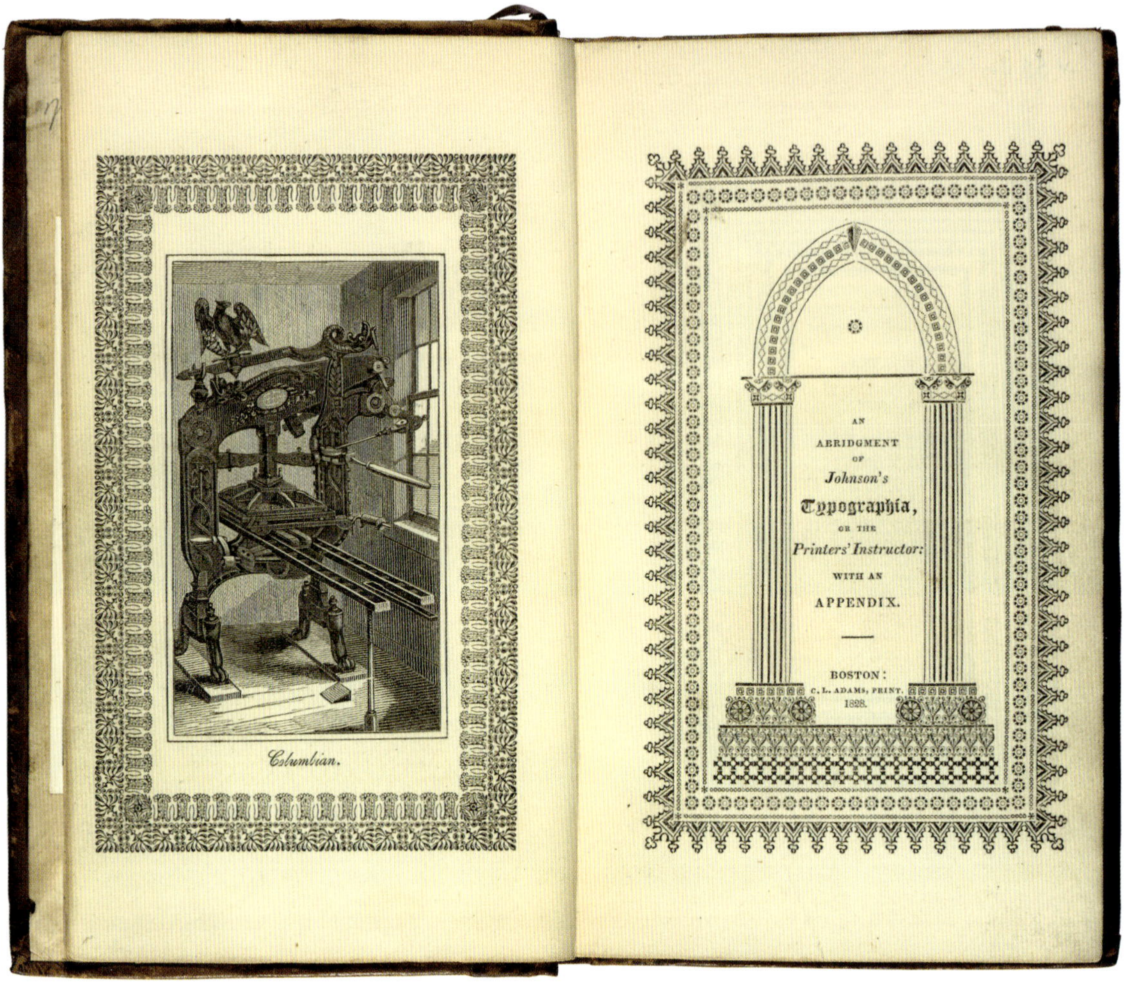


FIGURE 10 *Frontispiece and title page from John Johnson,* An Abridgment of Johnson's Typographia, or the Printers' Instructor: With an Appendix.
BOSTON: C.L. ADAMS, 1828

time, with the arched structure representing an entrance or "screen before a chapel or shrine."[37] The significance of the design in the mission's production, however, remains open-ended. Did Johnson's book, one of the first extensive anthologies on industrial printing techniques, represent a paragon of modernization to those working at the Press? Or were these producers also thinking in the neoclassical vein of the moment by featuring classical elements, implicitly inciting the reader to compare them with those of local archaeological sites (such as Anjar and Baalbak) that harked back to a "Golden Age" or origin of "Western civilization"? In the absence of any records related to the design program preferred by the American Press's printer and supervisor at the time, one can only conjecture.

37 This comes from a description of an engraving found on the inscription page of the second volume of the 1824 edition. See Johnson, *Typographia or the Printers' Instructor*, vol. 2 (London: Longman, Hurst, Rees, Orme, Brown, and Green, 1824). The title pages in the two volumes from 1824 differ from each other and from that of the 1828 edition. However, all title pages from 1824 and 1828 feature framed entrances/passageways. The title page from the first 1824 volume features the design of an arched opening in a brick wall, while the second volume shows a composition resembling a classical temple entrance made up of a triangular pediment surmounting two columns.

For instance, Johnson's book may simply have been readily available for the Press composers to emulate, while also serving as an example of the latest European trends in print designs and conventions. However, it could be argued that these elaborate visuals, which required painstaking labor, lent the book a certain amount of weight and importance, in hopes of elevating it to the level of its handwritten contemporaries. Specifically, as McKitterick argues with respect to fifteenth-century European incunabula,[38] these works were representations of what books were expected to look like during this period by the specific audience that the mission and its Press authors were targeting.

Although al-Yāzijī's grammar book, of all the books printed at this press, is the only of such an elaborately illustrated composition, the American Press publications' title pages from the 1830s featured more decorative styles than those printed in the 1840s and 1850s. For instance, the title page of the 1838 tract on self-examination (*Kitāb irshād al-masīḥī fī imtiḥān al-nafs*) mentioned above features a combination of three nested decorative borders framing the text's title with an excerpt from the Bible appearing below it. Interestingly, many of the pamphlets printed at the Press during this period also show a preference for title pages (despite the smaller page count). Most of these ephemeral examples, like the pamphlet on the treatment of cholera from 1837, employ a similar compositional formula of three ornamental borders, which vary in motif design, framing the title page content (Fig. 11 and Fig. 12).

### *Pagination and Organization*

The coming together of print and scribal practices in the American Press publications from this period is also manifest in the texts' organizational systems including aspects related to pagination, collating practices, and colophons. What is striking about such early works is the combination of printing and scribal conventions in the organization of these texts. This is most apparent in the use of catchwords simultaneously with page numbers. In these publications, catchwords frequently appear in the lower left corner of each individual leaf, displaying the first word of the subsequent page (see the bottom left corner of individual pages in Figures 3, 5, 6, 7, and 8). This clearly emulated existing systems in place for organizing and maintaining the sequence of manuscripts' folia and quires.[39] Aside from a few exceptions, the numbering of manuscript pages remained rare until after printing methods became prevalent during the late 1800s.[40]

Interestingly, in the American Press's publications from the 1830s, catchwords often appeared in conjunction with *abjad* numerals and running section headings at the top of each folio, which was typical of contemporary printed books. The practice of using both catchwords and page numbers seems rather redundant in these printed works, yet it was prevalent during this period and not at all limited to books. In fact, it is also seen in pamphlets, like the booklet on treating cholera, a mere twelve pages composed of no more than three folios (Fig. 8). Additionally, these books were printed using page signatures, a practice exclusive to print production where a pre-arranged group of pages is printed on the recto and verso of a single sheet of paper (taking into account how the pages will appear in the bound product once the sheets are cut and folded). This raises questions about why Press editors saw the need to include multiple pagination systems. It may be a matter of maintaining a visual (and an ideological) link between this emergent technology and regional bookmaking traditions, particularly with regard to how local readers expected texts to look.

Colophons also regularly appear in the mission's books from this period. Although from the mid-1860s onwards the American Press publications' title pages included the date, author, place of publication, and publisher, just as in Europe and the US, from the 1830s to the 1850s this information

38 McKitterick, 37.

39 Gacek, 50–51.

40 Ibid., 179.

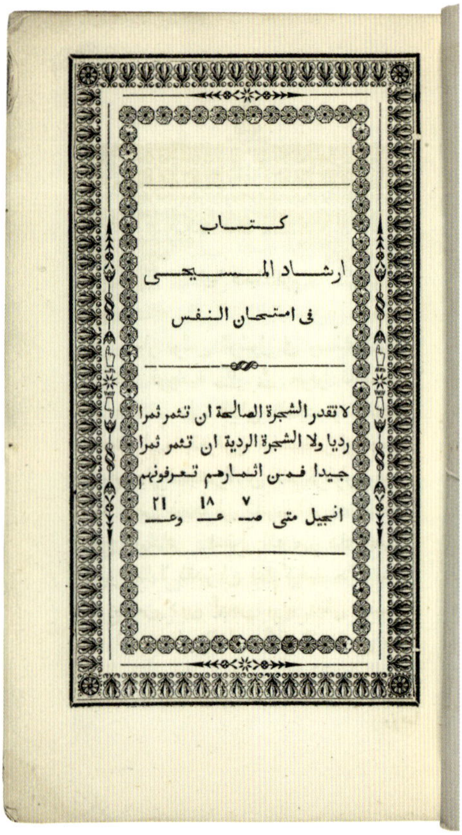

كتاب
ارشاد المسيحى
فى امتحان النفس
لا تقدر الشجرة الصالحة ان تثمر ثمرا
رديا ولا الشجرة الردية ان تثمر ثمرا
جيدا فمن اثمارهم تعرفونهم
انجيل متى ص ٧ ع ١٨ وع ٢١

FIGURE 11
*Title page from George B. Whiting,* Kitāb irshād al-masīḥī fī imtiḥān al-nafs.
BEIRUT, 1837

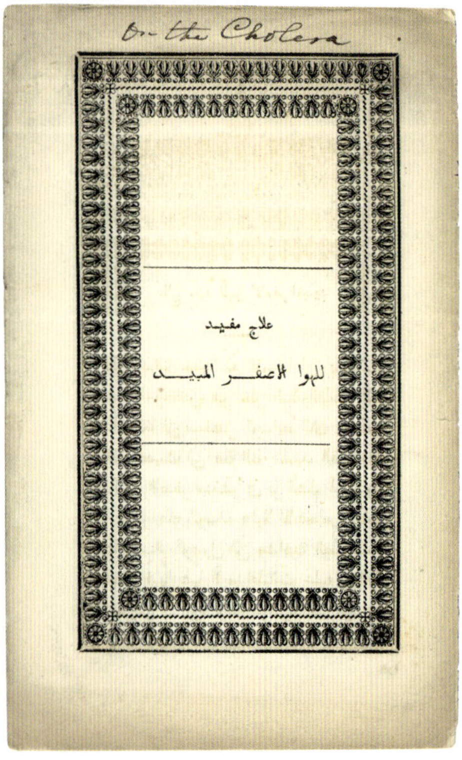

On the Cholera
علاج مفيد
للهوا الاصفر المبيد

FIGURE 12
*Title page from* ʿIlāj mufīd li-l-hawāʾ al-aṣfar al-mubīd.
BEIRUT: AMERICAN PRESS, 1837

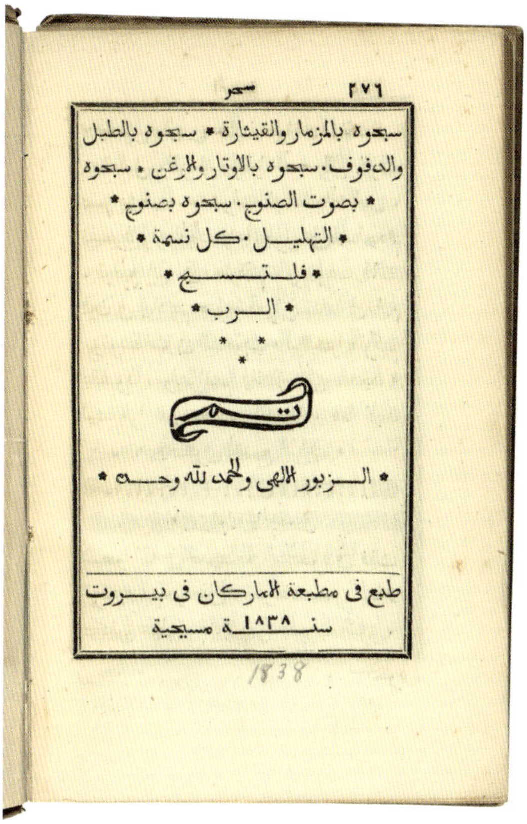
٢٧٦ سحر

سبحوه بالمزمار والقيثارة * سبحوه بالطبل
والدفوف . سبحوه بالاوتار والارغن * سبحوه
* بصوت الصنوج . سبحوه بصنوج *
* التهليل . كل نسمة *
* فلتسبح *
* الرب *

تم

* الزبور الالهي والحمد لله وحده *

طبع في مطبعة الاماركان في بيروت
سنة ١٨٣٨ مسيحية

1838

FIGURE 13
*Colophon with finis motif from* Kitāb al-zabūr al-ilāhī li-dāūd al-nabī.
BEIRUT: AMERICAN PRESS, 1838

(aside from author and title) was often reserved for the book's colophon. Positioned at the conclusion of the main text in a formulation that often tapered down to a v-shaped ending (similar to the conclusions of handwritten books), the printed colophons occupy a rectangular cartouche at the foot of the text block, setting them apart from other content on the page, sometimes including an Arabic finis motif (Fig. 13). While colophons frequently appeared in manuscripts, their location and design, which included rectangle, circular, or triangular shapes, varied from one book to the next. However, in the case of the mission's works, it is clear that certain elements from manuscript organizational methods found their way, in varying incarnations, onto the printed page. In almost all of the mission's early publications, the opening pages, chapter headings and introductions display multifarious forms of decorative motifs inspired by local manuscripts yet recreated within the means of letterpress printing.

While the Press's publications clearly tapped into the traditions surrounding handwritten books, they also varied greatly from local book-making traditions. In fact, although the Press's books ranged in size, the most sizable amongst them, such as the large-format editions of the Protestant Bible printed in the 1860s, were no more than 22 centimeters in length. The smallest books, which the missionaries referred to as "pocket editions," tended to be hymnals and copies of the New Testament without notes that measured at about 4.5 x 6 inches. Al-Yāzijī's *Kitāb faṣl al-khitāb*, for instance, which measures at approximately 5 x 7 inches and runs 168 pages long, would not necessarily be deemed a "pocket edition" by missionary standards. However, it was certainly much smaller than standard educational and religious manuscripts,[41] and in its ease of transportation

41 Manuscripts also ranged in size, with some coming in miniature sizes for travelers and talismanic purposes.

would have fulfilled one of the purposes of pocket book editions. Manuscript producers also paid much attention to binding methods and covers, which was an attitude not very apparent in the mission's publications. While several of the mission's earlier printed works have had their original covers replaced,[42] many were simple constructions since such work was chiefly done in-house until the early 1860s.[43] Some were made out of thick cardboard pieces glued to the body or attached with ribbons. Others (such as the smaller, thinner booklets) were simply bound with a light weight colored stock paper using saddle stitching. The most elaborate covers featured leather binding with some minimal, ornamental embossing (seen in the mission's Bibles from the 1860s).

### Considering Regional Printing Traditions

The emulations of scribal conventions commonly appeared in the works of other (Christian and Muslim) Arabic presses active in the region during print's nascent stage, and the Americans made use of such productions. An important Christian print shop was that of the Greek Catholic monastery of al-Shuwayr, active in Mount Lebanon from the late 1700s. Books printed at al-Shuwayr also featured decorative elements such as ornamental borders and rules, catchphrases, and calligraphic designs (Fig. 14). Although the inspirations for some aspects were of European origin, such as the appearance of robed angel motifs flanking titles in books printed during the 1700s, these books engaged with local Christian manuscript conventions and preferences. This is clear, for example, in the use of catchwords and the triangular tapering of text endings.[44]

Although the productions of this small press were never widely disseminated, members of the Syria mission were aware of its regional importance as a pioneering enterprise. In fact, the American missionaries working at the Press often relied on al-Shuwayr's books as sources for their own publications. For instance, a Psalter printed at al-Shuwayr was used as the basis for an early American Protestant translation of the Psalms.[45] Various graphic elements from al-Shuwayr's publications also appeared in the Protestants' books. One example is seen on the incipit pages of Whiting's tract "On Temperance" (Fig. 15), where the lead-engraved word *kitāb* that appears in the heading of the title page is an exact replica of that seen in books from al-Shuwayr (Fig. 14).

Publications from the state press in Būlāq, for example, also show a similar use of *sarlawḥ*s and calligraphic forms[46] that could have been an

However, the ones commonly used at mosques, monasteries, and seminaries were heavier and much larger than books printed at the American Press. For more on small-sized devotional manuscripts, particularly *sancak* (banner) Qur'ans, see Heather Coffey, "Between Amulet and Devotion: Islamic Miniature Books in the Lilly Library," in Gruber, *The Islamic Manuscript Tradition*, 79–115.

42 Most as a result of processing at international libraries and collections.

43 Press records show that there was an active, though slow, binding department in the print shop. See for instance "Quarterly Report of the Press," Oct-Dec 1844, PHS, RG 115-1-25. Leather-bound books produced during the 1860s often have an inner label that reads "Rosenweig Bookbinder, Beirut."

44 This is also seen in the inclusion of engravings depicting saints and evangelists, which appear in prayer books from al-Shuwayr press.

45 Copies of books printed at al-Shuwayr press were in the possession of the American missionaries and they might have been consulted for their graphic methods at some point. In a letter from a Press employee to Smith, for example, a copy of the Psalms printed at al-Shuwayr is discussed as a possible reference for the mission's edition. See ABC 50, Eli Smith Arabic Collection, Box 1, al-ʿĀzār to Smith, 8 Aug 1842.

46 See Cheng-Hsiang Hsu, "A Survey of Arabic-character Publications Printed in Egypt during the Period of 1238–1267 (1822–1851)," in *History of Printing and Publishing in the Languages and Countries of the Middle East*, ed. Philip Sadgrove (Oxford: Oxford University Press, 2004), 1–9; Fawzi M. Tadrus, *Printing in the Arab World with Emphasis on the Būlāq Press in Egypt* (Doha: University of Qatar, 1982); Richard N. Verdery, "The

كتاب

المجمع الانطاكى المنعقد بامر قدس السيد كيريوكيرا غابيوس
مطر البطريرك الانطاكى وساير المشرق الكلى الطوبى * وكان
التيامة في دير مارى انطونيوس الغرب الكاين في ساحل مدينة
بيروت وهو احد ادير رهبنة ماريوحنا الشوير * وقد طُبع بامر
ونفقة قدس السيد الكلى الغبطة المذكور اعلاه لكى يسهل
اقتناه لراغبه وتعم الافادة لكل مطالع فيه * وذلك في دير
القديس ماريوحنا السابق الملقب بالشوير من معاملة كسروان
بعل الرهبان القانونيين الباسيليين من طايفة الروم الملكية
سنة الف وثمانماية وعشرة مسيحية * ويرجو كل
من له تعب بمباشرة هذا العمل الصالح الدعا
بالرحمة والغفران * والحظوة بالقبول
والرضوان * من الرب الكريم المنان *
الذى له المجد والعزة والاكرام
الى ابد الابدين وفي
كل وقتٍ وحين
* امين *

(١)

FIGURE 14 *Title page from* Kitāb al-majmaʿ al-anṭākī.
BEIRUT: MAṬBAʿAT DAYR MĀR YŪḤĀNNA AL-MULLAQAB BI-L-SHUWAYR, 1810

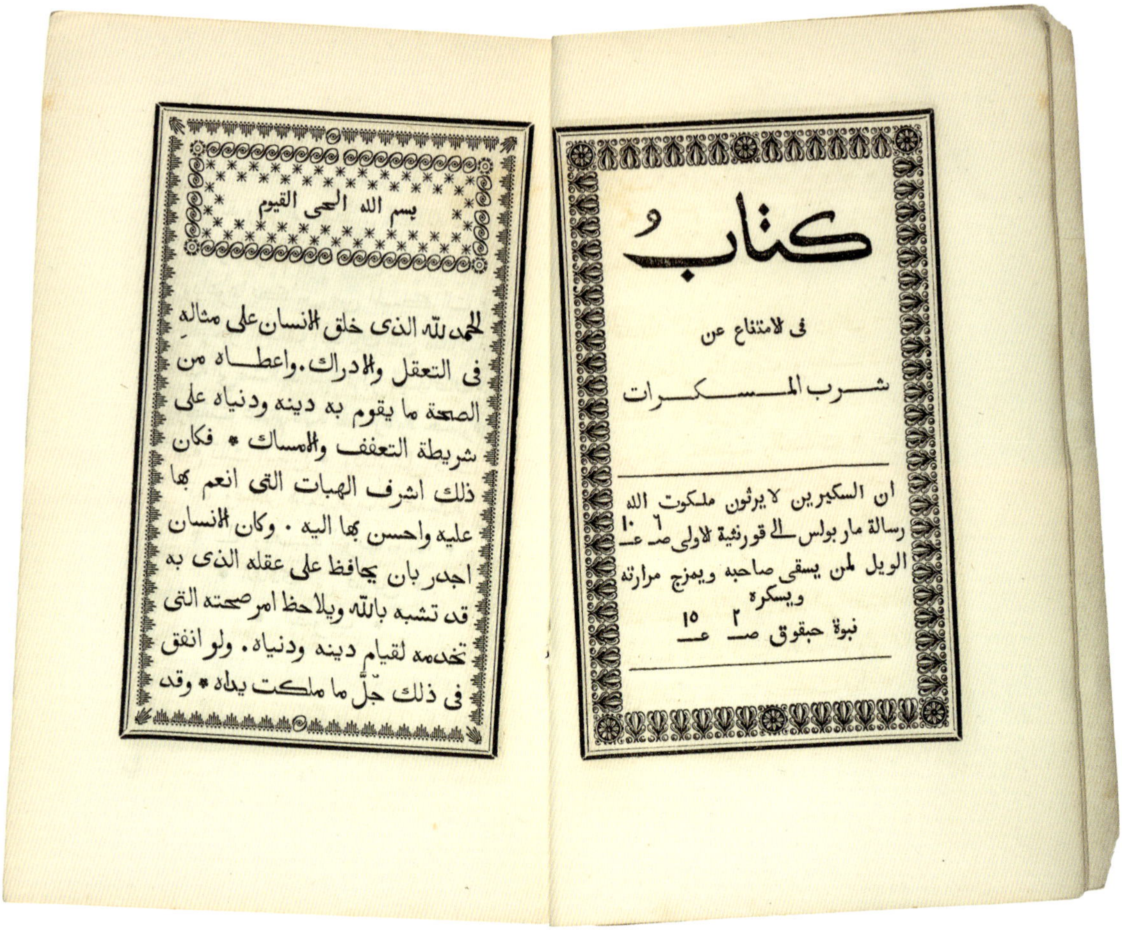


FIGURE 15 Right, *title page showing the word* kitāb *from George B. Whiting,* Kitāb fī al-imtināʿ ʿan shurb al-muskirāt [*sic*]. BEIRUT, 1838

additional source of inspiration for American Press works.[47] These Egyptian books displayed often elaborate headpieces within their *ʿunwān* pages, in addition to their reliance on catchwords and manuscript-style colophons.[48] Additionally, books by the short-lived Müteferrika press in eighteenth-century Istanbul utilized similar manuscript elements, along with their inclusion of hand-colored aquatints and gilding.[49] These books represent an example of how regional Arabic presses contended with local scribal traditions by forging a set of visual conventions and methods uniquely formulated for their particular readerships. The recreation of manuscript conventions

Publications of the Būlāq Press under Muḥammad ʿAlī," *Journal of the American Oriental Society* 91, no. 1 (1971): 129–32.

47 Eli Smith frequently updated his library with books from Būlāq; see ABC 50, Box 2, "List of books printed at Būlāq press."

48 One example of a book with headpiece elements in its chapter headings is *Dīwān ʿalī ibn abī ṭālib* (The Poetry of ʿAlī ibn Abī Ṭālib) printed at Cairo's Būlāq press in 1835. An original is held at the University of California, Berkeley. An online copy, which was digitized by Google, is available for viewing on www.hathitrust.org.

49 See Yasmin Gencer, "İbrahim Müteferrika and the Age of the Printed Manuscript," in Gruber, *The Islamic Manuscript Tradition*, 155–93.

via the letterpress technology resulted in an unconventional emulation of hand-drawn forms and designs in the "new" print medium. However, this approach was not limited to letterpress printing, and in fact is evident in nineteenth-century lithographic copies produced in Cairo as well as publishing centers in Qajar Iran, or Tabriz. Given the nature of lithography, which allows for continuity with manuscript traditions, the continued adherence to scribal visual modes would not be unusual.[50] The reliance of local presses (run by local Arabs) on manuscript conventions demonstrates a continuation of long-established traditions within the genealogies of the Arabic, specifically Islamic, book.

It should be noted that some early regional Christian presses seemed to eschew manuscript conventions in favor of visual tropes more in line with the establishments' religious programs. For instance, books printed at al-Shuwayr, such as *Kitāb al-majmaʿ al-anṭākī* (printed in 1810), show the use of figurative imagery as well as classical-style ornaments that one would associate with Renaissance engravings and printed books[51] (Fig. 14). However, what all of these examples from regional presses demonstrate is that Arabic publications during the early nineteenth century draw from a great variety of sources and techniques. Although this certainly speaks to the experimental nature of the medium at this time, it also shows how local and regional notions of books and their dimensions were in flux.

An important distinction to be made between the American Press in Beirut and its regional contemporaries is its non-Arab (or "foreign") status. While other regional presses that adopted scribal conventions were, for the most part, Muslim-led or funded, the American Press was (particularly during the 1830s) first and foremost an extension of the missionary apparatus. As such, since one would assume that the missionary Press editors in Beirut were more familiar with contemporary Western-style printing aesthetics and practices than with local Arab ones, their emulation of manuscript conventions and local Arabic writing styles shows an engagement with, and understanding of, local scribal traditions.

To a certain degree, the same can perhaps be said of the CMS press in Malta, where the press's early imprints demonstrate an overlap between printing and manuscript conventions. Books (some of which were distributed by the Americans in Beirut) printed by the CMS using the letterpress at this print shop at times displayed wood engraved images, illustrations, borders, and calligraphic styles. In an 1832 edition of a work on Biblical history for schools entitled *Kitāb al-tawārīkh al-ma'khūdha min al-kitāb al-muqaddas,* the title page uses some calligraphic engraving for the book title in addition to a contemporary European figural illustration beneath the subtitle (Fig. 16). The incipit page (*ʿunwān*) includes a Christian doxological phrase (*bism-l-ab wa-l-ibn wa-l-rūḥ al-qudus allāh wāḥid amın*) set in a typeface used in all of this press's publications before 1838 and supplied by Richard Watts[52] (Fig. 16). The *basmala* is enclosed within a triangle nested in a cartouche decorated with varied typographic ornamental metal sorts. Although this visual element certainly stems from an understanding of local manuscript traditions, it is distinct from the headpiece designs found in the American Press publications. The CMS publication's colophon (on page 33 of the booklet) also resembles those of traditional scribal conventions in the way that the ending text is tapered. These elements were not unique to this one CMS; such designs can be found in a number of other publications from this press.[53]

50 An explanation of the distinctions between these two technologies, and their visual and intellectual ramifications, is taken up in Chapter 5.

51 A copy of this text is held at the University of Bonn library, a digital version of which is available in their online database. Similar engravings can be found in other books printed at al-Shuwayr.

52 Roper, "Arabic Books Printed in Malta," 112–13.

53 Ibid., 111–30.

كتاب التواريخ الماخوذه من الكتاب المقدس

علي سبيل السوال والجواب

نفعه لاجل تعليم الشباب والاولاد

فاثبت انت علي ما تعلمت وايتمنت به فقد علمت ممن
تعلمت وانك من صبايك قد تعلمت الاسفار المقدسة
التي تقدر على ان تحكمت للخلاص بالايمان الذي
بيسوع المسيح* ٢ طيماثاوس ص٣ عدد١٤ و١٥

طبع في مالطة سنه ١٨٣٢

بسم
الاب والابن والروح
القدس الاه واحد * امين *

ما يتضمن هذا الكتاب وهو جزان

الجز الاول

تواريخ ماخوذة من كتب العهد العتيق

س* من هو خالق العالم
ج* الله القادر علي كل شي خلق السما والارض
وكل الاشيا التي فيها (تكوين فصل ١ عدد ١
وفصل ٢ عدد ١)
س* في كم يوم خلق الله العالم
ج* خلقه بكلمته في ستة ايام واستراح في اليوم
السابع وجعل ذلك النهار مقدسا (تكوين فصل ١
عدد ٣١ عبرانيين فصل ١١ عدد ٣ تكوين فصل
٢ عدد ٣ و خروج فصل ٣١ عدد ١٥ و١٧)

FIGURE 16 Right, *title page;* left, *first page from* Kitāb al-tawārīkh al-maʾkhūdha min al-kitāb al-muqaddas.
MALTA, 1832

What sets the visual conventions of the CMS publications apart from those of the American Press, however, is not that one press utilized scribal conventions more than the other. Rather, it is in the combined visual choices that clearly mark the works printed by the CMS in Malta as "Protestant" or "foreign" publications – while those printed at the American Press at the time did not include clear markers of the publisher and/or the press's religious/political affiliation. For example, going back to the title page from *Kitāb al-tawārīkh* (seen in Fig. 16), the inclusion of a Biblical quotation beneath the engraved figure clearly indicates the religious nature of the press (and publication). The European manner of dress and European-style depiction of the seated figure seen in the engraving would be clear to any local Arabic-speaking readers, once again highlighting the "Frankish" nature of this publication. Unlike al-Yāzijī's grammar, which did not list the name of the press, and included visual elements familiar to local Christian and Muslim readers, the non-Arab nature of CMS publications is foregrounded in these title pages, demonstrative of the direct proselytizing approach the British were adopting in the region at this time. In the case of books printed at the

American Press, deviating from common Presbyterian and American printing standards appears to have been an attempt at making the mission's books as attractive as possible using the visual and written language of the local "Other" in hopes of attracting multi-confessional audiences.

### A Tempered Evangelism

In order to understand the uses and meanings of these printed books, and to avoid a fetishization of the medium, it is necessary to read these visual features alongside textual content, as well as situating such works within the particular contexts of readership and circulation during the nineteenth century. To begin with, an intriguing fact about many of the first publications struck off the American Press (with the exception of al-Yāzijī's book and a few others) was that they were revisions of books first printed in Arabic by the CMS in Malta. For instance, the following books printed in Beirut from 1836–1837[54] share titles and some content with British works produced in Malta in 1836 and 1837: *Kitāb taʿlīm mukhtaṣar li-l-aṭfāl fī qawāʿid al-dīyāna wa-l-īmān* (A Short Children's Instruction on the Rules of Religion and Faith),[55] *Baʿḍ mazāmīr li-l-tarannum* (Some Psalms for Singing),[56] *Qiṣṣat ilīṣābāt ibnat al-labbān al-saʿīda* (The Story of Elizabeth the Dairyman's Happy Daughter, a tract more commonly known as *The Dairyman's Daughter*),[57] *Amthāl sulaymān* (The Proverbs of Solomon),[58] and *Waʿẓ al-masīḥ ʿala-l-jabal* (Christ's Sermon on the Mount).[59] A number of scholars agree that the key

54 All these appear on a list (composed by Eli Smith) of books printed at the American Press from 1836 to early (March) 1844: ABC 16.8.1, vol.1, "Books printed at the Mission Press in Beirut, Mar 1844 [?]."

55 Printed in Beirut in 1836 and translated from Isaac Watt's *The First Catechism for Children* (London, 1730). It was first printed in Arabic by the CMS in 1826 and 1832. Geoffrey Roper, "The Beginnings of Arabic Printing by the ABCFM, 1822–1841," *Harvard Library Bulletin* 9, no. 1 (1998): 63; Roper, "Arabic Printing in Malta 1825–1845: Its history and its place in the development of print culture in the Arab Middle East" (PhD Thesis, University of Durham, 1988), 331, 336; Alexander G. Ellis, *Catalogue of Arabic Books in the British Museum,* 3 vols. (London, 1894–1901), 2:757–58; A.L. Tibawi, *American Interests in Syria 1800–1901: A Study of Educational, Literary and Religious Work* (Oxford: Oxford University Press, 1966), 82.

56 These were Psalms versified by al-Yāzijī; this American Press version dates to 1836. An earlier edition from 1828 by the CMS press in Malta, *Baʿḍ mazāmīr ustukhrijat min al-lugha al-ʿibrāniyya ila-l-lugha al-ʿarabiyya wa nuzimat shiʿran li-l-tarnīm,* was versified for that press by Fāris al-Shidyāq. Roper, "The Beginnings of Arabic Printing," 64; Miroslav Krek, "Some Observations on Printing Arabic in America and by Americans Abroad," *Manuscripts of the Middle East* 6 (1992): 82; Roper, "Arabic Printing in Malta," 332; Tibawi, *American Interests*, 82.

57 The first version of this book was translated for the American mission by the Greek Catholic ʿĪsā Bītrū (Pappas Ysa Petros) during the early 1820s but it was first printed in 1826 by the CMS. According to Smith, this book was later "Corrected from the Malta edition." ABC 16.8.1, vol. 1, "Books printed at the Mission Press in Beirut, Mar 1844 [?]." The CMS edition is mentioned in Roper, "The Beginnings of Arabic Printing," 64; the ABCFM edition is mentioned in Ellis, *Arabic Books,* 2:519. For more on Bītrū's work with the early missionaries, see *The Missionary Register* 16 (1828): 237; William Jowett, *Christian Researches in Syria and the Holy Land, in MDCCCXXIII and MDCCCXXIV* (London: Richard Watts, 1825), 220–23.

58 According to the 1844 list, the American Press's edition was printed in 1837 "without alteration from the Romish version of the Bible." A revised edition was printed in 1842. ABC 16.8.1, vol. 1, "Books printed at the Mission Press in Beirut, Mar 1844 [?]." Roper states that this book was first printed by the CMS in 1834 based on the Arabic and Latin Bible printed in Rome in 1671. The CMS edition, however, contains Arabic and French text printed side by side, see Roper, "Arabic Printing in Malta," 338. The Malta edition is listed as "A Selection from the book of Proverbs, reprinted from the Bible in Arabic and Latin published at Rome in 1671, and accompanied by a French version" in Ellis, *Arabic Books*, 1:380.

59 The American Press edition was printed in 1837. The CMS edition, printed in 1826, included the "Ten Commandments" in addition to "Christ's Sermon on the Mount." See Roper, "Arabic Printing in Malta," 330.

reason behind the mission's reliance on Arabic imprints from the CMS press in Malta and from the BFBS in London[60] was the Americans' grappling with language barriers and Arabic printing.[61]

As mentioned in the previous chapter, throughout the missionary Press's early decades only two or three members of the mission were capable of writing and translating Arabic texts for print. Since most of its Protestant members came from the US or Britain, they may have studied Arabic in their home regions but for the most part had not yet acquired enough of a grasp on the language to compose texts on their own.[62] Members of the Syria Mission were aware of the actual level of fluency in the language needed to work effectively in the field. In 1839, for example, the mission's members asked then-Press editor and missionary Eli Smith (one of the few Americans at the time fluent in Arabic) to prepare an essay on the "importance of missionaries obtaining a thorough acquaintance with the languages of the people among whom they are to labour."[63] Mid-century records of the Press also show that many missionaries remained hesitant about taking on the testing task of Arabic composition.[64]

This explains why the mission printed books based on previous Arabic editions. However, it does not sufficiently address reasons behind their particular choices of text and subject matter. It is also important to examine further what the nature of such publications meant for the missionary enterprise as a whole at this time, and why there was a reliance on publishing this particular type of literature. Regardless of whether these works (already in production at Malta) were easier to translate/rework given the limited amount of "original" texts produced by the American missionaries at the time, the relevance of these publications to the mission's printing history and its operations during this early period should not be overlooked.

An important point is that almost all of the Syria Mission's ecclesiastical literature at this time avoided any explicit attacks on local religious practices, and instead focused on issues of ethics and godliness. For instance, the Press's production of religious fictions like *Qiṣṣat ilīṣābāt* illustrates the mission's uses of subtlety in the evangelical tone of its early publications. This text is an example of nineteenth-century morality-driven evangelical tales, rooted somewhere between sentimental fiction and social novels, that "illustrate the permeable nature of the barrier between secular and sacred texts."[65] Employing "novelistic devices" to deliver a religious message, these tracts were popular amongst nineteenth-century evangelical publishers (like the American Tract Society, a benefactor of the American Press) for use by missions – at home and abroad – as a way to secure mass readership of evangelical literature and, ultimately, conversions.[66] In 1839, the Press began printing *Khabarīyat hinrī al-ṣaghīr wa-ḥammālih* (The Story of Young Henry and his Bearer),[67] which had not been printed in Malta but was singled out

60 For more on this organization, see Leslie Howsam, *Cheap Bibles: Nineteenth-Century Publishing and the British Foreign Bible Society* (Cambridge: Cambridge University Press, 2002).

61 See Roper, "The Beginnings of Arabic Printing," 57–59; Tibawi, *American Interests*, 82; Krek, "Some Observations," 85.

62 The Syria Mission's struggles in the field due to its members' insufficient knowledge of Arabic go back to the mission's early days in 1824, as reported by Isaac Bird: "were we able to speak Arabic with fluency, I see nothing to hinder our 'speaking boldly'." *The Missionary Herald* 20 (1824): 216.

63 ABC 16.8.1, vol. 8, "Meeting at Whiting's," 27 Apr 1838.

64 According to a press report from 1855: "The most of our number, have little inclination to provide copy for the press – on the contrary, for the last years, the difficulty has been to induce members of the mission to provides treatises, when their great need was felt and acknowledge by all our number." "Report on the Printing Establishment," 1 Oct 1855, PHS, RG 115-1-25.

65 Cynthia S. Hamilton, "Spreading the Word: The American Tract Society, *The Dairyman's Daughter*, and Mass Publishing," *Book History* 14 (2011): 27.

66 Hamilton, "Spreading the Word," 27.

67 From the English original *The History of Little Henry and his Bearer*, by Mary Martha Sherwood, first printed in London in 1814.

(in addition to *Qiṣṣat ilīṣābāt*) by one of the first American missionaries to Syria, William Goodell, in 1828:

"I want to see 'Little Henry and his Bearer' in Arabick [sic]. I have translated it into Turkish and it is read, in manuscript, with prodigious interest. The 'Dairyman's Daughter' has been highly praised among the Arabs, and I think 'Little Henry' would be much more so.... I think such works ... are likely to be more useful at present than Tracts of any other character."[68]

Such books, certainly not unique to the Syria Mission or its Press, fit into the predetermined range of texts deemed by missionary boards to be most suitable for distribution amongst local Christian groups.[69] Additionally, other religious texts published by the Syria Mission related to issues of morality, such as the teachings of Christ's "Sermon on the Mount,"[70] or included tracts on godliness and temperance such as those by Whiting,[71] and the wisdom literature of Solomon's Book of Proverbs.[72] Other texts, such as an Arabic translation of John Chrysostom's *Homilies* printed at the American Press in 1837 as *Qaṭf maqālāt al-qiddīs yūḥannā fam al-dhahab ʿan muṭālaʿat al-kutub al-muqaddasa*, were not only well suited to the mission's proselytizing project but were probably also valued by local Greek Catholics and Maronites. These religious education books thus followed the themes of devout behavior and morality found in the works of spiritual fiction.[73] Furthermore, the mission's schoolbooks that were deemed of great necessity at the time at first avoided any potentially alienating religious undertones,[74] particularly in texts on geography, arithmetic, and Arabic grammar.

These early texts produced at the American Press, via their tempered evangelical message and locally-inspired manuscript conventions, appear to represent the Syria Mission's reaction to local attitudes towards and perceptions of the mission in particular, and Protestantism in general, at the time. These works, most of which relate more to issues of morality than to outright criticism of local religious practices, seemed ideally suited for missionaries in this religiously and politically volatile region. Specifically, through such publications, the mission seemed to be responding to a negative perception of their printed works amongst local readers, namely Maronite, Greek Catholic, and Greek Orthodox Christians.

## Pursuing Local Readers

The earliest members of the Syria Mission in the 1820s, who were the first Protestants to circulate books amongst the local communities of Mount Lebanon, distributed editions of the Protestant Arabic Bible produced in London by the BFBS. Works like these were notably met with disdain

68 *The Missionary Register* 16 (1828): 205.

69 Other missions abroad printed similar texts at the time. Editions for the ABCFM were translated into: Syriac, printed in Urumiyeh, ca. 1845; Marathi, printed by the Bombay Tract and Book Society in 1850; and Armeno-Turkish, printed by the ABCFM press in Malta in 1829. See William Goodell and Edward D.G. Prime, *Forty Years in the Turkish Empire: Or, Memoirs of Rev. William Goodell, D.D. Late Missionary of the A.B.C.F.M. at Constantinople* (New York: R. Carter and Bros., 1875), 221.

70 For instance, the previously mentioned *Waʿẓ al-masīḥ ʿala-l-jabal*, from 1837, and Thomas à Kempis's *Iqtitāf kitāb al-iqtidāʾ bi-l-masīḥ* (The Imitation of Christ), printed in 1837 and 1842.

71 Examples include the previously mentioned *Kitāb fī al-imtināʿ ʿan shurb al-muskirāt*[*sic*], of 1838, and *Kitāb irshād al-masīḥī fī imtiḥān al-nafs*, first printed in 1837 (then in 1843 and 1848).

72 *Amthāl sulaymān* (Beirut, 1837).

73 This approach was distinct from the Press's later works, which outwardly criticized the Catholic Church and its local "Papal sects." Such books appeared in the late 1840s and early 1850s.

74 Missionary papers and records deposited at Yale Divinity School Library, Manuscripts and Special Collections, Eli Smith Family Papers, Record Group 124 (hereafter cited as YDSL, RG 124) 6:34, "General Remarks on the Use of the Press in the East," 1830.

by the local Christian clergy. The Bible printed by the BFBS, and circulated by the American missionaries at the time, was a reprint of the Roman *Biblia Sacra Arabica* translated in 1671 by Maronites in Rome, minus the Apocrypha.[75] The British Bible's omission of these seven canonical books, viewed as sacred by the Maronite church, was seen as an anathema against these "divine texts." Not only were local clergy members appalled by the Protestant Bible's content, they were also wary of the indiscriminate way in which the American missionaries were distributing this work and others within local communities.[76] The tension culminated in a decree by the Maronite Patriarch in 1824 against the "Bible-men," their publications, and their schools, demanding a complete avoidance of the Americans and their books and activities. Pressure from local Catholic groups also led to the issuing of the firman (widely discussed by the Protestant missionaries at the time) in June 1824 by the Ottoman government against all Arabic Bibles imported from Europe (the land of the "Franks").[77]

What this meant for American missionaries evangelizing in the region was a need to reconsider the content of printed texts and their methods for distributing them. Initially, it seemed that some of the early missionaries maintained a seemingly unconcerned attitude regarding the nature and content of the 1824 Maronite Patriarch's decree and the Porte's firman. For instance, in a journal entry (dated August 12, 1824) Isaac Bird writes about the Sultan's firman against the circulation of foreign Bibles with some levity, stating that when Bird showed the document to the British Consul Peter Abbott, "he smiled at the Firman" stating "that a Firman of that sort might be bought at any time for a trifle."[78] However, it is clear that the Ottoman government's support of the local clergy's concerns and views led to changes in the American's proselytizing approach. In 1828, for instance, surreptitiously circulating manuscripts in small numbers was preferred to distributing printed books "profusely," lest they "share the fate of the Holy Bible – that is, are cast into the fire."[79] Rather than circulate printed controversial literature, the missionaries, believed that "the Press is much to be feared by our enemies in this land; and they will not fail to silence it if they can," felt it best "to let it [the Press] speak MILDLY."[80]

During the 1830s, the Syria Mission was cautioned against offending local beliefs and practices.[81] This certainly was a view linked to the events of the previous decade. However, the missionaries' designation of all local Christian sects as "nominal Christians" also led to tensions with the Greek Orthodox Church. In 1836 a letter signed by the church's patriarchs referred to the Protestant missionaries as "heretics," with their schools and books reviled as the "poison of heresy."[82] By 1836 the American mission's official stance was an "aim to avoid overt attacks upon religious peculiarities of the native Christian sects."[83] For instance, having learned from their mistakes during the 1820s, the

75 The Press director at the time discussed differences between this and the Protestant edition. YDSL, RG 124, 2:13, "Reports on the translation of the Scriptures into Arabic, 1844–1854."

76 Makdisi, *Artillery of Heaven: American Missionaries and the Failed Conversion of the Middle East* (Ithaca: Cornell University Press, 2008), 85–87, 94–99.

77 See, YDS, Isaac Bird Papers, MS 82, 2:24, "Journals," 1824 Jan-1830 Oct.

78 In an earlier entry from August 4, 1824, Isaac Bird writes that that, despite the anathema, many Maronites were still purchasing books from the Protestant missionaries. Bird writes that one such individual "and 20 others ... had determined to read [the Protestant's books] notwithstanding for their priests had hitherto been deceiving them. They had taught them to be idolaters contrary to the express command of God." For both entries see, YDS, Isaac Bird Papers, MS 82, 2:24, Journals, 1824 Jan-1830 Oct.

79 *The Missionary Register* 16 (1828): 205.

80 Quoted from a report by Bird, ibid.

81 *The Missionary Herald* 26 (1830): 18.

82 *The Missionary Herald* 33 (1837), 299, 397, 445, as cited in Tibawi, *American Interests,* 79, 79n3.

83 From "Records of the Syrian Mission, i (1836–53)" quoted in Tibawi, *American Interests*, 75n3. The records Tibawi consulted were in New York at the time, however they are presently held at the Presbyterian Historical Society, Philadelphia.

Americans decided to avoid attacks on the "religious peculiarities" of local Christian denominations and to focus instead on communicating issues of morality.[84] Concurrently, despite Islamic restrictions against proselytizing amongst the local Muslim populace,[85] the mission's records from the 1830s show plans for developing tracts for Muslims. Indeed, a desire to print books for Muslims consistently appears throughout the Syria Mission's accounts and records.[86] Additionally, Smith wrote and presented (at a meeting on April 17, 1838) an essay on the subject of a mission to Muslims, which was never published.[87]

Records from this period also demonstrate that the mission was grappling with the legalities of Druze conversions. Having met with much resistance from local Maronite, Greek Catholic, and Greek Orthodox groups in the 1820s and 1830s, the missionaries became interested in establishing relations with other, non-Christian, local groups, such as the Druze of Mount Lebanon. This was not easy, however, since members of the Druze community were considered unorthodox Muslims by the Egyptian state (which was in control of Beirut and nearby territories at this time), and thus proselytizing amongst them was problematic.[88] Records show that mission members were addressing these problems in 1836, when the first works were coming off the Press.[89] It appears that various baptisms of Druze men seeking to avoid military enlistment in the Egyptian-Ottoman wars occurred in 1839. The Americans feared if they turned these individuals away that they would "run to the bosom of Papal sects."[90] The subject of the mission's policy towards the Druze was also reconsidered in 1842 and during the 1860s.[91]

It is clear that during the 1830s, the newly instated American Press in Beirut was still hoping to improve the mission's standing amongst the region's Christian and Muslim groups, and thus produced its books with caution, to avoid alienating local readers or attracting controversy. What such records also demonstrate is that despite the wariness of local clergy towards the mission's work, as well as the illegality and difficulty of proselytizing among members of Ottoman Muslim communities, the mission had hopes of pursuing them as potential converts via publications. Read in parallel to the mission's goals and concerns at the time, the mission publications from the 1830s, in their visual, organization, and textual conventions, mirror this atmosphere of experimentation and ambivalence within the mission's own proselytizing methods in the 1830s.

## Considering Design Decisions and Direction

To completely attribute the visual and organizational choices made in these publications to the missionaries themselves would be a questionable approach. As an avid collector of manuscripts and print and a researcher of regional calligraphic traditions,[92] Eli Smith was well versed in local Arabic productions. However, it is unclear how involved he or other members of the mission were in every stage of a book's journey from composition to distribution. For one thing, Smith, the mission's lone expert in Arabic at the time, spent much of the 1830s and early 1840s on extended

84 ABC 16.8.1, vol. 8, "Meeting at Thompson's," 22 Apr 1836.

85 The nature of these restrictions is discussed in Chapter 2.

86 See *The Missionary Herald* 30 (1834), 421. Also see the following records: ABC 16.8.1, vol. 8, "Meeting," 12 Apr 1837; "Meeting," 7 Apr 1855.

87 See, ABC 16.8.1, vol. 8, "Meeting at Thomson's," 12 Apr 1837; "Meeting at Whiting's," 17 Apr 1838; "Meeting at Whiting's," 21 Apr 1838.

88 Due to Islamic laws on apostasy; see Tibawi, *American Interests*, 77.

89 ABC 16.8.1, vol. 8, "Meeting on 19 Apr 1836." See also an entry in *The Missionary Herald* 32 (1836): 460–61.

90 ABC 16.8.1, vol. 8, "Meeting at Thomson's," 3 Apr 1839.

91 ABC 16.8.1, vol. 8, "Meeting at Native Church," 19 Apr 1842.

92 At the time, Smith had begun work on designs for a new Arabic typeface for the Press. Numerous records from the 1830s indicate that he purchased local manuscripts for research. There are also some calligraphic samples amongst his Arabic papers at Harvard's Houghton Library. See for instance ABC 50, Box 1, "Calligraphic specimen of al-Naskhi script; Ownership Is God's," 1840 [?].

trips away from Beirut.[93] The head printer as of late October in 1836, George Percy Badger, only stayed on in the position (and in Beirut) for a little under two years. Although this means he saw the earliest publications come off the American Press, he was not doing this on his own, and had much local help.[94] His successor, Robert Thorn, took over three years later in 1839, though this was after a number of works had already been published.[95] Although it is not stated in mission's records, it is possible that – in addition to stalling production – efforts to familiarize each new printer with the Press's ins and outs fell on the shoulders of the handful of local laborers employed at the Press from its foundational years. Additionally, while the mission records in the 1830s remain mostly silent on the involvement of local Press employees in the design, organization, and supervision of Press productions, it seems to be that much of these duties were assumed by the mission's local copyists and authors.

The input and direction of such individuals, who during the 1830s were more familiar with scribal production methods than print, should not be overlooked. As discussed in Chapter 2, between the 1830s and 1840s American Press workers, copyists, and translators (of various ranks and positions) were ultimately the ones carrying most of the weight in the Press rooms.[96] While individuals like al-Yāzijī and Tānnūs al-Ḥaddād also worked as missionary Arabic tutors, with the latter frequently employed as a catechist after 1836, they performed varied important duties at the Press, including supervising and correcting presswork, translating English and/or Greek texts into Arabic, and producing original copy for the Press.[97]

As previously mentioned, for his part, al-Yāzijī composed two of the earliest publications that came off the Press during the 1830s: the Arabic grammar and versified Psalms. Of course, these are the two instances in which mission records and/or title pages clearly give al-Yāzijī as the author/composer; it is possible that he was involved in the production of more tracts during the 1830s, which were not clearly credited to him. Additionally, in his capacity as Press corrector, al-Yāzijī had some influence over the style and composition of the mission's publications, during the writing and editing process.[98] As discussed earlier in this chapter, he was closely involved throughout the Arabic grammar's numerous stages of production. On the level of design and visual conventions, it would be safe to suggest that the author also had much input in these layout decisions. Additionally, while the extent of their involvement in the publication process (beyond translating and correcting copy) is not well-documented in mission and press records, other mission employees, such as al-Ḥaddād and Antūniyyū al-Khayyāṭ, probably lent their expertise in scribal conventions to the production of early Press publications.

What this shows is that, at a time when it was still contending with consolidating its approach

93 The mid- to late 1830s saw Smith at Izmir working on procuring his new set of type. During the 1840s, he continued to take trips abroad – to the US and Germany – to supervise the production of this typeface. A number of journeys away from Beirut were also taken for health and family reasons (e.g. deaths of his wives – he was married four times). This included a well-publicized shipwreck in 1836; see *The Missionary Herald* 32 (1836): 464.

94 "Quarterly Report of the Superintendent of the Press," 30 Sep 1835, PHS, RG 115-1-25. For more on Badger, see Roper, "George Percy Badger (1815–1888)," *British Society for Middle Eastern Studies, Bulletin* 11, no. 2 (1984): 140–55.

95 For Thorn, see "Contract with Robert Thorn," 16 Oct 1835; "Quarterly Report on the State of the Press," 30 Sep 1836; "Quarterly Report on the Press," Dec 1836; "Original Report Respecting the Press," Apr 1842, PHS, RG 115-1-25. This is discussed further in Chapter 4.

96 "Quarterly Report of the Superintendent of the Press," 30 Sep 1835; "Report on the Press," 31 Dec 1836, PHS, RG 115-1-25.

97 These individuals, and their roles at the Press, are discussed in Chapter 2.

98 According to an 1855 press report: "The style of composition, owing in a good degree to the ability and taste of the Arab corrector [al-Yāzijī], is setting the standard of Modern Arabic writing, and creating a taste for reading where our books are circulated." "Report on the Printing Establishment," 1 Oct 1855, PHS, RG 115-1-25.

in a context dominated by manuscript traditions, the American Press, particularly via its earliest publications, saw much input in writing style and composition from local scholars and individuals in its employ. It would not be a far stretch to also suggest that such individuals, who were certainly versed in the visual and organizational aspects of manuscript conventions, also had some input in the way that these publications looked. That the missionaries agreed to such visual choices, and perhaps even encouraged or requested them, certainly mirrors the mission's tendency to tread lightly while casting a wide net in the proselytizing project. However, it also indicates that printed artifacts were the material bases upon which the mission negotiated its shifting conversion tactics in light of local prejudices and resistance. Thus the texts published by the American Press, in some ways, reflected the interests and concerns of their local readers.

## Conclusion

The design, content, and writing style of American Press publications during the 1830s illustrate the mission's attempts at appealing to readers of manuscripts and to an emergent print readership. These works also reflect the renewed policies the American missionaries had in place during the 1830s towards Christian communities, which reveal the Protestants' interests in casting a wide net in their conversion efforts. The roles Arab Christian individuals like al-Yāzijī, al-Ḥaddād, and al-Khayyāt had as translators, copyists, editors, and, at times, print supervisors, make it likely that these men's visual and textual preferences found their way into the final products coming off the Press. The 1830s can be seen as an experimental period for the American Press in which boundaries, visual conventions, and technologies were constantly in flux at a time when those laboring at the print shop were either not well-versed in Arabic (in the case of missionaries) or knew little about printing practices (such as the local hires). The Press's early books, which were also distinct from anything printed at the Syria Mission from 1840 onwards, are emblematic of this trial and error period. At a time when the question of readership was a broad and shifting one, these publications are also a paramount example of how the mission attempted to to avoid further alienating local communities and riling their clergy members and, by extension, state officials.

Despite their labored efforts, the Americans' publications, as well as the missionaries' proselytizing methods, failed to claim large numbers of local converts. After a series of international conflicts (where Beirut was a scene of military confrontations) as well as various class-related and intercommunal struggles, the mission began to rethink its conversion policies and approaches towards its local audience. With the Board in Boston exerting pressure for higher conversion rates, the mission and its Press underwent major overhauls after the mid-1840s. These changes (inadvertently) made way for new uses and meanings associated with its publishing methods and conventions amongst a growing local print readership.

CHAPTER 4

# Print for Shifting Alliances and Readers (1841–1851)

At the dawn of the 1840s books printed at the American Press shared very little with their earlier incarnations. While books produced during the Press's inaugural years emulate scribal modes and conventions found in decorative illuminated manuscripts, those printed from 1840 into the 1850s, notable for the absence of ornamentation and overall plain design, increasingly break with manuscript conventions. The Press's publications abandoned their previous decorative layout and design schemes in favor of a more minimalist aesthetic. Gone were the wide floriated borders, the elaborately embellished chapter headings, the catchword pagination system, and the hand-engraved calligraphic elements. In their place was a design that emphasized textual content and typographic variation while limiting any ornamental elements to simple borders, seemingly so as not to detract from the significance of the text (Fig. 17).

By the 1850s only a few elements in these books bore witness to the Press's past experimentations with scribal motifs, such as tapered text endings, occasional simple borders, and sparsely capped chapter headings. In fact, books printed at the American Press in the mid-1840s and into the 1860s appeared to fall more in line with what one would expect from a Presbyterian aesthetic: unadorned, text-emphasized layouts.[1] This disconnect from previous design practices is perhaps most strikingly apparent in an 1854 edition of Naṣīf al-Yāzijī's grammar, an earlier edition of which was treated in Chapter 3 (Fig. 18). In addition to the lack of excessive embellishment that prominently featured in the book's first edition, the book's incipit page featuring the requisite doxological *fātiḥa* (opening) abandons the explicitly Muslim incantation used in the past in favor of the more ambiguous *bismallāh al-fattāḥ* (in the name of God the Opener/Revealer).[2]

These simpler typographic compositions did not translate into the subdued evangelism of the 1830s. One can even say that from the mid-1840s until the late 1850s, the further the missionary publications' design program departed from the scribal tradition, the more controversial the books' textual content became. In addition to some secular works printed for the mission's schools, for instance, the Press produced a number of texts criticizing practices of the Catholic Church and its local supporters. Examples from the 1840s included: a translation of William Nevins's anti-Catholic *Thoughts on Popery*,[3] a letter to Syrian clergy stipulating the error of their ways,[4] Mikhāʾīl

1 See Appendix Two for titles discussed in this book that were printed during this period.

2 One of the ninety-nine names attributed to God (in Islam and Middle Eastern Christianity).

3 The English version was first published by New York's American Tract Society (ATS) in 1836. The Arabic edition is titled *Kitāb al-mabāḥith fī iʿtiqādāt baʿḍ al-kanāʾis* (Beirut: American Press, 1844). The book was initially suggested for printing at the Press in 1842. See American Board of Commissioners for Foreign Missions, deposited at Houghton Library, Harvard University, Cambridge, Mass. (hereafter cited as ABC), 16.8.1, Syria Mission (1823–1871), vol. 8, "Meeting at Native Chapel," 21 Apr 1842; ABC 16.8.1, vol. 1, "Books printed at the Mission Press in Beirut, 1844 [?]."

4 *Risālā ila aklīrūs kanāʾis sūriyya* (Beirut: American Press, 1846). Alexander G. Ellis, *Catalogue of Arabic Books in the British Museum*, vol. 2 (London: The British Museum, 1894–1901), 822. It was actually a translation of a tract by Thomas Kerns, a representative of the London Jews Society who served as a member of the mission's Aleppo station. See ABC 16.8.1, vol. 8, "Meeting in ʿAbay," 14 Sep 1846. "Semi-Annual Report of the Press," Jul-Dec 1846, United Presbyterian Church in the U.S.A. Syria Mission Records, 1808–1967, RG 115, box 1, folder 25, Presbyterian Historical Society, Philadelphia, PA (hereafter cited as PHS, RG 115-1-25).

 DOI 10.1163/9789004314351_005

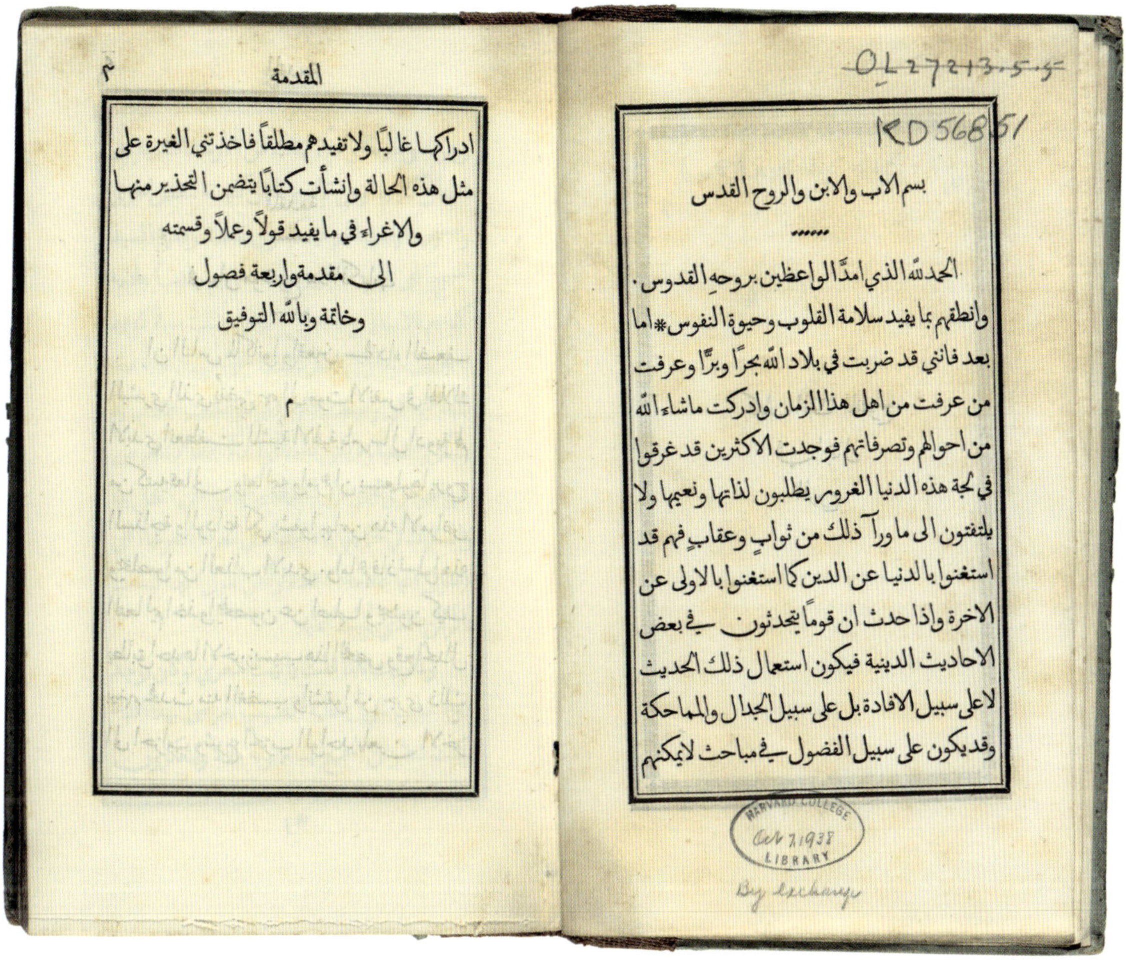
المقدمة ٣

ادراكها غالبًا ولا تفيدهم مطلقًا فاخذتني الغيرة على
مثل هذه الحالة وانشأت كتابًا يتضمن التحذير منها
والاغراء في ما يفيد قولًا وعملًا وقسمته
الى مقدمة واربعة فصول
وخاتمة وبالله التوفيق

بسم الاب والابن والروح القدس

الحمد لله الذي امدَّ الواعظين بروحه القدوس.
وانطقهم بما يفيد سلامة القلوب وحيوة النفوس * اما
بعد فانني قد ضربت في بلاد الله بحرًا وبرًا وعرفت
من عرفت من اهل هذا الزمان وادركت ما شاء الله
من احوالهم وتصرفاتهم فوجدت الاكثرين قد غرقوا
في لجة هذه الدنيا الغرور يطلبون لذاتها ونعيمها ولا
يلتفتون الى ما ورآ ذلك من ثواب وعقاب فهم قد
استغنوا بالدنيا عن الدين كما استغنوا بالاولى عن
الاخرة واذا حدث ان قومًا يتحدثون في بعض
الاحاديث الدينية فيكون استعمال ذلك الحديث
لا على سبيل الافادة بل على سبيل الجدال والمماحكة
وقد يكون على سبيل الفضول في مباحث لا يمكنهم



FIGURE 17 *Introduction from Buṭrus al-Bustānī and Eli Smith,* Kitāb al-bāb al-maftūḥ fī aʿmāl al-rūḥ.
BEIRUT, 1843

Mishāqa's (d. 1888) critique of the Catholic Church (including an account of this Greek Orthodox historian's conversion to Protestantism in 1848),[5] and *Kitāb al-thalath ʿashara risāla* (letters by early American missionaries Isaac Bird and Jonas King in which both men criticize Catholicism) printed in 1849.[6] The late 1840s was also when the mission decided to embark on the translation and production of its own version of the Arabic Bible specifically to compete with others in circulation (although it was not published until 1860).[7]

An argument could be made that the simplified visual conventions employed in the American

5 *Al-risāla al-mawsūma bi-l-dalīl ila ṭāʿat al-injīl* (Beirut: American Press, 1849).

6 This edition of the letters and addresses by Isaac Bird and Jonas King was revised from an earlier one printed for the mission in 1834 by the CMS in Malta. Although Smith complained that the CMS editions were rife with error, his revisions of this work were not made until the late 1840s. ABC 16.8.1, vol. 8, "Meeting at Native Chapel," 10 Mar 1843; PHS, RG 115-1-25, "Semi-Annual Report of the Press," Jan-Jun 1849; ABC 16.8.1, vol. 1, "Books printed at the Mission Press in Beirut, Mar 1844 [?]."

7 While this project did not actually commence until 1848, minutes from meetings of the Beirut station in 1844 show an increased interest in a new Bible translation, with Eli Smith presenting a report on the subject in March. See ABC 16.8.1, vol. 8, "Meeting at Mission House," 16 Mar 1844.

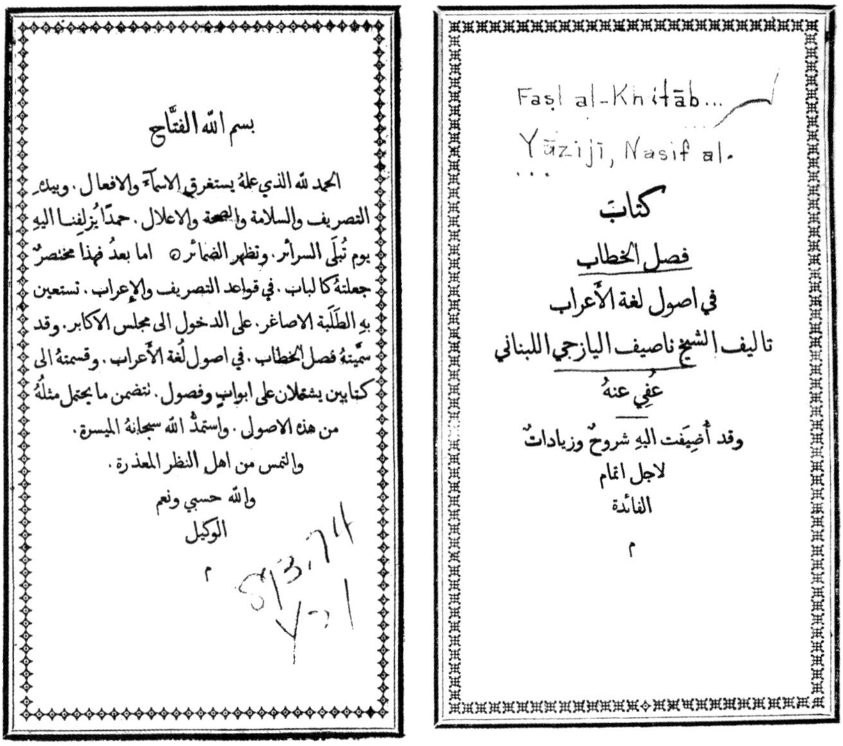
بسم الله الفتّاح

الحمد لله الذي علمهُ يستغرق الاسماء والافعال · وبيده التصريف والسلامة والصحة والاعلال · حمداً يزلفنا اليه يوم تُبلَى السرائر · وتظهر الضمائر ۝ اما بعدُ فهذا مختصرٌ جعلتهُ كالباب · في قواعد التصريف والإعراب · تستعين به الطَّلَبة الاصاغر · على الدخول الى مجلس الاكابر · وقد سمَّيتهُ فصل الخطاب · في اصول لغة الأعراب · وقسمتهُ الى كتابين يشتملان على ابوابٍ وفصول · تتضمن ما يحتمل مثلهُ من هذه الاصول · واستمدُّ الله سبحانهُ الميسرة · والتمس من اهل النظر المعذرة ·

والله حسبي ونعم الوكيل

Fasl al-Khitab...

Yaziji, Nasif al.

كتاب

فصل الخطاب

في اصول لغة الأعراب

تاليف الشيخ ناصيف اليازجي اللبناني

عُفي عنهُ

وقد أُضيفت اليهِ شروحٌ وزياداتٌ

لاجل اتمام

الفائدة

FIGURE 18 Right, *title page;* left, *first page from Nāṣīf al-Yāzijī,* Kitāb faṣl al-khiṭāb fī uṣūl lughat al-iʿrāb. BEIRUT, 1854

Press's publications from 1842 into the 1860s echoed the Protestants' disapproval of Catholic traditions. The missionaries' criticism of the Papacy, the rituals of "Eastern Churches," and the cult of saints (with its reliance on spiritual intermediaries), may be extended to the commonly held view that (Calvinist) Protestantism eschews any engagement with aesthetics. Claims of the Protestant rejection of iconography and the visual dimensions of Catholic and Orthodox ritual, coupled with the paucity in "Protestant aesthetic theory," serve to perpetuate the concept of a Puritanical, anti-visual "Protestant aesthetic."[8] However, scholars of Protestant history and theology have challenged these views. For instance, countering "a common assumption that Protestants have little interest in the fields of art and aesthetics,"[9] William A. Dyrness turns to an analysis of an implicit "aesthetic framework" in John Bunyan's *The Pilgrim's Progress* (from 1678). Dyrness claims that "the fact that the form [in Bunyan's text] does not intend to call attention to itself, does not keep it from embodying a specific aesthetic contour."[10] "[T]his indirection," Dyrness continues, "is one of the characteristics of the Protestant aesthetic form" whereby "sensible images are put in the service of edification."[11] Explaining the emphasis on simplicity in seventeenth-century British religious fiction for children, Jo Carruthers argues that "simplicity [as an English characteristic] is a peculiarly Protestant

8 Daniel T. Jenkins, "A Protestant Aesthetic? A Conversation with Donald Davie," *Journal of Literature & Theology* 2, no. 2 (1988): 153.

9 William A. Dyrness, "Dante, Bunyan and the Case for a Protestant Aesthetics," *International Journal of Systematic Theology* 10, no. 3 (2008): 285.

10 Dyrness, "Protestant Aesthetics," 285.

11 Ibid. See also, Dyrness *Reformed Theology and Visual Culture: The Protestant Imagination from Calvin to Edwards* (Cambridge: Cambridge University Press, 2004).

aesthetic and concept."[12] Carruthers states that "while seemingly innocent and benign [simplicity] is an aesthetic and concept that perpetuates a Reformed antagonism and that informs an equally oppositional sense of English identity."[13]

While both scholars are not discussing actual visual conventions but rather literary references to concepts of the aesthetic in seventeenth-century Protestant literature, their points may be extended to an understanding of the simplicity of the design conventions utilized in the American mission's publications from the 1840s onwards. The emphasis placed on the textual content, with an avoidance of illustrations or excessive ornamentation, may be viewed as being characteristic of Puritan simplicity. Yet, these conventions do not necessarily evidence an intrinsic lack of engagement with visual modes, nor can such a streamlined aesthetic be dismissed as proof of an innocuous simplicity. Furthermore, in the case of the Syria Mission's publications, what can be argued for the so-called "Protestant aesthetic" is that (during the nineteenth century) it is not a clearly defined and regulated set of visual guidelines or aesthetic program. It was also not a set of design rules that were transplanted from English or American traditions, and applied universally in a de facto manner to all of the ABCFM's publications. In particular, this blanket description for all Protestant activity in Ottoman Syria does not take into account the uncharacteristic nature of the mission's earlier prints and how they related to these abruptly dissimilar incarnations in the 1840s and beyond. Instead, the Press's visual and textual choices during the 1840s should be read as reflections of a new missionary policy towards local conversions, as well as responses to a changing religious landscape and an expanding print readership. In the case of this particular press, it can be argued that the documented transformations in its publications were influenced by developments in its local context.

This chapter explores how changes in books printed at the Press from 1842 onwards were responses to various local and external impulses. Such catalysts included developments in the Press's typographic and production standards, pressure from the American Board of Commissioners for Foreign Missions (ABCFM) in Boston for a decreased emphasis on printing/education in favor of mass conversion preaching tactics, a changing local religious landscape (e.g. increased competition with other foreign missions), a growing interest (at both the provincial and state level) in secular education, and, subsequently, a need for suitable textbooks. Each of these various motivators led to (repeatedly divergent) practices in the mission's book production and to views that differed from those adopted by the Press at the time of its inauguration.

## A Changing Political Landscape

The 1840s were a particularly tumultuous period for the Beirut and Mount Lebanon regions. The participation of British, Austrian, and French powers, at the request of the Ottoman state, in the removal of Egyptian forces in the Syrian province in October of 1840 (otherwise known as the Second Egyptian-Ottoman War)[14] resulted in a string of clashes within the province's communities. With the ousting of the Egyptian Viceroy came the end

12 Jo Carruthers, *England's Secular Scripture: Islamophobia and the Protestant Aesthetic* (New York: Continuum, 2010), 2.

13 Ibid., 3.

14 Virginia H. Aksan, *Ottoman Wars: An Empire Besieged* (Harlow: Pearson, 2007), 363–422; Efraim Karsh and Inari Karsh, *Empires of the Sand: The Struggle for Mastery in the Middle East, 1789–1923* (Cambridge, MA: Harvard University Press, 2001); Ussama Makdisi, *The Culture of Sectarianism: Community, History, and Violence in Nineteenth-Century Ottoman Lebanon* (Berkeley: University of California Press, 2000); Afaf Lutfi al-Sayyid Marsot, *Egypt in the Reign of Muhammad Ali* (Cambridge: University of Cambridge, 1983); Caesar E. Farah, "The Lebanese Insurgence of 1840 and the Powers," *Journal of Asian History* 1 (1967): 105–32.

of Shihābī rule in Mount Lebanon, which led to a precarious power vacuum in the area's mountain regions already divided between the factions of Maronite and Druze overlords. Various intercommunal battles arose between resident sectarian groups intermittently throughout this period, culminating in the violent civil wars of 1860.[15]

The 1840s was an extended trial period for the Syria mission, which was devoted to experimentation and preparation.[16] However, at the dawn of this decade the American Press seemed to finally gain a foothold in the realm of book production. Despite a brief printing hiatus during parts of 1839 into all of 1840 (a result of the Egyptian-Ottoman conflict),[17] the missionaries continued dividing essay and tract writing assignments amongst themselves, with the intention of preparing some for press.[18] Once back at work in 1841, the Press saw through the production of three books by that year's fourth quarter, with five more publications completed in 1842.

The paucity of this Press's output at the time becomes more pronounced when compared to the high-volume work of regional ABCFM presses like the one in Izmir. At this press devoted to printing in Turkish and Armenian, output rose from 1.9 million pages in 1836/7 to approximately 4.1 million by 1844.[19] In comparison, the Beirut station's press production numbers were far less impressive where, in 1847 for example, the total numbers of pages produced clocked in at a mere 693,000.[20] It should be noted that the missions in both Izmir and Istanbul were significantly larger (in its number of members) and considered more important[21] than the much smaller Syria Mission. Nonetheless, the American Press in Beirut's production numbers were not noteworthy even compared to the Press's paltry output from earlier years.[22] However, these numbers do indicate that activity continued at the Press despite the various political and internal obstacles throughout the 1840s. Beyond these meager numbers, the most striking aspects of this decade's publications was how much they diverged from the Press's inaugural endeavors in form and content. More importantly, when production resumed at the Press in 1841 its books exhibited the visibly more streamlined and standardized approach to organization, layout and design mentioned above. What were the triggers behind such noticeable aesthetic shifts in the Press's works after the 1830s?

15 Bashīr Shihāb II had supported the Egyptian takeover of parts of the Syrian province from the Ottoman state in the 1830s, and for this reason was removed from Mount Lebanon in 1840 once Egypt was driven out. He remained in exile in Istanbul until his death. For more, see Makdisi, *The Culture of Sectarianism*. See also Kamal Salibi, *A House of Many Mansions: The History of Lebanon Reconsidered* (London, I.B. Tauris, 1988).

16 A.L. Tibawi, *American Interests in Syria 1800–1901: A Study of Educational, Literary and Religious Work* (Oxford: Oxford University Press, 1966), 120.

17 Press records are spotty for these two years. It appears that two books were printed in 1839, one of which was a second edition of the 1837 *Waʿẓ al-masīḥ ʿala-l-jabal* (Christ's Sermon on the Mount). However, the Press had suspended all its work by 1840. See Geoffrey Roper, "The Beginnings of Arabic Printing by the ABCFM, 1822–1841," *Harvard Library Bulletin* 9, no. 1 (1998): 66. A report in the *Missionary Herald* claims: "The press has lain idle for a year, for want of a printer, and perhaps also for want of more missionaries and funds." *The Missionary Herald* 37 (1841): 6.

18 ABC 16.8.1, vol. 8, "Meeting at Mission Chapel," 4 May 1840.

19 J.F. Coakley, "Printing Offices of the American Board of Commissioners for Foreign Missions, 1817–1900: A Synopsis," *Harvard Library Bulletin* 9, no. 1 (1998): 14. For more recent work on the ABCFM press in Izmir, see Mehmet Ali Doğan, "The Missionary Activities of Elias Riggis in İzmir," *International Journal of Turcologia* 5, no. 10 (2010): 21–30.

20 ABC 16.8.1, Documents, Reports, Letters, vol. 4, "Annual Tabular View Report," 1847.

21 Rufus Anderson, Board Secretary, underscored the significance (in size and import) of the "Mission to the Armenians" at the time; see Anderson, *Report to the Prudential Committee of a Visit to the Missions in the Levant*, (Boston: T.R. Marvin, 1844), 12–13.

22 During the 1830s five to eight books were printed at the Press per year. For more, see Chapter 3.

### Reworked Visual Conventions

An important technical factor during this period was a major shift in production standards at the Press office, ushered in after two significant, and rather long-awaited, additions were made in 1841: a new and improved Arabic typeface from Leipzig (the history of which has been elaborated upon elsewhere[23]) and a full-time missionary printer, George C. Hurter. Both the printer and the typeface arrived in Beirut on the same ship in April 1841.[24] Designed by Smith in the late 1830s, the new typeface replaced the mission's defective British model, which the American Press had inherited after the dissolution of the ABCFM's station on Malta in 1833. The new typeface was cast and cut by a German foundry in 1840.[25]

The earlier British font, which was procured for the ABCFM press in Malta but was not used until the American Press began operating in Beirut in the 1830s, had been produced by Richard Watts's London-based foundry around 1829.[26] However, press records indicate that the Watts typeface fell short of the mission's expectations.[27] When the American missionaries compared their typeface to local handwritten scripts, they found that their Arabic prints were full of visual shortcomings and sorely lacking in the genuine calligraphic qualities necessary for attaining the approval of local educated readers[28] (Fig. 19). For example, in Arabic calligraphy, the scribe's hand and pen assure that the vertical stems (ascenders) of some letterforms generally follow the same angle, which the British typeface failed to do. Another issue with the Watts typeface was the opacity of certain letterforms' "needle eyes" (counters). In customary calligraphic practices such openings are not typically entirely filled in. Additionally, while not necessarily related to the design of the typeface, faulty casting is apparent in the fact that gaps appear within words; unlike in the seamless cursive of Arabic script.

There were also problems with type deficiencies. The set of type that the American Press received from the London-based foundry was incomplete upon its arrival. For instance, in a press report from 1835, Smith states: "Besides the smallness of the fount of types, it was found so deficient in a few letters and in leads, that we could not proceed with it."[29] Furthermore, there was much difficulty involved in replacing lacks in metal sets of type. Indeed, deficiencies in fonts of Arabic type at the time were not uncommon due to the sheer number of sorts required and – at times – the foundry's lack of knowledge in or experience with Arabic fonts. Unlike scripts based on the Latin alphabet, Arabic's basic twenty-eight letters retain forms conditional to where they appear in a word: beginning, middle, end, or isolated. Some letterforms also appear

23 See Dagmar Glass, *Malta, Beirut, Leipzig and Beirut Again: Eli Smith, the American Syria Mission and the Spread of Arabic Typography in 19th Century Lebanon*, ed. Angelika Neuwirth (Beirut: Orient-Institut der Deutschen Morgenländischen Gesellschaft, 1997).

24 Several sources state that the font arrived with Hurter (which he picked up in Izmir on his way from Boston to Beirut), including "Original Report Respecting the Press," Apr 1842; "Report on the Printing Establishment," ʿAbay, 1 Oct 1855, PHS, RG 115-1-25. See also *The Missionary Herald* 37 (1841): 393.

25 ABC 60, Eli Smith Papers, 1801–1857, Letters to Eli Smith, vol. 1, Tauchnitz to Smith, 16 Nov 1840.

26 According to Roper, the British typeface looked very similar to the one being used by the CMS in Malta. Both were apparently designed by Charles Wilkins (a British Orientalist) and cut by William Martin. See Roper, "The Beginnings of Arabic Printing," 51; "Arabic Printing and Publishing in England Before 1820," *British Society for Middle Eastern Studies, Bulletin* 12 (1985): 22–4.

27 See "Quarterly Report of the Superintendent of the Press," 30 Sep 1835; "Memoranda for Mr. Badger," 4 Aug 1835; "Report on the Printing Establishment," ʿAbay, 1 Oct 1855, PHS, RG 115-1-25.

28 See ABC 16.8.1 Reports, Letters, Journals, vol. 1, Smith to Anderson, 13 Jul 1835. See also "Quarterly Report of the Superintendent of the Press," 30 Sep 1835, PHS, RG 115-1-25.

29 "Quarterly Report of the Superintendent of the Press," 30 Sep 1835, PHS, RG 115-1-25.

FIGURE 19 *Problems with the Watts typeface indicated in red seen in Nāṣīf al-Yāzijī,* Kitāb faṣl al-khiṭāb fī uṣūl lughat al-iʿrāb. BEIRUT, 1836

combined as ligatures. As such, the number of sorts needed to complete an Arabic font in just one size was exorbitant. This was certainly an issue that the Press struggled with at the time, as Smith writes:

“To seek some way of supplying these deficiencies, Mr. [George] Badger [the American Press printer at the time] visited both the Jewish press at Safed and the Greek Catholic press at Shwair. But neither of them makes use of leads and the latter was judged to be unable to go on with its own operations for want of types.”[30]

Consequently, plans for the production of the new Smith-designed typeface (dubbed “American Arabic” by some scholars) were set in motion at the Press’s inception in 1835. This new typeface was designed from various calligraphic specimens collected by Smith between 1835 and 1836, with guidance from “the most learned judges at Cairo, Jerusalem, Beirut, Smyrna and Constantinople,” various scholars forming a collection that “was done with great care, after a comparison of a large number of the most beautiful specimens.”[31] From these, molds and matrices were

30 “Quarterly Report of the Superintendent of the Press,” 30 Sep 1835, PHS, RG 115-1-25..

31 *The Missionary Herald* 40 (1841): 171. Also discussed in Tibawi, *American Interests*, 81; Glass, *Malta, Beirut, Leipzig*, 20.

produced at the Izmir station by punch cutter Homan Hallock.[32] After several trials and tribulations,[33] the American Press finally had on hand a new set of fonts, cut and cast by a founder in Leipzig, Germany,[34] in 1841.[35] By 1844 the new typeface was made available in three sizes: a large size for body text,[36] a size for title pages, and one for captions.[37] This collection of fonts fulfilled the basic requirements for producing visually balanced Arabic books. The first set of metal sorts from 1842 had not included the font sizes necessary for references or title pages, which were acquired over the course of the next two years; the typeface's family of font sizes was completed in 1848 with the production of a fourth (small) size for reference notes.[38]

Visually speaking, the American Press's new typeface diverged significantly from the early Watts font in use during the 1830s, and the mission's books printed with the new metal type took on different graphic standards.[39] For instance, the American Arabic typeface was more compactly designed and allowed for fewer spaces between letters (Fig. 20), words, and sentences than the bulkier characters of the Watts design (seen in Fig. 6). The letterforms' various strokes in the American Arabic font also appear to be more uniform in shape and weight than those of their predecessor. The new script's metal sorts also better accommodated vocalization marks in line with the text, making it easier for the reader to discern which letter each vowel belonged to. This aspect was lacking in the typeface from Malta, which required that vowel points be set separately and at a distance from their corresponding letters.[40]

The new design conventions seen in the mission's publications during this period were not a complete abandonment of scribal conventions, but rather a changing visual language. As previously noted, there were still aspects of local manuscript traditions that survived, although they were less elaborate in design. For instance, some publications show the use of simple framing devices (for body texts and chapter openings), the inclusion of colophons, and the tapering of text endings. However, the emphasis had shifted from one on ornamental frameworks and headpieces to one

32 For more on Hallock, see Coakley, "Homan Hallock, Punchcutter," *Printing History* 45, no. 1 (2003): 18–41.

33 "Quarterly Report of the Superintendent of the Press," 30 Sep 1835, PHS, RG 115-1-25. A letter to Smith from Isaac Bird hints at the struggle and long-felt frustration with acquiring a new typeface. Bird writes: "Your second letter suggests the trying question of your going to America to complete our Arabic types, or rather our stock of type. You will know, dear Brother, how much my heart is set on this great object and that I shall scarcely be able ever to say 'Lord now those letters and thy servant depart in peace' until I shall have seen the Syrian Mission supplied with this desideration." ABC 60, vol. 1, Bird to Smith, 23 May 1836.

34 This sequence of events in the production of the typeface is outlined in a press report from 1855. "Report on the Printing Establishment," 'Abay, 1 Oct 1855, PHS, RG 115-1-25.

35 The font may have been ready before 1841, and simply awaiting passage to Beirut. According to a letter from Karl Tauchnitz (owner of the type foundry in Leipzig) to Smith from September 4, 1839, the former states that the completed typeface would be shipped off to Homan Hallock in Izmir, who was then to deal with ensuring its arrival to Beirut. This is verified in a subsequent letter to Smith, dating to November 16, 1840, in which the type-founder states: "Of the Arabic types I have heard nothing since I sent them to Smyrna. I hope they have kept them there so that they are now secured against the damages of war." ABC 60, vol. 1, Tauchnitz to Smith, 4 Sep 1839; Tauchnitz to Smith, 16 Nov 1840.

36 ABC 16.8.1, vol. 8, "Meeting at Native Chapel," 23 Apr 1842. Despite this success, however, the mission felt the type was too large for the purposes of its publications, and thus they commissioned the production of sorts in a smaller font size.

37 ABC 60, vol. 1, Hallock to Smith, 10 Oct 1843.

38 See, ABC 16.8.1, vol. 8, "Meeting at Native Chapel," 23 Apr 1842; ABC 16.8.1, vol. 1, "Report on Arabic Type, Press Property, and Foundry," 1844; ABC 16.8.1, vol. 8, "Meeting at Smith's," 9 Feb 1848.

39 Many of these visual differences are discussed in Geoffrey Roper's article on the subject; see Roper, "The Beginnings of Arabic Printing."

40 ABC 16.8.1, vol. 1, "Report on Arabic Type, Press Property, and Foundry," 1844.

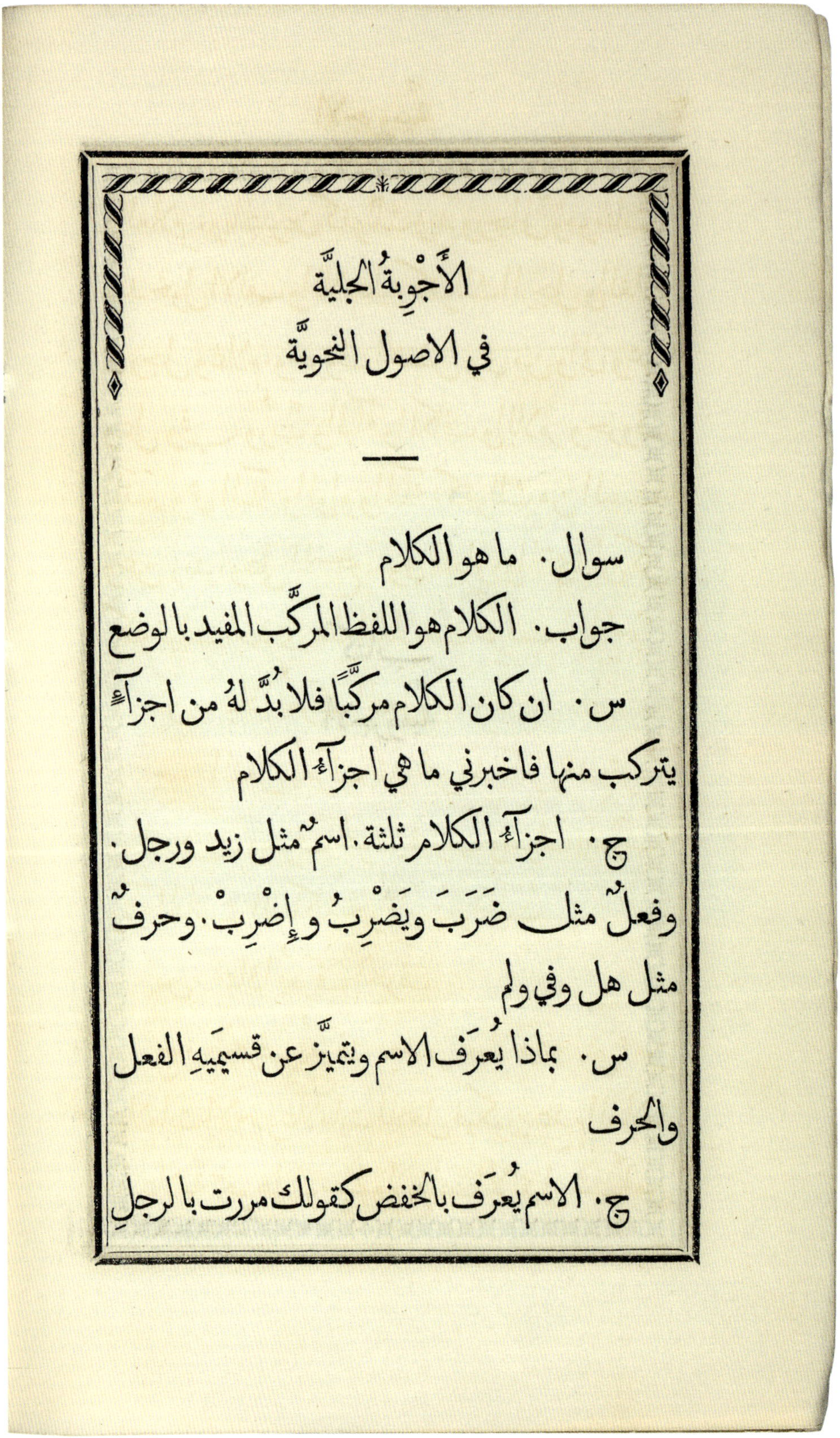

الأَجْوِبَةُ الجليّة
في الاصول النحويّة

—

سوال. ما هو الكلام
جواب. الكلام هو اللفظ المركّب المفيد بالوضع
س. ان كان الكلام مركّبًا فلا بُدَّ لهُ من اجزآءٍ
يتركب منها فاخبرني ما هي اجزآء الكلام
ج. اجزآء الكلام ثلثة. اسمٌ مثل زيد ورجل.
وفعلٌ مثل ضَرَبَ ويَضْرِبُ و إِضْرِبْ. وحرفٌ
مثل هل وفي ولم
س. بماذا يُعرَف الاسم ويتميّز عن قسيمَيهِ الفعل
والحرف
ج. الاسم يُعرَف بالخفض كقولك مررت بالرجلِ

FIGURE 20 *Example showing the new "American Arabic" typeface used in* Kitāb al-ājurrūmiyya.
BEIRUT, 1841

on the new typeface. In fact, the missionaries seem to have perceived their books, with the inclusion of the American Arabic typefaces, as models of local manuscript traditions. For instance, the ABCFM Board Secretary, Rufus Anderson, describes books printed at the American Press using the American Arabic typeface as being "based on the perfect calligraphy of the smaller Koranic manuscripts," and the printed pages as "resembling the manuscript, fall[ing] in line with the Arab prejudice."[41]

The impact of these typographic developments is noticeable in the cost, speed, and (at times) volume at which books began emerging off the Press in 1841, mere months after the typeface's arrival in April. Additionally, the fact that printing with this new, more condensed typeface would cost approximately eighteen percent less than previous ventures was not lost on the Board in Boston, or on the tract societies that funded the missionary publications.[42] Excitement over the Press's new developments during that year encouraged the American Tract Society (ATS) to fund the mission's first high-volume publication (at a run of 6000) of *Qiṣṣat ālām sayyidnā yasūʿ al-masīḥ* (The Story of Christ's Pain), a 16-page translation of the Passion of Christ that was actually a pamphlet, not a book.[43] Incidentally, this pamphlet was also rather popular in the two years after its publication, with approximately 1,488 copies (roughly the number of a standard press run) distributed by early 1844. Over the next decade, about 300–400 issues were disseminated each year. This was a significant amount since the number of books commonly sold per year averaged at a little over 400.[44] By 1843 books printed at the Press were often original works and translations by missionaries in Beirut, not the typical reprints and revisions, which was an indication that things were picking up.[45]

The second important addition to the Press was the arrival of the printer George Hurter at a most opportune time. In his youth, Hurter, who was born in Malta to a British mother and Swiss father, worked for the London Missionary Society there as well as in Corfu, where he assisted the Society in printing a Greek-Latin lexicon.[46] Prior to Hurter's employment at the American Press in Beirut the post of printer had remained vacant, on and off, since the departure of the mission's full-time printers George Badger in 1836 and his successor Robert Thorn in 1839.[47] Like Hurter, Badger and Thorn were British nationals with ties to Malta.[48] However,

41 Rufus Anderson, *Memorial Volume of the First Fifty Years of the American Board of Commissioners for Foreign Missions,* 4th ed. (Boston: Geo. C. Rand and Avery, 1861), 343. However, this may just have been an attempt at overselling the achievements of this station. Writing in 1861, twenty years after Smith worked on this typeface, the narrative being woven is clearly skewed to reflect the successful completion of the first editions of the mission's Arabic Bible.

42 Anderson, *Report to the Prudential Committee*, 29.

43 "Passion of Christ. The 27th chap. [sic] of Matthew with parts of the 26th and 28th. Expenses borne [sic] by a special donation to the Tract Society. Corrected from the Romish version." ABC 16.8.1, vol. 1, "Books printed at the Mission Press in Beirut, 1844 [?]."

44 See "Quarterly Report of the Press," Apr-Jun 1844; *Annual Report of the Press and Book Magazine*, Dec 1851, PHS, RG 115-1-25. See also ABC 16.8.1, vol. 4, *Annual Report of the Syria Mission*, 1851.

45 Such as *Kitāb al-bāb al-maftūḥ fī aʿmāl al-rūḥ,* which was translated into Arabic by Buṭrus al-Bustānī (the first of many books by him for the mission). ABC 16.8.1, vol. 1, "Books printed at the Mission Press in Beirut, Mar 1844 [?]"; Ellis, *Arabic Books*, 2:633.

46 Henry Harris Jessup, *Fifty Three Years in Syria*, 2 vols. (New York: Fleming H. Revell, 1910), 1:604.

47 For more on Badger, see Roper, "George Percy Badger (1815–1888)," *British Society for Middle Eastern Studies Bulletin* 11, no. 2 (1984): 140–55. For Thorn, see "Contract with Robert Thorn," 16 Oct 1835; "Quarterly Report on the State of the Press," 30 Sep 1836; "Quarterly Report on the Press," Dec 1836; "Original Report Respecting the Press," Apr 1842, PHS, RG 115-1-25.

48 Having grown up on Malta, Badger had worked with the island's British (Methodist and Anglican) church societies. See Roper, "Beginnings of Arabic Printing," 59; Roper, "George Percy Badger (1815–1888)," 140–55. Thorn, apparently younger and less experienced than

both were also unable to commit full-time to their work at the Press. For instance, Badger returned to Malta to serve as a typographer and translator for the CMS press before making his way to London where he was ordained as a parson in 1841.[49] Thorn's four-year service at the American Mission's Beirut station, from 1835 to 1839, included dividing his time between the Press and the mission's book storehouse. Initially Thorn worked between the Press and depository, completing some print works at the Press in September 1836, such as a set of lithographic spelling cards. He was officially made the Press foreman after Badger's departure in October 1836. However, according to some press records, Thorn was also reluctant to remain in Beirut; contracts with him consistently mention his desire to return to Malta at some future date.[50]

The Press's supervisor and editor, Eli Smith, was also continuously absent from his post and Beirut for long stretches of time up until 1847 due to numerous assignments and ill-fated events. After his arrival in Beirut in 1834, Smith took countless trips to the US and regional stations. For instance, in 1836 he set out to Izmir (accompanied by his ailing wife) to supervise the production of an Arabic typeface by punch cutter Homan Hallock. After only three days at sea, they were shipwrecked; his wife died of her illness a couple of months later. Smith left Beirut again in 1838 to tour parts of the region with his colleague, the American theological scholar Edward Robinson.[51] From 1839–1841 Smith journeyed between Leipzig and Boston (to procure a new typeface) with only occasional visits to Beirut. He returned to the station, newly remarried, in 1841 (shortly after Hurter's arrival) only to have his new wife die in Beirut a year later. He left again for the US in 1845, finally returning to settle in Beirut in 1847 accompanied by a third wife.[52] Aside from Smith's and others' comings and goings, the increasing regional conflicts, the mission's general unpopularity amongst local Christians, and the lack of sufficient operational funds had also taken a toll on the Americans' morale. An entry in the *Missionary Herald* states as much: "The past year has been to it a season of unprecedented excitement, distress and danger .... Straitened as we are for pecuniary means, you will hardly anticipate an appeal for men."[53] Hurter's enlistment meant that the mission finally had a permanent printer[54] able to devote most of his

his predecessor, also arrived to Beirut from Malta. "Contract with Robert Thorn," 16 Oct 1835, PHS, RG 115-1-25. Roper quotes letters from Smith to the Board secretaries in which Smith describes this second English printer from Malta as a "young man of 19 years of age not a master of any branch of business, and to whom we are obliged to give extravagant funds." However, Roper does not mention Thorn by name. See Roper, "The Beginnings of Arabic Printing," 59–60.

49 After he was ordained, Badger made several trips back to the region including visits to Iraq, Egypt, Iran, and Oman, as well as a residency in Bombay where he served as a minister for the Diocese; see Roper, "George Percy Badger," 142–43.

50 See "Contract with Robert Thorn," 16 Oct 1835; "Quarterly Report on the State of the Press," 30 Sep 1836; "Quarterly Report on the Press," Dec 1836; "Original Report Respecting the Press," Apr 1842, PHS, RG 115-1-25. Additionally, Thorn's colleagues saw his work ethic as less than exemplary. In 1837, for example, after agreeing to honor Thorn's request for a contract renewal, William Thomson – involved in book sales as well as Press activity when Smith was out of town – argued that Thorn needed to "bind himself to attend regularly and strictly in the [Press] office during the hours of labour." "Quarterly Report of the Press," 30 Jun 1837, PHS, RG 115-1-25. For more on Thorn's work at the mission, see letters from Thorn to Smith, ABC 60, vol. 1, Thorn to Smith, 1836–1839.

51 The results of this trip were published as *Biblical Researches in Palestine and Adjacent Countries: A Journal of Travels in the Years 1838 & 1852*, 3 vols. (London, 1856).

52 For a chronological list of these events, see Thomas Laurie, *Historical Sketch of the Syria Mission* (Boston: American Board of Commissioners for Foreign Missions, 1866), 21–29.

53 *The Missionary Herald* 37 (1841): 391–92.

54 Hurter's tenure as press printer lasted until 1861, when he and his family returned to the US once local intercommunal battles escalated. See Laurie, *Historical Sketch*, 29.

time to the Press and its publications. The missionaries enthused that the Press "will go into speedy operation ... [we] are in urgent need of books, both for the use of the mission and for distribution among the people, and trust that this essential branch of our operations will be adequately sustained."[55]

With a new printer in place there was bound to be some overhaul in the visual conventions and standards of books printed at the Press. Having worked as an Ohio news printer in 1839, Hurter's familiarity with Arabic printing was tangential and mostly based on his previous experience setting type in Greek and Hebrew,[56] and he was not as well versed as his predecessors in regional calligraphic and manuscript customs. It is probable, then, that this printer's experience with the styles and preferences of Midwestern American readers found its way into the Press's production and design standards. For one thing, books printed after 1842 (in addition to diverging from earlier books graphically) also displayed different organization methods, including the sole use of page numbers instead of their combination with catchwords, and a preference for title pages simpler in design, while continuing the past tradition of excluding publishing information like dates and location (Fig. 21).

All these visual changes, however, cannot simply be attributed to Hurter and his stylistic predilections. As was explained in Chapter 3, these books were never a one-person production, and the previously instated group of type compositors, correctors, and editors (including the Press editor, Eli Smith) still had a hand in the way these books ended up looking. The aesthetic choices reflected in the mission's books from 1842 onwards would have been all the more jarring when compared to contemporaneous works from other presses in the region, which continued to tap into the visual language of local manuscripts. Although changes within the Press certainly factored into the visual standards and textual content of its books at midcentury, an equally pertinent development at the time was Ottoman Syria's rapidly changing religious landscape and the rise of a local print readership.

### Competition for Readers

Although local ecclesiastic opposition to the American mission had never ceased since its inception in the 1820s, it did see a short-lived lull in the 1830s.[57] However, increasing intercommunal conflicts during the 1840s and 1850s created a tricky environment of simmering sectarian tensions and volatile political alliances. By exacerbating already taut dealings, these factional encounters did little to help the Syria Mission's position with local religious communities. For instance, having long desired a foothold amongst Mount Lebanon's Maronite and Druze-dominated communities,[58] the Americans attempted to take advantage of the mountain villages' shifting allegiances in 1841 (following the ousting of the Shihābī emir) by establishing a station in Dayr al-Qamar, a Druze stronghold. However, according to missionary records, a letter from the Maronite Patriarch compelled the village's Druze chieftain to ascertain the "sincerity of his friendship" and drive the *bīblīshiyyūn* (Bible-men) away to avoid any disturbances.[59] Similarly, in 1844, a number of

55 *The Missionary Herald* 37 (1841): 393.

56 Margaret Leavy argues that Hurter had no knowledge or experience in setting Arabic type. Leavy, *Eli Smith and the Arabic Bible* (New Haven: Yale Divinity School Library, 1993), 12. Rufus Anderson confirms Hurter's inadequacy in Arabic in an 1844 account in which the Board secretary states that said printer should take time off to "improve himself in the Arabic language." Anderson, *Report to the Prudential Committee*, 29.

57 During Egyptian rule a firman was issued that ordered "the relaxation of certain restrictions" on the non-Muslim religious communities in the region, including "foreign" residents. This policy seemingly led to the equal enforcement of "law and order" across all residential communities. Tibawi, *American Interests*, 60.

58 Tibawi, *American Interests*, 23–26. See also Chapter 1.

59 ABC 50, Eli Smith Arabic Collection, Box 1, Maronite Patriarch to Shaykh AbuNakad (translated from Arabic), 1841.

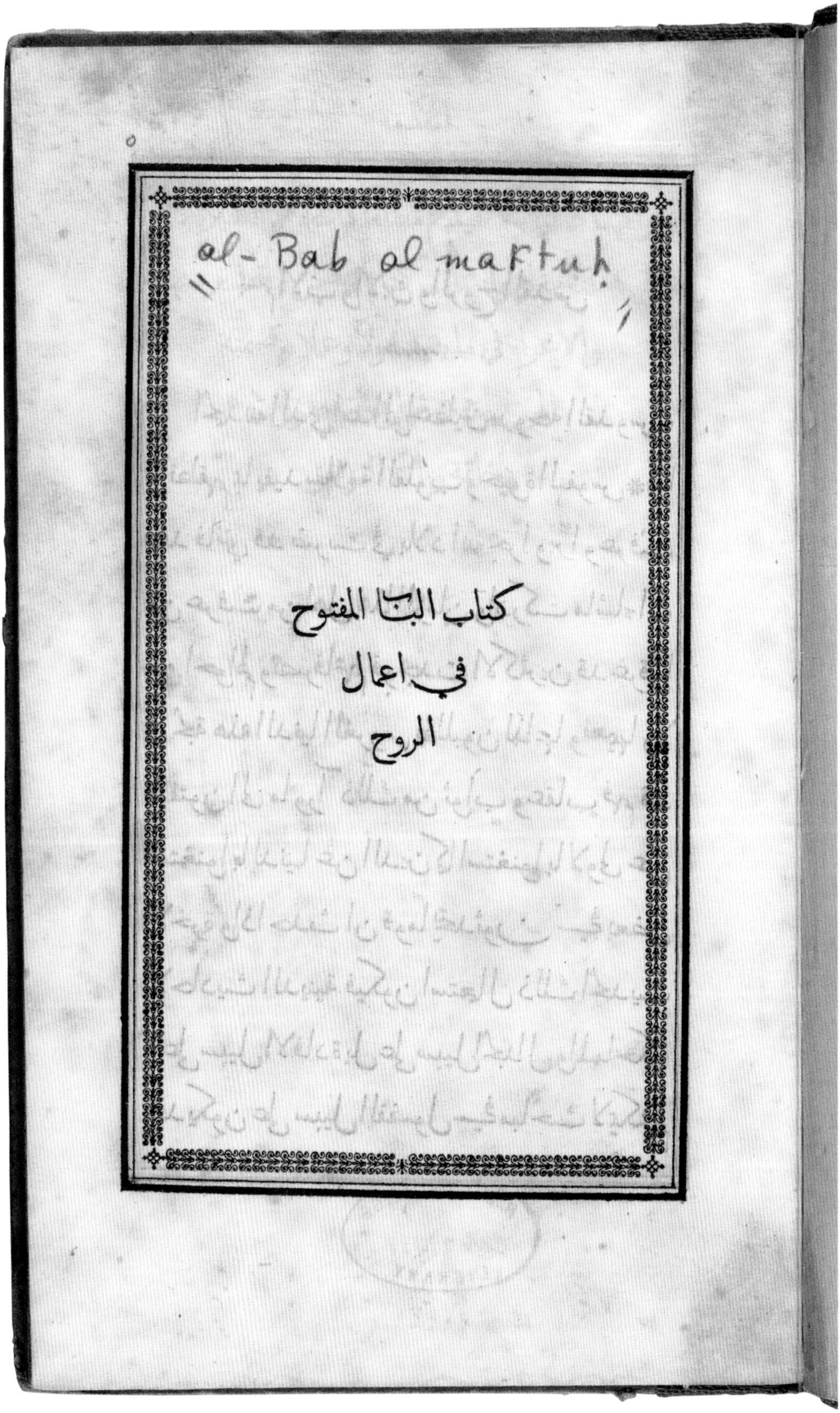


FIGURE 21 *Title page from Buṭrus al-Bustānī and Eli Smith,* Kitāb al-bāb al-maftūḥ fī aʿmāl al-rūḥ. BEIRUT, 1843

Greek Orthodox Christians from Ḥāṣbayya converted to Protestantism, for political and economic reasons.[60] This prompted a visit from their affronted Patriarch who chastened many back to their church. A letter addressed to Damascus's Governor from The Russian Consul has the latter remarking on the subject of Protestant converts in Ḥāṣbayya:

"[W]e have the right of protecting the Greek Church in the Ottoman dominions .... I protest against every proceeding which may lead to the humiliation of the Greek church at Hasbeiya, and to the encouragement of the pretended Protestants, especially as the Sublime Porte does not recognize among her subjects any such community."[61]

These events resulted in a series of conflicts that eventually culminated in the Druze-Maronite war of 1845. Missionary reports from 1844 underplay these catalyzing incidents as a "storm of persecution" which the Ḥāṣbayya Protestants weathered.[62] Things became more violent in July, when Smith made his second visit to Ḥāṣbayya (the first being in May), and seemed alarmed by the lack of political protection shown to Ḥāṣbayya's Protestant community, citing evidence of "favoritism" for the Greek Church.[63] This period of simmering tensions saw renewed challenges from local religious leaders who needed to save face by securing their numbers in an increasingly volatile political environment. With their covert conversion tactics, the Protestants thus found themselves at the receiving end of criticism from most local religious parties as a common enemy.

Further complicating matters for the Americans was mounting competition with other foreign missions, particularly La Compagnie de Jésus (the French Jesuits), already in the region at the time. While there were other Catholic missions to the region, such as the Lazarists (who had posts in Damascus, Jerusalem, and Beirut) and the Franciscans (whose stronghold was in Jerusalem where they had an active press),[64] the Jesuits were the most prominent, with their presence in the region dating to the 1600s. Founded in the 1530s, and recognized as an official Catholic order in 1540, the Jesuits began dispatching missionaries to work amongst Coptic Christians in Egypt in 1561.[65] By the 1630s, as part of capitulations (*imtiyāzāt*) between the French monarch and the Ottoman ruler, Jesuit missionaries were sent to Ottoman territories.[66] Prior to that period, in the mid-1500s, the Jesuit

60 Smith states that the mission told these individuals that forming a new "sect" was not the mission's aim, and any converts would not receive protection or exemption from the laws of the land, which required non-Muslim minorities to pay the *jizya* (head-tax). However, Smith mistakenly sees the situation as being favorable to local converts forming their own community, one that would be seen in the same light (and subject to the same protection/laws) as other non-Muslim religious communities in the eyes of the state. *The Missionary Herald* 40 (1844): 352.

61 As quoted in Isaac Bird, *Bible Work in Bible Lands; or, Events in the History of the Syria Mission* (Philadelphia: Presbyterian Board of Publication, 1872), 368. This document is also mentioned in Tibawi, *American Interests*, 111n3. This conflict and those ensuing are also outlined in a detailed account by the missionary George B. Whiting; see *The Missionary Herald* 41 (1845): 261–67.

62 *The Missionary Herald* 40 (1844): 354–5. See also *The Missionary Herald* 41 (1845): 149–51.

63 For more on this Protestant movement in Ḥāṣbayya, and subsequent conflicts, see Tibawi, *American Interests*, 108–14; Bird, *Bible Work in Bible Lands*, 348–402.

64 For more on competition amongst European Catholic missions in Ottoman Syria see Eleanor Tejirian and Reeva Simon, eds., *Conflict, Conquest, and Conversion: Two Thousand Years of Christian Missions in the Middle East* (New York: Columbia University Press, 2012), 94–114. For more on the Franciscan press in Jerusalem, see Ami Ayalon, *Reading Palestine, Printing and Literacy: 1900–1948* (Austin: University of Texas Press, 2004).

65 Tejirian and Simon, *Conflict, Conquest, and Conversion*, 63.

66 Ibid., 61. After the "suppression of the Jesuits" in Europe (roughly 1750–1780), its effects were felt in Ottoman territories in 1774, when members of Jesuit missions and stations in the region – including Aleppo, various Greek islands, Izmir, Istanbul, Damascus, Mount

order in Rome also had a regional presence via print, since they produced Arabic books at their press for regional distribution. Reports from Maronite and Greek Catholic Patriarchs in Syria,[67] as well as French residents in the region, warned of "les ministres anglais," who (according to such accounts) were becoming a problematic presence, particularly in their insistence on evangelizing in Mount Lebanon. For instance, an excerpt from an 1827 report on Protestant missionary activity, penned by Chevalier Reynault (the vice-consul of France stationed in Sidon), explicitly states that despite the firman against the circulation of "Frankish" bibles, and the subsequent forced relocation of the missionaries to Beirut, they were doing all they could to return to proselytizing in Mount Lebanon. Reynault calls on France and Rome to come to the aid of local Maronite communities.[68]

While various ideological conflicts with France complicated matters for Syria's small Jesuit mission during the 1830s,[69] by 1843, with the reinstatement of the mission's head at Ghazīr in Mount Lebanon, it was seen as a viable and perturbing threat to the Syria Mission's goals. Given their prior experience in the region, and the generally favorable attitudes towards them amongst local churches, the Jesuits more easily aligned themselves with local "Eastern" churches, aiming to unify the disparate groups (who, according to Jesuit reports, had lost their way) under Catholicism by helping them establish stronger links to Rome.[70]

The competition between these two foreign missionary bodies only increased when the Imprimerie des Pères Jésuites[71] printed its first work in 1848.[72] This inaugural publication was a fourteen-page lithographed version of Pope Pius IX's Encyclical "Epistle to the Easterns" (in Greek and Arabic), urging the clergy of local Orthodox churches, not in communion with the Vatican since the eleventh-century schism, to reestablish ties with Rome.[73] This letter's reception amongst

Lebanon, Tripoli, and Cairo, among other smaller towns – began to be recalled. See Sami Kuri, *Une histoire du Liban à travers les archives des Jésuites: 1816–1845*, vol. 1 (Beirut: Dār al-Mashriq, 1985), 11–12.

67 Mentioned in Kuri, *Les archives des Jésuites*, 1:11–12.

68 The text reads that the missionaries "employèrent tous les moyens possibles pour rentrer dans la montagne [Mt. Lebanon]. Des lettres furent envoyées au sultan, au grand vizir, au pacha, etc mais tout fut inutile." He goes on to urge the Jesuit order in France and Rome: "Il est donc plus nécessaire que jamais que les Cours de Rome et de France viennent au secours de ces enfants [members of the local Maronite communities] que l'ennemi [the Protestants] poursuit de toutes ses forces." See the letter reproduced in its entirety in Kuri, *Les archives des Jésuites*, 1:15–18.

69 A short-lived rift between the Jesuits in Beirut and France occurred when the missionaries sided with the Ottoman state during the 1839–1840 conflict (the Second Egyptian-Ottoman War). France initially backed the Egyptian forces in Syria but, in 1840, switched sides to aid the Ottomans, hoping to maintain their mercantile connections with Maronite-produced silk in Mount Lebanon. France's desire to maintain a strong French missionary presence in the region, even as anti-clerical sentiment grew at home, was thus tied to concerns of trade and industry. See Tejirian and Simon, *Conflict, Conquest, and Conversion*, 97–99. For a detailed account from the Jesuit mission's perspective, see Kuri, *Les archives des Jésuites*, 1:277–96.

70 Chantal Verdeil, "Between Rome and France, Intransigent and Anti-Protestant Jesuits in the Orient: The Beginning of the Jesuits' mission of Syria, 1831–1864," in *Christian Witness Between Continuity and New Beginnings*, eds. Martin Tamcke and Michael Marten (Berlin: LIT Verlag, 2006), 23–32.

71 By 1857 the press became better known as l'Imprimerie Catholique. Kuri, "Esquisse d'un catalogue des imprimés de l'imprimerie catholique de Beyrouth, 1848–1888," *Ḥawalīyāt maʿhad al-adāb al-sharqiyya* 7 (1993/1996): 76.

72 The Jesuit priests felt a dire need for books and first decided to purchase their own press in 1846. "Nous avons été tourmentés par le manque de livres. Nous sommes parvenus à nous mettre un peu plus à l'aise. Je vais demander au R.P. Provincial une pierre lithographique. Je crois qu'elle nous sera bien utile." Excerpt of letter from P. Benoit Planchet (Jesuit missionary) to P. Jean Roothan (the General Superior in Rome), dated April 16, 1846, and reproduced in Kuri, *Une histoire du liban à travers les archives des jésuites: 1846–1862*, vol. 2 (Beirut: Dār al-Mashriq, 1985), 15.

73 Kuri, "Catalogue des imprimés," 76, 81–82. This epistle's original title was *In suprema Petri apostoli sede* (On the

local Greek Orthodox patriarchs and clergy was far from warm and, in fact, was rejected outright as heretical.[74] Regardless of its impact on local Christian groups, to the Americans, the Pope's communiqué was perceived as an affront and warning to local Protestant efforts, particularly since the Americans were not well attuned to the complexities of varying ideologies amongst local Christian groups, frequently labeling such communities as undifferentiated members of "papal sects." Thus the fact that Greek Orthodox communities spurned Catholic missionary efforts, as they had done with the Protestants, seemed to matter little to the American mission's perceptions of Jesuit (therefore Catholic) activity in the region. It is clear from the anti-Catholic nature of books published by the Protestants during this time that Jesuits were seen as a viable threat, and the Jesuits reciprocated in kind.

Interestingly, while the American Press's equipment and experience printing in Arabic far surpassed that of the Catholic press, the Jesuits still managed to produce fifteen religious and educational publications (many of which countered works by the Protestants) on their lithographic press between 1848 and 1852.[75] Jesuit records indicate that by 1851 the French missionaries in Beirut expressed a dire need for an Arabic letterpress because they felt that the lithographic method only allowed for an average number of runs that was insufficient given the demands of local Christian readers.[76] Production took off once the Jesuits received their letterpress equipment from Paris in 1853. The Jesuit press proved to be a serious competitor in the Arabic printing industry.[77] This translated the situation into a full-scale war of words between these two foreign bodies, evident in the nature of their tracts.

Although the Jesuits also printed numerous secular works for their schools,[78] a number of their works were interpreted as open criticisms of the Protestants' publications. For instance, the first book the Jesuits printed on their new letterpress in 1854 was their version of *Kitāb al-iqtidāʾ bi-l-masīḥ wa huwa mushtamil ʿala arbaʿā asfār* ("The Imitation of Christ, a Book in Four Chapters," translated from the original seventeenth-century work by Thomas à Kempis).[79] First published at the American Press in 1837, the Protestant's rendition of this Latin text was reprinted in 1842 as

Supreme Throne of Peter the Apostle), and was published on January 6, 1848. For an online English translation of this document, see "Pope & Patriarchs: The 1848 Letters of Pope Pius IX and the Orthodox Patriarchs," *Orthocath: musings by a revert to the Orthodox Catholic faith* (blog), November 3, 2010, http://orthocath.wordpress.com/.

74 Members of the region's Greek Orthodox synod and its patriarchs responded to this Papal Bull in a letter of May 1848, in which they outwardly rejected the Vatican's supremacy, and reasserted the centuries-old debate between Eastern and Western churches regarding the Catholic *Filioque* clause (that the "Holy Ghost proceedeth from the Father and the Son," deemed heretical by Greek Orthodox doctrines which state that it only "proceedeth from the Father"). An English translation of this letter can be found online: Orthodox Christian Information Center, "Encyclical of the Eastern Patriarchs, 1848: A Reply to the Epistle of Pope Pius IX, 'to the Easterns,'" accessed October 15, 2012, http://orthodoxinfo.com/ecumenism/encyc_1848.aspx. The controversies surrounding this Papal encyclical are discussed in Aidan Nichols, *Rome and the Eastern Churches: A Study in Schism*, 2nd ed. (San Francisco: Ignatius Press, 2010), 351–53.

75 The Jesuits' lithographic press arrived in Beirut from Lyon sometime in October 1847. Kuri lists all fifteen publications produced on the Catholic mission's lithographic press in his "Catalogue des imprimés," 76n4, 82–83.

76 Kuri, *Les archives des jésuites*, 2:74-5n3. Their first letterpress arrived in 1853 and a second press was acquired in 1855, a donation from the Comité des Ecôles d'Orient in France. Kuri, "Catalogue des imprimés," 76n8. See also Lūwīs Shaykhū, *Tārīkh fan al-ṭibāʿa fī al-mashriq*, 2nd ed. (Beirut: Dār al-Mashriq, 1994), 58.

77 For a thorough list of all the letterpress printed books by the Jesuits from 1854 until the late 1880s, see Kuri, "Catalogue des imprimés," 84–137.

78 Kuri, "Catalogue des imprimés," 82–83.

79 Ibid., 76, 88. The press issued 2000 copies of this tract.

*Iqtiṭāf kitāb al-iqtidāʾ bi-l-masīḥ*.[80] According to Jesuits and local Catholic readers, the Protestants' version deliberately excluded the intrinsically Catholic message of this Latin work until "no truth remained of its Catholic origins."[81] While it appears that the original reason behind the Jesuit Press's publication of Kempis's text was to follow through on a condition placed by one of the Press's benefactors,[82] it is also probable that the need to reprint this text stemmed from a general desire by the Catholics to counter Protestant works in circulation.[83]

As far as nineteenth-century missionary literature goes, both Catholic and Protestant missions (along with others) turned to similar sources for their religious and secular works. Indeed, regardless of denominational variations in catechisms, homilies, extracts from scripture and new Bible translations,[84] all still belonged to the same religious genre popular amongst missionary presses at the time. Distinctions, if they were made, were clearly drawn in the introductions of these Jesuit and Protestant books, with each religious order calling out the other as heretical or false. One could also argue that another way in which the Protestants and Jesuits differentiated their respective works was via their visual attributes. Although extant examples of the early Jesuit lithographic books printed from 1848–1853 are difficult to locate,[85] if one goes by contemporaneous works printed off the region's other lithography presses,[86] these books relied on manuscript conventions in their layout and design. For instance, the Jesuit Press's reliance on a local Arabic calligrapher, the priest Ḥanna Ghoṣn, for its lithographic productions possibly meant that

80 ABC 16.8.1, vol. 1, "Books printed at the Mission Press in Beirut, Mar 1844 [?]."

81 One finds a dismissal of religious books printed at the American Press in a book on regional printing by Lūwīs Shaykhū, a turn of the century Arab Jesuit priest. See Shaykhū, 50. See also Joseph Nasrallah, *L'imprimerie catholique de Beyrouth, 1852–1966* (Beirut: l'Imprimerie Catholique, 1960).

82 Both Shaykhū and Jesuit records indicate that in 1853 "le conte de Trémond," a French tourist passing through Beirut during his visit to the "Holy Land," donated 6000 francs to the Jesuit mission towards their purchase of a letterpress and metal type. His one condition was that the first book issued off the press be an Arabic translation of Kempis' work, to be distributed for free amongst local Christians. Shaykhū, 57; Kuri, *Les archives des jésuites*, 2:119n6.

83 This remained an issue, as seen in Jesuit records from the 1850s and 1860s, which continually mention the Protestant threat, particularly the need to counter the American's "shamefacedly disguised" (*honteusement travesty*) and "brutally combative" books. For instance, another publication clearly aiming at undoing the American mission's work was *Kitāb al-daraj al-amīn ʿila al-ḥaq al-mubīn* (The Stairway to the Truth) (Beirut: al-Maṭbaʿa al-Kathūlīkiyya, 1858). According to Jesuit records, this book (a liberal translation from *Echelle de la foi*) is an addition to the fifty reasons that convinced the Lutheran Antoine-Ulrich de Brunschwich-Wolfenbuttle to convert to Catholicism in 1709. See letter dated 22 Mar 1860, from P. Louis-Xavier Abougit to P. Pierre Beckx, in Kuri, *Les archives des jésuites*, 2:247–48. See also Kuri, "Catalogue des imprimés," 108.

84 While Arabic renditions of the New Testament were long in circulation, such as the popular 1671 *Biblia Sacra Arabica* translated by Maronites in Rome and produced by the Sacra Congregatio de Propaganda Fide, both missions chose to produce new versions. In addition to illustrating the evident competition between the Protestants and Jesuits, this also clearly reflects contemporary developments in European and American ecclesiastic circles, the most prominent of which was the debate between defenders of the Greek *textus receptus* and the growing use of textual criticism (namely, eclecticism) in Bible translations. For more see Bruce M. Metzger and Bart D. Ehrman, *The Text of the New Testament: Its Transmission, Corruption and Restoration* (Oxford: Oxford University Press, 2005). For the Syria mission's perspective, see Eli Smith and Cornelius Van Allan van Dyck, *A Brief Documentary History of the Translation of the Scriptures into the Arabic Language* (Beirut: American Presbyterian Mission Press, 1900).

85 According to Shaykhū, 56.

86 For instance, books printed on lithography presses in Qajar Iran closely resembled their manuscript counterparts in layout, decoration, and calligraphic style. For a discussion of this, see Chapter 5.

scribal methods were employed in these preliminary works.[87]

Looking at later publications by the Jesuits and other local Catholic presses,[88] such as Jerusalem's Franciscan missionary press,[89] it is clear that such print shops favored decorative scripts and embellished borders in their books (Fig. 22 and Fig. 23). Admittedly, it could also be argued that these Catholic presses were simply more open to illustrations and embellishments than their Protestant counterparts, and thus channeled the typical design conventions of similar European presses. For instance, the publications seen in Figures 22 and 23 show the use of each religious group's respective standard insignia. These title pages, unlike the American Press's books at the time, include the date, publisher, and location, thus fitting the popular formula for contemporary Latin-script books.

As in the case of the American Press, however, other local missionary presses included or excluded certain design and organizational elements in response to various social, technical, and political impulses. In Jesuit publications, images of their earlier letterpress publications (printed in the 1850s) show a much simpler design aesthetic that resembles books printed by the Americans in the 1840s (Fig. 24). While this visual approach is later abandoned for the more ornate books from the 1870s (like the one seen in Figure 22), the earlier designs seem to mirror the Catholic Press's shortcomings during its initial attempts at Arabic letterpress work. The Jesuit press supervisor at the time, the priest Philippe Cuche, cites numerous technical and skill-related difficulties printing in Arabic during the 1850s, such as textual errors during typesetting, poor printing quality, and issues setting vocalization marks.[90] During the 1840s and the early 1850s, however, the Jesuit's lithographic publications resembled those of local scribal works, at least in the manner in which they were organized and their emphasis on calligraphic techniques – since all stone plates were produced via a calligrapher's hand. In this they greatly differed from the productions of the American Press at this time.

### A Shifting Missionary Policy

The increased Jesuit presence and the Protestants' failure to attract significant numbers to their cause did little to impress the Board secretary, Rufus Anderson, on his visit to the Mediterranean missions in 1844. In meetings with the Syria mission's members, a disgruntled Anderson, who found the mission's "labors wanting to a great degree,"[91] made clear his frustration at the Syria mission's lack of success in converting locals and establishing churches:

87 This calligrapher is briefly mentioned in sources on the subject. See Shaykhū, 57; Kuri, "Catalogue des imprimés," 76.

88 Other presses that emerged in Jerusalem at the time included the Anglican missionary and Greek Orthodox presses. Ami Ayalon, *Reading Palestine, Printing and Literacy: 1900–1948* (Austin: University of Texas Press, 2004), 50n53.

89 Established in 1846, the first book printed at this press was a catechism. For more, see an online letter (in English) dating to April 8, 1997 and penned by Giuseppe Nazzaro, the Franciscan guardian in Jerusalem. The Franciscans of the Holy Land and Malta, "Over 155 years of a socio-cultural ministry," *Franciscan Printing Press*, last modified April 8, 1997, accessed January 12, 2013, http://www.christusrex.org/www1/ofm/fpp/FPP150en.html. http://www.christusrex.org/www1/ofm/fpp/FPP150en .html. Information in this letter comes from original press records (in Italian), and a press catalog: Agustin Arce, *Catalogus descriptivus illustratus operum in Typographia Ierosolymorum Franciscali impressorum*, 1:1847–1880 (Jerusalem: 1969).

90 A letter written on June 19, 1856 by P. Philippe Cuche (a missionary and lexicographer who worked on the French-Arabic dictionary) relates the many difficulties facing the Catholic Press during this period: "… ces quelques livres…sont très mal imprimés et plein de fautes; …il [the type composer] ne sait composer que l'arabe simple; quand il a à composer de l'arabe avec des voyelles, il embrouille, il confond tout." Kuri, *Les archives des jésuites,* 2:154–56.

91 ABC 2.1.1, Letters: Foreign (Transcript series), 1836–1875, vol. 7, Anderson to Syria Mission, 23 Apr 1844.

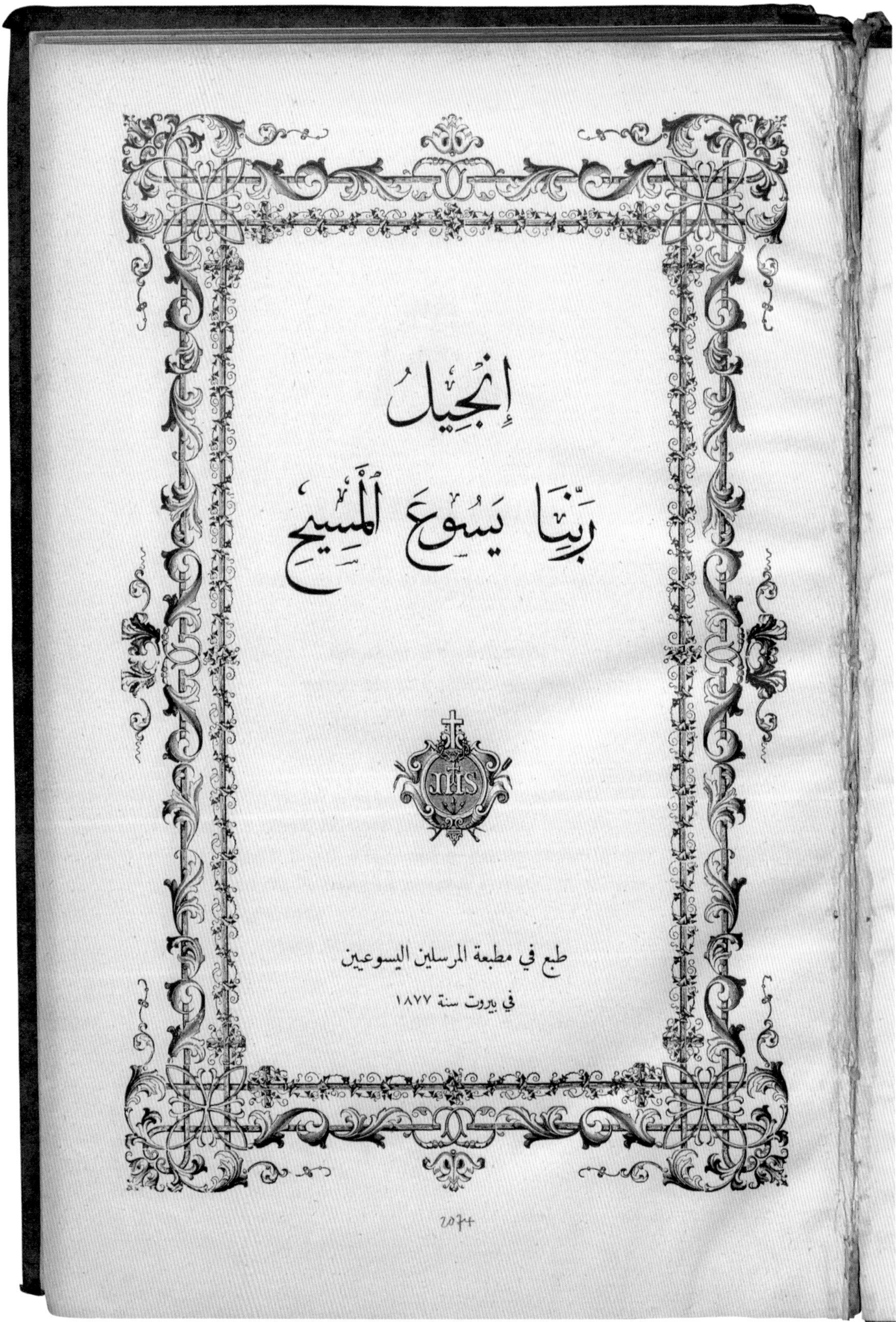


FIGURE 22 *Title page from* Injīl rabbinā yasūʿ al-masīḥ.
BEIRUT: L'IMPRIMERIE CATHOLIQUE, 1877

FIGURE 23 *Title page from* Kitāb al-ifkhūlūjiyyūn al-kabīr: istiʿmāl kahnat al-rūm al-kātūlīk.
JERUSALEM: THE FRANCISCAN MISSION PRESS, 1865

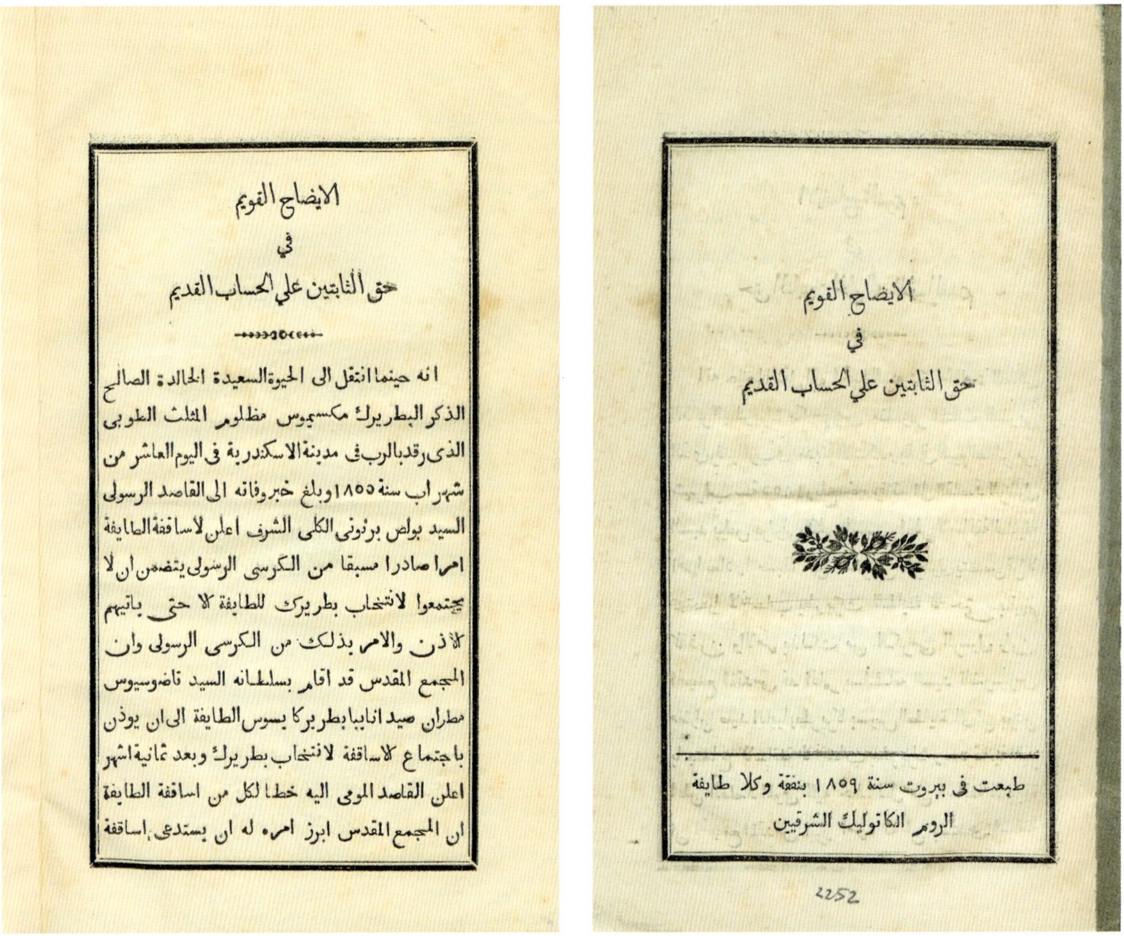
الايضاح القويم
في
حق الثابتين على الحساب القديم
انه حينما انتقل الى الحيوة السعيدة الخالدة الصالح
الذكر البطريرك مكسيموس مظلوم الثلث الطوبى
الذى رقد بالرب في مدينة الاسكندرية في اليوم العاشر من
شهر اب سنة ١٨٥٥ وبلغ خبر وفاته الى القاصد الرسولى
السيد بولس برونوني الكلي الشرف اعلن لاساقفة الطايفة
امرا صادرا مسبقا من الكرسي الرسولي يتضمن ان لا
يجتمعوا لانتخاب بطريرك للطايفة الا حتى ياتيهم
الاذن والامر بذلك من الكرسي الرسولي وان
المجمع المقدس قد اقام بسلطانه السيد تاضوسيوس
مطران صيدا نايبا بطريركيا بسوس الطايفة الى ان يوذن
باجتماع الاساقفة لانتخاب بطريرك وبعد ثمانية اشهر
اعلن القاصد المومى اليه خطا لكل من اساقفة الطايفة
ان المجمع المقدس ابرز امره له ان يستدعي اساقفة

الايضاح القويم
في
حق الثابتين على الحساب القديم
طبعت في بيروت سنة ١٨٥٩ بنفقة وكلا طايفة
الروم الكاثوليك الشرقيين
2252

FIGURE 24 Right, *title page;* left, *first page from* Al-īḍāḥ al-qawwīm fī ḥaqq al-thābitīn ʿalā al-ḥisāb al-qadīm.
BEIRUT: L'IMPRIMERIE CATHOLIQUE, 1859

"I think that this has had an effect on the policy of the mission and led to operating through the press and schools rather than the Pauline operation upon the hearts. The missionary has been afraid to strike because he did not know what to do next ... I do not think the present force of the mission is sufficient to carry on the three departments of preaching, press, and seminary. One or more must suffer at present. Shall it be preaching? No. It must be one of the others."[92]

Anderson ultimately called for the curtailment of all activities not related to preaching and prosyletizing, such as publishing and education (e.g. work at the mission's seminary),[93] claiming that the "absorbing demands of the press on some of the brethren; and of education on others" had been some of the prevented the

92 ABC 30, Rufus Anderson (Secretary, 1822–1866), vol. 10, "Meeting at the Mission house," Beirut, 11 Mar 1844.

93 At this point in the mission's history, their education program was limited to a seminary for male students and a boarding-style system for girls operated out of various missionary households – with the former focused on religious education and the latter (taught by wives of missionaries) dealing with home economics in addition to teachings of the scripture. By 1850, an official female boarding school was established at Henry De Forest's residence. For more see Tibawi, *American Interests*, 62–66.

mission's success amongst the masses.[94] He also viewed English instruction in the mission's schools and seminary as "inexpedient."[95]

Anderson's criticism was not limited to the Syria mission. In fact, he viewed such issues as prevalent across foreign missions, particularly those in the Indian Subcontinent. Speaking about his visits to ABCFM mission stations in Sri Lanka (Ceylon) and India in 1844 and 1855, Anderson shared similar sentiments, specifically towards the emphasis on English instruction at mission schools. He was eager for such missions to "give greater prominence in biblical instruction, and to create an enthusiasm in that direction which would check the tendencies in favor of English and science." He claimed that the mission understood the need to stop "cultivating" the local community's "excessive passion" for the English language.[96] The colonial ideology of the ABCFM is clearly reflected in Anderson's views on missionary activity focusing solely on conversions, and excluding activity that might be aimed at a broader intellectual, political, or economic benefit to local populations.

The Board secretary had even harsher words to say about the Syria mission's Press in a report to the ABCFM's Prudential Committee, published on his return to Boston in 1844:

"[The Press] is a bad master for preachers of the gospel. Strictly subordinate to the pulpit, it adds immensely to its power. But where there is only a small number of missionaries, its encroaching tendency on the oral instructions, and especially the more formal preaching, is almost uncontrollable. There is felt to be a necessity for keeping the machinery in motion, and therefore of furnishing at all events a certain amount of work; and thus what was designed to be merely a servant and aid of the preacher, becomes his dictator, and he sinks into an author and editor."[97]

It may be that this "author and editor" comment was directed at either Eli Smith or Cornelius Van Dyck. While Smith was initially hired as a press editor for the Malta and then Beirut stations, he was also an ordained member of the mission and was expected to perform his duties as a preacher (the same went for Van Dyck, who was a practicing physician, a prolific writer, and a preacher). In order to ensure that the mission heeded his concerns, Anderson had the Board distribute a circular to its foreign missionary presses, stipulating that all future funding requests to the Bible and Tract Societies – which had been submitted by the Press editor in the past – come from the Board in Boston and not missionary members.[98] Given this pressure from the Prudential Committee, compounded by dwindling convert numbers and mounting pecuniary struggles,[99] the mission suspended press activity to focus on gaining "access to the minds of the people" via direct preaching, and forming local-run churches to provide a "home" suitable for such efforts.[100]

Aside from publishing a small number of reprints and the "binding of books already printed enough to employ the apprentices,"[101] work at the Press significantly decreased by 1844. For instance, only two Press publications date to that year: a first edition of *Kitāb al-mabāḥith fī iʿtiqādāt baʿḍ al-kanāʾis* (an Arabic translation of William Nevins's

94 Anderson, *Report to the Prudential Committee*, 27.

95 For instance, when the seminary was reopened in 1846, English was no longer taught as a subject; see Tibawi, *American Interests*, 114.

96 Anderson, *The First Fifty Years*, 312.

97 Anderson, *Report to the Prudential Committee*, 33.

98 Anderson first proposed this in his *Report to the Prudential Committee*, 33. The circular was then printed in 1845; see ABC 60, vol.1, "Printed Circular from Prudential Committee to all Foreign Missions addressed to Rev. Eli Smith," 23 May 1845.

99 The need for funding is consistently voiced by the missionaries in records throughout the 1840s, even as late as 1848. See ABC 2.1.1, "Printed circular by ABCFM," 15 Jun 1848.

100 Ibid.; ABC 30, "Meeting at the Mission house," Beirut, 11 Mar 1844.

101 Anderson, *Report to the Prudential Committee*, 29.

criticism of Catholic practices[102]) and *Kitāb siyāḥat al-masīḥī*[103] (an Arabic translation of John Bunyan's *The Pilgrim's Progress*[104]). Press reports from 1844 also show that its workers were mostly occupied with a backlog of book binding – with some book pages dated to 1836.[105] Over the next three years, the Press did not pick up its pace beyond two annual print runs.[106] Minutes from a meeting in 1845 show that the Press's work was still "very much contracted and the mission [is] now more especially devoted to preaching."[107] The same went for the following year, when the missionaries decided that local assistants in the mission's employ be dispatched "as vigorously and constantly as possible" to nearby towns as catechists and preachers of the gospel.[108] The Press continued to be intermittently suspended because "the mission cannot with its present numbers and enfeebled health sustain the operations of the Press without interfering seriously with the preaching of the Gospel."[109]

With Press activities under close scrutiny from the Board, the mission's publication proposals clearly needed to demonstrate the use, impact and unambiguously Protestant nature of any books it wanted to print. For instance, although a printed edition did not come off the Press until 1860, the Protestant's Arabic Bible project that was translated and edited between 1847 and 1860[110] went from being an ambitious suggestion to serving as the Press's key selling point for the better part of the next two decades, and defining Smith's life work.[111] Indeed, records indicate that after Anderson's visit the production of the "Sacred Scriptures" in Arabic was promoted by the Beirut station as the central goal of the American Press in the hope of demonstrating to the Board the print shop's continued value as part of the missionary enterprise.[112]

102 Nevins, *Thoughts on Popery* (New York: American Tract Society, 1836). This had been translated into Arabic by missionary George B. Whiting a few years prior. ABC 16.8.1, vol. 8, "Meeting at Native Chapel," 21 Apr 1842. A second edition was printed in 1866.

103 This booklet was included in the list of tracts to be prepared for press in 1842. ABC 16.8.1, vol. 8, "Meeting at Native Chapel," 21 Apr 1842. It was printed in 1844, "Quarterly Press Report," Apr-Jun 1844, PHS, RG 115-1-25.

104 ABC 16.8.1, vol. 1, "Books printed at the Mission Press in Beirut, 1844 [?]." This list dates the book to 1843, though the book colophon shows 1844. Printing may have started in 1843 and been completed in 1844. For more on the regional translation of such works into Arabic, see Peter Hill, "Early Translations of English Fiction into Arabic: *The Pilgrim's Progress* and *Robinson Crusoe*," *Journal of Semitic Studies* 60, no. 1 (2015): 177–212.

105 "Quarterly Press Report," Apr-Jun 1844; "Quarterly Press Report," Jul-Sep 1844; "Quarterly Press Report," Oct-Dec 1844, PHS, RG 115-1-25.

106 For the titles of these books, see Appendix Two.

107 ABC 16.8.1, vol. 8, "Meeting at Mission House," 30 Jul 1845. A quarterly press report from this year only shows a reprint of "the shorter catechism" (printed as *Kitāb qawāʿid al-imān al-masīḥī*), which was an Arabic translation of a catechism by the Westminster Assembly. The first edition was printed at the American Press in 1843. A semi-annual press report from the same year states that "1000 Arabic lessons were also printed," which may have been lithographed. "Quarterly Report of the Press," Jan-Mar 1845; "Semi-Annual Report of the Press," Jan-Jun 1845, PHS, RG 115-1-25.

108 ABC 16.8.1, vol. 8, "Meeting at Mission House," 9 Jan 1846.

109 An additional factor that stymied Press activity was Smith's absentee status – for health reasons, he returned to the United States in 1845 and did not resume work at the mission until 1847 – thus leaving the Press without an editor. For more on the Press's suspension that year see ABC 16.8.1, vol. 8, "Meeting at Mission House," 9 Jan 1846; "Meeting at Lanneau's," 16 Jan 1846; "Meeting in ʿAbay," 15 Sep 1846.

110 The translation project was officially approved in January. ABC 16.8.1, vol. 8, "Meeting at Mission House," 20 Jan 1847.

111 Smith worked on translating the Old and New Testaments from 1848 until his death in 1857, after which fellow missionary Cornelius van Dyck continued with the project. As per Smith's death-bed declaration, he was only responsible for the translations from Genesis up to Exodus (except for the last chapter); see Isaac Hall, "The Arabic Bible of Drs. Eli Smith and Cornelius V.A. Van Dyck," *Journal of the American Oriental Society* 11 (1882–1885): 279.

112 This is evident in a report on the Press's activity stating that the editor (Smith) remains occupied with the

Also aligned with this new policy were ecclesiastical works that pointed out the flaws and errors of local churches, which would certainly have qualified as necessary tracts, especially when religious identities, in an increasingly unstable local political setting, were in flux. Concurrently, as Arabic translations of contemporary radical thought – many of which were of popular writings that emerged from the French Revolution[113] – were taken up by local readers, the American Press editor underscored the need to print Protestant books as "antidotes" to these European works that were "allied with infidelity."[114] Certainly, from the Syria Mission and Board's perspective, this was not the time for ambiguity or subtlety in message if the Protestants were to influence this nebulous print readership.

With the focus on religious material, as in the new Bible translation, the production of most secular publications decreased dramatically. For instance, aside from a book of Arabic lessons (1846),[115] a revised pamphlet on the treatment of cholera,[116] and an arithmetic textbook by Buṭrus al-Bustānī[117] (both produced in 1848), the scant number of books printed at the Press during the mid- to late 1840s pertained almost exclusively to religious instruction. Incidentally, although al-Bustānī's was printed in 1848, it had initially been slated for publication between 1842–1843 (before Anderson's visit),[118] and was thus put aside in line with the mission's revised policy, despite its usefulness to the mission's schools and seminary.[119]

It is also highly probable that the mission's insistence on valuing the publication of religious tracts over secular ones was met with some resistance, at least from Smith, given his long-standing view regarding the importance of secular publications – specifically Arabic grammars – for a largely illiterate populace.[120] A letter from al-Yāzijī to Smith (who was still in the United States at the time) indicates as much. In it, al-Yāzijī complains to the missionary that the ABCFM's new policy to only fund religious works meant that there was no financial support for

translation of the Bible. ABC 16.8.1, vol. 4, *Annual Report of the Syria Mission*, 1855.

113 For more on the spread of radical thought amongst and by the local Ottoman readers, see Ilham Khuri-Makdisi, *The Eastern Mediterranean and the Making of Global Radicalism, 1860–1914* (Berkeley: University of California Press, 2010).

114 ABC 16.8.1, vol. 4, *Annual Report of the Syria Mission*, 1850.

115 Book of "Arabic lessons," 1000 copies, which were possibly lithographed. "Semi-Annual Report of the Press," Jan-Jun 1846, PHS, RG 115-1-25.

116 *ʿIlāj mufīd li-l-hawā al-aṣfar al-mubīḍ* (A useful treatment of the fatal Cholera), composed by the mission's Dr. Azariah Smith, 17 pages, 1000 copies; see ABC 16.8.1, vol. 8, "Meeting at ʿAbay station," 4 Oct 1848. The tract is listed as printed in the "Semi-Annual Report of the Press," Jul-Dec 1848, PHS, RG 115-1-25.

117 *Kitāb kashf al-ḥijāb fī ʿilm al-ḥisāb* (A Book on the Demystification of Arithmetic), consisting of 1000 copies printed, included parts of Smith's earlier book on the subject (*Kitāb dalīl al-ṣawāb fī uṣūl al-ḥisāb,* printed in 1837). See Tibawi, *American Interests*, 85; "Semi-Annual Report of the Press," Jul-Dec 1848, PHS, RG 115-1-25; Ellis, *Arabic Books*, 1:429.

118 It was first listed for production in 1842, then again a year later. See ABC 16.8.1, vol. 8, "Meeting at Native Chapel," 21 Apr 1842; "Meeting at Native Chapel," 10 Mar 1843.

119 The earlier edition by Smith (the version used by the seminary and schools at the time) was deemed unsatisfactory, and Smith himself recommended the production of a more elaborated text. See ABC 16.8.1, vol. 1, "Books printed at the Mission Press in Beirut, Mar 1844 [?]."

120 Smith's opinions on this matter are first voiced in an article from 1830 on the importance of secular publications amongst the illiterate masses, stating: "ignorance impedes the motions of the press. What then shall we do but employ the press itself to remove this obstacle: Let a series of *elementary school-books* be placed in the list of its publications." He goes on to specify that: "there are some classes of school-books, whose nature does not allow of their being made the vehicle of much religious instruction." Smith clearly supported the production of non-religious works to aid with educating potential converts in the basics of language needed to read the Gospel. Yale Divinity School Library, Manuscripts and Special Collections, Eli Smith Family Papers, Record Group 124 (hereafter cited as YDSL, RG124) Series V. Research Materials of Margaret Russell Leavy, Writings of Eli Smith, Box 6/34, "Use of the Press in the East," 1830.

printing the lexicon and Arabic grammar that the author was working on for the mission under Smith's supervision.[121] Additionally, while the Press's editing committee, essentially constituting of Smith and Cornelius van Dyck, showed an interest in producing such secular books on "Grammar and Rhetoric" with al-Yāzijī's help for the seminary in 1848,[122] these books were not authorized for publication by the author until 1854.[123]

The mission's new focus on religion and preaching over printing and education also impacted the employment of certain local workmen at the Press. In particular, at various intervals during the mid-1840s and later decades, some missionary members demonstrated a changing attitude towards the Press employees (as well as those working within the mission's apparatus) who adamantly maintained an affiliation with local religious communities. For instance, during a meeting in 1845, a report by a special committee (made up of missionaries George Whiting and Thomas Laurie) is read on the subject of the Greek Orthodox al-Yāzijī's continued employment given the mission's dwindling funds and the Press's suspension, in which the committee states that:

> "[F]unds placed at our disposal by the church are a sacred deposit to be used for the promotion of the Kingdom of Christ & for that only. [T]he individual in question [Yāzijī] is not friendly to the Evangelical Religion, has regularly absented himself from our Sabbath services and forbidden his son from attending the Sabbath school ... we cannot conscientiously recommend that he be continued on his present permanent salary. [W]e consider it our duty in view of all the facts detailed above permissible to employ the said corrector hereafter only when we have appropriate work for him to do."[124]

While some missionaries continued to express their discontent with al-Yāzijī in later years,[125] the notes from this particular meeting illustrate an important shift at the time in the Press's policy relating to the mission's goals of "promoting the Kingdom of Christ," one that extended to their local employees.[126]

121 ABC 50, Box 2, al-Yāzijī to Smith, 3 Feb 1846. This issue is also brought up in an earlier letter to Smith, dating to August 15, 1845. For details from this letter, see Tibawi, *American Interests*, 116, 117n1.

122 Smith and Van Dyck are asked "to examine the works ... on Grammar & Rhetoric and if they find them proper for text books in the seminary ... examine existing works on Prosody...request al-Yāzijī to compose a work on that subject for a text book." See ABC 16.8.1, vol. 8, "Meeting at Smith's," 11 Feb 1848.

123 ABC 16.8.1, vol. 8, "Meeting in Beirut," 2 Nov 1854. The book was eventually published in two volumes: *Majmūʿ al-adab fī funūn al-ʿarab: Kitāb ʿiqd al-jumān fī ʿilm al-bayān*, 1855, 165 pages; see ABC 16.8.1, vol. 8, "Meeting in Beirut," 2 Nov 1854. The book's title and information is listed in Ellis, *Arabic Books*, 2:415. The second part was printed later that same year as *Majmūʿ al-adab fī funūn al-ʿarab: nuqṭat al-dāʾira*, which is also listed in Ellis, *Arabic Books*, 2:417–18.

124 ABC 16.8.1, vol. 8, "Meeting at Mission House," 30 Jul 1845. This report is also discussed in Chapter 2.

125 This became most evident after Van Dyck took over the project of translating the Bible into Arabic upon Smith's death in 1857. While al-Yāzijī was very involved in copying, correcting, and translating the work under Smith's supervision, Van Dyck did not work with al-Yāzijī on this project. According to Van Dyck, a condition of the contract between Smith and his local assistants "was that in case of the death of either party, the contract became null and void. The Mission was not bound thereby." Van Dyck's discontent with al-Yāzijī's work in particular, however, was clearly underscored: "in doing this work [the Bible translation] he [al-Yāzijī] was not faithful...The fact that he cared little whether the work was accurate in grammar or not became evident to some others." See Eli Smith and Cornelius Van Allen van Dyck, *A Brief Documentary History of the Translation of the Scriptures into the Arabic Language* (Beirut: American Presbyterian Mission Press, 1900), 14, 29.

126 In addition to al-Yāzijī, another local the mission had issues with at the time was Bishāra al-Khūrī, a Maronite employed as an instructor at the mission's seminary. See Tibawi, *American Interests*, 99–100.

This issue appears to have been unique to the mid- to late 1840s, around the time when Anderson continuously attempted to micromanage the mission and its publishing activities from afar. During the 1830s, for instance, it did not seem pertinent to the mission whether local hires working at the Press or otherwise converted to the mission's cause. In fact, many of those working at the American Press, including some who were closely involved in the translation and printing of books, belonged to local religious sects. It was also not a policy that was very consistently enforced in later years. For example, despite briefly limiting his employment at the Press during the mid-1840s, the mission kept al-Yāzijī within their employ until at least June 1860.[127] Another instance in which the mission contradicted its 1840s stance was its employment of Yūsuf ibn ʿAql al-Asīr al-Ḥusaynī in 1860 to assist Van Dyck in the Arabic Bible translation after Smith's death in 1857.[128] The fact that al-Asīr, who had studied in Damascus and at Cairo's al-Azhar mosque, was a Muslim was actually viewed as an added advantage. Specifically, Van Dyck thought that an educated Muslim scholar would have no biased assumptions about how Biblical passages should read, and would thus focus on the purity of the Arabic writing.[129] Additionally, Henry Harris Jessup (d. 1910) of the Beirut station, in his historical account of the mission's first fifty-three years, praised al-Asīr as a "Muhammedan scholar of high repute ... whose purely Arabic tastes and training fitted him to pronounce on all questions of grammar, rhetoric and vowelling."[130] It is probable, then, that the mission's religious discrimination towards local hires, and its stringent evangelical views in general, were ways in which missionary members tried to appease the Prudential Committee at a time when the Press's (and even the mission's) very existence was in jeopardy.

## An Emergent Print Readership

Despite the American Press's varied attempts from the 1830s to the late 1850s at either luring or reprimanding local readers into entering Protestantism's hallowed gates, many of its books gathered dust on shelves at the Press or in the mission's book depot. Oftentimes, if large numbers were distributed, they were religious works for use by neighboring missionary stations.[131] How much of an impact these books actually had on elite readers during the Press's nascent period (from 1835 until at least 1860) is difficult to gauge due to inconsistent sales records, which often did not distinguish between purchases made by local residents or outlying missions. In the mission's Annual Reports, the number of books issued by the Press and book magazine (or storehouse) is often tallied into lump sums. For instance, while 3,406 books were issued from the Press in 1850, it is not clear if they were actually sold locally or simply shipped off en masse to neighboring stations.[132]

127 It appears that the scholar's connection with the mission ended in June of 1860. See ABC 16.8.1, vol. 8, "Meeting in Beirut," 3 Apr 1860.

128 For more on this poet and intellectual, see John A. Thompson, *The Major Arabic Bibles: Their Origin and Nature* (New York: American Bible Society, 1956), 23–24.

129 Hall, "The Arabic Bible," 280.

130 Henry Harris Jessup, *Fifty Three Years in Syria*, 2 vols. (New York: Fleming H. Revell, 1910), 1:75. Also see YDSL, RG 124, Box 3/5, Series II. Writings, Writings of Others, Data Furnished by Dr. C.V.A. Van Dyck with Reference to the Translation of the Scriptures into the Arabic Language under the Auspices of the American Mission in Syria and the American Bible Society, 1885; Smith and Van Dyck, *A Brief Documentary History*, 29.

131 One rather popular tract at the time was the mission's "Passion of the Christ" booklet (printed in 1844). In 1852, for instance, 315 copies were sold to the ABCFM station in Mosul. "Annual Report of Press and Magazine," Dec 1851, PHS, RG 115-1-25.

132 ABC 16.8.1, vol. 4, *Annual Report of the Syria Mission*, 1850. Press and magazine records held at the Presbyterian Historical Society provide a slightly more nuanced view of book distribution. However,

From the few documents available it certainly appears that throughout this period the mission's publications hardly attained a mass readership. In the second half of its 1846 fiscal year, for instance, the Press only sold fifteen prints of ecclesiastic works to "natives" while about forty-one copies of secular writings (the most popular being *Kitāb al-ājurrūmiyya: al-ajwiba al-jaliyya fī al-uṣūl al-naḥawiyya*[133]) were purchased.[134] Of the publications distributed in 1851 from the mission's book depot in Beirut's mercantile center, which was the preferred point of purchase for local urban class readers,[135] the bestsellers were an edition of the Psalms[136] (fifty-two copies sold) and *Kitāb al-ājurrūmiyya* (thirty-two sold).[137] Despite these rather paltry sales figures, which would see major improvements into the second half of the century, it is clear that local readers were mostly interested in secular works; as would be expected, works like catechisms and published missionary sermons seemed to pique little interest.[138]

Although the mission had by 1855 recognized the changing political landscape and print readers' preference for secular publications (a problem the Jesuit press had started addressing at this time as well), the Press's production of such works did not significantly increase. Eli Smith was able to justify the need for occasional volumes of Arabic grammar, arithmetic, and geography for use in the mission's schools and seminary.[139] However, for most of the 1850s, even into the early 1860s, the Press's policies remained tied up with restrictions on book production set by the ABCFM in Boston. In a letter to the mission from 1851, for instance, Anderson states: "Are you losing ground, or are you gaining, at Beirut and ʿAbay?... We should regard it as highly inauspicious to your mission should Beirut become, like Smyrna, chiefly a *book-making* station."[140] The process of translating and printing the first editions of the Bible, as well as other religious works, remained the mission's star projects with respect to their Press. This shift in priorities was still evident in 1855, as seen in a press report from that year, in which Smith states that despite the great need for educational publications

available documents are incomplete, with several years missing.

133 "The Ajurrumiyya: Answers to the Basics of Arabic Grammar" (Beirut: American Press, 1841) was adapted from the thirteenth-century text by Muḥammad al-Ṣanhājī b. ʿĀjurrūm, and remained one of the mission's most popular publications with at least 2,000–3,000 issues printed in 1841, 1853, 1857, 1874, and 1886. See publishing details in ABC 16.8.1, vol. 1, "Books printed at the Mission Press in Beirut, Mar 1844 [?]"; vol. 4, *Annual Report of the Syria Mission*, 1853; vol. 4, *Annual Report of the Syria Mission*, 1856. Some editions are listed in Ellis, *Arabic Books*, 2:236.

134 "Semi-Annual Report of the Press," Jul-Dec 1846, PHS, RG 115-1-25.

135 Although a book depot was first set up in 1835, the mission split the sales of its books between the depot and Press offices until 1865, when all books were transferred to the depot. ABC 16.8.1, vol. 8, "Special Meeting in ʿAbay," 9 Aug 1865.

136 First printed in 1842 then 1851, this was a revised edition of an earlier 1838 translation by al-Yāzijī and an issue from the press in al-Shuwayr. The publication served as a popular textbook for missionary schools, and perhaps remained one of the least controversial of the Protestant's liturgical texts in circulation. The 1842 edition is listed in ABC 16.8.1, vol. 1, "Books printed at the Mission Press in Beirut, Mar 1844 [?]." A letter from an American Press workman shows that the mission was using both the al-Yāzijī and al-Shuwayr texts as sources, ABC 50, Box 1, al-ʿĀzār to Smith, 8 Aug 1842.

137 *Annual Report of Press and Magazine*, Dec 1852, PHS, RG 115-1-25.

138 It should be noted here that, according to records of the book magazine/depot, most books, even the smaller booklets, were sold. It was rare for books to be given away free of charge. However, some publications were sent to the mission's schools for students to use.

139 A number of these books were written by Van Dyck, such as a work on algebra in 1853 and an Arabic translation of Euclid's *Elements of Geometry* in 1856. ABC 16.8.1, vol. 4, "Annual Report of the Syria Mission," 1853; "Annual Report of the Syria Mission," 1857.

140 ABC 2.1.1, vol. 15, Anderson to Syria Mission, 6 Nov 1851.

(school books, grammars, etc.), "the probability is, that years will elapse before any one of our number shall find time to supply the demand."[141] Rather than reducing the significance of the American Press within a growing regional printing culture, the decreased missionary involvement in the Press's activity opened up the possibility for increased local involvement.

## Conclusion

A complex web of external and internal impulses shaped the design and content of the mission's publications in the 1840s and early 1850s. When compared to the mission's earlier efforts, it is clear that the mission's policy regarding its Press and publications in the 1840s cannot simply be explained away as a transplantation of Presbyterian Protestant aesthetics, texts, and ideology. Seen in this light, the choices for the American mission's books from the 1840s reflect its revamped proselytizing goals and efforts, at a time of mounting foreign missionary competition and local ecclesiastical opposition. Books that pointed out the errors of local churches, and clearly outlined the Protestants' worldview in design and content, may have been deemed essential for the mission's participation in an increasingly unstable political setting where religious identities and communal concerns were in flux.

At the same time, in presenting the narrative of this missionary press during the 1840s, this study has set up a framework for a broader consideration of the American Press's significance to an emergent print readership. In particular, the technical, administrative, and ideological changes that took place at the mission and the Press at this time, chiefly in response to the region's shifting socio-political landscape, positioned the Press on an unintended path as a local publisher. This allowed for a varied and non-traditional inclusion of subject matter reflective of the ground-shifting cultural, social, and political concerns beginning to influence Arab Christian intellectual spheres.

141 "Report on the Printing Establishment," ʿAbay, 1 Oct 1855, PHS, RG 115-1-25.

CHAPTER 5

# Protestant Ideals and Arab Intellectual Ambitions (1852–1867)

By the early to mid-1850s the importance of the American Press had extended well beyond the missionary apparatus. In particular, at a time when missionaries were unable to compose, edit, and print books for use by the mission, its Press found itself (inadvertently) taking on the role of a secular publisher by printing works of established and emergent Arab scholars in Beirut.[1] In a request to purchase its first steam-powered press in 1852, for instance, the mission's description of the Press's activity clearly demonstrates a key shift in the nature of the work being produced on its premises: "[A] good deal of the press work consists of jobs for merchants and different departments of government ... it occupies no missionary time, helps support the establishment and gains us favor with the people and with those who are in authority."[2] With the mission's subsequent purchase of a steam press by 1855, which far surpassed the efficacy of the Press's older equipment,[3] the Press was "employed, more than formerly, in printing books for the natives of the country, at their own expense."[4] This continued well into the 1860s. For instance, a report from 1867 explains that funding for missionary publications (namely the Protestant Bible) was coming in not from the Prudential Committee but from the American Bible Society (ABS), which was paying the salaries of at least two pressmen at a time and the cost of electrotyping plates for new editions of the Bible.[5]

Changes from the 1850s to the mid-1860s would become important to an expanding print readership that would flourish as the much discussed intellectual milieu of the late 1800s. Although the Press continued to sporadically publish ecclesiastical works for use by the mission, as well as numerous early editions and proof copies of the new Bible translation, the Americans increasingly resorted to loaning out the Press to members of an expanding print intelligentsia who sought to publish their own works (often funded by local elite sponsors).[6] Long-time employees Nāṣīf al-Yāzijī and Buṭrus al-Bustānī took full advantage of this moment by producing a string of their own writings, in addition to translating classical manuscripts of poetry, literature and history into print. While these "job work" publications by local Arab intellectuals diverged from the religious nature of books commonly commissioned by the Protestant mission, they surprisingly resembled the mission's products in their visual language and organizational methods. More importantly, although both scholars were aligned with the Christian faith, their work at this time excluded explicitly Christian references, in order to engage a multi-confessional audience.

One could argue that a burgeoning print intelligentsia embraced the American Press's design program, through its typeface, layouts,

1 See Appendix 1 for the number of annual publications produced at the Press during this period.

2 Records of the American Board of Commissioners for Foreign Missions deposited at Houghton Library, Harvard University, Cambridge, Mass. (hereafter cited as ABC), 16.8.1, Syria Mission (1823–1871), vol. 4, Syria Mission to Anderson, 27 Jul 1852.

3 See "Report on the Printing Establishment," ʿAbay, 1 Oct 1855, United Presbyterian Church in the U.S.A. Syria Mission Records, 1808–1967, Record Group 115, box 1, folder 25, Presbyterian Historical Society, Philadelphia, PA (hereafter cited as PHS, RG 115-1-25).

4 ABC 16.8.1, vol. 4, *Annual Report of the Syria Mission*, 1855.

5 ABC 16.8.1, vol. 6, *Annual Report of the Beirut Station*, 1867.

6 ABC 16.8.1, vol. 4, *Annual Report of the Syria Mission*, 1855. For a list of some titles printed at the Press during this period, see Appendix 2.

 | DOI 10.1163/9789004314351_006

and formatting preferences, while avoiding any obvious association with the Protestant mission and its evangelical message. Scholars who have researched the subject of the American Press's regional impact have taken up the popularity of the Press's typeface as one aspect of these visual borrowings. In a lecture on the subject published in 1997, Dagmar Glass traces the use of this set of fonts, and some ornamental borders and rules, by private Christian and Muslim presses in Syria and beyond from the late 1850s onwards. Highlighting books by local Arab scholars, who likely purchased sets of the Americans' typeface, she credits Smith and his letterforms' success with bridging scribal and print culture for this widespread adoption.[7] This sentiment is reiterated in a later publication by Glass and Geoffrey Roper, in a joint article detailing the development of Arabic printing in the Arab world and emphasizing the importance of the mission's typeface to emergent private presses.[8]

In printing books at the American Press during this period, individuals like al-Bustānī and al-Yāzijī likely utilized the American Arabic typeface because of its aesthetic solutions, practicality and availability. The visual appeal and technical efficiency of this typeface certainly explains its widespread popularity during the 1850s and 1860s. However, in order to locate the printed word within the larger visual vehicle of the book and its production it is also necessary to examine the overall layout, organization, and visual compositions of these printed works, instead of focusing exclusively on the typography. Thus the aim of this chapter is not to try to attribute certain visual practices or designs of typefaces to one or more sources in order to underscore the significance of the mission in this context. Rather, I aim to understand how the popularity of the American Press's aesthetics and production standards related to changing local perceptions, at mid-century, of books and their visual dimensions. More specifically, what needs to be explored are the functions that stylistic methods prominent in the mission's publications served as local scholars adopted the nascent print medium to further their own political, social, and intellectual agendas. Evidently, other agents were able to deploy the visual features of the Press's books for other purposes, and these features were received quite differently from previous missionary works that followed the same template.

In addition to examining the visual and textual dimensions of secular books coming off the Press in the 1850s, this chapter considers the roles of local agents in utilizing the American Press, its design programs, and typefaces to publish works to further their own visions and agendas. Indeed, during this period, the Press was quickly becoming a well-known venue for the publication of secular works by members of an emergent print intelligentsia, whose writing reflected local interests in "reviving" past literary works as well as concepts of a multi-confessional Syrian identity. The dialogism between missionaries and local agents becomes most apparent in the publications from this period produced, funded, and/or written by local Arab scholars. This chapter thus examines how the Press, with its changing role within the missionary framework, provided an opportunity for such projects beyond the Syria Mission's proselytizing goals. Furthermore, it proposes possible explanations for certain aesthetic choices and how these graphic conventions were likely negotiating broader social and political concerns.

7 Dagmar Glass, *Malta, Beirut, Leipzig and Beirut Again: Eli Smith, the American Syria Mission and the Spread of Arabic Typography in 19th Century Lebanon*, ed. Angelika Neuwirth (Beirut: Orient-Institut der Deutschen Morganländischen Gesellschaft, 1997), 25–34.

8 Roper and Glass, "The Printing of Arabic Books in the Arab World," in *Middle Eastern Languages and the Print Revolution: A Cross-Cultural Encounter*, eds. Eva-Maria Hanebutt-Benz et al. (Mainz: Gutenberg-Museum, 2002), 192–94.

### A Chasm between Bookmaking and Evangelizing

During the early 1850s the Press continued to struggle with internal problems, mostly resulting from the editor's failing health, and external issues. Throughout this period, the Board in Boston persevered in its attempts at curbing the Press's activities and placed restrictions on book production, described in the previous chapter.[9] The translation of the Bible remained the mission's central project for its Press in the 1850s. However, it soon proved to be an all-consuming task for a terminally ill Smith,[10] and allowed him little time for writing, editing, or translating any other works.[11] Given Smith's inability to act as both Press editor and Bible translator during this period, requests were made for a new Press editor from 1855 until shortly before Smith's death in 1857.[12] Unsurprisingly, given the American Board of Commissioners for Foreign Missions' (ABCFM) continued tightening of its expenditures[13] and their general dismissal of missionary press activity, it appears that the Board did not heed these appeals.[14]

Board Secretary Rufus Anderson still maintained a staunch stance regarding the Press as a subordinate auxiliary to other missionary activity. Indeed, the missionaries' decreased involvement in press activity at the time did little to assuage the Board's concerns. Anderson's position regarding the Press did not change from his earlier views in the 1840s, even as the mission pushed for more ecclesiastical works as opposed to secular publications.[15] For instance, shortly after Smith's death, Anderson addressed the Syria Mission with a request that a non-missionary author, a Dr. Reiggs, take over the Bible translation project and not a member of the mission (e.g. Cornelius van Dyck) "with all the active labors among the people which are and must be incumbent upon you [the missionaries]." His letter made it clear that no excess time be spent on

9 Approval from the Board for funding the production of books remained a key issue, as discussed in a letter from Smith addressed to a Priest, Qusṭa al-Gharghūr, in Jerusalem. ABC 50, Eli Smith Arabic Collection, Box 3, Smith to al-Gharghūr, 31 May 1853.

10 Smith, who is described as "pale" with a "delicate frame" in some missionary accounts, was plagued with health issues throughout his work in Beirut. In 1855 cancer rapidly took hold of his health. He died on January 11, 1857. See Henry Harris Jessup, *Fifty Three Years in Syria*, vol. 1 (New York: Fleming H. Revell, 1910), 53. His increasingly poor health during the mid-1850s is also indicated in letters from Press employees (particularly al-Yāzijī) as well as minutes from meetings. For some examples, see ABC 16.8.1, vol. 8, "Meeting in Beirut," 1 Apr 1856; "Meeting in Beirut," 5 Apr 1856. See also ABC 50, Box 1, al-Yāzijī to Smith, 21 Jul 1856; al-Yāzijī to Smith, 4 Dec 1855.

11 ABC 16.8.1, vol. 4, *Annual Report of the Syria Mission*, 1855.

12 The 1855 press report, for instance, explains that the translation of the Bible may be delayed given Smith's need to serve as Press editor – thus implying the desire to hire a new editor. "Report on the Printing Establishment," ʿAbay, 1 Oct 1855, PHS, RG 115-1-25. This is brought up again more explicitly in a letter addressed to Anderson in 1856. ABC 16.8.1, vol. 4, Syria Mission to Anderson, 8 Apr 1856.

13 ABCFM budgetary issues came to a head in 1861, with the unfolding of the American Civil War that directly impacted the Presbyterian mission via enlistments, taxation, and the sectionalism of denominations. In a letter to the mission from Anderson, the Board secretary urged the mission to limit its expenses to "relieve the [ABCFM] Treasury" due to increased war taxes and decreased commercial activity. The letter also asks the mission to rally for "native contributions and efforts and obtaining aid where ever you can from foreigners." ABC 16.8.1, vol. 8, Anderson to Syria Mission, 31 Jul 1861.

14 There are no indications in the missionary records that any new editors were hired during the three years prior to Smith's death. Shortly after his death in 1857, all Press-related tasks, including the Bible translation project, were handed off to Cornelius Van Dyck (previously of the Sidon station). ABC 16.8.1, vol. 4, *Annual Report of the Syria Mission*, 1857.

15 This is clear in a letter to the mission from 1851. See ABC 2.1.1 Letters: Foreign (Transcript series), vol. 15, Anderson to Syria Mission, 6 Nov 1851.

producing the Bible, or any other publications.[16] Perhaps Anderson felt that with the passing of Smith, the Press's steadfast advocate,[17] the Press could finally be pushed to the periphery of the mission's operations, thus allowing for a renewed (and more successful?) focus on preaching and strengthening the foundations for "native churches."

The Press's outpouring of controversial religious works in previous years had backfired by further damaging Protestant-local ties at a time when inter-communal strife escalated to dangerous levels. Inter-communal tensions of the 1840s continued into the late 1850s. These culminated in the widespread civil wars of 1860 in the villages of Mount Lebanon when the local Maronite peasantry revolted against the *muqāṭaʿjī* (provincial) families, the intermediaries between the peasants and their feudal landlords (traditionally elite members of the Druze community). While conflicts between Druze and Maronite groups were centered in the mountain towns,[18] nearby Damascus and Ottoman Syrian coastal cities saw battles ensue between resident Muslims and non-Muslim minorities. These peripheral conflicts were largely fueled by struggles between Ottoman-supporters and an emergent Christian merchant class, and included the intervention of European powers. Historians of these conflicts are divided over their exact causes. For a time, they were seen as part of an inherent divide between Muslims and Christians that was set off by the Ottoman Tanzimat (orderings), which instituted a view that all sects were equal in the eyes of the state. More recent scholarship, which rightly repudiates the notion of a primordial Muslim-Christian divide, cites economic issues, particularly the widening gap between the elites and disenfranchised peasantry, as well as growing European hegemony in the region, as catalysts of these conflicts.[19]

Looming civil struggles, and the impediment they posed to proselytizing activity, directly impacted members of the mission and their small pockets of Protestant communities at this time. For instance, records indicate that during the 1850s, there were various incidents between Protestants in Sidon and members of the Sunni community, which resulted in the Christians fleeing the city for fear of persecution.[20] While the

16 ABC 16.8.1, vol. 8, Anderson to Syria Mission, 13 Mar 1857. The Syria mission responded to Anderson's request a few months later. The mission argued that Van Dyck was uniquely qualified for the task, which required that the Protestant Bible be written in a style familiar to the local (specifically Muslim) residents. ABC 16.8.1, vol. 4, Syria Mission to Anderson, 12 May 1857.

17 This idea has also been posited by A.L. Tibawi, see *American Interests in Syria: 1800–1901: A Study of Educational, Literary and Religious Work* (Oxford: Oxford University Press, 1966), 134.

18 Struggles in Mount Lebanon were not strictly along sectarian lines; the Maronite church, which was also a feudal landowner at the time, rebuffed the peasant revolts. For a concise listing of the various factors fueling these conflicts, see Nadia Bou Ali, "Buṭrus al-Bustānī and the Shipwreck of the Nation," *Middle Eastern Literatures: incorporating Edebiyat* 16, no. 3 (2013): 267.

19 For more on these conflicts and their far-reaching political and social implications see: Eugene L. Rogan, "Sectarianism and Social Conflict in Damascus: The 1860 Events Reconsidered," *Arabica* 54, no. 4 (2004): 493–511; Ussama Makdisi, "After 1860: Debating Religion, Reform, and Nationalism in the Ottoman Empire," *International Journal of Middle East Studies* (hereafter cited as *IJMES*) 34, no. 4 (2002): 601–17; *The Culture of Sectarianism: Community, History, and Violence in Nineteenth-Century Ottoman Lebanon* (Berkeley: University of California Press, 2000); Leila F. Tarazi, *An Occasion for War: Civil Conflict in Lebanon and Damascus in 1860* (Berkeley: University of California Press, 1994); "The City and the Mountain: Beirut's Political Radius in the 19th Century as Revealed in the Crises of 1860," *IJMES* 16, no. 4 (1984): 489–95.

20 William W. Eddy, an American missionary resident of Sidon, relayed the increased tensions between Christian and Muslim groups in the port-city via letters to the mission as well as published accounts in the US. Records of the Syria Mission, of the American Board of Commissioners of Foreign Missions, deposited at Jafet Memorial Library Archives and Special Collections, American University of Beirut, Lebanon, American Missionaries, AA: 7.5, Box 1, File 11(hereafter cited as

late 1850s were only the start of a series of drawn out, violent conflicts, Anderson and members of the Board were kept abreast of these simmering tensions and their potential hindrance to the mission's goals. Anderson was closely involved with the mission's work, having paid the region a third visit in 1855.[21] Letters from the Syria Mission with updates on the tensions were regularly published in the *Missionary Herald*. In an issue from 1859, for instance, a letter claims: "The affairs of Syria are in a rather disturbed state."[22] All these developments likely factored into Anderson's desire to keep the Press on the sidelines, lest its time-consuming and expensive activities derail the entire missionary establishment in Beirut, particularly at a time when missionary protection and sustainability seemed most precarious.[23]

The Board's request to remove the Press from Beirut in 1858 was initially agreed to by members of the Syria Mission,[24] however its members quickly reneged on this decision and provided an alternate suggestion, detailed in an eight-page letter to Anderson.[25] The missionaries in Syria argued that while they understood that the Press needed to be kept "in its place as a secondary instrumentality," they believed it was a necessity as a "front" for the mission's cause and goals, as well as a way to make money to offset its cost. They suggested it remain in operation, via job works, with the intention that it be eventually turned over "to private hands and thus relieve the Board and mission of all care and responsibility" for it.[26] Press-related funding remained a critical issue in the 1860s, given the war in the US and the local situation.[27] This paved the way for the increased involvement of local scholars in the Press's activity, as seen in a Press report from 1861 stating that "a good share of job works" had been completed,[28] while the mission did not print any books for its own use save for "a few Sabbath school tracts."[29] The printing establishment was thus set on a course that allowed it to exist, and even successfully thrive,[30] outside the missionary apparatus.

Such developments at the Press during the 1850s and the 1860s allowed for the closer involvement of al-Yāzijī and al-Bustānī as independent authors and publishers, not just as Press translators and correctors. For instance, al-Yāzijī took this opportunity to publish a number of works. These included a collection of his poetry in 1853,[31] a two-volume compendium of Arabic poetry and prose,[32] and *Kitāb majmaʿ al-baḥrayn* (in 1856),

AUB Archives AA7.5-1-11), Eddy to Van Dyck, 18 Oct 1858; "Persecution of Protestants in Syria," 18 Dec 1858; Eddy to N. Moore (British Consul), Sidon, 18 Mar 1859; Eddy to N. Moore (British Consul), Sidon, 17 Sep 1859.

21 Tibawi, *American Interests*, 139.

22 *The Missionary Herald* 55 (1859): 28.

23 Although the Sublime Porte had granted the Protestants some stay and protection via a formal recognition of the religious group as part of the empire's *milal* (religious communities) system in 1850 – which had come about with the help of the British Consul and other connections in Istanbul – this did not mean local residents accepted this new group of converts as legitimate. ABC 16.8.1, vol. 8, "Meeting at Mission House," 19 Jan 1847. This was the firman issued on 6 November 1850, cited in Tibawi, *American Interests*, 109.

24 ABC 16.8.1, vol. 8, "Meeting at Press Library," 1 Apr 1858.

25 ABC 16.8.1, vol. 4, Syria Mission to Anderson, 6 May 1858.

26 Ibid.

27 ABC 16.8.1, vol. 6, *Annual Report of the Syria Mission*, 1860.

28 ABC 16.8.1, vol. 6, *Annual Report of the Beirut Station*, 1861.

29 ABC 16.8.1, vol. 6, *Annual Tabular View Report*, 1861.

30 Financially, printing job works was certainly a lucrative venture: in 1862, the Press made 28,554.30 piastres, while in 1863 the Press's income saw an approximate 30% gain with a total of 37,030.27 piastres. ABC 16.8.1, vol. 6, *Annual Report of the Beirut Station*, 1863.

31 *Nabdha min dīwān al-shaykh nāṣīf al-yāzijī* (Selections from the Collection of Poems by Nāṣīf al-Yāzijī) (Beirut, 1853), funded by Anṭūnīyūs al-Amyūnī. See A.G. Ellis, *Catalogue of Arabic Books in the British Museum*, vol. 2 (London: The British Museum, 1901), 415.

32 *Majmūʿ al-adab fī funūn al-ʿarab: Kitāb ʿiqd al-jumān fī ʿilm al-bayān*, vol. 1 (Beirut, 1855), and *Majmūʿ al-adab fī funūn al-ʿarab: nuqṭat al-dāʾira*, vol. 2 (Beirut, 1855); see Ellis, *Arabic Books*, 2: 415–18.

which was a collection of sixty anecdotes written in the literary style of al-Ḥarīrī's[33] *Maqāmāt* (Sessions),[34] itself an example of one of the most important genres of pre-modern Arabic literature. Al-Bustānī also produced a number of key publications at this time.[35] Such works included the first edition of the proceedings of the "Syrian Society for the Study of the Sciences and Arts" (*Al-jamʿiyya al-sūriyya l-iktisāb al-ʿulūm wa-l-funūn*) published in 1852,[36] Maronite Christian Tānnūs ibn Yūsuf al-Shidyāq's (d. 1861) account of Mount Lebanon's history (edited and supervised by al-Bustānī),[37] and the story of Tānnūs's brother Asʿad al-Shidyāq,[38] an early Protestant convert who was persecuted by his Maronite community and eventually died in captivity. Other individuals to take advantage of producing job works at the Press included Ibrāhīm Sarkīs, Salīm ibn Mūsa Busṭrus (d. 1882 or 1883),[39] and Iskandar ibn Yaʿqūb Abkariyyūs (d. 1885),[40] to name a few. Of these three, Sarkīs, a Protestant convert of Armenian origin, was the only one employed by the mission (he was hired as an Arabic type compositor at the Press on Dec 8, 1851).[41] In addition to typesetting books, such as the mission's first Arabic Bible, Sarkīs also composed tracts for the mission and published numerous works, including his *Kitāb ṣawṭ al-nafīr fī aʿmāl iskandar al-kabīr* in 1864.[42]

Although the topic of job works appears ubiquitously in mission records of the time, there are no documents that define exactly what constituted a job work and how they were differentiated from mission publications, beyond that the former were usually funded externally (by local elites). This division was further complicated by the fact that

33 Abū Muḥammad al-Qāsim ibn ʿAlī al-Ḥarīrī (d. 1122).

34 Described as "rhetorical anecdotes, composed in imitation of those of al-Ḥarīrī. With explanatory notes by the author." See Ellis, *Arabic Books*, 2:417. See also ABC 16.8.1, vol. 4, *Annual Report of the Syria Mission*, 1856.

35 Other books worth mentioning include "an historical lecture on the culture of the Arabs"; see Ellis, *Arabic Books*, 1:430. Al-Bustānī also printed a rendition of Daniel Defoe's *Robinson Crusoe*, *Kitāb al-tuḥfa al-bustāniyya fī al-aṣfār al-kurūziyya ʿan riḥlat rūbinṣun kurūzī* (Beirut, 1861); see Ellis, *Arabic Books*, 1:429. An earlier edition was published in 1835 by the CMS in Malta as *Qiṣṣat rūbinṣun kurūzī*.

36 This inaugural issue covered the group's proceedings from 1847–1852, including essays by Smith and other missionaries. For a reprint, see Yūsuf Khūrī, *Al-jamʿiyya al-sūriyya li al-ʿulūm wa-l-funūn 1847–1852* (Beirut: Dār al-Hamrā, 1990). This society was initially formed in 1842, and it first appears in mission records from 1842. See ABC 16.8.1, vol. 8, "Meeting at Mission House," 7 Apr 1849. Its publication is brought up in ABC 16.8.1, vol. 5, Hurter to Anderson, 5 Apr 1852; ABC 16.8.1, vol. 8, "Meeting at Native Chapel," 21 Apr 1842.

37 Tānnūs al-Shidyāq, *Kitāb akhbār al-aʿyān fī jabal lubnān*, 3 vols. (Beirut, 1859). It is listed in Luwīs Shaykhū, *Tārīkh fann al-ṭibāʿa fī al-mashriq*, 2nd ed. (Beirut: Dār al-Mashriq, 1995), 50.

38 *Qiṣṣat asʿad al-shidyāq bākūrat sūriyya* (Beirut, 1860). Al-Bustānī discusses working on this publication, which was a translation of the English account that appeared in an earlier edition of the *Missionary Herald*, in a letter to Anderson in Jan 1860. See ABC 16.8.1, vol. 6, al-Bustānī to Anderson, 25 Jan 1860. The publication is listed in ABC 16.8.1, vol. 6, *Annual Report of the Beirut Station*, 1860. A different version was printed in 1833 by the CMS in Malta as *Khabariyyat asʿad shidyāq* (The Tale of Asʿad al-Shidyāq), which was probably written by both al-Shidyāq and Isaac Bird (of the ABCFM mission).

39 An Arab traveler who wrote a book on his journeys in Egypt and Europe: *Kitāb al-nuzha al-shahiyya fī al-riḥla al-salīmiyya* (Beirut, 1856). It was referred to in missionary records as "a book of Travels by a native merchant." See ABC 16.8.1, vol. 4, *Annual Report of the Syria Mission*, 1856.

40 *Kitāb rawḍat al-adab fī ṭabaqāt shuʿarāʾ al-ʿarab* (Beirut, 1857) is described in the mission's annual report as "a volume of Poems by a native/job work." See ABC 16.8.1, vol. 4, *Annual Report of the Syria Mission*, 1857.

41 *Annual Report of the Press and Magazine*, 1851, PHS, RG 115-1-25.

42 Shahīn Sarkīs, the author's brother, funded the book. At one point in the mid-1860s, Ibrāhīm Sarkīs was also instated (albeit temporarily) as the head printer/press supervisor when Van Dyck was in the United States working on electrotyping editions of the mission's Arabic Bible. See ABC 16.8.1, vol. 6, *Annual Report of the Syria Mission*, 1865.

mission employees were some of the main authors of these job works. Thus, it is difficult to tell from Press records which of the publications produced as job works were also sold or used by the mission and which were not. Some books are clearly listed in the mission's annual reports as having been published by the Press, while others are vaguely mentioned in passing or ignored all together. For instance, al-Yāzijī's numerous works on grammar and prose, such his *Kitāb quṭb al-ṣināʿa fī uṣūl al-manṭiq* (*al-taḍkira fī uṣūl al-manṭiq*)[43] and *Kitab majmaʿ al-baḥrayn,* appear in annual reports as works published by the Press.[44] Similarly many of al-Bustānī's earlier texts used by the mission's schools (such as his arithmetic[45]) and books related to Protestantism (such as the story of Asʿad al-Shidyāq) are highlighted in the Press's reports.[46]

When it came to secular works not specific to the mission's needs they were rarely elaborated on and the author was hardly ever named. For instance, an 1856 report alludes to al-Bustānī's publication of Tānnūs al-Shidyāq's history simply as a "history of Lebanon by a native."[47] While some job works were mentioned by title or referred to in Annual Mission and Tabular Reports, most were not even tallied in the usual increments of numbers of volumes or pages, but rather were indiscriminately categorized under the vague descriptor "job works." If these reports are to be taken at face value, one would (incorrectly) assume that the Press saw very little activity during this period. Was downplaying the significance and size of such works (al-Shidyāq's three-volume history ran at about 720 pages!) a way to circumvent any potential issues with the Board? Had they known the nature of such publications coming off the Press, would members of the Board have also objected to all job works and local bookmaking efforts?[48]

It is unlikely that the Board approved funding applications for any secular works during the 1850s, unless they were deemed of utmost necessity for missionary progress in the region. However, it is clear that what was a "need" in the mission's view was not necessarily seen as such by the Board, thus representing a significant fissure between perceptions of the mission in Beirut and Boston. In a letter to Anderson from 1861, Van Dyck states that copies of books needed for mission stations and schools (such as Smith and al-Bustānī's "The Office and Work of the Holy Spirit" first printed in 1843[49]) were out of print, yet the mission did not have funds for reprints. Van Dyck pleads: "What shall we do? I know you will sympathize with us most deeply, yet we must call out – what shall we do?"[50] It does seem that the mission is granted some reprieve regarding key religious works, yet it does not come until 1863 (Smith's book that is mentioned here, for instance, gets reprinted during that year).[51]

It is equally unclear how profits from these non-missionary job work publications were allocated. Since funding was limited, and books were needed, it is probable that some job works, though not officially approved by the Board and not fitting with the Protestants' agenda, were incorporated into the mission's libraries and book depots. Did the

43 "A Book on Logic" printed in 1857, 48 pages. See ABC 16.8.1, vol. 4, *Annual Report of the Syria Mission*, 1857; Ellis, *Arabic Books*, 2:416.

44 For instance, ABC 16.8.1, vol. 4, *Annual Report of the Syria Mission*, 1857; ABC 16.8.1, vol. 4, *Annual Report of the Syria Mission*, 1856. Additionally, Salīm Busṭrus's book on travels was noted in ABC 16.8.1, vol. 4, *Annual Report of the Syria Mission*, 1856.

45 *Kitāb kashf al-ḥijāb fī ʿilm al-ḥisāb* was printed in 1848 and 1859. "Semi-Annual Report of Press," Jul–Dec 1848, PHS, RG 115-1-25; ABC 16.8.1, vol. 4, *Annual Report of the Syria Mission*, 1858.

46 Al-Bustānī's *Qiṣṣat asʿad al-shidyāq* is listed in ABC 16.8.1, vol. 6, *Annual Report of the Beirut Station*, 1860.

47 ABC 16.8.1, vol. 4, *Annual Report of the Syria Mission*, 1856.

48 For instance, Tānnūs al-Shidyāq, unlike his brothers Asʿad and Fāris (another Protestant convert), remained Maronite. His history was meant to emphasize this community's regional significance, possibly to regain favor with the Maronite Patriarch. Which makes its publication at the American Press rather interesting.

49 *Kitāb al-bāb al-maftūḥ fī aʿmāl al-rūḥ*.

50 ABC 16.8.1, vol. 7, Van Dyck to Anderson, 24 Jul 1861.

51 ABC 16.8.1, vol. 6, *Annual Report of the Beirut Station*, 1863.

authors of such works receive any printing discounts or subsidies for permitting the mission to sell such books to fund the Protestants' own projects? Perhaps as a more likely scenario, particularly in the case of al-Yāzijī, whose books frequently appear on annual reports, some special arrangement was in place regarding publications by Press employees and the mission's rights to a percentage of them. Whatever the nature of the mission's involvement in job works, currently unclear in available press records, this overlap of conflicting views, projects, and interests within the space of the Press demonstrates negotiations and tensions between the mission's proselytizing goals and the emergent secular publishing endeavors of local Arab scholars.

### The Visual Conventions of "Job Works"

Although these "job work" publications by local authors diverged from the religious nature of books commonly commissioned by the Protestant mission, they surprisingly resembled the mission's products, particularly the Press's post-1830s visual language and organizational methods. While there are numerous job works from the period that illustrate these methods, this chapter focuses on select works by al-Yāzijī and al-Bustānī, since these two scholars were the most prolific writers employed by the Press at this time, and their terms of employment between mission and press provide unique examples for study. For instance, al-Yāzijī's *Majmaʿ al-baḥrayn* from 1856 (Fig. 25), sponsored by the renowned Greek Orthodox literary elite Nakhla al-Mudawwar (d. 1899), and his *Nabdha min dīwān al-shaykh nāṣīf al-yāzijī* of 1853 (Fig. 26), funded by Anṭūnīyūs al-Amyūnī,[52] maintained similar proportions and layout styles to those of ecclesiastic books printed at the American Press during this period. One can say the same about books by al-Bustānī from this period, such as his *Kitāb misbāḥ al-tālib fī baḥth al-maṭālib,* from 1854[53] (Fig. 27). Like the Press publications from the 1830s, the visual programs of books and ephemeral works like pamphlets did not differ drastically from each other, as can be seen from al-Bustānī's *Khuṭba fī ādāb al-ʿarab* (Fig. 28), a lecture of his published in pamphlet format in 1859.[54]

Commonalities are clear when comparing the typography, layout design, and organizational conventions of the above mentioned publications by al-Yāzijī and al-Bustānī to those of the mission from the 1840s, like *Kitāb al-ājurrūmiyya* from 1841 (Fig. 20) or *Kitāb al-bāb al-maftūh fī aʿmāl al-rūh* from 1843 (Fig. 17). For starters, all of these printed examples use the various font sizes of the "American Arabic" typeface. The significance of this typeface for local scholars will be touched upon shortly. For the moment, suffice it to say that the prevalence of this typeface owes both to its availability at the Press during this period, and to its increasing popularity, as the American Press was quickly becoming popular amongst local print producers. However, the similarities do not stop there and should not be limited to a discussion of typeface.

Like the mission's works proper at this time, these publications by al-Yāzijī and al-Bustānī also display a minimalist design that demonstrates an emphasis on text and typography within which any ornamental elements are limited to simple borders. For instance, in al-Yāzijī's *Majmaʿ al-baḥrayn* a simple, thin-weight frame of two lines surrounds the text, while a three-sided border of small diamond-shaped motifs crowns the page heading and subheading within the upper quadrant of the text box. A similar, equally simplified, headpiece can be seen in the author's *Nabdha,* although the actual motif design varies. These streamlined framing devices can also be found at the opening of introduction and dedication pages in al-Bustānī's works. While the simple headpieces pictured in *Kitāb*

52 Ellis, *Arabic Books*, 2:415.

53 *Kitāb misbāḥ al-ṭālib fī bahth al-maṭālib: mutāwwal fī al-ṣarf wa-l-naḥū wa-ʿilm al-ʿarūd wa-l-qawāfī* (Beirut, 1854), 454 pages; see Ellis, *Arabic Books*, 1:429; Shaykhū, *Tārīkh fann al-ṭibāʿa*, 51.

54 *Khuṭba fī ādāb al-ʿarab* (Beirut, 1859), 40 pages; see Ellis, *Arabic Books*, 1:430.

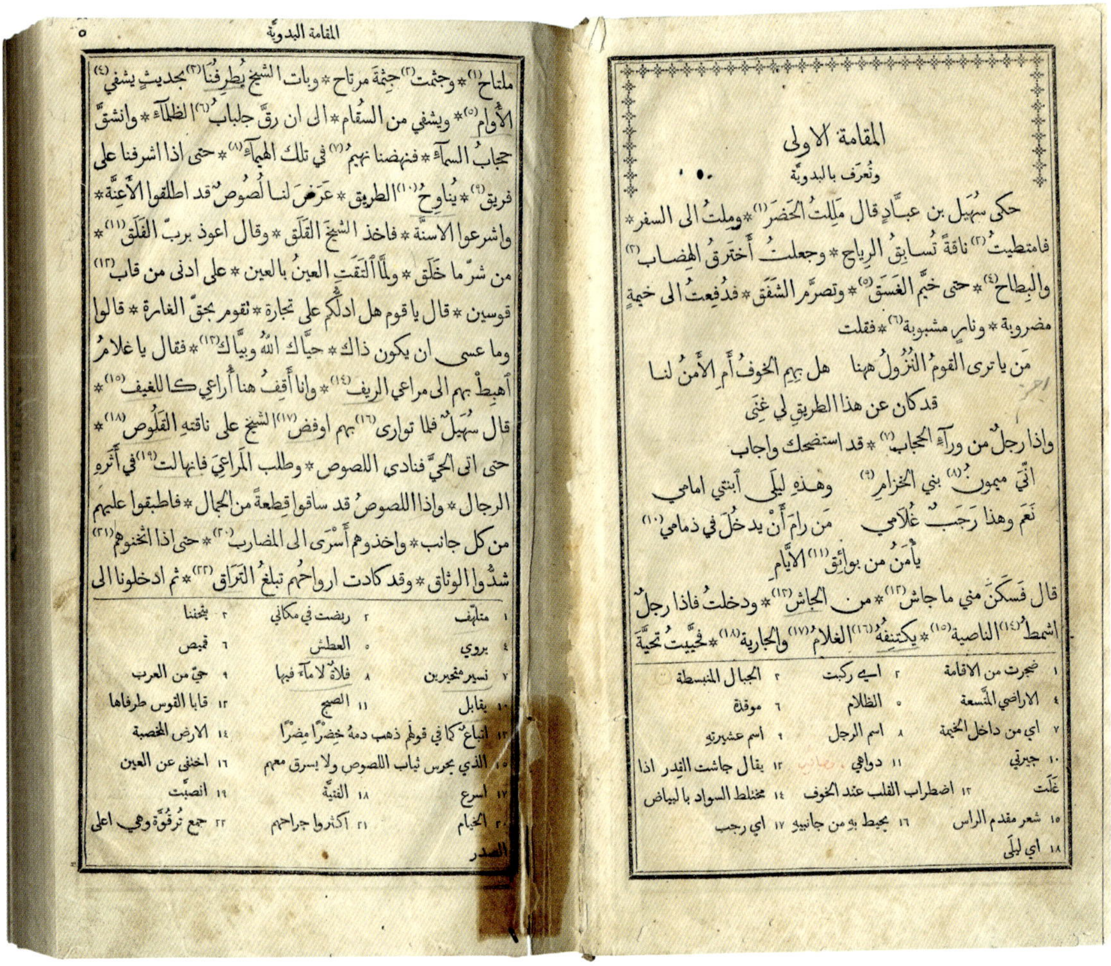
المقامة البدوية

المقامة الاولى

وتعرف بالبدوية

FIGURE 25 *Opening pages of Chapter 1 from Nāṣīf al-Yāzijī,* Kitāb majmaʿ al-baḥrayn. BEIRUT, 1856

*misbāḥ al-tālib* and *Khuṭba fi ādāb al-ʿarab* (Figs. 27 and 28) are certainly more ornamental than the preceding two examples, their size, shape and location are consistent with those of al-Yāzijī. These three-part ornamental borders certainly mirror the ones at the opening pages of missionary publications from the 1840s, such as in *Kitāb al-ājurrūmiyya*, where the three-part, simplified headpiece is made up of a border with a twisted-chord motif (Fig. 20). It would appear that these small framing devices are all that remain from the more elaborately designed *sarlawḥ* compositions of Press publications from the 1830s (see, for example, Figs. 5–8). In some cases, such as al-Bustānī's *Qiṣṣat asʿad al-shidyāq*, these ornamental devices have completely disappeared.

Alignment with the conventions of the mission's post-1830s publications does not stop there. Like the mission's texts from the 1840s, works by al-Yāzijī and al-Bustānī (as well as the other job works printed at this Press) show no traces of catchwords. Page numbers and running headings are used exclusively in such productions. Although remnants of scribal traditions do appear in some of these works, for example

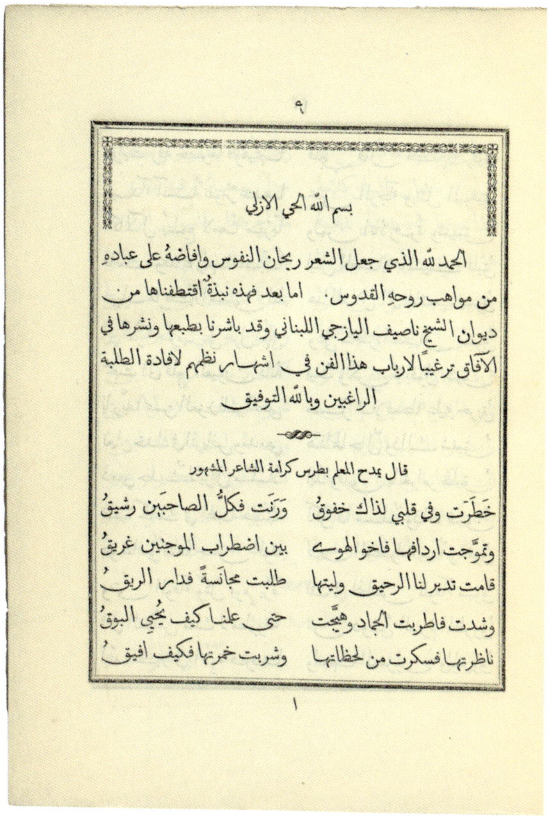
٩

بسم الله الحي الازلي

الحمد لله الذي جعل الشعر ريحان النفوس وافاضهُ على عبادهِ
من مواهب روحهِ القدوس. اما بعد فهذه نبذةٌ اقتطفناها من
ديوان الشيخ ناصيف اليازجي اللبناني وقد باشرنا بطبعها ونشرها في
الآفاق ترغيباً لارباب هذا الفن في اشهار نظمهم لافادة الطلبة
الراغبين وبالله التوفيق

قال يمدح المعلم بطرس كرامة الشاعر المشهور

خَطَرَت وفي قلبي لذاك خفوقُ     ورَنَت فكلُّ الصاحبَين رشيقُ
وتموَّجت اردافها فاخو الهوى     بين اضطراب الموجتين غريقُ
قامت تدير لنا الرحيق وليتها     طلبت مجانسةً فدار الريقُ
وشدت فاطربت الجماد وهيَّجت     حتى علمنا كيف يُحيِي البوقُ
ناظرتها فسكرت من لحظاتها     وشربت خمرتها فكيف افيقُ

١

FIGURE 26 *First page from Nāṣīf al-Yāzijī,* Nabdha min dīwān al-shaykh nāṣīf al-yāzijī.
BEIRUT, 1853

the tapering of chapter/section endings into an inverted-triangular form, which can be seen in al-Yāzijī's *Kitab majmaʿ al-baḥrayn* (Fig. 25), links to scribal conventions in these publications are no longer as immediately apparent as they were in Press works from the 1830s. At the same time, most of the job works printed during this period exhibit simpler title pages than those seen in the 1830s. A number of these works, for instance, simply employ a single line of ornamental sorts as a border for the title page, with the title and, sometimes, the author, publisher and date of publication centered within the page's rectangular frame (Fig. 29 and Fig. 30).

What is particularly interesting is the fact that these simple borders are made up of the same metal borders and sorts as the ones use to recreate elaborate, illumination-inspired frames on the title pages and within the headpieces of Press productions from the 1830s. In some cases, like the title page seen in al-Bustānī's *Kitāb misbāḥ al-ṭālib* (from 1854), some links can still be established with an interest in visually experimenting with sorts to create unique page borders (Fig. 31). However, the post-1830s publications in general eschew the most obvious manuscript conventions from past productions in favor of a sleek, simplified aesthetic that is equally experimental and innovative. Arguably, these visual and organizational choices could be seen as simple implementations of the standards and practices, set by the Americans' print shop, that the Press's compositors, printers, and other laborers were most familiar with. Indeed, one could argue that local authors perhaps felt it most convenient and cost effective to rely on pre-set methods and designs to complete the task at hand. However, the importance of the design programs adopted by al-Yāzijī, al-Bustānī, and other local intellectuals for their works lay neither in the Press's typeface, nor in other de facto implementations of production standards and aesthetics. Rather, the significance of such visual conventions is in the way in which they evidence an engagement with varying perspectives on what books should look like during a period that saw a heightened push-pull dynamic between customary modes of book production and printing practices.

## The Regional Visual Conventions of Print at Mid-Century

The fact that Arab Christians in the mission's employ were trained as copyists and scribes within local monastic scribal settings, and/or with access to books from regional presses, meant that most were quite familiar with early practices within the local publishing industry, where manuscript conventions were often adapted to the printed page. Given their close involvement at the Press, and their access to

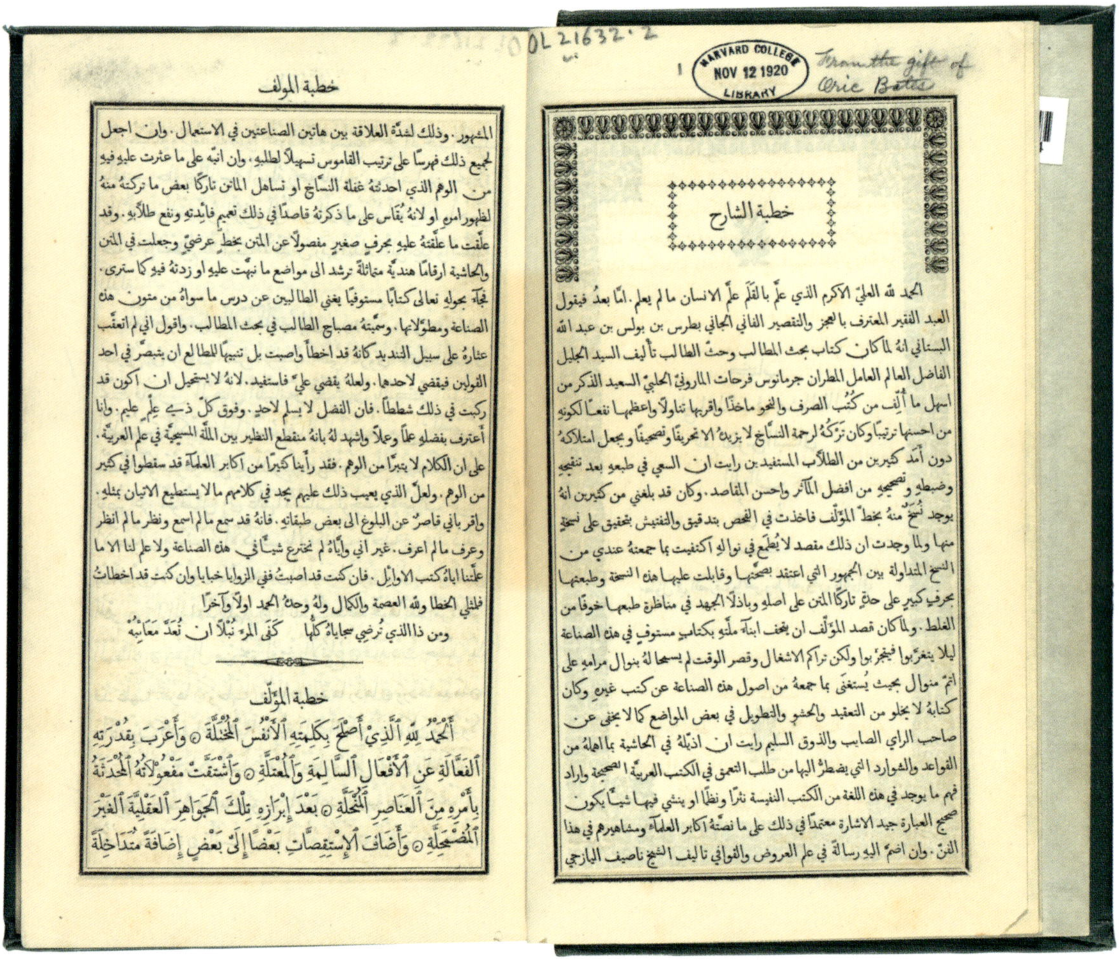

FIGURE 27 *Opening pages from Buṭrus al-Bustānī,* Kitāb misbāḥ al-tālib fī baḥth al-maṭālib. BEIRUT, 1854

and/ or involvement in its works from the 1830s, both al-Yāzijī and al-Bustānī were certainly aware of alternative approaches to Arabic printing practices. Any visual or organizational choices made in publications by these scholars could not simply have been instances of co-opting standard practices at the American Press. Rather, their significance lay in the studied decisions made by these individuals to incorporate certain conventions and to exclude others.

This becomes clear when comparing the visual dimensions of works by al-Yāzijī with those of contemporaneous printed books in circulation. One example is a letterpress book on travels in Egypt, Turkey, and Europe, by Ibrāhīm ibn Khalīl al-Najjār (d. 1864), the chief military surgeon in Beirut at the time,[55] printed in 1855.[56] The book's title page, for instance, shows numerous decorative elements

55 The following description of the author appears on his book's title page: "Ibrāhīm Afandī al-ṭabīb al-awwal li-l-'asākir al-Shāhāniyya fī madīnat Bayrūt." Taken from a copy held at the Archives and Special Collections, Jafet Library, American University of Beirut (CA956 N16A vol.1: c.1).

56 *Kitāb miṣbāḥ al-sārī wa nuzhat al-qārī* (Beirut, 1855). Ellis, *Arabic Books*, 1:723. He published an earlier travelogue while in Europe as *Hadiyyat al-Aḥbāb wa Hidāyat al-Ṭullāb* (Marseillies, 1850). Al-Najjār also went on to found his own press, *al-Maṭba'a al-Sharqiyya* (the Oriental Press), in Beirut in 1858. Thanks to Anthony Edwards for provided me with a short biographic entry on al-Najjār.

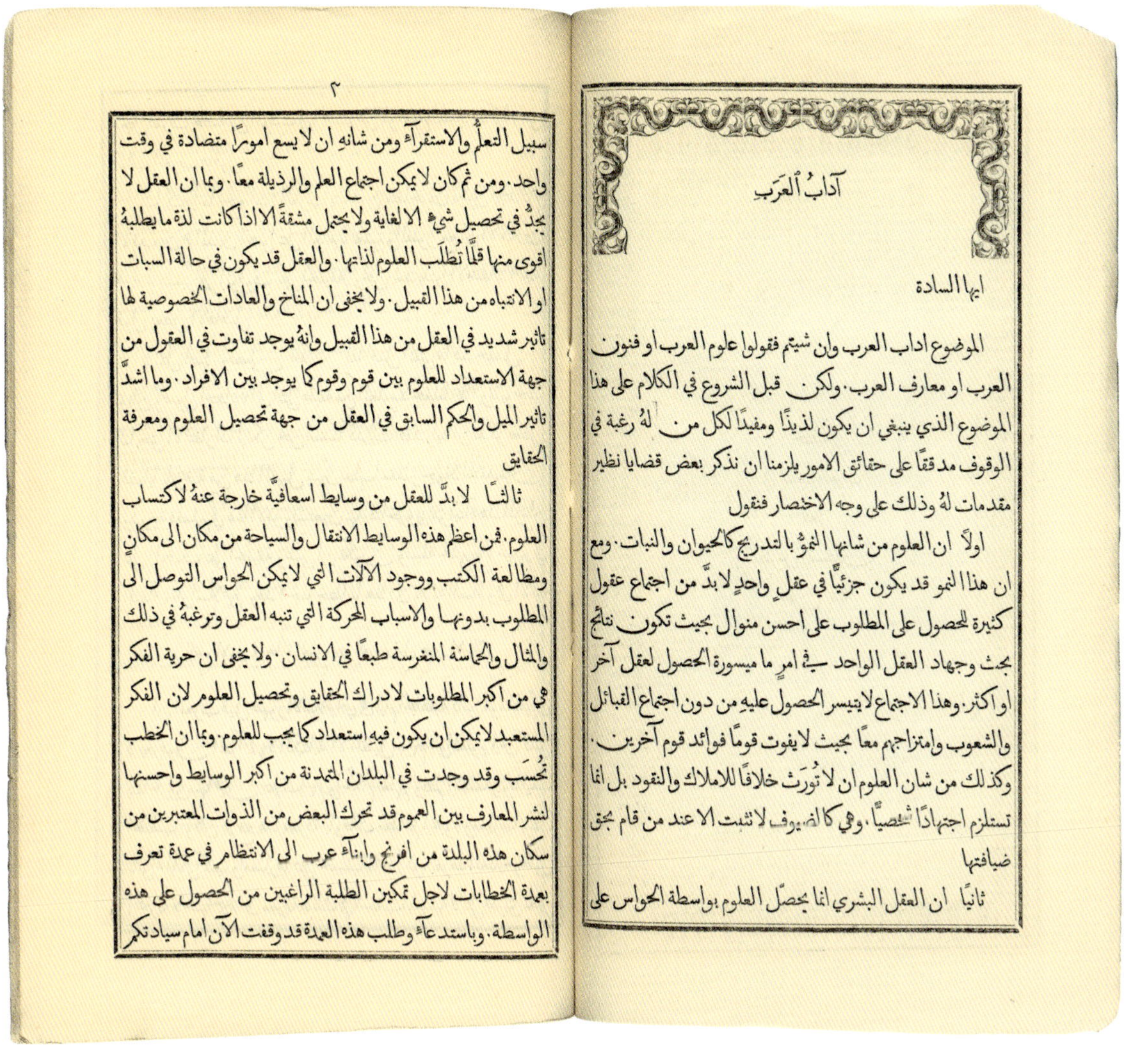

آداب العرب

ايها السادة

الموضوع اداب العرب وان شيتم فقولوا علوم العرب او فنون
العرب او معارف العرب. ولكن قبل الشروع في الكلام على هذا
الموضوع الذي ينبغي ان يكون لذيذًا ومفيدًا لكل من له رغبة في
الوقوف مدققًا على حقائق الامور يلزمنا ان نذكر بعض قضايا نظير
مقدمات له وذلك على وجه الاختصار فنقول
اولًا ان العلوم من شانها النموّ بالتدريج كالحيوان والنبات. ومع
ان هذا النمو قد يكون جزئيًا في عقلٍ واحدٍ لا بدّ من اجتماع عقول
كثيرة للحصول على المطلوب على احسن منوال بحيث تكون نتائج
بحث وجهاد العقل الواحد في امرٍ ما ميسورة الحصول لعقل آخر
او اكثر. وهذا الاجتماع لا يتيسر الحصول عليهِ من دون اجتماع القبائل
والشعوب وامتزاجهم معًا بحيث لا يفوت قومًا فوائد قوم آخرين.
وكذلك من شان العلوم ان لا تورّث خلافًا للاملاك والنقود بل انما
تستلزم اجتهادًا شخصيًا. وهي كالضيوف لا تثبت الا عند من قام بحق
ضيافتها
ثانيًا ان العقل البشري انما يحصّل العلوم بواسطة الحواس على

٣

سبيل التعلّم والاستقراء ومن شانهِ ان لا يسع امورًا متضادة في وقت
واحد. ومن ثم كان لا يمكن اجتماع العلم والرذيلة معًا. وبما ان العقل لا
يجدّ في تحصيل شيء الا لغاية ولا يحتمل مشقة الا اذا كانت لذة ما يطلبهُ
اقوى منها قلّما تُطلب العلوم لذاتها. والعقل قد يكون في حالة السبات
او الانتباه من هذا القبيل. ولا يخفى ان المناخ والعادات الخصوصية لها
تاثير شديد في العقل من هذا القبيل وانهُ يوجد تفاوت في العقول من
جهة الاستعداد للعلوم بين قوم وقوم كما يوجد بين الافراد. وما اشدّ
تاثير الميل والحكم السابق في العقل من جهة تحصيل العلوم ومعرفة
الحقايق
ثالثًا لا بدّ للعقل من وسايط اسعافية خارجة عنهُ لاكتساب
العلوم. فمن اعظم هذه الوسايط الانتقال والسياحة من مكان الى مكان
ومطالعة الكتب ووجود الآلات التي لا يمكن الحواس التوصل الى
المطلوب بدونها والاسباب المحركة التي تنبه العقل وترغبهُ في ذلك
والمثال والحماسة المغروسة طبعًا في الانسان. ولا يخفى ان حرية الفكر
هي من اكبر المطلوبات لادراك الحقايق وتحصيل العلوم لان الفكر
المستعبد لا يمكن ان يكون فيهِ استعداد كما يجب للعلوم. وبما ان الخطب
تُحسب وقد وجدت في البلدان المتمدنة من اكبر الوسايط واحسنها
لنشر المعارف بين العموم قد تحرك البعض من الذوات المعتبرين من
سكان هذه البلدة من افرنج وابناء عرب الى الانتظام في عمدة تعرف
بعمدة الخطابات لاجل تمكين الطلبة الراغبين من الحصول على هذه
الواسطة. وباستدعاء وطلب هذه العمدة قد وقفت الآن امام سيادتكم

FIGURE 28 *Opening pages from Buṭrus al-Bustānī,* Khuṭba fī ādāb al-ʿarab. BEIRUT, 1859

which do not appear in its counterparts from the American Press, such as the use of vegetal ornamental corners that are connected by borders made of rosette-like sorts, some of which are used to flank lines of the centered title-page text (Fig. 32). While it is not clear at which Beirut-based press this book was printed (no publisher is listed), it is apparent, from the typeface and style of ornaments used, that it did not come off the American Press and differed from its publications' design program. Two later editions of the same book (from 1858 to 1860) were also published in Beirut, with no publisher listed. It may be that this work was printed at the Jesuit press, which, as previously mentioned, began operating its letterpress in 1854. What this example illustrates is that while some publications from this period and region imply a growing trend towards the incorporation of title pages (in the "Western" sense of the tradition, meaning that the page includes the title, author, date and/or publisher[57]), the visual conventions used vary. Some presses continued employing

57 The significance of title pages, particularly their connection to the emergence of printing practices in Europe and the Middle East, is discussed in Chapter 3.

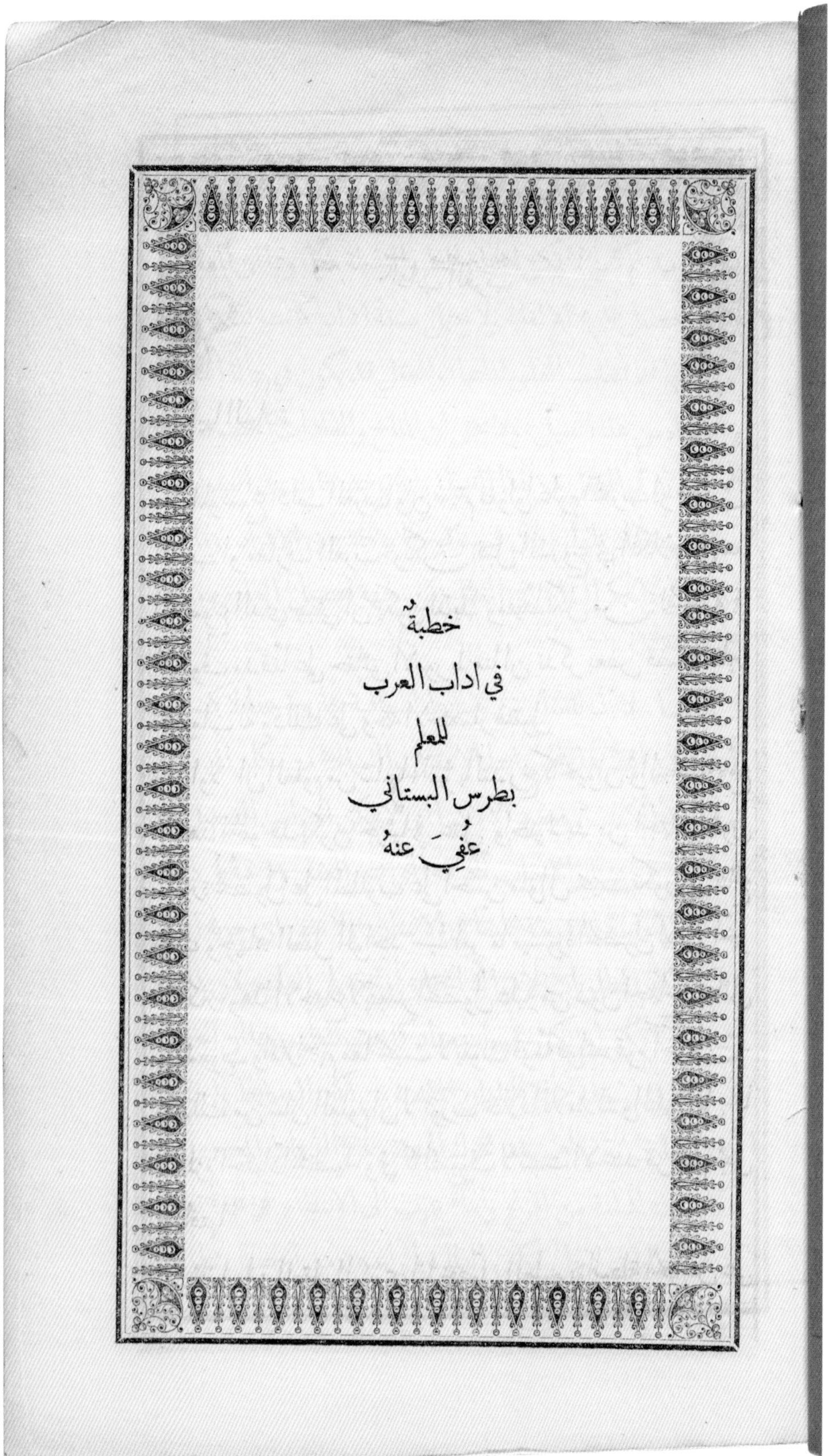
خطبةٌ
في اداب العرب
للمعلم
بطرس البستاني
عُفِيَ عنهُ

FIGURE 29 *Title page from Buṭrus al-Bustānī,* Khuṭba fī ādāb al-ʿarab.
BEIRUT, 1859

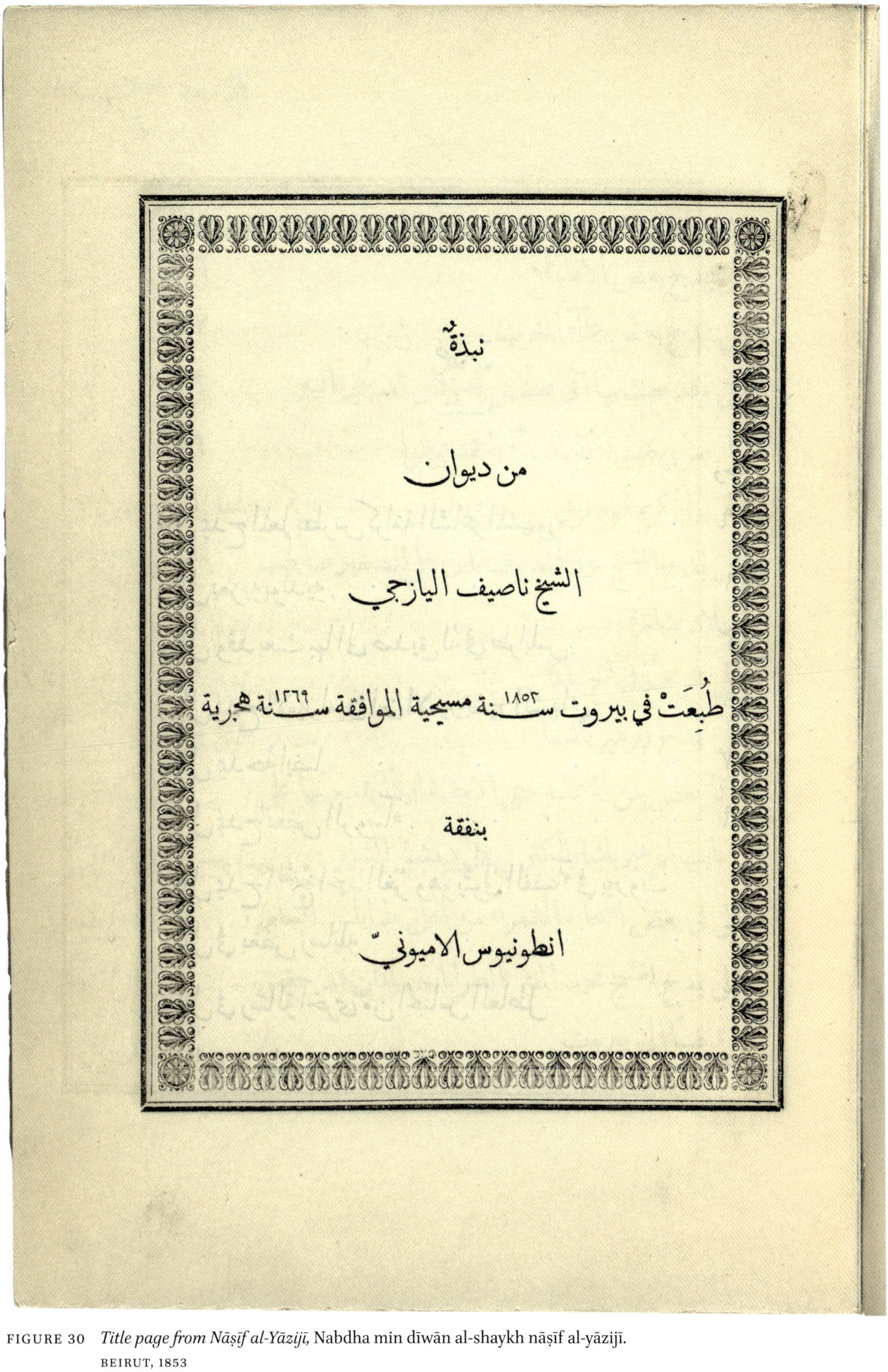

نبذةٌ

من ديوان

الشيخ ناصيف اليازجي

طُبِعَتْ في بيروت سنة ١٨٥٣ مسيحية الموافقة سنة ١٢٦٩ هجرية

بنفقة

انطونيوس الاميونيّ

FIGURE 30 *Title page from Nāṣīf al-Yāzijī,* Nabdha min dīwān al-shaykh nāṣīf al-yāzijī.
BEIRUT, 1853

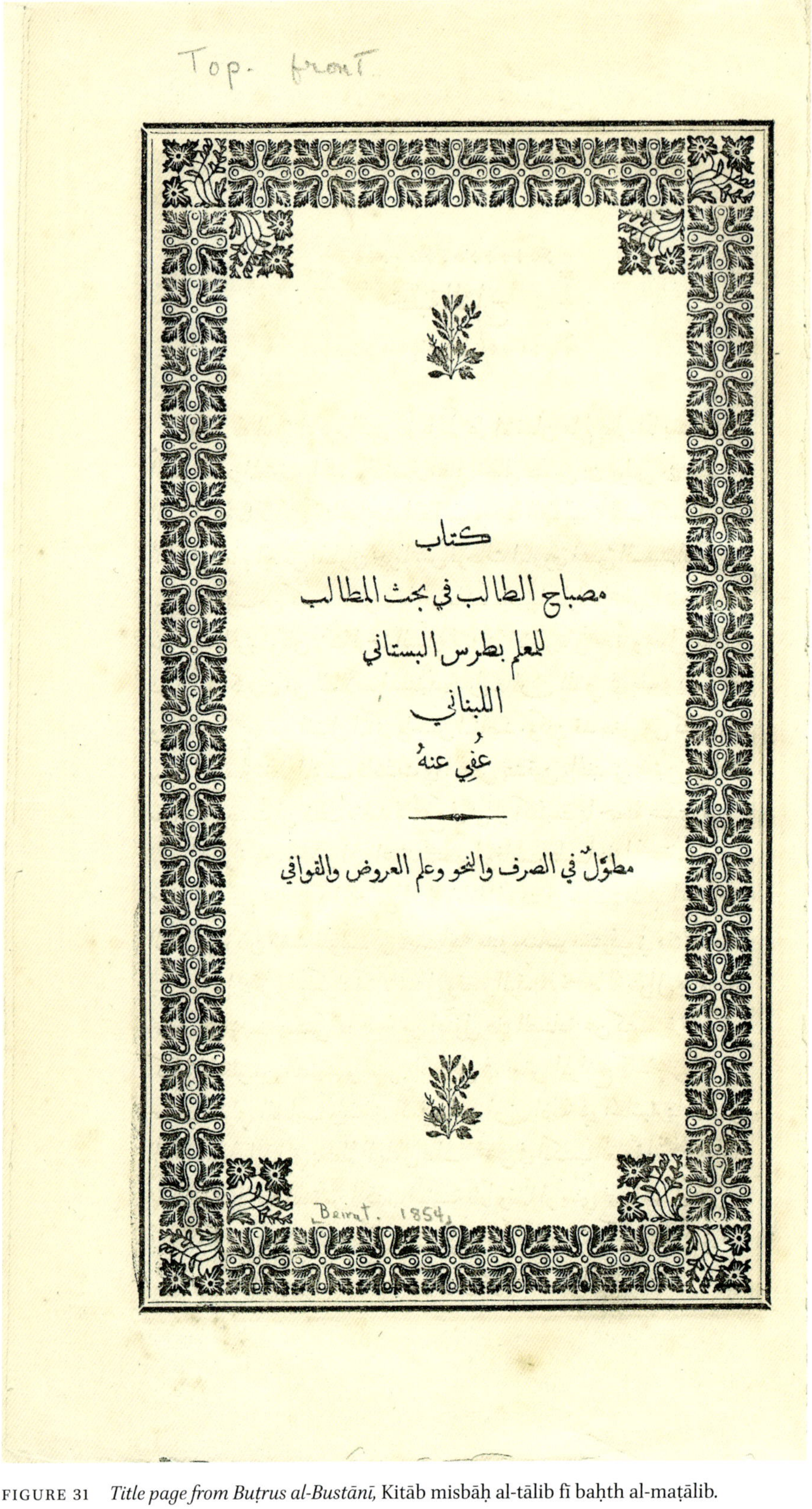
Top- front

كتاب
مصباح الطالب في بحث المطالب
للمعلم بطرس البستاني
اللبناني
عُفِي عنهُ

مطوَّلٌ في الصرف والنحو وعلم العروض والقوافي

Beirut. 1854

FIGURE 31 *Title page from Buṭrus al-Bustānī,* Kitāb misbāḥ al-tālib fī baḥth al-maṭālib.
BEIRUT, 1854

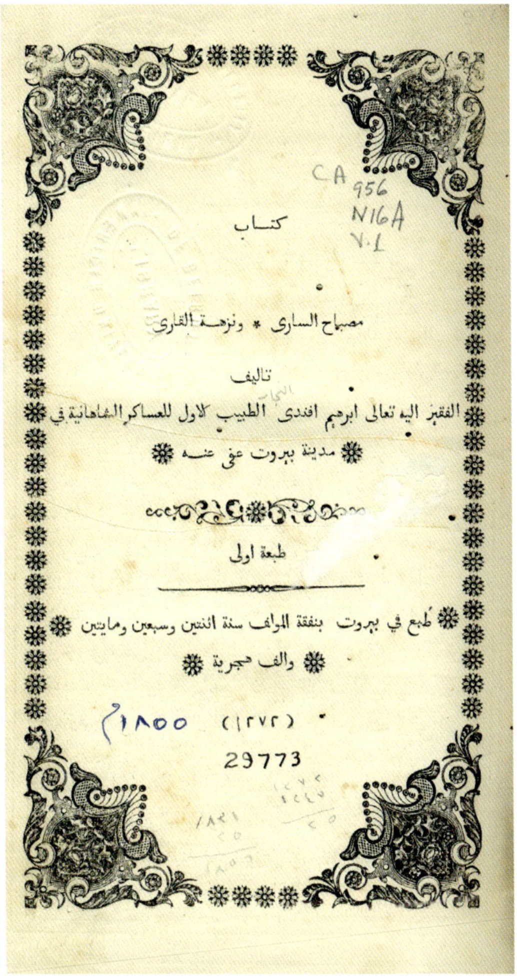


FIGURE 32 *Title page from Ibrāhīm ibn Khalīl al-Najjār,* Kitāb miṣbāḥ al-sārī wa nuzhat al-qārī. BEIRUT, 1855

ornamental elements (see the Jesuit and Franciscan examples, Fig. 22 and Fig. 23), many of which were throwbacks to scribal customs, while others, like the American Press, seemed to move further away from manuscript traditions.

More germane to the comparison with al-Yāzijī's *Kitāb majmaʿ al-baḥrayn* are the contemporaneous editions of al-Ḥarīrī's *Maqāmāt* that were printed from 1856–1857 at Muslim-owned, state-funded presses in neighboring and outlying cities.[58] One such example was printed in 1856 via letterpress at *Dār al-Ṭibāʿa*, Cairo (Fig. 33), while another (a lithograph version) was produced at the ʿAbbās Mirza-sponsored presses in Tabriz between 1856/7 (Fig. 34). The fact that varied editions of this text were issued in the span of one year from three different presses hints at the fact that this historic literary work resonated with audiences across regions during this era, particularly so for intellectuals interested in translating classical texts into products of print technologies. This relates to the growing popularity of the classical literary genre amongst such agents at the time.

Interestingly, unlike al-Yāzijī's publications from the 1850s, these editions produced on Muslim-owned presses bear great resemblances to the products of scribal conventions. For instance, in the example from Cairo, a highly decorated *sarlawḥ* made up of ornamental metal sorts caps the book's introductory page, a practice reminiscent of al-Yāzijī's first printed work from 1837 that the scholar now seemed to have abandoned. Such works from regional presses also clearly continue the tradition of marginal glosses or scholia, popular in regional manuscripts, which present a culmination of textual corrections, interpretations, explanations, and inter-textual readings. In scribal practices, the manner of adding textual glosses (*taḥshiyya*) frequently entailed writing interlinear annotations and/or including such commentary at (sometimes varying) angles from the primary orientation of the text.[59] In this way, these printed elements reflect the kind of handwritten exegeses that would normally populate the margins of manuscripts. This practice is most noticeable in the lithographed example from Tabriz, which exhibits the intricate layers of

58 The popularity of al-Ḥarīrī's *Maqāmāt* amongst an emergent print readership certainly parallels the genre's resurgence during the eighteenth-century, when illustrated versions of this text were being copied in large numbers. See Jaakko Hämeen-Anttila, "An Old-Fashioned Genre – Maqāma in the 18th Century," *Rocznik Orientalistyczny* LXV, no. 2 (2012): 5–12.

59 For more on the different categories of glosses and the methods in which they were written, see Adam Gacek, *Arabic Manuscripts: A Vademecum for Readers* (Leiden: Brill, 2009), 114–17.

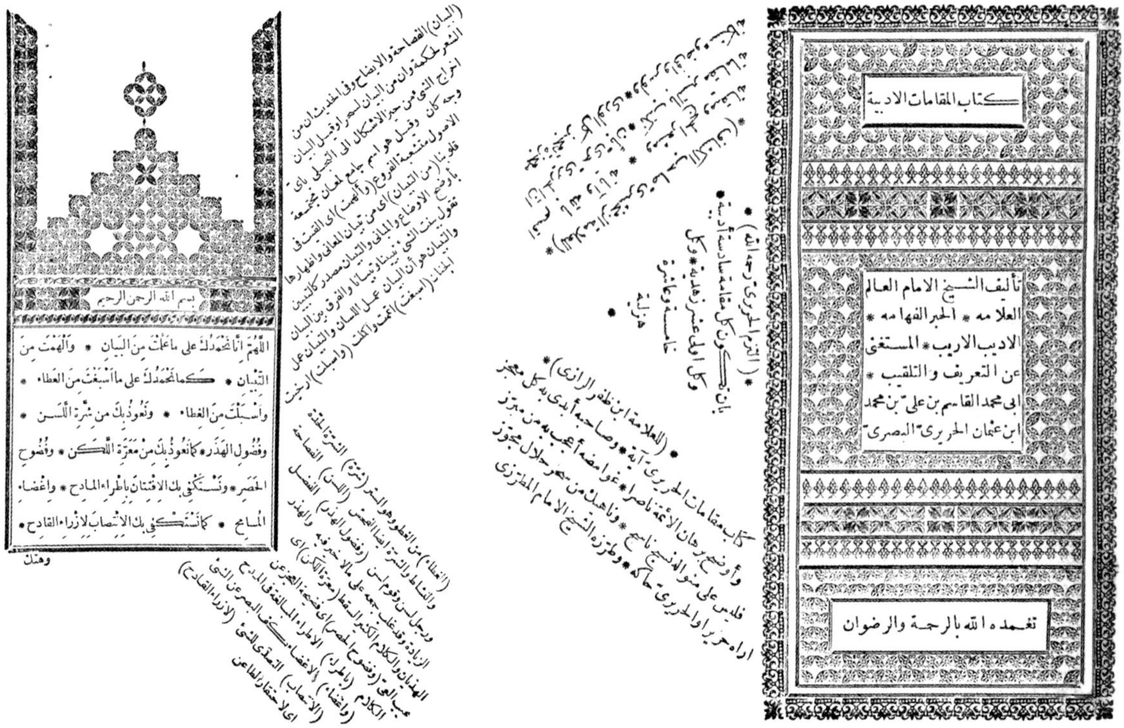


FIGURE 33 Right, *title page;* left, *first page from* Maqāmāt al-ḥarīrī fī al-lugha al-ʿarabiyya wa-l-funūn al-adabiyya. CAIRO: DĀR AL-ṬIBĀʿA, 1856

writing created when multiple lines of marginal interpretation punctuate and interface with the body text, lending an unexpected visual dimension to the complexities of the Barthesian "writerly text."[60]

Al-Yāzijī's *Majmaʿ al-baḥrayn*, on the other hand, falls in line with both the simplicity of the American Press's design program at the time and with its presentation of external references in the form of footnotes, which were common to contemporary Western print traditions.[61] The appearance of the footnote in Arabic books at this time was likely limited to the realm of print, with manuscripts mostly utilizing marginal notes for their exegeses. For example, footnotes in Arabic historical chronicles made an appearance in nineteenth-century publications as aspects of "historicism" became increasingly popular in history and narrative genres during an age of modernization.[62]

### The Question of Technology

In considering Arabic-script books from other presses in the region, it is necessary to make note

60 See Roland Barthes, *S/Z* (Oxford: Blackwell Publishing, 2002), 4–6.

61 Experimentations with footnotes in European book production can be seen in incunabula from the pre-sixteenth century period. See Elizabeth Eisenstein, *The Printing Revolution in Early Modern Europe* (Cambridge: Canto, 1993), 22.

62 Yoav Di-Capua, *Gatekeepers of the Arab Past: Historians and History Writing in Twentieth-Century Egypt* (Berkeley: University of California Press, 2009), 44. For a general overview of the footnote's connection to modern forms of historical writing, see Anthony Grafton, *The Footnote: A Curious History* (Cambridge, MA: Harvard University Press, 1997).

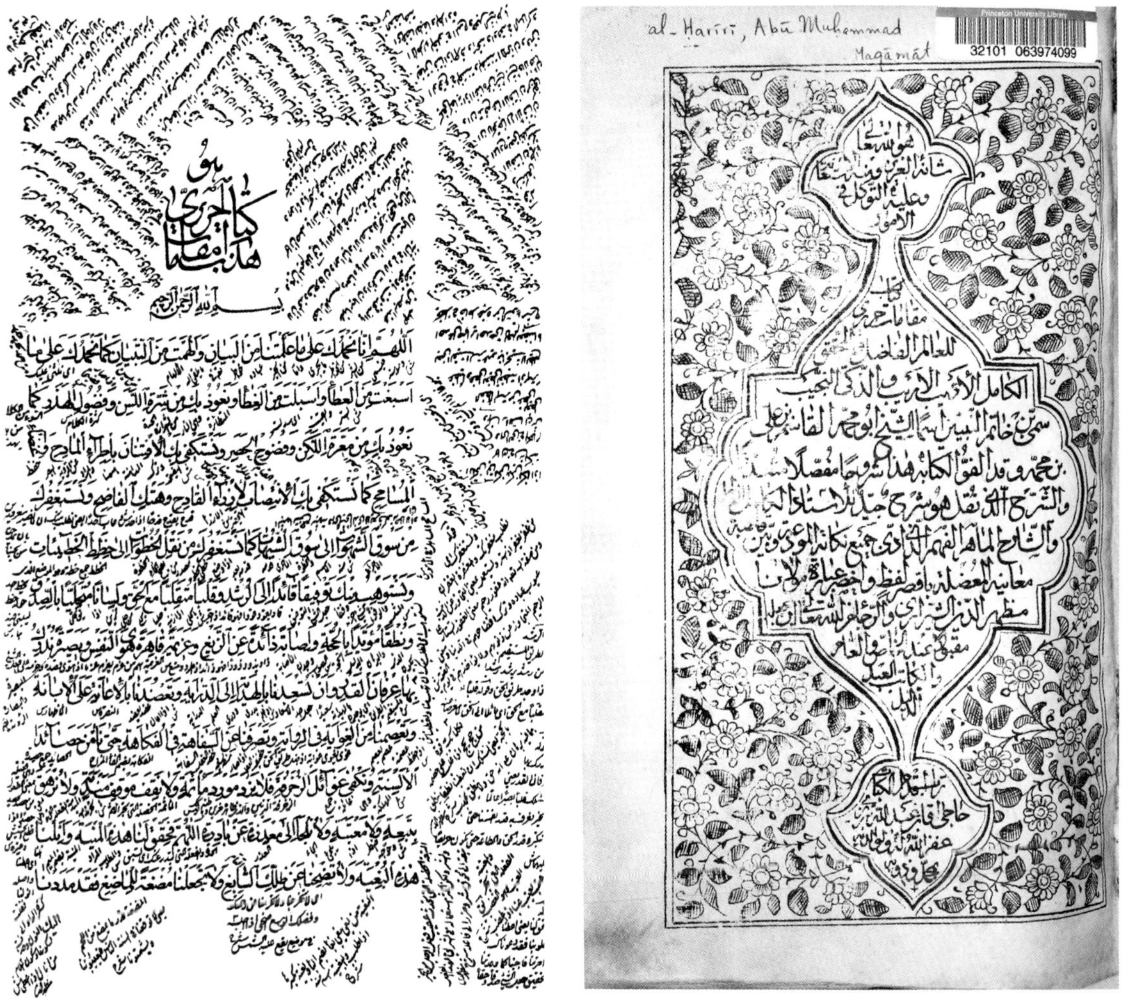


FIGURE 34 Right, *title page;* left, *first page from* Maqāmāt al-ḥarīrī [maʿa] sharḥ … muẓhir al-dīn al-shīrāzī. TABRIZ, 1856/7

of the relationship between visual elements and technological limitations. Books produced in Qajar Iran, such as the edition of al-Ḥarīrī's *Maqāmāt* from Tabriz, were printed on lithographic presses and letterpress ones. Persian lithographic printing centers during the nineteenth century included cities like Tabriz and Tehran,[63] as well as in surrounding urban centers like Lucknow at the Muslim press of Naṣīr al-Dīn Haydar, and presses in Bombay and Lahore.[64] The importance of Tabriz, in addition to its being known for lithographic printing from at least the early 1830s, is

63 Tabriz was known for lithographic printing from the 1830s. See Marzolph, "Illustrated Persian Lithographic Editions of the Shahname" *Edebiyat* 13, no. 2 (2003), 178. This was also the site of the earliest examples of Persian printing with moveable type in the region. See Nile Green, "Persian Print and the Stanhope Revolution: Industrialization, Evangelicalism, and the Birth of Printing in Early Qajar Iran," *Comparative Studies of South Asia, Africa and The Middle East* (hereafter cited as *CSSAAME*) 30, no. 3 (2012): 480. However, most publishing houses in Qajar Iran were in Tehran.

64 For more, see O.P. Scheglova, "Lithograph Versions of Persian Manuscripts of Indian Manufacture in the Nineteenth Century," *Manuscripta Orientalia* 5, no. 1 (1999): 12–22.

that it was where the first lithographed version of the Qur'an was published in the 1832/4.[65] Tabriz was also the site of the earliest examples of Persian printing with moveable type in the region, which began around 1817 through the work of the printer Mirza Zayn al-ʿAbidīn.[66] Although a large number of books produced in Qajar Iran were printed via the letterpress,[67] this technology was abandoned from the late 1850s until at least the 1870s in favor of lithography.[68]

Visually speaking, one would expect that books printed using the lithographic press would recall manuscript conventions more closely than those printed on letterpresses. The translation of paper-based scribal skills and techniques, such as those used for illuminations, calligraphy, and figural illustrations, was much better suited to lithography. In this printing method, the artwork was drawn on specially treated paper that would then be transferred to the lithographic stone. As a result, books coming off lithographic presses in the region demonstrated more calligraphic fluidity, finer details, and more elaborate ornamentation than their letterpress-printed equivalents, which had to rely on the use of rigid metal type and preset grids, the latter necessary for establishing the location of margins and body text.

Given the frequently cumbersome nature of setting multiple lines of Arabic type with the inclusion of vocalization marks, one may wonder why lithographic printing was not the default method used for all of the region's print shops. The American mission even considered this possibility in 1833, as demonstrated in a letter from the ABCFM Board Secretaries to Eli Smith, telling the young missionary bound for Beirut that he would have "use of a lithographic press … the value of which for printing in the Arabic and Syriac languages, your knowledge of the lithographic art will enable you very speedily to determine."[69] However, although a few items were printed on a lithographic press at the American Press, namely sets of calligraphic alphabet and spelling cards for use in the mission's elementary schools, lithography was not turned to as a serious book-making mechanism. Initially, this may have been because the two lithographic presses were faulty, with one eventually fixed by 1836.[70] At the same time, while facilitating the emulation of scribal conventions, lithography did not provide the same "fail-safes" when it came to the production of critical texts. Specifically, letterpress printing provided multiple opportunities for correcting and proofreading texts. Composing texts with moveable type provides the option to correct texts during the early and the later stages of the printing process. With lithography, however, corrections would need to be included in the margins, as the original text could not be altered once transferred to the stone. Producing lithographed books was also more expensive than letterpress printing at the time. For instance, lithographic presses from this period (unlike letterpress machinery) did not utilize steam technology (which made printing more efficient). Additionally, producing lithographed books that adhered to scribal conventions required labor skilled in calligraphy, illuminations, and illustrations (much like the labor employed in manuscript workshops). Another point to consider is how the role of this printing method (at least from the Americans' perspective) may have mirrored that of its contemporaries in the United States and Europe: as a tool for larger prints, images, advertisement posters, and maps. Based on press records from 1836, for instance, it seems that this printing method was

65 Marzolph, "Persian Lithographic Editions," 178.

66 Green, "Persian Print and Stanhope," 480.

67 At least sixty Persian books were printed by letterpress in Iran up to 1856. See Ulrich Marzolph, "Persian Incunabula: A Definition and Assessment," *Gutenberg-Jahrbuch* 82 (2007): 205–20.

68 Marzolph, "Persian Lithographic Editions," 178.

69 ABC 60, Eli Smith Papers, 1801 1857, Letters to Eli Smith, vol. 1, Board Secretaries to Smith, 7 Sep 1833.

70 "Quarterly Report of the Superintendent of the Press," 30 Sep 1835, PHS, RG 115-1-25.

only viewed as capable of producing low-volume, single printed sheets and not complete books.[71]

Nonetheless, various regional presses chose to propagate scribal customs, even while others (such as the American Press) seemed to move further away from manuscript traditions despite the limitations of print technologies. For instance, while including multi-directional marginal glosses was relatively easy for the press in Tabriz, in the letter-pressed example from Cairo (Fig. 33) the inclusion of peripheral text on diagonal lines with metal type was probably more difficult. However, as evidenced in numerous books printed on presses in Cairo, this technological hurdle did not necessarily prevent the inclusion of some ornamental elements and marginal notes. The fact that these presses were state-funded (for which funding, at the time, was more consistent than that of private printing establishments) also means that certain luxuries could be afforded in the layouts of their respective publications. Thus, while books printed in Cairo and Tabriz relied on different technologies, they both indisputably continued turning to scribal sources for inspiration, even as they formulated a visual language distinct to the printed Arabic-script book.

## The "Lure" of a Typeface

Some important questions to consider regarding the conventions of choice amongst local Arab scholars are: did the "unique" design of the American Press's typeface set its publications apart from others in circulation? Moreover, to what extent was the Press's overall design program appealing to emergent local printers, and why? Scholars have attributed the significance of the American Press in local printing efforts to its typeface, the "American Arabic" family of fonts first acquired by the mission in 1841. The general scholarly consensus on the subject of the Arab press is that the American mission's set of types was (at least from 1842 to the 1860s) more desirable than other local or European-produced alternatives.[72] Focusing on the appeal and efficiency of this typeface in a narrow interpretation, however, does not locate the printed word within the larger visual vehicle of the book, its production, and its socio-political significance. Additionally, some scholarship on the American Mission that highlights the key roles of local agents within the missionary framework are highlighted, nevertheless perpetuates a unilateral, missionary narrative when it comes to the American Arabic typeface.[73] At times, Eli Smith is situated as a "pioneer" of Arabic type and printing advancements that "set the standard for nineteenth-century Arabic printing."[74] Such reductionist statements overplay Smith's contributions to these achievements, while (perhaps inadvertently) overlooking the equally significant roles of local Press employees.

It does appear that this typeface garnered plenty of attention from locals eager to print their own books. The Greek Orthodox scholar Khalīl al-Khūrī (d. 1907), who was also an early entrepreneur, future state official,[75] and publisher

71 "Quarterly Report on the state of the Press," 30 Sep 1836; "Report on the Press," 31 Dec 1836, PHS, RG 115-1-25.

72 Dagmar Glass lists numerous books printed in Beirut, at private local presses, which clearly used copies of the mission's American Arabic, stating that this typeface's availability resulted in "a remarkable increase in the output of Arabic publications in Lebanon." See Glass, *Malta, Beirut, Leipzig and Beirut Again*, 27.

73 For instance, sociologist Samir Khalaf cites an article published in 1964 that claims Eli Smith's Arabic typeface design "provid[ed] the Arabic world stretching from Morocco to the Philippines with an aesthetically pleasing and orthographically correct typeface." Robert L. Daniel, "American Influences in the Near East before 1861," *American Quarterly* 16, no. 1 (1964): 81, cited in Khalaf, *Protestant Missionaries in the Levant: Ungodly Puritans, 1820–1860* (Oxford: Taylor and Francis, 2012), Kindle edition, 205.

74 Discussed in Ussama Makdisi, "'Anti-Americanism' in the Arab World: An Interpretation of a Brief History," *Journal of American History* 89, no. 2 (2002): 542.

75 After the Maronite-Druze civil wars of 1860, he served as a secretary for the Ottoman minister of Foreign

(in 1858) of one of the region's first newspapers, *Ḥadīqat al-akhbār* (The Garden of News), wrote to Smith in 1856 about procuring a copy of the American Arabic typeface.[76] Even before then, in 1853, Smith received requests from locals for copies of this font. In a letter to Anderson, Smith explains that a group of locals had formed a company interested in establishing their own printing press, and hoped to purchase types from the mission.[77] Press catalogs, which listed books for sale, also included advertisements for different sizes of typefaces, thus indicating that the Press regularly cast and sold sets of type to local and regional presses.[78]

Interest in the typeface was not limited to independent scholars and entrepreneurs but also extended to other missionary presses, such as the Dominican mission in Mosul,[79] as well as the Jesuits, the Americans' main "rivals." According to the Jesuit priest Lūwīs Shaykhū, the Catholic press in Beirut purchased a "simple" set of the American typeface (*ḥurūfān amerkiyya basīṭa*) in 1868.[80] This is corroborated by American missionary accounts,[81] which further claim that "the type of our press is taking the precedence of the other kinds formerly in use."[82] In addition to bolstering the Press's reputation locally, the sale of typefaces was also a lucrative endeavor for an establishment that constantly needed to reassert its value to the Board at home. For example, in his account of type sales to the mission in Mosul, the missionary Henry Harris Jessup (d. 1910) states that the Dominicans spent as much as $300 on their purchase in 1870. At present-day rates that amounts to a little over $5,300.[83] Notably, this was also the basic yearly salary for al-Bustānī's mission-related services.[84]

The popularity of American Arabic, while attributed in missionary records to the "beauty" or "uniform nature" of its letters that closely emulated calligraphic writing,[85] stemmed from its solutions to the myriad problems that had long plagued attempts at Arabic-language printing, including its cursive nature and its use of vocalization marks. Unlike scripts of Latin origin, which allow for spaces

---

Affairs in Syria, Fu'ād Pasha. See Philip C. Sadgrove, "al-Khūrī, Khalīl (1836–1907)," in *Encyclopedia of Arabic Literature*, vol. 2., eds. Julie Meisami and Paul Starkey (London: Routledge, 1998), 448.

76 ABC 50, Box 3, al-Khūrī to Smith, 9 Jun 1856.

77 ABC 16.8.1, vol. 5, Smith to Anderson, 26 Dec 1853.

78 Many examples of these catalogs date to the late nineteenth century. For instance, see *Catalogue and Price List of Publications of the American Mission Press* (Beirut: American Press, 1884). The Press also printed type specimen booklets, such as *Specimens of Arabic Founts* (Beirut: American Mission Press, 1885), a copy of which is held the Archives and Special Collections, Jafet Library, American University of Beirut (CA686.2 S741s).

79 "At the earnest solicitation of the agent of the Dominican Convent at Mosul, we cast, for that Convent, three fonts of type." *The Missionary Herald* 66 (1870): 160. It is apparent from the Arabic pages of this Catholic mission's Bible (*Biblia Sacra Versio Arabica*) printed in 1874 by Josephi David (Yūsuf Dāwūd) that it used the American Arabic typeface. See Michael Albin, "A Preliminary Bibliography of Arabic Books Printed by the Dominican Fathers in Mosul," *Mélanges de l'Institut Dominicain d'Études Orientales* 16 (1983): 247–60.

80 Shaykhū, *Tārīkh fann al-ṭibāʿa*, 61. Given Shaykhū's bias as a Jesuit priest, however, he makes a point of downplaying the American typeface's use and value to the Catholic Press, stating that the Jesuits continued their efforts to procure a better font than the Americans'. This was done in the 1870s, on site at the press, and the first Jesuit book printed with their new typeface was their Bible in 1876. While Shaykhū does not mention the typeface's designer, the process involved Ibrāhīm al-Yāzijī, a printer, editor, and translator working at the Jesuit press, who also happened to be Nāṣīf al-Yāzijī's son and who would have learnt the craft at the hands of his father.

81 "We have also furnished the Jesuit Convent of Beirut with new specimen types from which to make electrotype matrices." *The Missionary Herald* 66 (1870): 160.

82 Ibid.

83 Jessup, *Fifty-Three Years in Syria*, vol. 1 (New York: Fleming H. Revell, 1910), 362.

84 ABC 16.8.1, vol. 8, "Meeting at Van Dyck's," ʿAbay, 28 Sep 1847.

85 ABC 16.8.1, vol. 1, "Report on Arabic Type, Press Property, and Foundry, Mar 1844 [?]."

(or kerning) between each letterform, Arabic is written with connected characters, meaning that even a hairline between letters would be noticeable and distracting. While this was a common problem across the board in Arabic printing at the time, the American Arabic typeface was cut in a way that minimized this issue.[86] This is most apparent when comparing works printed with this font to those displaying the mission's earlier Watts typeface (discussed in Chapter 4). This new font family also allowed for better capability to print vocalization marks. Vowel marks, appearing above and below letterforms in most locally produced Arabic (specifically religious) manuscripts, are not critical to reading or understanding Arabic writing. However, vowel symbols play a key role in eliminating ambiguity in meaning and pronunciation, and thus found standard use in devotional books like the Qur'an (as well as some examples of poetry).

Aware of these marks' significance to certain local reading practices (mainly amongst Muslim denominations), the missionaries hoped to produce copies of vocalized texts as a way to attract such readers. As such, their new typeface adopted an "expedient" in printing vocalization marks.[87] Reports describe this as "[Smith's] invention of the Grooved Mould by which types cast from it were to receive the vowels & the nice adjustment of the face of the letter to enable the vowels to come over and under."[88] Basically, the new metal type contained grooves into which compositors could insert metal sorts with vowel mark glyphs, in this way bringing each vowel closer to its respective letter. In the older models, such as the Watts typeface used at the American Press during the 1830s, the vowels were printed on separate lines above and below the lines of text. This made it confusing to discern which letter each vocalization mark belonged to. The Americans felt that including vocalization marks in their publications would not only speak to the authenticity of their texts, but could also serve as a graphic custom familiar to local readers.

However, from reports sent to the American Bible Society (ABS), it almost sounds as if the missionaries were selling the importance of vowel marks as necessary visual attributes that emulated the Qur'an's "style," and were not just linguistic features. For instance, in a report from 1864 requesting funding for electrotyping vocalized editions of its then completed Protestant Arabic Bible, members of the mission stated that vocalized editions of the Bible: "are more particularly intended for the Mohammedans, to conform to their idea of what a sacred book should be, and to stand fairly for comparison beside their Koran."[89] A second entry, by the missionary Henry Jessup, reads: "A Mohammedan…on seeing the vowelled edition of the [Protestant Bible] gave out word that the lost *Enjeel* or New Testament [of the Qur'an] was found."[90] It may have been that the mission's entries in these reports, which highly exaggerated the centrality of vocalization marks to reading Arabic, were geared towards an American audience, largely unfamiliar with the "Near East," let alone the Arabic language. Thus these reports were likely the missionaries' attempts at facilitating the "sale" of the importance of vocalization marks for their newly minted Bible.[91]

Although the ability to include vowel marks likely appealed to local Arab scholars, it is doubtful

86 ABC 16.8.1, vol. 1, "Report on Arabic Type, Press Property, and Foundry, Mar 1844 [?]."

87 Ibid.

88 ABC 16.8.1, vol. 5, Hurter to Anderson, 17 Aug 1857. For a more detailed description of this mechanism, see J.F. Coakley, "Homan Hallock, Punchcutter," *Printing History* 45, no. 1 (2003): 26–27.

89 The report was published by Joseph Holdich and William J.R. Taylor as *The Arabic Scriptures* (New York: American Bible Society, 1864), 4.

90 *The Arabic Scriptures*, 7.

91 Rana Issa argues that these "exaggerated jubilations [of the need for vocalization marks] were intended for American donors, whose financial support guaranteed technological upgrades at the press." Issa, "The Bible as Commodity: Modern Patterns of Arabic Language Standardization and Bible Commoditization in the Levant" (PhD Diss., University of Oslo, 2014), 127.

that such marks were seen as imperative to successful Arabic publishing. Aside from religious writing and incantations, for instance, fully vocalized texts hardly made an appearance in books printed at the American Press from this period, largely because there was no real need for or interest in vocalization within scribal traditions at the time. Some examples using complete vowel marks include sermons and similar texts translated into print verbatim from original manuscripts, such as al-Bustānī's production of the Maronite Archbishop Jibrīl Farḥāt's sermon in al-Bustānī's *Kitāb misbāḥ al-ṭālib fī baḥth al-maṭālib* (see bottom left of Fig. 27). It appears that the way in which vowel marks were set via the "grooved molds" of the American Arabic typeface still made composing lines of fully vocalized text an extensively time-consuming task fraught with potential for error. Attempts at printing a vocalized edition of the Protestant Bible in 1860, for instance, proved too time consuming and difficult.[92] In a letter from 1864 addressed to the ABS it is stated that setting the vowel marks for a single Bible took the Press type compositor over a year.[93] Additionally, there seemed to be a number of issues with producing variations in typeface designs that still used this method for vowel marks. For instance, Smith mentions inconsistencies between small (body text) fonts and larger ones for use in headings and titles, which he erroneously described as "thuluth" in style.[94] It appears that the numerous versions and sizes of American Arabic produced between the 1840s and the 1860s contained various inconsistencies, particularly in the inclusion of vowel marks.[95]

There is also the question of the over-selling of the aesthetic and technical value of this particular typeface at this point in time. Although it did show much improvement over older incarnations in its production of a cursive Arabic script that was both legible and visually balanced, it was not without occasional errors. Usually the result of faulty casting, gaps between letterforms were still common recurrences in works printed by Arab scholars at the American Press (Fig. 35). This remained an issue in Arabic letterpress printing until the invention of typecasting and typesetting machinery during the late 1800s. In particular, equipment by Linotype and the Monotype machine allowed for more intricate overlaps between separate letterforms. These technologies also improved the process of composing and printing texts with complete vocalization marks.[96]

While its efficacy as a tool for textual communication certainly contributed to its positive reception, the popularity of the American Arabic typeface amongst surrounding missions and local printers was largely due to the fact that the Press, over the years, had acquired the equipment necessary to cast and cut fonts of this typeface in-house, making it easier and cheaper to order. Since there were only a handful of presses operating regionally at the time, some at quite some distance from Beirut, there were few local type foundries, and even fewer options for highly legible and relatively well-designed typefaces. The Jesuit press and other

92 ABC 16.8.1, vol. 7, Van Dyck to Anderson, 12 Apr 1860. It was not until the mid-1860s that the Press succeeded in producing fully vocalized Bibles in multiple editions by relying on electrotype plates. Initially suggested in 1862, electrotyping the mission's newly completed Bible with vowel marks first took place in 1864. Since the plate-making technology was still not in use by local presses, plates for the vocalized Bible were produced in New York under Van Dyck's supervision and then shipped to Beirut. See ABC 16.8.1, vol. 8, Hallock to Hurter, 15 Mar 1862; "Meeting in Beirut," 23 Jan 1865; ABC 16.8.1, vol.7, Van Dyck to Anderson, 8 Sep 1865; ABC 16.8.1, vol. 8, "Meeting," 20 Mar 1866.

93 Holdich and Taylor, 7.

94 ABC 16.8.1, vol. 5, Smith to Anderson, 15 Feb 1849; Smith to Anderson, 31 Jul 1849.

95 For a detailed outline of these different versions, see Coakley, "Homan Hallock," 18–41.

96 Huda Smitshuijzen-Abifares, *Arabic Typography: A Comprehensive Sourcebook* (London: Saqi, 2001), 79–80, 131–32.

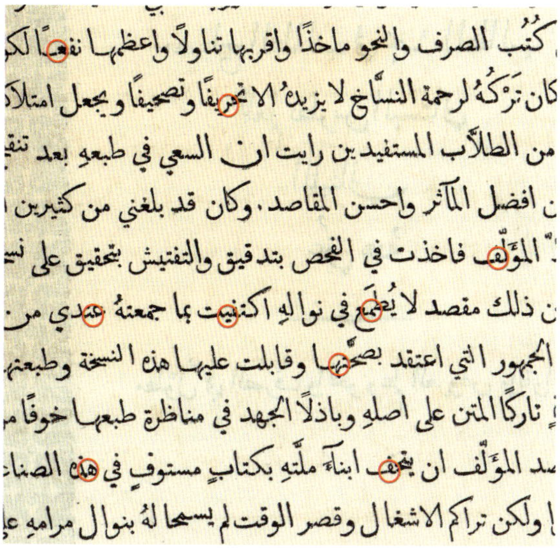
كتب الصرف والنحو ماخذًا واقربها تناولاً واعظمها نفعًا لكو
كان تركهُ لرحمة النسّاخ لا يزيدهُ الا تحريفًا وتصحيفًا ويجعل امتلا
من الطلّاب المستفيدين رايت ان السعي في طبعهِ بعد تنقي
افضل المآثر واحسن المقاصد. وكان قد بلغني من كثيرين
المؤلّف فاخذت في الفحص بتدقيق والتفتيش بتحقيق على نس
ذلك مقصد لا يُطمع في نوالهِ اكتفيت بما جمعتهُ عندي من
الجمهور التي اعتقد بصحّتها وقابلت عليها هذه النسخة وطبعته
تاركًا المتن على اصلهِ وباذلاً الجهد في مناظرة طبعها خوفًا م
المؤلّف ان يتحف ابناء ملّتهِ بكتابٍ مستوفٍ في هذه الصنا
ولكن تراكم الاشغال وقصر الوقت لم يسمحا لهُ بنوال مرامهِ ع

FIGURE 35 *Erroneous gaps between letterforms (circled) from the introduction of Buṭrus al-Bustānī,* Kitāb misbāḥ al-tālib fī baḥth al-maṭālib.
BEIRUT, 1854

missionary establishments did not manage to cast their own sets of type in-house until the 1870s. Even the American mission's own attempts at locating a reliable foundry during the 1830s met with minimal success, having relied on a type-caster in Safed, a Rabbi not well-versed in Arabic printing.[97] Other presses with foundries included al-Shuwayr, but the typeface used at this press (as is apparent from its earlier publications) resembled and had some of the same aesthetic, legibility, and casting problems as the Watts typeface used by the American Press in the 1830s.[98] The American Press was the most practical and affordable choice when it came to locals purchasing their own typefaces. In printing books at the American Press during this period, individuals like al-Bustānī and al-Yāzijī likely utilized the American Arabic typeface because of its aesthetic solutions, practicality and availability. However, the real significance of the design programs adopted for these works by local scholars was not in their reliance on this typeface. Rather, as previously mentioned, their import lay in the studied choices made by these locals to incorporate certain conventions (e.g. those of the Protestants' books from the 1840s onwards) and to exclude others (e.g. those which demonstrated literal emulations of scribal traditions).

### The *tughrāʾ*: A Perennial Motif

Interestingly, what a close examination of the visual dimensions and organization of the American Press publications does is raise questions about the shifting roles the Press played as an enterprise caught between missionary goals and independent secular publishing. This also complicates the dominant narratives associated with mid-nineteenth century regional Arab presses that emerged in the 1850s. A case in point is a printed copy of the famed tenth-century Abbasid poet Aḥmad ibn al Ḥusayn al-Mutanabbī's collection of poetry *Dīwān abu al-ṭayyib aḥmad ibn al-ḥusayn al-mutanabbī,* which was compiled, edited, and printed by al-Bustānī in 1860 (Fig. 36). The simplified design layout, lack of any elaborate borders, and use of footnotes all recall the mission's ecclesiastical products and al-Yāzijī's *Majmaʿ al-baḥrayn*. What is particularly striking about this publication is found on its opening pages: the doxological calligraphic *basmala tughrāʾ* motif from al-Yāzijī's grammar of 1836. Although al-Bustānī did not technically begin working at the Press until the early 1840s, he was certainly aware of this book's earliest design programs, particularly the original context that this *tughrāʾ* appeared in, and this choice clearly demonstrates al-Bustānī's preference for a minimally embellished layout more in line with the mission's mid-century works. The reappearance of this *tughrāʾ* in books that mirrored the Press's layout conventions from this period illustrates (on a visual level) the ways in which al-Bustānī, and scholars who produced works with a similar aesthetic, were negotiating their fluctuating perceptions of books during a period of technological

97 "Memoranda for Mr. Badger," 4 Aug 1835; "Quarterly Report of the Superintendent of the Press," 30 Sep 1835; "Report on the Press," 31 Dec 1836, PHS, RG 115-1-25.
98 The Watts typeface is discussed in Chapter 4.

ولد ابو الطيب احمد بن الحسين المتنبي بالكوفة في كندة سنة ثلث وثلثماية هجرية . ولما اشتد ساعده هاجر الى العلماء . ولقي اصحاب المبرد ابي العباس محمد بن يزيد فقرا على اكابرهم منهم ابو اسحق الزجاج وابو بكر بن السراج وابو الحسن الاخفش . ولقي اصحاب ابي العباس احمد بن يحيى بن ثعلب فقرا على ابي موسى الحافظ وابي عمرو الزاهد وابي نصر . ولقي اصحاب ابي سعيد البكري فقرأ على نفطويه وابن درستويه . ثم لقي ابا بكر محمد بن دريد فقرأ عليه ولزمه . ولقي بعده اكابر اصحابه منهم ابو علي الفارسي وابو القاسم عمر بن سيف البغدادي وابو عمران موسى . قال الواحدي في شرح ديوان ابي الطيب وان الناس منذ عصر قديم قد ولوا جميع الاشعار صفحة الإعراض مقتصرين منها على شعر ابي الطيب المتنبي نائين عما يروى لسواه وان فاته وجاز في الاحسان مداه وليس ذلك الا لبخت اتفق له فعلا فبلغ المدى وقد قال هو

هو الجد حتى تفضل العين اختها    وحتى يكون اليوم للامس سيدا

على انه كان صاحب معان مخترعة بديعة ولطائف ابكار منها لم يسبق اليها دقيقة . ولقد صدق الشيخ ابو القاسم مظفر بن علي المظفر بن الطبلسي حيث يقول

ما رأى الناس ثاني المتنبي    كيف ثان يرى لبكر الزمان
هو في شعره نبي ولكن    ظهرت معجزاته في المعاني

ولهذا خفيت معانيه على اكثر من روى شعره من اكابر الفضلاء والائمة العلماء . ونشأ المتنبي بالشام والبادية وقال الشعر صبيا فمن اول قوله في الصبا

ابلى(۱) الهوى اسفا يوم النوى(۲) بدني    وفرق الهجر بين الجفن والوسن(۳)
روح تردد(٤) في مثل الخلال اذا    اطارت الريح عنه الثوب لم يبن(٥)
كفى بجسمي نحولا انني رجل    لولا مخاطبتي اياك لم ترني

وقال ايضا في صباه ارتجالا

بأبي من وددته فافترقنا    وقضى الله بعد ذاك اجتماعا
فافترقنا حولا(٦) فلما التقينا    كان تسليمه علي وداعا

وقال ايضا في صباه يمدح محمد بن عبيد الله العلوي

اهلا بدار سباك اغيدها(۷)    ابعد ما بان(۸) عنك خردها(۹)
ظلت(۱۰) بها تنطوي على كبد    نضيجة فوق خلبها(۱۱) يدها
يا حادبي(۱۲) عيسها(۱۳) واحسبني    اوجد ميتا قبيل افقدها

۱ غير ۲ الفراق ۳ النوم ٤ تردد اي تروح وتجي ٥ بظهر ٦ سنة
۷ الاغيد الناعم البدن ۸ فارق ۹ جمع الخريدة وهي البكر ۱۰ ظللت اي دمت ۱۱ غشا
الكبد يقول ظللت بتلك الدار تنثني على كبدك واضعا يدك فوق غشائها ۱۲ ـ ابي ۱۳ جمالها

FIGURE 36 *Opening pages from Buṭrus al-Bustānī,* Dīwān abu al-ṭayyib aḥmad ibn al-ḥusayn al-mutanabbī. BEIRUT: AL-MAṬBAʿA AL-SŪRIYYA, 1860

change. Indeed, this motif's reappearance in later ephemeral pamphlets and booklets, particularly those produced at local Syrian presses that become touchstones for scholarship on the Arab *nahḍa,* can be read as a re-mediation with past traditions, while concurrently positing a continuity of reading practices during a period of modernization.

Before further considering the broader implications of this *tughrāʾ* (which I elaborate on towards the end of this chapter), it is worth noting how the visual conventions at play in these publications, which were less ornamental, varied from those of regional presses. For instance, al-Bustānī's *Dīwān al-mutanabbī*, like al-Yāzijī's *Majmaʿ al-baḥrayn*, differed on a visual level from other regional productions of the same subject matter. As with the case of the *Maqāmāt*, compilations al-Mutanabbī's writings were also being printed simultaneously in other locations, thus providing compelling examples for comparison. One edition printed in 1870 at Cairo's *Dār al-Ṭibāʿa* (The House of Print),[99] for instance, continued

99 *Sharḥ al-tibyān li-l-ʿukbarī ʿala dīwān abī al-tayyib aḥmad ibn ḥusayn al-mutanabbī* (Cairo: Dār al-Ṭibāʿa, 1870).

the emulation of scribal conventions through the use of a decorative *ʿunwān* in its incipit pages and the addition of extra-textual marginal notes (Fig. 37). Pictured here is the book's opening page, which shows an elaborately decorated headpiece, complete with a calligraphic *basmala* nested within a cartouche. Also seen in this figure is an inner page from this book (left), which shows the continued presence of references, readings, and notes in the large margins, in addition to the use of both catchwords and page numbers, much as in the contemporary editions of the *Maqāmāt* discussed above.

Going back to al-Bustānī's *Dīwān al-mutanabbī*, another intriguing factor about it is that despite its clear utilization of the American Arabic typeface and its adherence to the American Press visual program, the book's title page lists a different press as its publisher. Unlike his earlier works that did not make note of a specific publisher (although they were clearly printed at the American Press), in al-Bustānī's *Dīwān al-mutanabbī* the publisher is given as *al-Maṭbaʿa al-Sūriyya*, or the Syrian Press (Fig. 38). Seemingly inconsequential, the appearance of this press's name on this particular work raises numerous questions. The well-known story of the Syrian Press is that it was founded by Khalīl al-Khūrī in 1857 for the purposes of printing his weekly *Ḥadīqat al-akhbār*[100] and supplied with equipment from the Greek Orthodox metropolitan purchased with the help of a wealthy merchant (Mikhāʾīl al-Mudawwar).[101] This is corroborated in various sources, including Tibawi and others.[102] However, this press's equipment when it was first established, specifically the nature and quality of its typefaces and ornamental sorts, were not likely at the level needed for the press to have produced Bustānī's *Dīwān al-mutanabbī*.

The theory that this book was independently produced at the Syrian Press becomes problematic when one examines the typography, decorative elements, and design of the book itself. For instance, it was clearly printed with the American Arabic typeface, and includes a number of ornamental metal-type sorts from the American Press (in addition to the engraved *tughrāʾ*). Additionally, al-Bustānī did not acquire his own print shop until 1867, when he established *Maṭbaʿat al-Maʿārif* (The Knowledge Press) with Khalīl Sarkīs (d. 1915).[103] It may well be that, as a mission/Press employee, most of the books al-Bustānī printed until then were either produced at the American Press or relied heavily on its equipment. Tibawi, in his discussion of al-Bustānī's *Dīwān al-mutanabbī*, also asserts that it was printed at the Protestants' Press, but devotes no attention to the broader implications of this connection.[104]

Further problematizing the dominant narrative of *al-Maṭbaʿa al-Sūriyya* is the possibility that al-Khūrī first printed his groundbreaking newspaper, at least during its first few years, with the American Arabic typeface. In a letter addressed to Smith dated to June 1856, al-Khūrī discusses *Ḥadīqat al-akhbār* and his license from Istanbul to publish it with Mikhāʾīl al-Mudawwar, his sponsor. In order to

100 Al-Khūrī went on to establish *al-Matbaʿa al-Adabiyya* (The Literary Press) in 1874. Tibawi, "The American Missionaries in Beirut and Buṭrus al-Bustānī," *St. Anthony's Papers* 16, *Middle Eastern Affairs* 3 (1963), 174.

101 Ami Ayalon, *The Press in the Arab Middle East: A History* (Oxford: Oxford University Press, 1995), 31, 199.

102 A.L. Tibawi, *American Interests*, 166. Konrad Hirschler names this press as the publisher of *Dīwān al-mutanabbī*, although he does not mention al-Bustānī, and states that the book was advertised in al-Khūrī's early issue of *Ḥadīqat al-akhbār*; see Hirschler, *Medieval Arabic Historiography: Authors as Actors* (London: Routledge, 2006), 118–19. See also, Adel Beshara, *The Origins of Syrian Nationhood: Histories, Pioneers and Identity* (London: Routledge, 2011), 77n52.

103 For a discussion of this press see Ayalon, "Private Publishing in the *Nahḍa*," *IJMES* 40, no. 4 (2008): 561–77.

104 Tibawi gives the book's title and mentions the *basmala*. He also states that the work was "among the first-fruits of the [Syrian Society of Arts and Sciences] association." Tibawi, "American Missionaries and al-Bustānī," 166n102.

FIGURE 37 *Opening pages from* Sharḥ al-tibyān li-l-ʿukbarī ʿala dīwān abī al-tayyib aḥmad ibn ḥusayn al-mutanabbī. CAIRO: DĀR AL-ṬIBĀʿA, 1870

spare the expense of printing equipment and typefaces during the first year, al-Khūrī states that he was looking into renting out equipment from the American Press or, at least, its typeface.[105] The American Arabic typeface is evident in the earliest available editions of *Ḥadīqat al-akhbār*, further corroborating the argument that the earliest publications of al-Khūrī's Syrian Press relied upon equipment, materials, and labor from the American Press. For instance, the typeface used in the January 5, 1860 issue of the journal very closely resembles that of the American Press used at this time (showing the same letterform characteristics and design flaws).[106] Although it is difficult to pinpoint such aspects, al-Khūrī's letters to Smith on the subject of typefaces, and the fact that the letterforms of the small-sized text-body font in early issues of *Ḥadīqat al-akhbār* resemble the small-sized font amongst the Press's holdings, complicate the picture enough to raise questions about the nature of *al-Maṭbaʿa al-Sūriyya* at the time.

Perhaps a clue to this puzzle lies in the fact that the *basmala tughrāʾ* makes at least five more appearances in publications from the 1860s. One example is in a copy of *Al-darārī al-sabʿ: ay*

105 ABC 50, Box 3, al-Khūrī to Smith, 9 Jun 1856.

106 Thanks to Antoine (Anthony) Edwards for sharing duplicates of this journal's earliest editions.

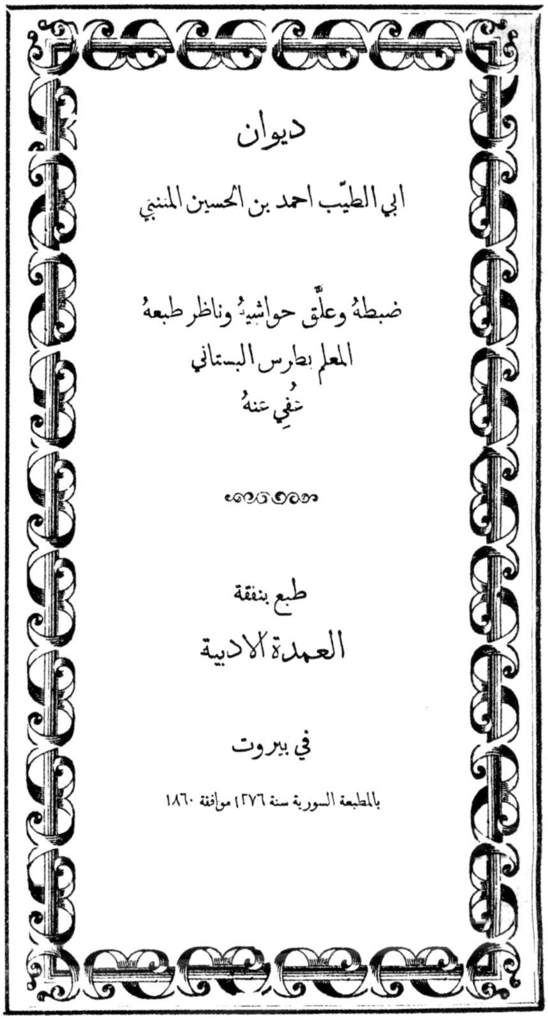
ديوان
ابي الطيّب احمد بن الحسين المتنبي
ضبطهُ وعلّق حواشيهُ وناظر طبعهُ
المعلم بطرس البستاني
عُفي عنهُ
طبع بنفقة
العمدة الادبية
في بيروت
بالمطبعة السورية سنة ١٢٧٦ موافقة ١٨٦٠

FIGURE 38 *Title page from Buṭrus al-Bustānī,* Dīwān abu al-ṭayyib aḥmad ibn al-ḥusayn al-mutanabbī. BEIRUT: AL-MAṬBAʿA AL-SŪRIYYA, 1860

*al-muwashaḥāt al-andalūsiyya* (The Seven Pearls; or The Andalusian Stanzas), which was printed in Beirut in 1864, most probably at the American Press (Fig. 39). This anthology of poetry includes posthumous works by Bashīr Shihāb II's court poet and minister Buṭrus Karāmī (d. 1851), a Greek Catholic, exiled to Istanbul with the Shihābī emir in 1839/40.[107] According to the booklet's title page, it was published and funded by Khalīl and Amīn Sarkīs. While one may assume that this work was produced at Khalīl Sarkīs's *Maṭbaʿat al-Maʿārif*, this was not the case, since Sarkīs's press was not operational until three years later.[108] Additionally, an edition of this booklet can be found in a collection of pamphlets and small books printed at the American Press at Harvard University's Houghton Library.[109] Furthermore, in addition to similarities in typeface and layout to Press works from the 1850s, this booklet's cover stock and binding bear a remarkable resemblance to an earlier pamphlet produced at the American Press, an 1837 edition of George Whiting's tract "On Self-Examination," which uses the same exact binding techniques and materials (Fig. 40 and Fig. 41).

The *basmala tughrā*ʾ makes various other appearances in booklets from 1866 to 1868. For example, it is found in a printed edition of the thirteenth-century writings of the Mamluk Sultan al-Ashraf Khalīl (d. 1293) published by the Beirut-based scholar and private press owner

107 This was possibly the first printed edition of poems by Karāmī, which he produced (in manuscript form) while exiled in Istanbul, prior to his death in 1851. Thanks to Stephen Sheehi, who generously provided some of this information. The anthology includes a number of contributions by local Arab Muslim and Christian scholars and poets including Yūsuf al-Asīr, who was employed as the American mission press corrector and translator at the time. For more on the Shihābī emir's exile, see Ceasar E. Farah, *Politics of Interventionism in Ottoman Lebanon, 1830–1861* (London: I.B. Tauris, 2000). Some excerpts from Karāmī's poems also appear in Yaziji's *Nabdha min dīwān al-shaykh nāṣīf al-yāzijī* from 1853 (Fig. 26). For more on the reception of Karāmī's work during this period, see Charbel Dagher, *Al-ʿarabiyya wa-l-tamaddun* (Beirut: Dār al-Nahār, 2008), 27–29.

108 For a discussion of this press, see Ayalon, "Private Publishing," 561–77.

109 *Missionary pamphlets in Arabic from the library of the American Board of Commissioners for Foreign Missions* (Beirut, 1850–1910), held at the Houghton Library, Harvard University, Cambridge, Mass. (*98Miss-168).

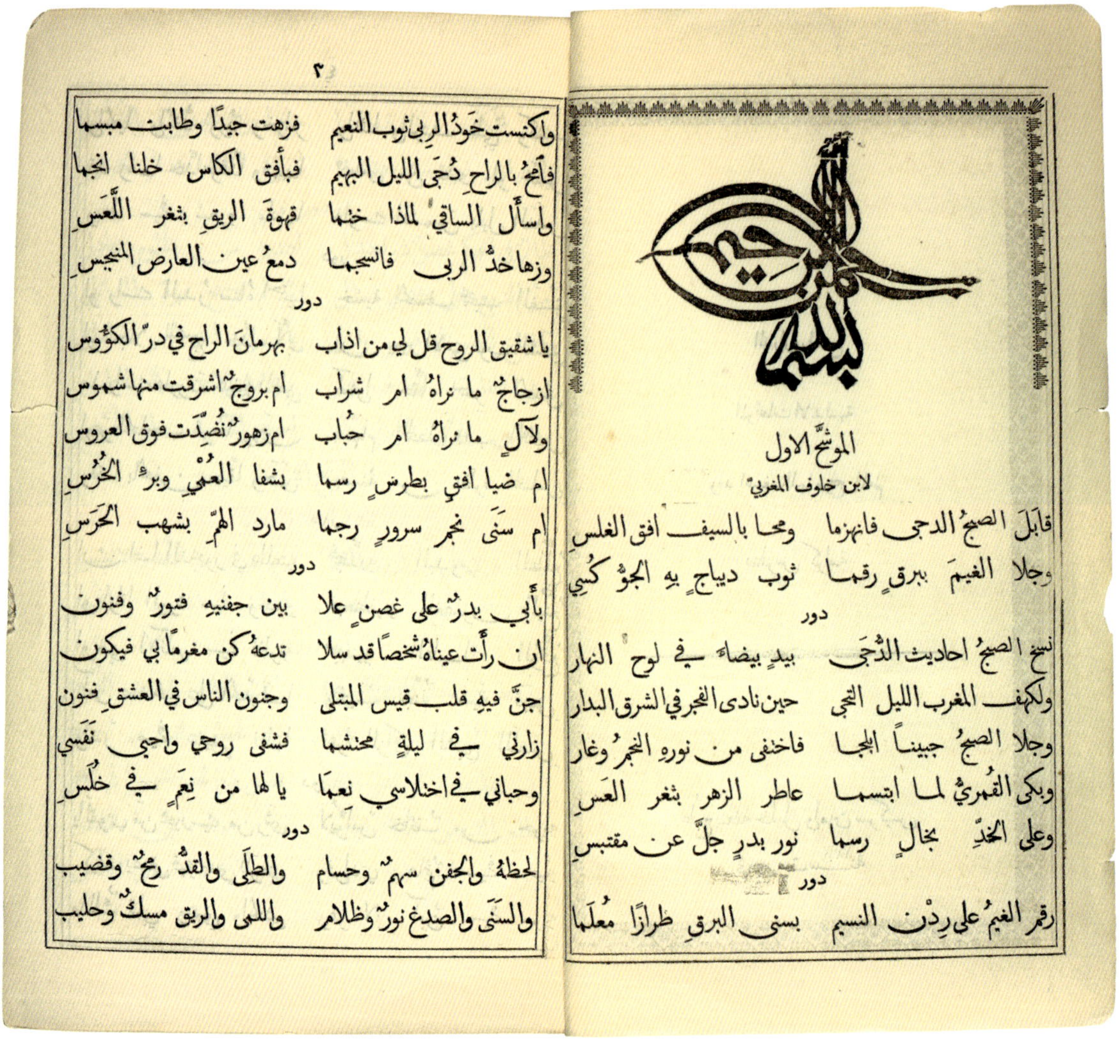


FIGURE 39 *Opening pages from Buṭrus Karāmī, Khalīl Sarkīs, and Amīn Sarkīs,* Al-darārī al-sabʿ: ay al-muwashaḥāt al-andalūsiyya.
BEIRUT, 1854

Yūsuf ibn Fāris Shalfūn (d. 1895).[110] The same *tughrāʾ* design emerges again in at least two works printed at *al-Maṭbaʿa al-Waṭaniyya* (The National Press) in Beirut: *Tazyīn nihāyat al-arab fī akhbār al-ʿarab* (Embellishing the End of Hope in the Chronicles of Arabs) printed in 1867,[111] and *Kitāb tārīkh iskandar dhī al-qarnayn al-makdūnī,* (The History of Alexander the Great) printed in 1868.[112] In addition to the now familiar *tughrāʾ,*

110 This is *Diwān al-qasīd al-jalīl min niẓām al-sulṭān khalīl ṭāb thurāh,* published in Beirut in 1866 by Yūsuf ibn Fāris Shalfūn, owner of *al-Maṭbaʿa al-ʿUmūmiyya* (The Public Press), as a part of a series. Thanks to Ami Ayalon for sharing a reproduction.

111 Iskandar Abkāriyyūs, who previously published a volume of Arabic poetry at the American Press in 1857/8, was the author of this book, see note 39 in this chapter. The edition consulted here was accessed on www.HathiTrust.org as Google-digitized book (hereafter cited as HathiTrust) from an original copy held at the University of Michigan library (PJ7611.I82).

112 The copy of the 158-page book consulted here is available for viewing at the British Library (14560.a.12).

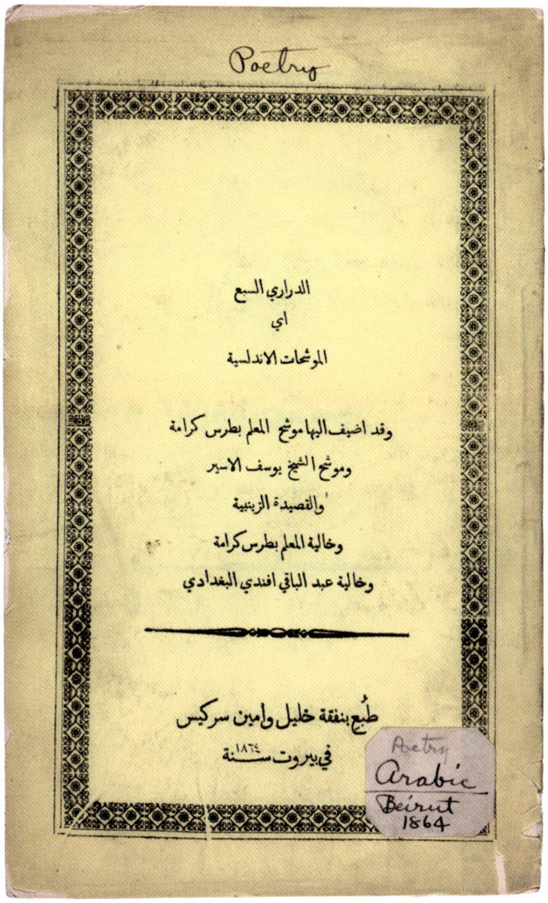


FIGURE 40 *Front cover from Buṭrus Karāmī, Khalīl Sarkīs, and Amīn Sarkīs,* Al-darārī al-sabʿ. ay al-muwashaḥat al-andalūsiyya.
BEIRUT, 1854

the overall design of these booklets, including the typefaces and fleurons/ornamental sorts used, very closely resembles those appearing in books and pamphlets from the American Press. Interestingly, *al-Maṭbaʿa al-Waṭaniyya* was also where Naṣīf al-Yāzijī's eldest child, Ḥabīb al-Yāzijī (d. 1870), published *Kitāb al-lāmiʿa fī sharḥ al-jāmiʿa* (A Book Illuminating al-Jāmiʿa) in 1869, a commentary that accompanied his father's metrical *urjūza* (rajaz poem) entitled *Al-jāmiʿa fī ʿilm al-ʿarūḍ wa-l-qawāfī* (A Collected Study of Prosody and Rhymes).[113] The former's layout also recalls aspects of those produced at the American Press, specifically the use of the American Arabic typeface and the minimal appearance of ornamental elements. While this book does not use the same *basmala tughrā*ʾ mentioned above, it does include an engraved *basmala* motif as a headpiece on the dedication page.[114] Although Ḥabīb, like his younger brother Ibrāhīm, was involved with the Jesuit mission and press,[115] and not the American missionaries and their enterprises, it is possible that Naṣīf's experiences with the American Press and the books he produced there played a large role in the design and visual programs used as references and models by his sons, as well as by his daughter Warda, for their own productions.[116]

It may well be that these works were produced at the press listed on their respective title pages, and not on the American Press's premises. However, it is clear that these examples of print engaged with the visual conventions and typographic elements popular in the Press's publications. Specifically, these numerous iterations of the Press's *tughrā*ʾ (possibly carved in the 1830s) attest to the frequent overlaps occurring within the nascent publishing industry in Beirut at the time. This certainly raises many questions. How far-reaching were the American Press's conventions amongst local presses at the time? For some local private print shops, the American Press publications seemed to have served as ready-to-hand models. Was the Press renting out not only its physical space, but also its materials at

113 Ellis describes Naṣīf al-Yāzijī's book as: "Al-Jāmiʿat. A metrical treatise on Arabic prosody, accompanied by a commentary entitled al-Lāmiʿat, by the author's son, Ḥabīb al-Yāzijī." Ellis, *Arabic Books*, 2:416. See also *Arabic Books*, 1:599.

114 The edition consulted was accessed on HathiTrust, digitized from an original copy held at the University of Michigan library (PJ7541.Y34/Y35).

115 Ibrāhīm is briefly discussed in Chapter 2. Ḥabīb was a member of *al-Jamʿiyya al-Sharqiyya fī Bayrūt* (The Eastern Society of Beirut) that was established by the French Jesuits in the 1850s. See Abdulrazzak Patel, *The Arab Nahḍah: The Making of the Intellectual and Humanist Movement* (Edinburgh: Edinburgh University Press, 2013), 217-18n52.

116 Marilyn Booth, "al-Yāzijī, Warda (1838–1924)," in Meisami and Starkey, *Encyclopedia of Arabic Literature*, 2:813.

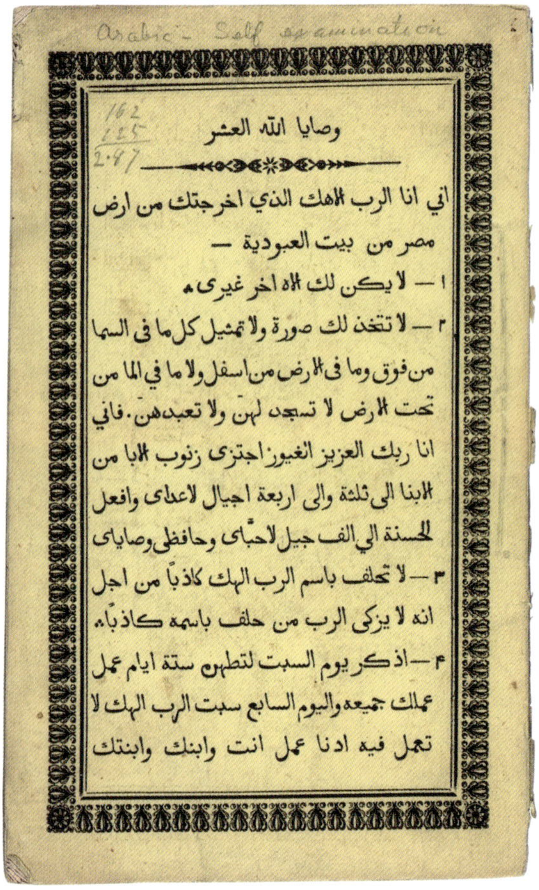


FIGURE 41 *Front cover from George B. Whiting,* Kitāb irshād al-masīḥī fī imtiḥān al-nafs.
BEIRUT, 1837

the time, in addition to casting and selling copies of its American Arabic typeface? From the movement of the *tughrā*ʾ from one press to the other (which, admittedly, could imply that engraved copies of it were made), this would appear to be the case. However, this was not a clear-cut instance of simply purchasing copies of fonts and ornamental sorts, or using American Press publications as visual and organizational references. When the visual conventions of these publications are evaluated – in their overall layouts and binding – it becomes clear that the relationships between private presses (or their sponsors) and the American Press were nuanced and prevalent. Additionally, one can read this *tughrā*ʾ as a perennial motif that concurrently demonstrates the dependence of early Arabic printing on the visual conventions of scribal markets, while also representing a reframing of customary practices within the multifaceted (and fractured) lens of technology and modernization.

### Secularizing the American Press

Although emergent *nahḍa* scholars used the American Press's premises and employed its production standards and visual conventions, these authors seemed eager to underplay any association with the Press and its mission. Understandably, given their independent nature, none of the books printed by scholars as "job works" list this Press as the printer or publisher. In fact, the Press is rarely mentioned by name in any of its publications, even those produced with mission funds in the 1830s. The few times the Press is explicitly mentioned as the publisher is on some ecclesiastic texts or the first edition of the booklet on treating cholera. This may well be a practice instated since the early years of the Press in the hopes of deflecting attention away from the missionary goal of its publications (seeing as the local attitudes towards the books initially circulated by the American missionaries were strongly unfavorable[117]).

Through their publishing efforts at the American Press, these Arab Christian scholars also dissociated themselves from the Syria Mission's worldview through an engagement with other Christian and Muslim intellectuals, Islamic texts, and prominent discourses on Arab heritage and identity. For instance, although many scholars using the American Press were Christians, the choice of subject matter and genre in their publications clearly demonstrates how these scholars were striving to situate their works within the lineage of classical Arabic writing, often by Muslim authors. Al-Yāzijī's personal spin on the classical

117 Such responses are discussed in Chapter 3.

writing style of al-Ḥarīrī's *Maqāmāt*, and his self-bestowed title of "al-Shaykh" before his name on his earliest publications (prior to his later days of literary fame), certainly demonstrates his drive to locate himself and his writings as a continuation of classical traditions within the forward-looking realm of print. Indeed, the simultaneous production of texts like al-Mutanabbī's poetry or *Maqāmāt al-ḥarīrī* at different Arabic or Muslim presses provides the sense that these historic literary works by Muslim thinkers of the past resonated with audiences across regions during this era, particularly for intellectuals first interested in translating classical texts into print. Furthermore, during the 1860s, al-Bustānī chaired *al-jamʿiyya al-ʿilmiyya al-sūriyya li-l-fūnūn wa-l-ʿulūm* (The Syrian Society of Knowledge for the Arts and Sciences), which counted a number of prominent Christian and Muslim scholars as its members, and played an active role promoting the secular writings and nationalist ideals at the crux of the *nahḍa*.[118] The organization was originally co-founded by Arab Christian intellectuals and American missionaries, with al-Bustānī listed as its secretary.[119] Al-Bustānī took on a more active role at the Syrian society's helm, after its reformulation in the 1860s when it included Muslim intellectuals (and excluded missionary scholars).

Perhaps the most explicit expressions of al-Yāzijī and al-Bustānī's political and intellectual leanings come in the form of the Islamic idioms and pan-religious verbal and visual lexicon frequenting the pages of their publications. In some of al-Yāzijī's books on Arabic poetry and literature,[120] for instance, his opening pages include boilerplate thanksgivings and incantations that are not specific to any religious sect. Most notable is the use of *bismallāh al-fattāḥ*, "in the name of God the Opener," which characteristically does not mention Christ or the Holy Spirit. Al-Bustānī's works take things a step further by borrowing phrases from the Qur'an. For instance, in his rendition of Maronite Patriarch of Aleppo Jirmānūs Farḥāt's *Baḥth al-maṭālib fī ʿilm al-ʿarabiyya*, al-Bustānī opens the introduction with a verse reminiscent of a key *sūra* (chapter) from the Qur'an: *al-ḥamdu li-l-lāh al-ʿaliyy al-akram alladhī ʿallama bi-l-qalam ʿallama al-insān mā lam yaʿlam* or "Praise be to God the High, the most Generous, who taught by the Pen, taught Man that which he knew not"[121] (see the first line of text on the right page of the book's foreword, pictured in Fig. 26). Like most other printed works from this early period, the popularity of Farḥāt's grammar was grounded in both the scribal realm of the 1700s[122] and the nineteenth-century world of print. There was certainly a growing interest during the nineteenth century in the genre of Arabic grammar and composition, particularly in relation to concepts of an Arab heritage and the push-pull between the growing popularity of colloquialism and a desire to preserve past linguistic traditions and rules. The regional pertinence of Farḥāt's work, of which the

118 Although often discussed in scholarship on the *nahḍa*, this society's timeline, publications, and names are not always consistent. This book follows Yūsuf Khūrī's research on this society. See Khūrī, *Al-jamʿiyya al-sūriyya li al-ʿulūm wa al-funūn 1847–1852* (Beirut: Dār al-Hamrā, 1990); *Aʿmāl al-jamʿiyya al-ʿilmiyya al-sūriyya lil-fūnūn wal-ʿulūm 1868–1879* (Beirut: Dār al-Hamrā, 1990).

119 A selection of the Syrian Society's first proceedings (from 1847–1852) was printed in January 1852 as *Al-jiz' al-awwal min aʿmāl al-jamʿiyya al-sūriyya*. Al-Bustānī is listed as *kātib al-waqāyaʿ* (secretary). Missionaries listed in this first issue include Eli Smith, Henry De Forrest, and Cornelius Van Dyck (among others). For more on the missionaries' early involvement in the society, see Edward Salisbury, "11. Syrian Society of Arts and Sciences," *Journal of the American Oriental Society* 3 (1853): 477–86.

120 These include the two volumes of *Majmūʿ al-adab fī funūn al-ʿarab* (Beirut, 1855). However, this was not the case for his *Nabdha min dīwān al-shaykh nāṣīf al-yāzijī* (Beirut, 1853), see Fig. 26.

121 This comes from the Qur'an's *Sūrat al-ʿalaq* (The Clot), verses 96:3–5.

122 Farḥāt produced two versions of this text, one in 1705 and an abridgement in 1707. The latter edition was what scholars like al-Bustānī reproduced in print form. See Patel, 49.

missionaries may have been aware, can also be seen in the different versions of it that were published in Malta in 1832, 1836, and 1841.[123] Al-Bustānī likely turned to Farḥāt's manuscript, as well as to these earlier printed editions, for his book.[124]

It is not clear from Press and mission records whether al-Bustānī's book was used at the American mission's schools as an Arabic textbook, although it was likely not produced with that intention in mind.[125] Certainly, the inclusion of Qur'anic phrases in a missionary publication (had it been one) during this period would not have been supported.[126] The practice of including Islamic verses and/or incantations, such as the *basmala,* in manuscript anthologies of poetry by Muslim writers, however, was not uncommon in local seminary and monastery workshops, something al-Bustānī was surely familiar with.[127] However, in the case of this publication by al-Bustānī, the Qur'anic-style verse appears within his commentary, and not copied from another text. What is particularly interesting about al-Bustānī's rendition, then, is locating Farḥāt's work (which was formulated based on Christian texts as sources and produced for a Christian readership[128]) within the frameworks Islamic idioms, thus calling out to a Muslim readership. Concurrently, this allowed al-Bustānī to position himself (as a Protestant Christian) within the ranks of this readership as one of its scholars. Interestingly, a similar Qur'anic phrase appears in the incipit pages of Ḥabīb al-Yāzijī's *Kitāb al-lāmiʿa fī sharḥ al-jāmiʿa*. In this case, the variation on the verse from the Qur'an reads: *al-ḥamdu li-l-āhi alladhī bi-l-qalami qad ʿallama al-insāna mā lam yaʿlami* (thanks be to God who with a pen taught man what he does not know). What this shows is a growing trend amongst Arab Christian intellectuals towards locating their work within a predominantly Muslim Arabic literary heritage.

This approach certainly tied into his vision for a multi-confessional Syrian society, which included members of other Christian communities, particularly Maronites, from among whom he was excommunicated when he converted to Protestantism. Certainly this can be seen in his production of Farḥāt's Arabic grammar, as well as in al-Bustānī's work on editing and printing Ṭānnūs al-Shidyāq's history (mentioned earlier in this chapter) of

123 The 1832 and 1841 editions were abridgements of the text produced in a simplified question-and-answer format. I thank the second anonymous reviewer for this clarification.

124 Tibawi briefly mentions this book and its noteworthy choice of opening phrase. See Tibawi, "American Missionaries and al-Bustānī," 160–61. For more on its importance in manuscript production from the late eighteenth century on, see Dana Sajdi, "Print and Its Discontents: A Case for Pre-Print Journalism and Other Sundry Print Matters," *The Translator* 15, no. 1 (2009): 105–38.

125 Although Tibawi makes the claim that it was, I have not located any evidence in support of this assertion. The *Annual Report* from 1854 does not list this book as one of the Press's publications. However, there is mention of "one book of 438 pages … printed at the expense of private publishers." This is may be referencing al-Bustānī's book (which is 454 pages long) since the press rarely published books of this length and certainly could not afford such an expense during this period of limited funding. See ABC 16.8.1, vol. 4, *Annual Report of the Syria Mission*, 1854. For Tibawi, see "American Missionaries and al-Bustānī," 161.

126 There did not seem to be an explicit American missionary interest in Muslim readers during the 1850s. This changed when the Americans' Bible was published in the 1860s. However, the mission was clearly against adopting "Islamic idioms" in work on its Bible. Jessup stated as much in his account of the "style of Arabic adopted" in the Bible translation: "Some would have preferred the style 'Koranic' … Islamic, adopting idioms and expressions peculiar to Mohammedans. *All native Christian scholars* decidedly objected to this." Jessup, *Fifty-Three Years*, 1:75.

127 One example is a manuscript copy of Niqūla ibn Yūsuf al-Turk's poetry (*Kitāb dīwān al-shāʿir niqūla al-turk*) copied in Tripoli by Fransīs ibn Isḥāq Tarabay in 1833 and held at the Central Library of the Université Saint-Esprit de Kaslik, Lebanon. For information on this copy see Philippe Roisse, *Al-makhṭūṭat al-ʿarabiyya fī lubnān: iltiqāʾ al-thaqāfāt wa-l-adyān wa-l-maʿārif* (Beirut: CEDRAC, 2010), 204–13.

128 Patel, 50.

Mount Lebanon from a Maronite's perspective. Another example of the trend towards locating Arab Christian work within a predominantly Muslim Arabic literary heritage was al-Bustānī's *Qiṣṣat as'ad al-shidyāq*, of which he had proposed a reprint in his own terms to Rufus Anderson.[129] This controversial memoir was the well-known tale of the martyred Arab Christian, As'ad al-Shidyāq, originally a Maronite, who allegedly became the Americans' first Protestant convert. Through the story of a casualty of ideology, in which brother was turned against brother, al-Bustānī's book did not privilege the American missionaries' role in the affair nor its regional presence, but strove to bring forth a discourse of unity across denominations. As Ussama Makdisi argues, the core importance of this production was:

"not its idealization of the Protestant martyr but the deliberate manner in which Bustani used the story of As'ad to evoke an unprecedented ecumenism, and later a new liberal pluralism as intolerable to American missionaries as it was to the Maronite Church."[130]

## Diverging Ideologies

Al-Bustānī's and al-Yāzijī's break from the mission's views and Protestant framework was not just intellectual. During the period when they were actively publishing their own works at the mission's Press, their importance as mission employees was also changing. Al-Bustānī remained employed as a permanent "native helper" for the Press (in addition to his responsibilities, as a Protestant convert, teaching, and preaching for the mission) until 1852, when his status became that of a contractor paid by the job.[131] During this period, there were various developments and conversations regarding whether or not al-Bustānī would be ordained as a minister in connection with the Syria Mission.[132] In the fall of 1854 it was decided that al-Bustānī was not a suitable candidate, and the mission declined his application.[133]

While this rejection did not lead al-Bustānī to abandon his work with the mission, his interactions with its members became fraught.[134] Tibawi, in his writing on al-Bustānī's ties to the mission, arrives at a similar conclusion. While Tibawi does not delve into the details of al-Bustānī's publications at the time, he too reads this moment as one in which al-Bustānī was "in half veiled terms, challenging the missionary view."[135] By the late 1850s al-Bustānī's involvement with Press-related work had significantly diminished – particularly with the death of Smith, who was not only his employer but also his long-time confidant. However, al-Bustānī's ties to the mission continued through his role as an "elder" in the local Protestant church

129 ABC 16.8.1, vol. 6, al-Bustānī to Anderson, 25 Jan 1860.

130 Makdisi, *Artillery of Heaven: American Missionaries and the Failed Conversion of the Middle East* (Ithaca: Cornell University Press, 2008), 181.

131 ABC 16.8.1, vol. 4, *Annual Report of the Syria Mission*, 1852.

132 An interest in preparing al-Bustānī for the ministry surfaces in records from 1844; see ABC 16.8.1, vol. 1, "Report on Native Helpers," 1844. A.L. Tibawi provides a detailed account of the back and forth involving Bustānī's ordination, commencing with Smith's long-held interest in the local convert as an ideal candidate for this process. See A.L. Tibawi, "American Missionaries and al-Bustānī," 158–159. Although initially interested in the possibility, al-Bustānī declined sometime in 1844/45, possibly due to pecuniary concerns – the salary for potential local pastors was not enough for living expenses. See Uta Zeuge-Buberl, "Misinterpretations of a Missionary Policy? The American Syria Mission's Conflict with Buṭrus al-Bustānī and Yuḥannā Wurtabāt," *Theological Review* 36 (2015): 31–32, 34, 34n38.

133 When the subject of ordination was brought up again in 1854, this time at al-Bustānī's and the local Protestant church's request, the mission's members debated it over the course of several months, leading to an eventual rejection of his application. See ABC 16.8.1, vol. 8, "Afternoon meeting," 29 Aug 1854; ABC 60, Eli Smith Papers, 1801–1857, vol. 1, Thompson to Smith, 10 Oct 1854.

134 Al-Bustānī took offense at this decision (particularly since he was not given a clear reason), yet came to his own conclusions on the matter. See Zeuge-Buberl, 35–37.

135 Tibawi, "American Missionaries and al-Bustānī," 166.

until 1878[136] and in his employment as an interpreter for the American consul. This included, for a brief period, al-Bustānī working as the unofficial acting consul.[137]

After the inter-communal conflicts that plagued the region in 1860, which made a lasting impression on him, al-Bustānī's writing and commitments took on a broader concern with the socio-political condition of his locale. In 1860 he began printing his now-famous collection of eleven political pamphlets, *Nafīr sūriyya* (The Clarion of Syria),[138] in which he (anonymously) called for a diffusion of sectarianism amongst his fellow Syrians in an effort towards a multi-confessional Syrian society. Nadia Bou Ali argues these booklets in fact manifested al-Bustānī's "imaginary concept of nation," a direct product of the 1860 violence, which glossed over the origins and history of these in favor of a universal concept of *al-waṭan* (the nation) "as an exit from a state of 'savagery and barbarism' into an age of 'civilization.'"[139] Al-Bustānī furthered his vision of *al-waṭan* by establishing *al-Madrasa al-Waṭaniyya* (the National School) in 1863, an "interdenominational Christian" school for boys.[140] This school later served as the "preparatory program"[141] for students interested in continuing their education at the American's Syrian Protestant College (SPC).[142] By 1867, in addition to his role in the Protestant community's "Native Church," al-Bustānī's connection to the mission remained almost exclusively defined through the SPC's "Principal of the Preparatory Department."[143] By this time, al-Bustānī's social and intellectual commitments had clearly diverged from those of the missionaries. Records from 1867, and publications by al-Bustānī in the years to follow, show a widening divide between al-Bustānī's pluralistic vision and the American mission's evangelical outlook.[144] Yet al-Bustānī's continued association with the mission through its educational institution helped to maintain his access to the American Press, since in 1867 he had two pressmen on his own

136 Zeuge-Buberl, 37.

137 Tibawi describes the situation as an ad-hoc arrangement resulting from the American consul taking leave from his position, which was seemingly filled by the British consul, Noel Moore. Yet al-Bustānī, according to Tibawi, was actually doing all the legwork and making payments out-of-pocket (and through loans) for all consulate-related expenses, including Moore's compensation. For more, see Tibawi, "American Missionaries and al-Bustānī," 167–68.

138 No publisher is listed on these pamphlets. However, based on its publication dates and the design layout, the booklets may have been printed at the American Press. Nonetheless, further research is needed to verify this.

139 For more, see Bou Ali, "Buṭrus al-Bustānī," 267–68.

140 Tibawi explains that this was "not 'national' in the strict meaning of the word." Tibawi, *American Interests*, 163n5. See also, Jens Hanssen, *Fin de Siècle Beirut: The Making of an Ottoman Provincial Capital* (Oxford: Clarendon Press, 2005), 164–69; Makdisi, *Artillery of Heaven*, 207–08. For more on al-Bustānī's philosophy on a interdenominational education, see Khalil Abou Rjaili, "Boutros al-Boustani (1819–83)," *Prospects: The Quarterly Review of Comparative Education*, UNESCO 23, no. 1/2 (1993): 125–33.

141 Tibawi, *American Interests*, 164.

142 This mission's university opened its doors in 1864 and by the 1920s its name was changed to the American University of Beirut. See Ellen Fleischmann, "Evangelization or Education: American Protestant Missionaries, the American Board, and the Girls and Women of Syria (1830–1910)," in *New Faith in Ancient Lands: Western Missions in the Middle East in the Nineteenth and Early Twentieth Centuries*, ed. Heleen Murre-Van den Berg (Leiden: Brill, 2006), 263–80; Fruma Zachs, "From the Mission to the Missionary: The Bliss Family and the Syrian Protestant College (1866–1920)," *Die Welt Des Islams* 45, no. 2 (2001): 145–73.

143 Makdisi, *Artillery of Heaven*, 209. Al-Bustānī held this title until at least 1867, as mentioned in the SPC's records. See AUB Archives AA7.5-1-13, Black to al-Bustānī, 9 Jul 1867.

144 Tibawi, "American Missionaries and al-Bustānī," 137–82. A number of letters, held at the AUB Archives, between the missionary James Black and al-Bustānī show that a Special Committee (headed by Black) at the SPC was looking into certain accusations/issues brought forth by al-Bustānī (although it is not clear from these records what the nature of these issues was). See AUB Archives AA7.5-1-13, al-Bustānī to Black, 6 Mar 1867; Black to al-Bustānī, 20 Jul 1867.

payroll printing his Arabic lexicon and Arabic grammar.[145]

Similarly, while he remained exclusively employed within the realm of the Press, al-Yāzijī's relationship with the mission became strained after Smith's death (particularly since, of all the American missionaries, Smith was likely his greatest supporter and advocate). Having maintained his allegiance to the Greek Orthodox Church, al-Yāzijī did little to endear himself to the other missionaries, least of all Cornelius van Dyck, the new Press editor. For instance, in an account of the Bible translations, Van Dyck claims that upon Smith's death, the contract with both al-Bustānī and al-Yāzijī regarding the translation project was "null and void."[146] Van Dyck goes on to rather explicitly voice his discontent with al-Yāzijī's work in general.[147] Thus, when Van Dyck opted to hire his own translator, Yūsuf al-Asīr, for the Bible project,[148] al-Yāzijī was edged out of any new, mission-funded presswork. Minutes from a meeting in April 1860 indicate that al-Yāzijī's employment with the mission was to end in the summer of that year.[149] Nonetheless, this scholar continued to make use of the Press for his own work until at least 1863.[150]

### Considering a "Modern" Aesthetic

Although long in the mission's employ, the scholarship of individuals like al-Yāzijī and al-Bustānī helped them grow in stature and achieve recognition. By the mid-1800s, such scholars had little stake in the Protestant mission. One could argue that the real reasons behind their eventual exclusion from the American missionary apparatus were their later, largely secular commitments and their growing popularity as important, well-published scholars. Through their work, they were forming their own visions of a "modern" nation founded on concepts of social progress (*ḥadāra*) and civilization (*tamaddun*) in which local religious communities would transcend their differences through the commonalities of an Arab-Syrian identity.[151] As numerous scholars on this period agree, such commitments were particularly apparent in the case of al-Bustānī, as indicated by projects like his nationalist school and publications from 1860 onwards.

Although most of these projects have been extensively discussed elsewhere, perspectives regarding al-Bustānī's socio-political commitments remain varied.[152] Some historians identify al-Bustānī as a radical figure who called for a break from a hegemonic Tanzimat-driven Ottoman regime of toleration.[153] Others posit that al-Bustānī was not necessarily a revolutionary figure, yet belonged to an emergent group of elite secularist scholars interested in "a modern Syro-Lebanese Arab" identity.[154] Still others have emphasized al-Bustānī's support of the Ottoman state and identity, evidenced in the dedication of his first dictionary to

145 These books were his text on elementary Arabic grammar, *Kitāb miftāḥ al-miṣbāḥ fī uṣūl al-ṣarf wa-l-naḥū* (printed as a job work in 1862), and his now-famous Arabic lexicon, *Kitāb muḥīṭ al-muḥīṭ: ay qāmūs muṭawwal li-l-lugha al-ʿarabiyya* (with both volumes printed as job works between 1867–1870). A second, enlarged edition of his Arabic grammer, *Kitāb miftāḥ al-miṣbāḥ*, was also produced at the Press in 1867; see ABC 16.8.1, vol. 6, *Annual Report of the Beirut Station*, 1862, 1863, and 1867.

146 Eli Smith and Cornelius V.A. van Dyck, *A Brief Documentary History of the Translation of the Scriptures into the Arabic Language* (Beirut: American Presbyterian Mission Press, 1900), 14.

147 Some of these issues are briefly mentioned in Chapter 2 and in more detail in Chapter 4. See also Smith and Van Dyck, *A Documentary History*, 29.

148 Smith and Van Dyck, *A Documentary History*, 25, 29.

149 ABC 16.8.1, vol. 8, "Meeting in Beirut," 3 Apr 1860.

150 For instance, he published a text on Arabic grammar, *Kitāb nār al-qura fī sharḥ jawf al-farā*, at the American Press (as a job work) in 1863; see ABC 16.8.1, vol. 6, *Annual Report of the Beirut Station*, 1862 and 1863.

151 See, for instance, a discussion of these concepts in al-Bustānī, *Khuṭba fī ādāb al-ʿarab* (Beirut, 1859).

152 For more recent perspectives on al-Bustānī, see Adel Beshara, ed., *Butrus al-Bustani: Spirit of the Age* (Melborne: Iphoenix Publishing, 2014).

153 Ibid., 201–11.

154 Stephen Sheehi, "Inscribing the Arab Self: Buṭrus al-Bustānī and Paradigms of Subjective Reform," *British Journal of Middle Eastern Studies* 27, no. 1 (2000): 10.

Sultan ʿAbdul-Azīz (d. 1876).[155] What can be argued in all cases, however, is that through his writing, views on the Arabic language, and educational projects, al-Bustānī was interested in locating his ideas within a nexus of multi-confessional perspectives, which was informed by regional events.

The secularist interests in al-Bustānī's concept of nationhood (*waṭaniyya*) in fact included situating Christianity within the discourse on national identity and Arab heritage, in order to displace Islam's hold (under Ottoman rule) on these discourses. It has been argued that al-Bustānī's "national imagination" was rooted in the "assertion of Christianity's role" in its construction.[156] In fact, his views on modernity and its language of *al-ʿilm* (science) were "secular" only if this term "is to be read with the recognition of its theological basis," and were "embedded within a complex theological framework."[157] In his *Nafīr sūriyya*, al-Bustānī's response to the conflicts of 1860 illustrates his conception of the "love of the nation" (*ḥub al-waṭan*) as the only solution to "overcoming the 'barbaric and savage' violence [...] and is the only source for 'harmony and unity.'" These views of "love" and "acts of faith," are certainly a response to his "hatred of a past that had already defined his nation."[158]

Through his universalist interests, though clearly Christian, al-Bustānī sought a nation built on the foundations of civilization, modernization (through schools, presses, etc.), commonalities, and inter-confessional unity.[159] Recalling the *tughrā'* in al-Bustānī's *Dīwān abu al-ṭayyib* (Fig. 36), unlike its earlier appearance in the mission-sanctioned Arabic grammar by al-Yāzijī (Fig. 2), its use in the later works should not simply be read as a nod to Islamic calligraphic practices with the aim of attracting Muslim readers. Rather, its aims are conflicted, fractured and multivalent.[160] The *tughrā'* in al-Bustānī's text can be read as a motif that explicitly calls to Arab Muslim intellectuals (members of his ideal Syrian nation) with the intent of including this group, who were simultaneously excluded as infidel others and desired as elusive converts by the Americans, in a broader discourse on the historical formation of a shared Arab language and heritage. Concurrently, by employing this visual device, al-Bustānī was locating himself, as a Protestant Syrian Christian, within the Arab classical literary tradition – typically dominated by Islamic thinkers – which was a genre with much resonance amongst an emergent print readership.

155 Tibawi, "American Missionaries and al-Bustānī," 179–80. While Makdisi acknowledges this and other events, he calls them token offerings, and remains unable to reconcile "the imperial state" with "liberal subjects like al-Bustānī"; see Makdisi, *Artillery of Heaven*, 208. For other perspectives, see Ashraf Eissa, "Majallat al-jinān: Arabic Narrative Discourse in the Making," *Quaderni di Studi Arabi* 18 (2000): 41–49; Butrus Abu-Manneh, "The Christians between Ottomanism and Syrian Nationalism: The Ideas of Butrus Al-Bustani," *IJMES* 11, no. 3 (1980): 287–304.

156 As argued in Rana Issa, "The Arabic Language and Syro-Lebanese National Identity Searching in Buṭrus al-Bustānī's *Muḥīṭ al-Muḥīṭ*" (unpublished manuscript, August 25, 2015), Microsoft Word file. Special thanks to this author for sharing her unpublished article. Emphasizing the dialogism evident in al-Bustānī's writing, Sheehi argues that this scholar's "ideal national subject" is in fact "mired in an inescapable Hegelian, master-slave struggle with the West." Sheehi, "Al-Bustānī and Subjective Reform," 10.

157 Bou Ali, "Collecting the Nation: Lexicography and National Pedagogy in *al-nahda al-ʿarabiyya*," in *Archives, Museums and Collecting Practices in the Modern Arab World*, eds. Sonja Mejcher-Atassi and John P. Schwartz (Farnham: Ashgate, 2012), 43.

158 Bou Ali, "Buṭrus al-Bustānī," 277. Emphasizing the dialogism evident in al-Bustānī's writing, Sheehi argues that this scholar's "ideal national subject" is in fact "mired in an inescapable Hegelian, master-slave struggle with the West" (10) in which a "bifurcation in national selfhood" is evident and "where the willful and enlightened native Self dissociates himself from his 'fanatical' and 'ignorant' compatriot Other." Sheehi, "Al-Bustānī and Subjective Reform," 12.

159 Such views are discussed in his *Khuṭba* and *Nafīr*.

160 Much like Bou Ali's description of "the gritty, mutable, and conflicted surface from which the Nahda mirror reflects a seemingly univocal image." Bou Ali, *Collecting the Nation*, 44.

The *tughrā*ʾ is also a clear link to calligraphic conventions, particularly those made popular through the works of scribes employed within the imperial, Ottoman realm. Thus, one may also suggest that the image of the Ottoman sovereign, or al-Bustānī's own re-negotiation of his subject-hood within a changing political context, is at work in this visual motif.[161] The significance of al-Bustānī's employment of this visual form can certainly be related to its subsequent appearance in publications from the 1860s. In the other examples, which are also publications by Arab Christian authors, the *tughrā*ʾ not only recalls scribal traditions within the new context of print, but also locates these works within the context of a multi-confessional readership. These multiple appearances of the *tughrā*ʾ illustrate what print intellectuals in Beirut perceived printed texts should look like at a time of rapid social and technological change.

Considering the ways in which several publications printed at the American Press (and some of its contemporaries in Beirut) during the 1850s-1860s emulated the Press's design and organizational program, one could argue that the Press's streamlined aesthetic and simplified typeface appealed to local Arab scholars' intellectual commitments. It is clear that the above examples of al-Yāzijī's and al-Bustānī's independent publications were important to the early and late nineteenth-century *nahḍa*. They were also possibly valued for their visually innovative, non-traditional, and industrial style, a style representative of a contemporary moment whose religious, political, and intellectual pillars were in flux. In their almost unadorned layouts, with traces of scribal conventions, these works demonstrate an interest in moving beyond the customary visual language of manuscripts in favor of new graphic representations that incorporated Western publishing practices and contributed to an emergent "modern" aesthetic. These scholars' preferred visual conventions illustrate emergent notions of what printed books should look like at a transformative moment, shortly before private Arab Christian and Muslim presses began to take hold throughout the region.

## Conclusion

The 1850s and 1860s saw an unconventional interface between the mission's American Press and local Arab intellectuals. Due to various funding and administrative considerations, the Protestants in Beirut frequently rented out their American Press and its equipment to local Muslim and Christian scholars interested in publishing their own works. In this way, the American Press, through its job works, was quickly becoming an anonymous (and unintentional) publisher of literature calling for a "revival" of past literary works, promoting nationalist ideals, and a multi-confessional Arab identity. Links between the American mission and an emergent Syrian identity have been frequently dealt with in historical and literary scholarship on the subject.[162] Such

161 For instance, Sheehi argues that in al-Bustānī's discussion of the national subject and social reform, "the subject-nation configuration depends on the intervention of a mediating leader" (the Ottoman sultan, in this case) "who is both external and internal to the native subject." Sheehi, "Al-Bustānī and Subjective Reform," 12."

162 These include (but are by no means limited to): Adel Beshara, *The Origins of Syrian Nationhood*; Ellen Fleischmann, "Evangelization or Education"; Fruma Zachs, *The Making of a Syrian Identity: Intellectuals and Merchants in Nineteenth Century Beirut* (Leiden: Brill, 2005); Zachs, "Toward a Proto-Nationalist Concept of Syria? Revisiting the American Presbyterian Missionaries in the Nineteenth-Century Levant," *Die Welt des Islams* 41, no. 2 (2001): 145–73; Adnan Abu-Ghazaleh, *American Missions in Syria: A Study of American Missionary Contribution to Arab Nationalism in 19th Century Syria* (Brattleboro: Amana Books, 1990); Tibawi, "The Genesis and Early History of the Syrian Protestant College," *American University of Beirut Festival Book*, eds. Fouad Sarruf and Suha Tamim (Beirut: American University of Beirut, 1967), 257–94; Munir A. Bashshur, "Higher Education and Political Development in Syria and Lebanon," *Comparative Education Review* 10, no. 3 (1966): 451–61.

sources emphasize the pivotal role of the mission's Syrian Protestant College and its missionary schools. The American Press, particularly during the period when almost all works it printed – besides the Bible – were produced by local Arab scholars and elites, also played an important (and unplanned) role for early scholars of the *nahḍa* period. In utilizing its premises and tools for the physical means of producing their books, local intellectuals also derived inspirations from this Press's visual language to shape and mold their works and image as actors in a changing intellectual, religious, and political landscape.

What the changing visual conventions of these early Arabic publications imply is how books functioned as dynamic sites of creative production that demonstrate the broader artistic concerns of this period in the Islamic world. This was a moment that saw the coming together of industrialized global modernization practices and the perseverance of local customary modes of visual production. In particular, the works discussed in this chapter illustrate the aesthetic manifestations of the interests of local Arab scholars in an engagement with modernization and their commitment to the formation of an inter-confessional Syrian national identity.

# Epilogue

While numerous examples of the mission's secular and religious publications were explored in the present study, these did not include one of the mission's most significant works, its Arabic Protestant Bible. This Bible, which was translated over the course of thirteen or so years (1847–1860), saw its first edition come off the press in 1860. It remained one of the mission's most significant publications, printed in numerous versions and editions throughout the late 1800s and the twentieth century. Indeed, this translation, which is commonly referred to as the "Van Dyck Bible," remains one of the key texts in use today by Arab Protestant communities in Lebanon, Egypt, and neighboring regions. This Bible's currency in these communities raises questions about its role within the framework of the *nahḍa* period and illuminates the significance of printed books in the region at the end of the nineteenth century.

This study was initially conceived as an examination of this Bible, an exemplar of an emergent "modern" aesthetic that paralleled the American translation's lexigraphy. The Bible is noteworthy in how it negotiated the re-imagining of past scribal customs and shifting perceptions of the uses, meanings, and aesthetics of the book, at a time when debates on modernity were becoming increasingly popular amongst Arab *nahḍa* intellectuals in Beirut. However, in the interest of emphasizing an earlier phase in the history of the American Press and in shedding much-needed light on the preliminary works of important Arab Christian intellectuals, the study was ultimately focused on a time leading up to that period in the mission's history. The Bible's importance to local readers only became evident during the 1870s, with the growth of the Arab Protestant communities. But its visual conventions and production, via collaborations between missionaries and local Arab scholars, had their origins in the mission's and the Press's earlier efforts.

In fact, in the early stages of research, what was most striking about the Van Dyck Bible was its seemingly unremarkable aesthetic composition. Much like the books printed at the American Press from the 1840s onwards, its various formats – from the small pocket book edition to the larger "royal" sizes – eschew any decorative margins, ornamental elements, or overtly calligraphic headings. Instead, the main focus is the text itself, composed via the popular American Arabic typeface, taking on what one might erroneously classify as a "Protestant aesthetic."

However, the non-ornamental set of visual conventions must be read in light of the mission's earlier, rather decorative, publications from the 1830s, and the role of these publications as sites of contestation of intersecting worldviews. A study of these seemingly unremarkable books highlights the shortcomings of the predominant narrative of the missionary press's history and its productions, namely the emphasis on the contributions of individual "visionaries" like Eli Smith. By tracing the story of these books using their materiality and design as starting points, what comes to light are their multi-dimensional components, the labor involved in their production, and their history as sites of negotiation between missionary ideals and Arab cultural and socio-political engagements.

By the 1860s Beirut was a dynamic site of multi-confessional convergence and contention bearing witness to widespread political, social, and intellectual change. The echoes of the devastating civil wars of the 1860s reverberated amongst local residents and altered the region's socio-political dynamics. Perhaps the most significant result of these conflicts, particularly with regard to present-day Lebanon, was the designation of Mount Lebanon as a protectorate in 1862. By 1870 sections of neighboring regions, including the coastal cities of Sidon, Beirut, and Tripoli, formerly parts of their own *wilāyas* (governorates), were reorganized within the borders of the *wilāya* of *sūriyya* (The Syrian Province). With these Tanzimat of the

 | DOI 10.1163/9789004314351_007

1860s, communal notions of a Syrian, or even a proto-Lebanese, identity began manifesting in physical (albeit shifting) boundaries.

Global developments, such as the growing interest in radical and socialist thought and the writings inspired by the French revolution of 1830, found their way into the discussions and debates within the public forums of these increasingly autonomous regions. Reading rooms, cafes, and town centers were the settings were these intellectual currents informed a local elite intelligentsia's emergent views on issues of political identity, class struggle, women's rights, and secular education. Arabic newspapers, pamphlets, journals, and books printed in key centers like Beirut, Cairo, and Alexandria emerged as the media through which these various perspectives intersected and overlapped.

It is not surprising, then, that the majority of the scholarship on this period deals with the ramifications and central ideas of the fin-de-siècle *nahḍa* period. However, as argued in this book, many of the ideas that circulated during the later *nahḍa* era had their origins in printed books from the early to mid-nineteenth century. This study excavates the import of this history, through the earlier works of individuals like Nāṣīf al-Yāzijī and Buṭrus al-Bustānī. These examples explore the physical means through which individuals grappled with guiding the formation of a contemporary vision of an Arab heritage and a multi-confessional Syrian identity.

In this story of the formative role of the pre- or early *nahḍa*, the printed Arabic book has a special significance. This significance tends to be sidelined in studies of the later period, which emphasize the increasingly popular mass-produced formats of newsprints and journals. Although books were more expensive and time consuming to produce, they were also sites of the earliest mediations between scribal traditions and emergent printing practices. They helped establish visual conventions for the nascent Arab printing industry. The results of these investigations were later parlayed by local private presses into the production standards and design layouts of the later popular periodicals. This study of the American Press's early secular and religious publications thus contributes to the recent scholarship on the early *nahḍa*, which refutes its exclusivity to the late 1800s and to that period's publishing industry. It is in this sense that this book concludes with the 1860s, which constitutes the starting point for the majority of scholarship on the subject of printed books, publishing, and the *nahḍa*. A study of the mission's publications as primary source materials, complemented by an evenhanded reading of the missionary records, lends evidence to a dynamic moment in missionary and local Arab encounters, which allowed for experimental overlaps between myriad visual modes, intellectual ideals, and sociopolitical concerns that were negotiated on the printed pages of these publications.

# *Appendices*

# Annual Number of Arabic Publications from the American Press, 1836–1867

The following is the total number of publications produced at the American Press based on figures from official records of the Syria Mission, such as Annual Reports of the Syria Mission, Annual Reports of the Beirut Station, Annual Tabular View Reports, and various Reports of the Press. Due to gaps and inconsistencies in these records, some publications may have been inadvertently left off of this list. For instance, it is possible that a number of works that were printed in pamphlet form were not noted in the missionary records. Additionally, since job works were not consistently included in these records, they are not always reflected in the numbers below.

| Year | Number of publications completed |
|---|---|
| 1836 | 8 |
| 1837 | 6 |
| 1838 | 5 |
| 1839 | 2 |
| 1840 | 0 |
| 1841 | 3 |
| 1842 | 5 |
| 1843 | 6 |
| 1844 | 2 |
| 1845 | 2 |
| 1846 | 3 |
| 1847 | 2 |
| 1848 | 5 |
| 1849 | 5 |
| 1850 | 1 |
| 1851 | 3 (1 is a possible job work) |
| 1852 | 4 |
| 1853 | 6 (1 is a possible job work; unspecified number of broad sheets printed) |
| 1854 | 6 (unspecified number of job works printed) |
| 1855 | 4 (2 are possible job works) |
| 1856 | 8 (3 are possible job works) |
| 1857 | 10 (1 is a confirmed job work) |
| 1858 | 3 (1 is a possible job work) |
| 1859 | 7 (17 editions of small pamphlets for children were also produced) |
| 1860 | 9 (1 is a possible job work) |
| 1861 | 0 (unspecified number of job works printed) |
| 1862 | 7 (1 is a confirmed job work) |
| 1863 | 3 (2 are confirmed job works) |
| 1864 | 4 (unspecified number of job works printed) |
| 1865 | 13[1] (1 is a confirmed job work; unspecified number of job works printed) |
| 1866 | Unspecified; tallied by number of pages (unspecified number of job works printed) |
| 1867 | 6 (2 are confirmed job works; unspecified number of job works printed) |

1 It is not clear whether all thirteen works were actually completed during this year.

 | DOI 10.1163/9789004314351_008

APPENDIX 2

# List of Arabic Publications Produced at the American Press, 1836–1867

The following is a list of works printed at the American Press in Beirut between 1836 and 1867 that are mentioned or discussed in this book. This is not a complete list of publications produced at the American Press. Some useful notes concerning this list are:

- The publications are grouped by year of production, with repeat entries for each subsequent edition.
- When available or known, the names of the missionary or Arab author(s), translators, and/or editors are given.
- If a publication has not been located and/or the Arabic title is unknown, then the English title from missionary records is used instead.
- Since many of these publications are discussed in this book, the translations and citations can be found elsewhere in this study. Notes are provided for any publications that were not directly dealt with in this book.
- Publications that were job works are indicated as such.
- Unless otherwise noted, all works were published in Beirut at the American Press. In cases where a different publisher is listed on the title page, the name of this alternate publisher is included alongside an indication that the book may have been produced at the American Press.

### Publications from Chapter 3: 1834–1840

- "Arabic spelling cards for spelling lessons." 1835 or 1836.[1]
- "Arabic copy books for writing." Lithographed. 1836.[2]
- *Kitāb taʿlīm mukhtaṣar li-l-aṭfāl fī qawāʿid al-dīyāna wa-l-īmān.* 1836.
- "Models of Arabic calligraphy"; or "Arabic alphabet cards." 1836. Lithographed.[3]
- *Qaṭf maqālāt al-qiddīs yūḥannā fam al-dhahab ʿan muṭālaʿat al-kutub al-muqaddasa.* Translated by ʿĪsā Bītrū. 1836.
- *Qiṣṣat ilīṣābāt ibnat al-labbān al-saʿīda.* 1836.
- al-Yāzijī, Nāṣīf. *Baʿḍ mazāmīr li-l-tarannum.* 1836.
- al-Yāzijī, Nāṣīf. *Kitāb faṣl al-khiṭāb fī uṣūl lughat al-iʿrāb.* 1836.
- *Amthāl sulaymān.* 1837.
- Homes, Henry A. *ʿIlāj mufīd li-l-hawāʾ al-aṣfar al-mubīd.* 1837.
- *Iqtiṭāf kitāb al-iqtidāʾ bi-l-masīḥ.* 1837.
- Smith, Eli. *Kitāb dalīl al-ṣawāb fī uṣūl al-ḥisāb.* 1837.
- *Waʿẓ al-masīḥ ʿala-l-jabal.* 1837.
- Whiting, George B. *Kitāb irshād al-masīḥī fī imtiḥān al-nafs.* 1837.
- *Kitāb al-zabūr al-ilāhī li-dāūd al-nabī.* 1838.
- *Kitāb taʿlīm al-awlād ʿan al-nafs, al-qism al-awal.* 1838.
- Thomson, William. *Sūrat al-īmān al-qawīm ʿala mūjib al-injīl al-karīm.* 1838.
- Whiting, George B. *Kitāb fī al-imtināʿ ʿan shurb al-muskirāt* [sic]. 1838.

1 "Report on the Press," 31 Dec 1836, United Presbyterian Church in the U.S.A. Syria Mission Records, 1808–1967, RG 115, box 1, folder 25, Presbyterian Historical Society, Philadelphia, PA (hereafter cited as PHS, RG 115-1-25).

2 "Quarterly Report on the Press," 29 Jun 1836, PHS, RG 115-1-25.

3 "Report of the Operation of the Press," 6 Apr 1836; "Report on the Press," 31 Dec 1836; "Quarterly Report on the state of the Press," 30 Sep 1836, PHS, RG 115-1-25. One card is amongst the holdings of the Houghton Library, Harvard University, Cambridge, MA (*98Miss168).

 | DOI 10.1163/9789004314351_009

- *Kitāb taʿlīm al-awlād ʿan al-nafs, al-qism al-thānī.* 1839.
- *Waʿẓ al-masīḥ ʿala-l-jabal.* 2nd ed. 1839.

### Publications from Chapter 4: 1841–1851

- *Kitāb al-ājurrūmiyya: al-ajwiba al-jaliyya fī-l-uṣūl al-naḥawiyya.* 1841.
- *Qiṣṣat ālām sayyidnā yasūʿ al-masīḥ.* 1841.
- *Khabarīyat hinrī al-ṣaghīr wa-ḥammālih.* 1839–1842.
- *Amthāl sulaymān al-ḥakīm ibn dāūd.* Revised ed. 1842.
- *Iqtitāf kitāb al-iqtidāʾ bi-l-masīḥ.* Revised ed. 1842.
- *Kitāb al-zabūr al-ilāhī li-dāūd al-nabī.* 1842.
- "Arabic spelling cards for spelling lessons." 2 cards. 2nd ed. 1843.[4]
- al-Bustānī, Buṭrus, and Eli Smith. *Kitāb al-bāb al-maftūḥ fī aʿmāl al-rūḥ.* 1843.
- Whiting, George B. *Kitāb irshād al-masīḥī fī imtiḥān al-nafs.* 2nd ed. 1843.
- *Kitāb al-mabāḥith fī iʿtiqādāt baʿḍ al-kanāʾis.* 1844.
- *Kitāb siyāḥat al-masīḥī.* 1844.
- *Kitāb qawāʿid al-imān al-masīḥī.* 2nd ed. 1845.
- *Kitāb taʿlīm mukhtaṣar li-l-aṭfāl fī qawāʿid al-dīyāna wa-l-īmān.* 2nd ed. 1845.
- *Risālā ila aklīrūs kanāʾis sūriyya.* 1846.
- "Book of Arabic Lessons." 1846. May have been lithographic copies.[5]
- al-Bustānī, Buṭrus. *Kitāb kashf al-ḥijāb fī ʿilm al-ḥisāb.* 1848.
- Smith, Azariah. *ʿIlāj mufīd li-l-hawāʾ al-aṣfar al-mubīd.* 1848.
- Whiting, George B. *Kitāb fī al-imtināʿ ʿan shurb al-muskirāt* [sic]. 2nd ed. 1848.
- Whiting, George B. *Kitāb irshād al-masīḥī fī imtiḥān al-nafs.* 3rd ed. 1848.
- Bird, Isaac, and Jonas King. *Kitāb al-thalath ʿashara risāla.* 1849.
- Mishāqa, Mikhāʾīl. *Al-risāla al-mawsūma bi-l-dalīl ila ṭāʿat al-injīl.* 1849.
- al-Bustānī, Buṭrus, Eli Smith, and Nāṣīf al-Yāzijī. *Sifr al-takāwīn* (Genesis; Bible, Old Testament). 1851. Proof copies.[6]

### Publications from Chapter 5: 1852–1867

- al-Bustānī, Buṭrus (and Eli Smith?), ed. *Al-jizʾ al-awwal min aʿmāl al-jamʿiyya al-sūriyya.* 1852.
- *Kitāb taʿlīm masīḥī.* 2nd ed. 1852.
- al-Yāzijī, Nāṣīf. *Nabdha min dīwān al-shaykh nāṣīf al-yāzijī.* 1853. Job work.
- *Kitāb al-ājurrūmiyya: al-ajwiba al-jaliyya fī-l-uṣūl al-naḥawiyya.* 2nd ed. 1853.
- *Kitāb tarnīmāt lil ʿibāda* (A Book of Hymns for Worship). Revised ed. 1853.[7]
- al-Bustānī, Buṭrus. *Kitāb misbāḥ al-tālib fī baḥth al-maṭālib: mutāwwal fī al-ṣarf wa-l-naḥū wa-ʿilm al-ʿarūd wa-l-qawāfī.* 1854.
- al-Yāzijī, Nāṣīf. *Kitāb faṣl al-khiṭāb fī uṣūl lughat al-iʿrāb.* 2nd ed. 1854.
- al-Yāzijī, Nāṣīf. *Majmūʿ al-adab fī funūn al-ʿarab: kitāb ʿiqd al-jumān fī ʿilm al-bayān.* vol. 1. 1855. Job work.
- al-Yāzijī, Nāṣīf. *Majmūʿ al-adab fī funūn al-ʿarab: nuqṭat al-dāʾira.* vol. 2. 1855. Job work.
- *Kitāb qawāʿid al-imān al-masīḥī.* Revised ed. 1855.[8]

---

4 Records of the American Board of Commissioners for Foreign Missions deposited at Houghton Library, Harvard University, Cambridge, Mass. (hereafter cited as ABC), 16.8.1 Syria Mission (1823–1871), vol. 4, *Annual Report of the Syria Mission*, 1853.

5 "Semi-Annual Report of the Press," Jan-Jun 1846, PHS, RG 115-1-25.

6 A few hundred proof copies of this new translation were printed for review; see ABC 16.8.1, vol. 5, "Letter accompanying first Genesis proofs," 15 Jul 1851; vol. 4, *Annual Report of the Syria Mission*, 1851.

7 ABC 16.8.1, vol. 4, *Annual Report of the Syria Mission*, 1853.

8 "Westminster Assembly's Shorter catechism in Arabic: with references." From the listing of the copy held at Harvard University libraries (OCLC 32961875).

- *Qiṣṣat hinrī al-ṣaghīr wa-ḥammālih.* 2nd ed. 1855.
- al-Yāzijī, Nāṣīf. *Kitāb majmaʿ al-baḥrayn.* 1856. Job work.
- Busṭrus, Salīm. *Kitāb al-nuzha al-shahiyya fī al-riḥla al-salīmiyya.* 1856. Job work.
- Whiting, George B. *Kitāb fī al-imtināʿ ʿan shurb al-muskirāt*[sic]. 3rd ed. 1856.
- *Kitāb al-ājurrūmiyya: al-ajwiba al-jaliyya fī al-uṣūl al-naḥawiyya.* 3rd ed. 1857.
- Abkariyyūs, Iskandar ibn Yaʿqūb. *Kitāb rawḍat al-adab fī ṭabaqāt shuʿarāʾ al-ʿarab.* 1857.[9] Job work.
- *Kitāb tarnīmāt lil ʿibāda.* 2nd ed. 1857.
- al-Yāzijī, Nāṣīf. *Kitāb quṭb al-ṣināʿa fī uṣūl al-manṭiq* (*al-taḍkira fī uṣūl al-manṭiq*). 1857. Job work.
- *Kitāb taʿlīm mukhtaṣar li-l-aṭfāl fī qawāʿid al-dīyāna wa-l-īmān.* 3rd ed. 1858.
- *Kitāb qawāʿid al-imān al-masīḥī.* 2nd ed. 1858.[10]
- al-Shidyāq, Tānnūs ibn Yūsuf, and Buṭrus al-Bustānī. *Kitāb akbār al-aʿyān fī jabal lubnān.* 2 vols. 1859. Job work.
- al-Bustānī, Buṭrus. *Kitāb kashf al-ḥijāb fī ʿilm al-ḥisāb.* 2nd ed. 1859.
- al-Bustānī, Buṭrus. *Khuṭba fī ādāb al-ʿarab.* 1859. Job work.
- *Kitāb siyāḥat al-masīḥī.* Translated by Buṭrus al-Bustānī. Revised ed. 1859.[11]
- al-Bustānī, Buṭrus. *Qiṣṣat asʿad al-shidyāq bākūrat sūriyya.* 1860. Job work (?).
- al-Bustānī, Buṭrus. *Dīwān abu al-ṭayyib aḥmad ibn al-ḥusayn al-mutanabbī.* Beirut: al-Maṭbaʿa al-Sūriyya, 1860. Possibly printed at the American Press. Job work.
- [al-Bustānī, Buṭrus]. *Nafīr sūriyya.* Possibly printed at the American Press. 1860. Job work.
- al-Bustānī, Buṭrus. *Kitāb al-tuḥfa al-bustāniyya fī al-aṣfār al-kurūziyya ʿan riḥlat rūbinṣun kurūzī.* 1861. Job work (?).[12]
- al-Bustānī, Buṭrus. *Kitāb miftāḥ al-miṣbāḥ fī uṣūl al-ṣarf wa-l-naḥū.* 1862. Job work.
- Karāmī, Buṭrus, Khalīl Sarkīs, and Amīn Sarkīs. *Al-darārī al-sabʿ: ay al-muwashaḥāt al-andalūsiyya.* 1864. Job work.
- Sarkīs, Ibrāhīm. *Kitāb ṣawṭ al-nafīr fī aʿmāl iskandar al-kabīr.* 1864. Job work.
- *Kitāb al-mabāḥith fī iʿtiqādāt baʿḍ al-kanāʾis.* 2nd ed. 1866.
- al-Yāzijī, Nāṣīf. *Kitāb nār al-qura fī sharḥ jawf al-farā.* 1863. Job work.
- al-Bustānī, Buṭrus. *Kitāb miftāḥ al-miṣbāḥ fī uṣūl al-ṣarf wa-l-naḥū.* 2nd ed. 1867. Job work.
- al-Bustānī, Buṭrus. *Kitāb muḥīṭ al-muḥīṭ: ay qāmūs muṭawwal li-l-lugha al-ʿarabiyya.* 2 vols. 1867–1870.

9 ABC 16.8.1, vol. 4, *Annual Report of the Syria Mission*, 1857.

10 Second of edition printed with "proofs" (or references). ABC 16.8.1, vol. 4, *Annual Report of the Syria Mission*, 1858.

11 Ibid.

12 It is not mentioned in the Beirut station's annual report for that year. ABC 16.8.1, vol. 6, *Annual Report of the Beirut Station*, 1858.

# Bibliography

## Primary Sources


Anderson, Rufus. *Report to the Prudential Committee of a Visit to the Missions in the Levant*. Boston: T.R. Marvin, 1844.

———. *Memorial Volume of the First Fifty Years of the American Board of Commissioners for Foreign Missions*. 4th ed. Boston: Geo. C. Rand and Avery, 1861.

Bird, Isaac. *Bible Work in Bible Lands; or, Events in the History of the Syria Mission*. Philadelphia: Presbyterian Board of Publication, 1872.

al-Bustānī, Buṭrus. *Nafīr sūriyya*. Beirut, 1860. Edited by Karam Rizk. Beirut: Dār al-Fikr lil-Abḥāth wa-l-Nashr, 1999.

Ellis, Alexander G. *Catalogue of Arabic Books in the British Museum*. 3 vols. London: The British Museum, 1894–1901.

Goodell, William and Edward D.G. Prime. *Forty Years in the Turkish Empire: Or, Memoirs of Rev. William Goodell, D.D. Late Missionary of the A.B.C.F.M. at Constantinople*. New York: R. Carter and Bros., 1875.

Hall, Isaac. "The Arabic Bible of Drs. Eli Smith and Cornelius V.A. Van Dyck." *Journal of the American Oriental Society* 11 (1882–1885): 276–86.

Holdich, Joseph and William J.R. Taylor. *The Arabic Scriptures*. New York: American Bible Society, 1864.

Jessup, Henry Harris. *Fifty-Three Years in Syria*. 2 vols. New York: Fleming H. Revell, 1910.

Johnson, John. *Typographia or the Printers' Instructor*. 2 vols. London: Longman, Hurst, Rees, Orme, Brown, and Green, 1824.

———. *An Abridgment of Johnson's Typographia, or the Printers' Instructor: With an Appendix*. Boston: C.L. Adams, 1828.

Jowett, William. *Christian Researches in Syria and the Holy Land, in MDCCCXXIII and MDCCCXXIV*. London: Richard Watts, 1825.

Khūrī, Yūsuf, ed. *Al-jamʿiyya al-sūriyya li al-ʿulūm wa al-funūn 1847–1852*. Beirut: Dār al-Hamrā, 1990.

———. *Aʿmāl al-jamʿiyya al-ʿilmiyya al-sūriyya lil-fūnūn wal-ʿulūm 1868–1879*. Beirut: Dār al-Hamrā, 1990.

Kuri, Sami. *Une histoire du Liban à travers les archives des Jésuites: 1816–1862*. 3 vols. Beirut: Dār al-Mashriq, 1985.

Laurie, Thomas. *Historical Sketch of the Syria Mission*. Boston: American Board of Commissioners for Foreign Missions, 1866.

*The Missionary Herald* 20–66 (1824–1870).

*The Missionary Register* 16 (1828).

*Report of the American Board of Commissioners for Foreign Missions* 10–16 (1819–1825).

Robinson, Edward, and Eli Smith. *Biblical Researches in Palestine and Adjacent Countries: A Journal of Travels in the Years 1838 & 1852*. 3 vols. London, 1856.

Salisbury, Edward E. "II. Syrian Society of Arts and Sciences." *Journal of the American Oriental Society* 3 (1853): 477–86.

Shaykhū, Luwīs. *Tārīkh fann al-ṭibāʿa fī al-mashriq*. 2nd ed. Beirut: Dār al-Mashriq, 1995.

al-Shidyāq, Tānnūs ibn Yūsuf, and Fu'ād Ifrām al-Bustānī. *Kitāb akbār al-aʿyān fī jabal lubnān*. Beirut, 1859. 2 vols. Beirut: Dār Nāḍīr ʿAbbūd, 1995.

Smith, Eli, and Cornelius Van Allen van Dyck. *A Brief Documentary History of the Translation of the Scriptures into the Arabic Language*. Beirut: American Presbyterian Mission Press, 1900.


## Secondary Sources


Abou Rjaili, Khalil. "Boutros al-Boustani (1819–83)." *Prospects: The Quarterly Review of Comparative Education*. UNESCO 23, no. 1/2 (1993): 125–33.

Abou Rjeily, Rana. *Cultural Connectives*. London: Mark Batty Publisher, 2011.

Abraham, Antoine J. *Lebanon at Mid-Century, Maronite-Druze Relations in Lebanon 1840–1860: A Prelude to Arab Nationalism*. Washington, D.C.: University Press of America, 1981.

Abu-Ghazaleh, Adnan. *American Missions in Syria: A Study of American Missionary Contribution to Arab Nationalism in 19th Century Syria*. Brattleboro: Amana Books, 1990.

Abu Husayn, Abdul Rahim. *The View from Istanbul: Ottoman Lebanon and the Druze Emirate*. London: I.B. Tauris, 2004.

Abu-Manneh, Butrus. "The Christians between Ottomanism and Syrian Nationalism: The Ideas of Butrus Al-Bustani." *International Journal of Middle East Studies* 11, no. 3 (1980): 287–304.

Aksan, Virginia. *Ottoman Wars: An Empire Besieged*. Harlow: Pearson, 2007.

Albin, Michael W. "The Iranian Publishing Industry: A Preliminary Appraisal." *Libri* 36, no. 1 (1986): 1–23.

———. "A Preliminary Bibliography of Arabic Books Printed by the Dominican Fathers in Mosul." *Mélanges de l'Institut Dominicain d'Études Orientales* 16 (1983): 247–60.

Anderson, Gerald H., ed. *Biographical Dictionary of Christian Missions*. Grand Rapids: William B. Eerdmas, 1999.

Antonius, George. *The Arab Awakening*. 2nd ed. London: Hamish Hamilton, 1945.

Arce, Agustin. *Catalogus descriptivus illustratus operum in Typographia Ierosolymorum Franciscali impressorum*. Vol. 1. 1847–1880. Jerusalem, 1969.

Ashur, Radwa, Ferial J. Ghazoul, and Hasna Reda-Mekdashi, eds. *Arab Women Writers: A Critical Reference Guide, 1873–1999*. Cairo: The American University of Cairo Press, 2008.

Atiyeh, George, ed. *The Book in the Islamic World: The Written Word and Communication in the Middle East*. Albany: State University of New York, 1995.

Ayalon, Ami. *The Press in the Arab Middle East; A History*. Oxford: Oxford University Press, 1995.

———. *Reading Palestine, Printing and Literacy: 1900–1948*. Austin: University of Texas Press, 2004.

———. "The Syrian Educated Elite and the Literary *nahḍa*." In *Ottoman Reform and Islamic Regeneration*, edited by Fruma Zachs and Itzchak Weismann, 127–66. London: I.B. Tauris, 2005.

———. "Private Publishing in the *Nahḍa*." *International Journal of Middle East Studies* 40, no. 4 (2008): 561–77.

ʿAzab, Khālid Muḥammad, and Aḥmad Manṣūr. *Al-kitāb al-ʿarabī al-maṭbūʿ: min al-judhūr ila maṭbaʿat būlāq*. Cairo: Dār al-Miṣriyya al-Lubnāniyya, 2008.

Badr, Habib. "American Protestant Missionary Beginnings in Beirut and Istanbul: Policy, Politics, Practice and Response." In Murre-van den Berg, *New Faith in Ancient Lands*, 211–40.

Badran, Margot. "The Origins of Feminism in Egypt." In *Current Issues in Women's History*, edited by Arina Angerman, Geerte Binnema, Annamieke Keunen, Vefie Poels, and Jacqueline Zirkzee, 153–70. 2nd ed. London: Routledge, 2012.

al-Bagdadi, Nadia. "Print, Script and the Limits of Free-Thinking in Arabic Letters of the 19th Century: The Case of al-Shidyaq." *Al-Abhath* 44–49 (2000): 99–122.

Barthes, Roland. *S/Z*. Oxford: Blackwell Publishing, 2002.

Bashkin, Orit. "Why Did Baghdadi Jews Stop Writing to Their Brethren in Mainz? Some Comments about the Reading Practices of Iraqi Jews in the Nineteenth Century." In Sadgrove, *History of Printing and Publishing*, 95–110.

Bashshur, Munir A. "Higher Education and Political Development in Syria and Lebanon." *Comparative Education Review* 10, no. 3 (1966): 451–61.

Bawardi, Basilius. "*Hadiqat al-Akhbar* Newspaper and Its Pioneering Role in the Arabic Narrative Fiction." *Die Welt der Islam* 48 (2008): 170–95.

Behrens-Abouseif, Doris, and Stephen Vernoit, eds. *Islamic Art in the 19th Century: Tradition, Innovation and Eclecticism*. Leiden: Brill, 2006.

Bein, Amit. *Ottoman Ulema, Turkish Republic: Agents of Change and Guardians of Tradition*. Stanford: Stanford University Press, 2011.

Ben Cheikh, Abdelkader. *Book Production and Reading in the Arab World*. Paris: UNESCO, 1982.

———. *Communication et société: pouvoir lire et développement culturel*. Tunis: Publications du centre de recherches en bibliothéconomie et sciences de l'information, 1986.

Benjamin, Walter. "The Work of Art in the Age of Mechanical Reproduction." In *Illuminations*, 211–44. London: Pimlico, 1999.

Berger, Lutz. "Zur Problematik der späten Einfuhrung des Buchdrucks in der islamischen Welt." In *Das gedruckte Buch im Vorderen Orient*, edited by Ulrich Marzolph, 15–28. Dortmund: Verlag für Orientkunde, 2002.

Beshara, Adel. *The Origins of Syrian Nationhood: Histories, Pioneers and Identity*. London: Routledge, 2011.

———. *Butrus al-Bustani: Spirit of the Age*. Melborne: Iphoenix Publishing, 2014.

Bhabha, Homi. *The Location of Culture*. London: Routledge, 1994.

Blair, Sheila. *Islamic Calligraphy*. Edinburgh: Edinburgh University Press, 2006.

Bloom, Jonathan. *Paper Before Print: The History and Impact of Paper in the Islamic World.* New Haven: Yale University Press, 2001.

Boogert, Maurits H. van den. "The Sultan's Answer to the Medici Press? Ibrahim Muteferrika's Printing House in Istanbul." In *The Republic of Letters and the Levant*, edited by Maurits van den Boogert, Alastair Hamilton, and Bart Westerweel, 265–91. Leiden: Brill, 2005.

Booth, Marilyn. "al-Yāzijī, Warda (1838–1924)." In *Encyclopedia of Arabic Literature*, vol. 2, edited by Julie S. Meisami and Paul Starkey, 813. London: Routledge, 1998.

Bosworth, Clifford E., ed. *Encyclopedia of Islam.* vol. 6. Leiden: Brill, 1989.

Bou Ali, Nadia. "Collecting the Nation: Lexicography and National Pedagogy in al-nahda al-ʿarabiyya." In *Archives, Museums and Collecting Practices in the Modern Arab World*, edited by Sonja Mejcher-Atassi and John P. Schwartz, 33–56. Farnham: Ashgate, 2012.

———. "Buṭrus al-Bustānī and the Shipwreck of the Nation." *Middle Eastern Literatures: Incorporating Edebiyat* 16, no. 3 (2013): 266–81.

Braude, Benjamin, and Bernard Lewis, eds. *Christians and Jews in the Ottoman Empire*. London: Holmes and Meier Publishers, 1982.

Brown, Michelle. *Understanding Illuminated Manuscripts: A Guide to Technical Terms*. Malibu: J. Paul Getty Museum, 1994.

Buheiry, Marwan. "The Peasant Revolt of 1858 in Mount Lebanon: Rising Expectations, Economic Malaise, and the Incentive to Arm." In *Land Tenure and Social Transformation in the Middle East*, edited by Tarif al-Khalidi, 291–302. Beirut: American University of Beirut, 1984.

Carruthers, Jo. *England's Secular Scripture: Islamophobia and the Protestant Aesthetic*. New York: Continuum, 2010.

Chartier, Roger. *Cultural History: Between Practices and Representations*. Translated by Lydia G. Cochrane. Ithaca: Cornell University Press, 1988.

———. "Texts, Printing, Readings." In *The New Cultural History*, edited by Lynn Hunt, 154–75. Berkeley: University of California Press, 1989.

———. *The Order of Books: Readers, Authors, and Libraries in Europe between the Fourteenth and Eighteenth Centuries*. Cambridge: Polity Press, 1994.

———. "The Printing Revolution: A Reappraisal." In *Agent of Change: Print Culture Studies after Elizabeth L. Eisenstein*, edited by Sabrina A. Baron, Eric N. Lindquist, and Eleanor F. Shevlin, 397–408. Amherst: University of Massachusetts Press, 2007.

Chevallier, Dominique. "Non-Muslim Communities in Arab Cities." In Braude and Lewis, *Christians and Jews*, 159–65.

Çinar, Alev. *Modernity, Islam, and Secularism in Turkey: Bodies, Places, and Time*. Minneapolis: University of Minnesota Press, 2005.

Clegg, Cyndia S. "History of the Book: An Undisciplined Discipline?" *Renaissance Quarterly* 54, no. 1 (2001): 221–45.

Coakley, J.F. "Printing Offices of the American Board of Commissioners for Foreign Missions, 1817–1900: A Synopsis." *Harvard Library Bulletin* 9, no. 1 (1998): 5–34.

———. "Homan Hallock, Punchcutter," *Printing History* 45, no. 1 (2003): 18–41.

Coffey, Heather. "Between Amulet and Devotion: Islamic Miniature Books in the Lilly Library." In Gruber, *The Islamic Manuscript Tradition*, 79–115.

Cohen, Mark R. *Under Crescent and Cross: The Jews in the Middle Ages*. Princeton: Princeton University Press, 1994.

Cole, Juan R.I. "Printing and Urban Islam in the Mediterranean World, 1890–1920." In Fawaz and Bayly, *Modernity and Culture*, 344–64.

Cox, Jeremy. *Imperial Fault Lines: Christianity and Colonial Power in India, 1818–1940*. Stanford: Stanford University Press, 2002.

———. "Master Narratives of Imperial Missions." In *Mixed Messages: Materiality, Textuality, Missions*, edited by Jamie S. Scott and Gareth Griffiths, 3–18. Hampshire: Palgrave Macmillan, 2005.

———. *The British Missionary Enterprise since 1700*. London: Routledge, 2008.

Dagher, Charbel. *Al-ʿarabiyya wa-l-tamaddun*. Beirut: Dār al-Nahār, 2008.

Daines, Mike. "Arabic Calligraphy, from Reed Pen to Mouse." *Baseline International Typographic Magazine* 15 (1992): 12–17.

Daniel, Robert L. "American Influences in the Near East before 1861." *American Quarterly* 16, no. 1 (1964): 72–84.

Darton, Robert. "What is the History of Books?" *Daedalus* 111, no. 3 (1982): 65–83.

Deeb, Lara. *An Enchanted Modern: Gender and Public Piety in Shiʿi Lebanon*. Princeton: Princeton University Press, 2006.

Di-Capua, Yoav. *Gatekeepers of the Arab Past: Historians and History Writing in Twentieth-Century Egypt*. Berkeley: University of California Press, 2009.

Dirlik, Arif. "Whither History? Encounters with Historicism, Postmodernism, Postcolonialism." In *History after the Three Worlds: Post-Eurocentric Historiographies*, edited by Arif Dirlik, Vinay Bahl, and Peter Gran, 241–58. Latham: Rowman and Littlefield Publishers, Inc., 2000.

Doğan, Mehmet Ali. "The Missionary Activities of Elias Riggis in İzmir." *International Journal of Turcologia* 5, no. 10 (2010): 21–30.

Drucker, Johanna. *The Visible Word: Experimental Typography and Modern Art, 1909–1923*. Chicago: The University of Chicago Press, 1994.

———. *Graphesis: Visual Forms of Knowledge Production*. Cambridge, Mass.: Harvard University Press, 2014.

Dunch, Ryan. "Beyond Cultural Imperialism: Cultural Theory, Christian Missions, and Global Modernity." *History and Theory* 41, no. 3 (2002): 301–25.

Dyrness, William A. *Reformed Theology and Visual Culture: The Protestant Imagination from Calvin to Edwards* (Cambridge: Cambridge University Press, 2004).

———. "Dante, Bunyan and the Case for a Protestant Aesthetics." *International Journal of Systematic Theology* 10, no. 3 (2008): 285–302.

Eisenstadt, S.N. "Multiple Modernities." *Daedalus* 129, no. 1, Multiple Modernities (2000): 1–29.

Eisenstein, Elizabeth L. *The Printing Press as an Agent of Change: Communications and Cultural Transformations in Early Modern Europe*. 2 vols. Cambridge: Cambridge University Press, 1979.

———. *The Printing Revolution in Early Modern Europe*. Cambridge: Canto, 1993.

Eissa, Ashraf. "Majallat al-jinān: Arabic Narrative Discourse in the Making." *Quaderni di Studi Arabi* 18 (2000): 41–49.

El-Ariss, Tarek. *Trials of Arab Modernity: Literary Affects and the New Political*. The Bronx: Fordham University Press, 2013.

El-Enany, Rasheed. *Arab Representations of the Occident: East-west Encounters in Arab Fiction*. London: Routledge, 2006.

Elsharky, Marwa. "The Gospel of Science and American Evangelism in Late Ottoman Beirut." *Past and Present* 19, no. 6 (2007): 173–214.

Ersoy, Ahmet. *Architecture and the Late Ottoman Historical Imaginary: Reconfiguring the Architectural Past in a Modernizing Empire*. Farnham: Ashgate Publishing, 2015.

Farah, Caesar E. "The Lebanese Insurgence of 1840 and the Powers." *Journal of Asian History* 1 (1967): 105–32.

———. *Politics of Interventionism in Ottoman Lebanon, 1830–1861*. London: I.B. Tauris, 2000.

Fawaz, Leila Tarazi. *Merchants and Migrants in Nineteenth-Century Beirut*. Cambridge, Mass.: Harvard University Press, 1983.

———. *An Occasion for War: Civil Conflict in Lebanon and Damascus in 1860*. Berkeley: University of California Press, 1994.

Fawaz, Leila Tarazi, and C.A. Bayly, eds. *Modernity & Culture: From the Mediterranean to the Indian Ocean*. New York: Columbia University Press, 2002.

Febvre, Lucien Paul Victor, and Henri-Jean Martin. *L'apparition du livre*. Paris: Albin Michel, 1958.

———. *The Coming of the Book: The Impact of Printing 1450–1800*. Translated by David Gerard, and edited by Geoffrey Nowell-Smith and David Wooton. London: N.L.B., 1976.

Fisher, Joshua B., and Rebecca Steinberger, eds. *Encountering Ephemera 1500–1800: Scholarship, Performance, Classroom*. Cambridge: Cambridge Scholars Publishing, 2012.

Fleischmann, Ellen. "Evangelization or Education: American Protestant Missionaries, the American

Board, and the Girls and Women of Syria (1830–1910)." In Murre-van den Berg, *New Faith in Ancient Lands,* 263–80.

Flood, Finbarr B. "From the Prophet to Postmodernism? New World Orders and the End of Islamic Art." In *Making Art History: A Changing Discipline and its Institutions*, edited by Elizabeth Mansfield, 31–53. London: Routledge, 2007.

———. *Objects of Translation: Material Culture and the Medieval "Hindu-Muslim" Encounter.* Princeton: Princeton University Press, 2009.

Gacek, Adam. *Arabic Manuscripts: A Vademecum for Readers*. Leiden: Brill, 2009.

Gaonkar, Dilip Parameshwar, ed. *Alternative Modernities.* Durham: Duke University Press, 2001.

Gdoura, Wahid. *Bidāyat al-ṭibāʿa al-ʿarabiyya fī isṭānbūl wa-bilād al-shām: taṭawwur al-muḥīt al-thaqāfī, 1706–1787*. Riyadh: Maktabat al-Malik Fahd al-Waṭaniyya, 1993.

Gencer, Yasmin. "İbrahim Müteferrika and the Age of the Printed Manuscript." In Gruber, *Islamic Manuscript Tradition,* 155–93.

Ghosh, Anindita. *Power in Print: Popular Publishing and the Politics of Language and Culture in Colonial Society, 1778–1905*. Oxford: Oxford University Press, 2006.

Glass, Dagmar. *Malta, Beirut, Leipzig and Beirut Again: Eli Smith, the American Syria Mission and the Spread of Arabic Typography in 19th Century Lebanon*. Edited by Angelika Neuwirth. Beirut: Orient-Institut der Deutschen Morganländischen Gesellschaft, 1997.

———. "Die *nahḍa* und ihre Technik im 19. Jahrhundert: Ärabische Druckereien in Ägypten und Syrien." In *Das gedruckte Buch im Vorderen Orient*, edited by Ulrich Marzolph, 50–84. Dortmund: Verlag für Orientkunde, 2002.

Göçek, Fatma Müge. *East Encounters West: France and the Ottoman Empire in the Eighteenth Century*. Oxford: Oxford University Press, 1987.

———. "Ethnic Segmentation, Western Education, and Political Outcomes: Nineteenth-Century Ottoman Society." *Poetics Today* 14, no. 3 (1993): 507–38.

———. *Rise of the Bourgeoisie, Demise of Empire: Ottoman Westernization and Social Change*. Oxford: Oxford University Press, 1996.

———. "Decline of the Ottoman Empire and the Emergence of Greek, Armenian, Turkish, and Arab Nationalisms." In *Social Constructions of Nationalism in the Middle East,* edited by Fatma M. Göçek, 15–84. Albany: State University of New York Press, 2002.

Golding, Peter, and Phil Harris, eds. *Beyond Cultural Imperialism: Globalization, Communication and the New International Order*. London: Sage, 1996.

Grafton, Anthony. *The Footnote: A Curious History*. Cambridge, Mass.: Harvard University Press, 1997.

Gran, Peter. *Beyond Eurocentrism: A New View of Modern World History*. Syracuse: Syracuse University Press, 1996.

Graves, Margaret. "Feeling Uncomfortable in the Nineteenth Century." *Journal of Art Historiography* 6 (June 2012): 1–27.

Green, Nile. "Journeymen, Middlemen: Travel, Transculture, and Technology in the Origins of Muslim Printing." *International Journal of Middle East Studies* 41, no. 2 (2009): 203–24.

———. "Persian Print and the Stanhope Revolution: Industrialization, Evangelicalism, and the Birth of Printing in Early Qajar Iran." *Comparative Studies of South Asia, Africa and the Middle East* 30, no. 3 (2012): 413–90.

Gruber, Christiane, ed. *The Islamic Manuscript Tradition: Ten Centuries of Book Arts in Indiana University Collections*. Bloomington: Indiana University Press, 2010.

Hafiz, Sabry. *The Genesis of Arab Narrative Discourse: A Study in the Sociology of Modern Arabic Literature*. London: Saqi, 1993.

Hakim, Carol. *The Origins of the Lebanese National Idea, 1840–1920*. Berkeley: The University of California Press, 2013.

Hämeen-Anttila, Jaakko. "An Old-Fashioned Genre – Maqāma in the 18th Century." *Rocznik Orientalistyczny* LXV, no. 2 (2012): 5–12.

Hamilton, Cynthia S. "Spreading the Word: The American Tract Society, *The Dairyman's Daughter*, and Mass Publishing." *Book History* 14 (2011).

Hanebutt-Benz, Eva, Dagmar Glass, and Geoffrey Roper, eds. *Middle Eastern Languages and the Print Revolution: A Cross-Cultural Encounter*. Mainz: Gutenberg-Museum, 2002.

Hanna, Nelly. *In Praise of Books: A Cultural History of Cairo's Middle Class, Sixteenth to the Eighteenth Century*. Syracuse: Syracuse University Press, 2003.

Hanssen, Jens. *Fin de Siècle Beirut: The Making of an Ottoman Provincial Capital*. Oxford: Clarendon Press, 2005.

Harris, Elizabeth M. *Printing Presses in the Graphic Arts Collection*. Washington, D.C.: The National Museum of American History, Smithsonian Institution, 1996.

Hill, Peter. "Early Translations of English Fiction into Arabic: *The Pilgrim's Progress* and *Robinson Crusoe*." *Journal of Semitic Studies* 60, no. 1 (2015): 177–212.

Hirschler, Konrad. *Medieval Arabic Historiography: Authors as Actors*. London: Routledge, 2006.

———. *The Written Word in the Medieval Arabic Lands: A Social and Cultural History of Reading Practices*. Edinburgh: Edinburgh University Press, 2012.

Hitti, Philip K. *History of the Arabs*. London: Macmillan, 1937.

Hourani, Albert. *Arabic Thought in the Liberal Age*. 2nd ed. Cambridge: Cambridge University Press, 1983.

Howsam, Leslie. *Cheap Bibles: Nineteenth-Century Publishing and the British Foreign Bible Society*. Cambridge: Cambridge University Press, 2002.

———. *Old Books & New Histories: An Orientation to Studies in Book and Print Culture*. Toronto: University of Toronto Press, 2006.

Hsu, Cheng-Hsiang. "A Survey of Arabic-Character Publications Printed in Egypt during the Period of 1238–1267 (1822–1851)." In Sadgrove, *History of Printing and Publishing*, 1–16.

Huntington, Samuel. *The Clash of Civilizations and the Remaking of World Order*. New York: Touchstone, 1997.

Hutchinson, William. *Errand to the World: American Protestant Thought and Foreign Missions*. Chicago: University of Chicago Press, 1987.

Issa, Rana. "The Bible as Commodity: Modern Patterns of Arabic Language Standardization and Bible Commoditization in the Levant." PhD diss., University of Oslo, 2014.

———. "The Arabic Language and Syro-Lebanese National Identity: Searching in Buṭrus al-Bustānī's *Muḥīṭ al-Muḥīṭ*." Unpublished manuscript, last modified August 25, 2015. Microsoft Word file.

Jardine, Lisa, and Anthony Grafton. "'Studied for Action': How Gabriel Harvey Read His Livy." *Past and Present* 129 (November 1990): 30–78.

Jenkins, Daniel T. "A Protestant Aesthetic? A Conversation with Donald Davie." *Journal of Literature & Theology* 2, no. 2 (1988): 153–62.

Johns, Adrian. *The Nature of the Book: Print and Knowledge in the Making*. Chicago: University of Chicago Press, 1998.

Kahale, Joseph. *ʿAbd-allāh zākhir, mubtakir al-maṭbaʿa al-ʿarabiyya*. Aleppo: Markaz al-Inmāʾ al-Ḥaḍārī, 2002.

Karsh, Efraim, and Inari Karsh. *Empires of the Sand: The Struggle for Mastery in the Middle East, 1789–1923*. Cambridge, Mass.: Harvard University Press, 2001.

Kasprzak, Natalia. "Quranic Matters: Media and Materiality." PhD diss., University of North Carolina at Chapel Hill, 2014.

Kassir, Samir. *Beirut*. Translated by Malcolm B. Debevoise. Berkeley: University of California Press, 2010.

Kerr, Robert M., and Thomas Milo, eds. *Writings and Writing from Another World and Another Era: Investigations in Islamic Text and Script in Honour of Dr Januarius Justus Witkam Professor of Codicology and Paleography of the Islamic World at Leiden University*. Cambridge: Archetype, 2013.

Khalaf, Samir. *Protestant Missionaries in the Levant: Ungodly Puritans, 1820–1860*. Oxford: Taylor and Francis, 2012. Kindle edition.

———. "Communal Conflict in 19th-Century Lebanon." In Braude and Lewis, *Christians and Jews*, 107–34.

Khalid, Adeeb. "Printing, Publishing, and Reform in Tsarist Central Asia." *International Journal of Middle East Studies* 26, no. 2 (1994): 187–200.

Khater, Akram Fouad. "She Married Silk: A Rewriting of Peasant History in 19th Century Mount Lebanon." PhD diss., University of California Berkeley, 1993.

Khuri-Makdisi, Ilham. *The Eastern Mediterranean and the Making of Global Radicalism, 1860–1914*. Berkeley: University of California Press, 2010.

Khūrī, Yūsuf. *Al-jamʿiyya al-sūriyya li al-ʿulūm wa-l-funūn 1847–1852*. Beirut: Dār al-Hamrā, 1990.

Kreiser, Klaus, ed. *The Beginnings of Printing in the Near and Middle East: Jews, Christians, and Muslims.* Weisbaden: Harrassowitz Verlag, 2001.

Krek, Miroslav. "Some Observations on Printing Arabic in America and by Americans Abroad." *Manuscripts of the Middle East* 6, no. 8 (1992): 71–87.

Kuran-Burçoğlu, Nedret. "Osman Zeki Bey and His Printing Office the *Matbaa-i Osmaniye*." In Sadgrove, *History of Printing and Publishing*, 35–58.

Kuri, Sami S.J. "Esquisse d'un catalogue des imprimes de l'Imprimerie Catholique de Beyrouth, 1848–1888." *Ḥawalīyāt maʿhad al-adāb al-sharqiyya* 7 (1993/1996): 75–134.

Leavy, Margaret R. *Eli Smith and the Arabic Bible.* New Haven: Yale Divinity School Library, 1993.

Mahdi, Muhsin. "From the Manuscript Age to the Age of Printed Books." In Atiyeh, *The Book in the Islamic World*, 1–16.

Makdisi, Ussama. "Reclaiming the Land of the Bible: Missionaries, Secularism, and Evangelical Modernity." *The American Historical Review* 102, no. 3 (1997): 680–713.

———. *The Culture of Sectarianism: Community, History, and Violence in Nineteenth-Century Ottoman Lebanon.* Berkeley: University of California Press, 2000.

———. "After 1860: Debating Religion, Reform, and Nationalism in the Ottoman Empire." *International Journal of Middle East Studies* 34, no. 4 (2002): 601–17.

———. "'Anti-Americanism' in the Arab World: An Interpretation of a Brief History," *Journal of American History* 89, no. 2 (2002): 538–57.

———. *Artillery of Heaven: American Missionaries and the Failed Conversion of the Middle East.* Ithaca: Cornell University Press, 2008.

Marsot, Afaf Lutfi al-Sayyid. *Egypt in the Reign of Muhammad Ali.* Cambridge Middle East Library. Cambridge: Cambridge University Press, 1984.

Marzolph, Ulrich. "Adab in Transition: Creative Compilation in Nineteenth-Century Print Tradition." *Israel Oriental Studies* 19 (1999): 161–72.

———. *Narrative Illustration in Persian Lithographed Books Handbook of Oriental Studies/Handbuch Der Orientalistik.* Leiden: Brill, 2001.

———, ed. *Das gedruckte Buch im Vorderen Orient.* Bremen: Verlag für Orientkunde, 2002.

———. "Illustrated Persian Lithographic Editions of the Shahname." *Edebiyat* 13, no. 2 (2003): 177–98.

———. "Persian Incunabula: A Definition and Assessment." *Gutenberg-Jahrbuch* 82 (2007): 205–20.

Marzolph, Ulrich, and Anja Pistor-Hatam. "Early Printing History in Iran (1817–ca. 1900)." In Hanebutt-Benz, *Middle Eastern Languages*, 249–72.

Masters, Bruce. *Christians and Jews in the Ottoman Arab World.* Cambridge: Cambridge University Press, 2001.

McKenzie, David F. "Printers of the Mind: Some Notes on Bibliographical Theories and Printing-House Practices." *Studies in Bibliography* 22 (1969): 1–75.

———. *Bibliography and the Sociology of Texts.* London: The British Library, 1986.

McKitterick, David. *Print, Manuscript and the Search for Order 1450–1830.* Cambridge: Cambridge University Press, 2003.

Messick, Brinkley. *The Calligraphic State: Textual Domination and History in a Muslim Society.* Berkeley: University of California Press, 1993.

Metzger, Bruce M., and Bart D. Ehrman, *The Text of the New Testament: Its Transmission, Corruption and Restoration.* Oxford: Oxford University Press, 2005.

Milo, Thomas. "Towards Arabic Historical Script Grammar: Through Contrastive Analysis of Qur'an Manuscripts." In Kerr and Milo, *Writings and Writing*, 248–92.

———. "Arabic Script and Typography: A Brief Historical Overview." In *Language Culture Type: International Type Design in the Age of Unicode*, edited by John D. Berry, 112–27. Zurich: Graphis Press, 2002.

Mitchell, Timothy, ed. *Questions of Modernity.* Minneapolis: University of Minnesota Press, 2000.

Moosa, Matti. *The Origins of Modern Arabic Fiction.* Boulder: Lynne Rienner Publishers, Inc., 1997.

Moran, James. *Printing Presses: History and Development from the Fifteenth Century to Modern Times.* Berkeley: University of California Press, 1973.

Moylan, Michele, and Lane Stiles, eds. *Reading Books: Essays on the Material Text and Literature in America.* Amherst: University of Massachusetts Press, 1996.

Murphy, Kevin, and Sally O'Driscoll, eds. *Studies in Ephemera: Text and Image in Eighteenth-Century Print*. Lanham: Bucknell University Press, 2013.

Murre-van den Berg, Heleen. *New Faith in Ancient Lands: Western Missions in the Middle East in the Nineteenth and Early Twentieth Centuries*. Leiden: Brill, 2006.

Nasrallah, Joseph. *L'imprimerie au Liban*. Beirut: l'Imprimerie de Saint-Paul, 1948.

———. *L'Imprimerie Catholique de Beyrouth, 1852–1966*. Beirut: l'Imprimerie Catholique, 1960.

Nassi, Gad, ed. *Jewish Journalism and Printing Houses in the Ottoman Empire and Modern Turkey*. Istanbul: Gorgias Press, 2001.

Neill, Stephen. *A History of Christian Missions*. 2nd ed. Westminster: Penguin Books, 1987.

Neumann, Christoph K. "Book and Newspaper Printing in Turkish, 18th–20th Century." In Hanebutt-Benz, *Middle Eastern Languages*, 227–48.

Nichols, Aidan. *Rome and the Eastern Churches: A Study in Schism*. 2nd ed. San Francisco: Ignatius Press, 2010.

Ogborn, Miles. *Indian Ink: Script and Print in the Making of the English East India Company*. Chicago: University of Chicago Press, 2007.

Osborn, J.R. (Wayne). "The Type of Calligraphy: Writing, Print, and Technologies of the Arabic Alphabet." PhD diss., UC San Diego, 2008.

Özbek, Nadir. "Defining the Public Sphere During the Late Ottoman Empire: War, Mass Mobilization and the Young Turk Regime (1908–18)." *Middle Eastern Studies* 43, no. 5 (2007): 795–809.

Patel, Abdulrazzak. *The Arab Nahḍah: The Making of the Intellectual and Humanist Movement*. Edinburgh: Edinburgh University Press, 2013.

Pedersen, Johannes. *The Arabic Book*. Translated by Geoffrey French and edited by Robert Hillenbrand. Princeton: Princeton University Press, 1984.

Pehlivanian, Meliné. "Mesrop's Heirs: The Early Armenian Book Printers." In Hanebutt-Benz, *Middle Eastern Languages*, 53–92.

Philipp, Thomas. "Bilād al-Šām in the Modern Period: Integration into the Ottoman Empire and New Relations with Europe." *Arabica* 54, no. 4 (2004): 401–18.

Phillips, Clifton J. *Protestant America and the Pagan World: The First Half-Century of the American Board of Commissioners for Foreign Missions, 1810–1860*. Cambridge, Mass.: Harvard University Press, 1969.

Pratt, Mary L. "Arts of the Contact Zone." *Profession* 91 (1991): 33–40.

———. *Imperial Eyes: Travel Writing and Transculturation*. London: Routledge, 1992.

Quataert, Donald. *Ottoman Manufacturing in the Age of the Industrial Revolution*. Cambridge: Cambridge University Press, 1993.

———. *The Ottoman Empire: 1700–1922*. Cambridge: Cambridge University Press, 2005.

Reeves-Ellington, Barbara. *Domestic Frontiers: Gender, Reform, and American Interventions in the Ottoman Balkans and the Near East*. Boston: University of Massachusetts Press, 2013.

Riḍwān, Abū al-Futūḥ. *Tārīkh maṭbaʿat būlāq: wa-lamḥa fī tārīkh al-ṭibāʿa fī buldān al-sharq al-awsaṭ*. Cairo: al-Maṭbaʿa al-Amīriyya, 1953.

Roberts, Mary. *Intimate Outsiders: The Harem in Ottoman and Orientalist Art and Travel Literature*. Durham: Duke University Press, 2007.

Robinson, B.W. "The Teheran Nizami of 1848 and Other Qajar Lithographed Books." In *Islam in the Balkans: Persian Art and Culture of the 18th and 19th Centuries*, edited by Jennifer M. Scarce, 61–65. Edinburgh: Royal Scottish Museum, 1979.

Robinson, Francis. "Technology and Religious Change: Islam and the Impact of Print." *Modern Asian Studies* 27, no. 1 (1993): 229–51.

Roehner, B.M. "Jesuits and the State: A Comparative Study of Their Expulsions." *Religion (London Academic Press)* 27, no. 2 (1997): 165–82.

Rogan, Eugene L. "Sectarianism and Social Conflict in Damascus: The 1860 Events Reconsidered." *Arabica* 54, no. 4 (2004): 493–511.

Roisse, Philippe. *Al-makhṭūṭat al-ʿarabiyya fī lubnān: iltiqāʾ al-thaqāfāt wa-l-adyān wa-l-maʿārif*. Beirut: CEDRAC, 2010.

Roper, Geoffrey. "George Percy Badger (1815–1888)." *British Society for Middle Eastern Studies, Bulletin* 11, no. 2 (1984): 140–55.

———. "Arabic Printing and Publishing in England before 1820." *British Society for Middle Eastern Studies, Bulletin* 12 (1985): 12–32.

———. "Arabic Printing in Malta 1825–1845: Its History and Its Place in the Development of Print Culture in the Arab Middle East." PhD thesis, Durham University, 1988.

———. "The Beginnings of Arabic Printing by the ABCFM, 1822–1841." *Harvard Library Bulletin* 9, no.1 (1998): 50–68.

———. "Fāris al-Shidyāq and the Transition from Scribal to Print Culture in the Middle East." In Atiyeh, *The Book in the Islamic World*, 209–31.

———. "The Printing Press and Change in the Arab World." In *Agent of Change: Print Culture Studies after Elizabeth L. Einstein*, edited by Sabrina A. Baron, Eric N. Lindquist, and Eleanor F. Shevlin, 251–67. Amherst: University of Massachusetts Press, 2007.

———. "An Autograph Manuscript of Ahmad Faris As-Sidyaq: Prepared by him for the Press." In *Writings and Writing from Another World and Another Era*, edited by Robert M. Kerr and Thomas Milo, 341–56. Cambridge: Archetype, 2013a.

———. "History of the Book in the Muslim World." In *The Book: A Global History*, edited by Michael F. Suarez, S.J., and H.R. Wooudhuysen, 524–52. Oxford: Oxford University Press, 2013b.

———. "Arabic Books Printed in Malta 1826–42: Some Physical Characteristics." In Sadgrove, *History of Printing and Publishing*, 111–29.

———. "Early Arabic Printing in Europe." In Hanebutt-Benz, *Middle Eastern Languages*, 129–50.

Roper, Geoffrey, and Dagmar Glass. "The Printing of Arabic Books in the Arab World." In Hanebutt-Benz, *Middle Eastern Languages*, 192–94.

Round, Phillip. *Removable Type: Histories of the Book in Indian Country, 1663–1880*. Chapel Hill: The University of North Carolina Press, 2010.

Roxburgh, David. *The Persian Album, 1400–1600: From Dispersal to Collection*. New Haven: Yale University Press, 2005.

Ruggles, D. Fairchild. *Islamic Art & Visual Culture: An Anthology of Sources*. West Sussex: Wiley-Blackwell Publishing, 2011.

Ṣabbāt, Khalīl. *Tārīkh al-ṭibā*ʿ*a fī al-sharq al-*ʿ*arabī*. Cairo: Dār al-Maʿārif, 1958.

Sabev, Orlin. "Waiting for Godot: the formation of Ottoman print culture." In *Historical Aspects of Printing and Publishing in Languages of the Middle East*, edited by Geoffrey Roper, 101–20. Leiden: Brill, 2014.

Sadgrove, Philip. "Al-Khūrī, Khalīl (1836–1907)." In *Encyclopedia of Arabic Literature*, vol. 2, edited by Julie Meisami and Paul Starkey, 448. London: Routledge, 1998.

———, ed. *History of Printing and Publishing in the Languages and Countries of the Middle East*. Oxford: Oxford University Press, 2005.

Safadi, Yasin H. "Printing in Arabic." *The Monotype Recorder* 2 (September 1980): 2–7.

Said, Edward. *Orientalism*. New York: Vintage Books, 1978.

———. *Culture and Imperialism*. New York: Vintage Books, 1993.

Sajdi, Dana. "Print and Its Discontents: A Case for Pre-print Journalism and Other Sundry Print Matters." *The Translator* 15, no. 1 (2009): 105–38.

———. *The Barber of Damascus: Nouveau Literacy in the Eighteenth-Century Ottoman Levant*. Stanford: Stanford University Press, 2013.

Salibi, Kamal. *A House of Many Mansions: The History of Lebanon Reconsidered*. London: I.B. Tauris, 1988.

Sanders, Paula. *Creating Medieval Cairo: Empire, Religion, and Architectural Preservation in Nineteenth-Century Egypt*. Cairo: The American University in Cairo Press, 2008.

Sardar, Ziauddin. "Print, Printing and Compact Disks: The Making and Unmaking of Islamic Culture." *Media, Culture and Society* 15 (1993): 43–59.

al-Sayyid, Jihān. *Al-biblīyūghrāfiyya al-taḥlīliyya: dirāsa fī awā*ʾ*il al-maṭbū*ʿ*āt al-*ʿ*arabiyya*. Alexandria: Dār al-Thaqāfa al-ʿIlmiyya, 2000.

Schaefer, Karl. *Enigmatic Charms: Medieval Arabic Block Printed Amulets in American and European Libraries and Museums*. Leiden: Brill, 2006.

———. "Arabic Printing before Gutenberg: Block-Printed Arabic Amulets." In Hanebutt-Benz, *Middle Eastern Languages*, 123–28.

Scheglova, O.P. "Lithograph Versions of Persian Manuscripts of Indian Manufacture in the Nineteenth Century." *Manuscripta Orientalia* 5, no. 1 (1999): 12–22.

Scheid, Kirsten. "Necessary Nudes: *ḥadātha* and *mu ʿāṣira* in the Lives of Modern Lebanese." *International Journal of Middle East Studies* 42 (2010): 203–30.

———. "The Agency of Art and the Study of Arab Modernity." *MIT-Electronic Journal of Middle East Studies* 7 (Spring 2007): 6–23.

Schulze, Reinhard. "The Birth of Tradition and Modernity in 18th and 19th Century Islamic Culture: The Case of Printing." *Culture & History* 16 (January 1997): 29–72.

Schwartz, Kathryn. "Meaningful Mediums: A Material and Intellectual History of Manuscript and Print Production in Nineteenth Century Ottoman Cairo." PhD diss., Harvard University, 2015.

Scott, Jamie, and Griffiths, Gareth, eds. *Mixed Messages: Materiality, Textuality, Missions*. London: Palgrave Macmillan, 2005.

Shannon, Jonathan Holt. *Among the Jasmine Trees: Music and Modernity in Contemporary Syria*. Middletown, Conn.: Wesleyan University Press, 2006.

Sharkey, Heather, ed. *Cultural Conversions: Unexpected Consequences of Christian Missionary Encounters in the Middle East, Africa and South Asia*. Syracuse: Syracuse University Press, 2013.

———. "Christian Missions and Colloquial Arabic Printing." In Sadgrove, *History of Printing and Publishing*, 131–49.

Shaw, Wendy. *Ottoman Painting: Reflections of Western Art from the Ottoman Empire to the Turkish Republic*. London: I.B. Tauris, 2011.

Sheehi, Stephen. "Inscribing the Arab Self: Buṭrus al-Bustānī and Paradigms of Subjective Reform." *British Journal of Middle Eastern Studies* 27, no. 1 (2000): 7–24.

———. *Foundations of Modern Arab Identity*. Gainesville: University Press of Florida, 2004.

———. "Arabic Literary-Scientific Journals: Precedence for Globalization and the Creation of Modernity." *Comparative Studies of South Asia, Africa and the Middle East* 25, no. 2 (2005): 438–48.

Smitshuijzen-Abifares, Huda. *Arabic Typography: A Comprehensive Sourcebook*. London: Saqi, 2001.

Somekh, Sasson. "Biblical Echoes in Modern Arabic Literature." *Journal of Arabic Literature* 26, no. 1/2 (1995): 186–200.

Stoler, Ann Laura, Carole Mc Granahan, and Peter C. Perdue, eds. *Imperial Formations*. Santa Fe: School for Advanced Research Press, 2007.

Strauss, Johann. "Who Read What in the Ottoman Empire (19th–20th Centuries)?" *Middle Eastern Literatures* 6, no. 1 (2003): 39–76.

Sutherland, John A. "Publishing History: A Hole at the Center of Literary Sociology." *Critical Inquiry* 14 (Spring 1988): 574–89.

Tadrus, Fawzi M. *Printing in the Arab World with Emphasis on the Būlāq Press in Egypt*. Doha: University of Qatar, 1982.

Tamari, Ittai Joseph. "Jewish Printing and Publishing Activities in the Ottoman Cities of Constantinople and Saloniki at the Dawn of Early Modern Europe." In Kreiser, *The Beginnings of Printing*, 9–10.

al-Ṭanāḥī, Maḥmūd M. *Al-kitāb al-maṭbūʿ bi-misr fī al-qarn al-tāsiʿ ʿashir: tārīkh wa taḥlīl*. Cairo: Dār al-Hilāl, 1996.

Tarrāzī, Fīlīb dī (Philippe de Tarrazi). *Tārīkh al-ṣiḥāfa al-ʿarabiyya*. 4 vols. 2nd ed. Beirut: al-Maṭbaʿa al-Adabiyya, 1914.

Tejirian, Eleanor, and Reeva Simon, eds. *Altruism and Imperialism: Western Cultural and Religious Missions in the Middle East*. New York: Columbia University Press, 2002.

———. *Conflict, Conquest, and Conversion: Two Thousand Years of Christian Missions in the Middle East*. New York: Columbia University Press, 2012.

Thompson, John A. *The Major Arabic Bibles: Their Origin and Nature*. New York: American Bible Society, 1956.

Tibawi, A.L. "The American Missionaries in Beirut and Buṭrus al-Bustānī." *St. Anthony's Papers* 16. *Middle Eastern Affairs* 3 (1963): 137–82.

———. *American Interests in Syria 1800–1901: A Study of Educational, Literary and Religious Work*. Oxford: Oxford University Press, 1966.

———. "The Genesis and Early History of the Syrian Protestant College." In *American University of Beirut*

*Festival Book*, edited by Fouad Sarruf and Suha Tamim, 257–94. Beirut: American University of Beirut, 1967.

Traboulsi, Fawwaz. *A History of Modern Lebanon*. London: Pluto Press, 2007.

Verdeil, Chantal. "Between Rome and France, intransigent and anti-Protestant Jesuits in the Orient: The beginning of the Jesuits' mission of Syria, 1831–1864." In *Christian Witness between Continuity and New Beginnings*, edited by Martine Tamcke and Michael Marten, 23–32. Berlin: LIT Verlag, 2006.

Verdery, Richard N. "The Publications of the Būlāq Press under Muḥammad ʿAlī." *Journal of the American Oriental Society* 91, no. 1 (1971): 129–32.

Vernoit, Stephen. *Occidentalism: Islamic Art in the Nineteenth Century*. London: Nour Foundation in association with Azimuth Editions and Oxford University, 1997.

Walbiner, Carsten. "Monastic Reading and Learning in 18th-Century Bilād Al-Šām: Some Evidence from the Monastery of Al-Šuwayr." *Arabica* 51, no. 4 (2004): 462–77.

———."Ktobō d-mazmūrē d-Dawīd malkō wa-nbīyō." In Kreiser, *The Beginnings of Printing*, 22–23.

Watenpaugh, Keith David. *Being Modern in the Middle East: Revolution, Nationalism, Colonialism, and the Arab Middle Class*. Princeton: Princeton University Press, 2006.

Watson, William J. "İbrahim Müteferriḳa and Turkish Incunabula." *Journal of the American Oriental Society* 88, no. 3 (1968): 435–41.

Weismann, Itzchak. *Taste of Modernity: Sufism, Salafiyya, and Arabism in Late Ottoman Damascus*. Leiden: Brill, 2001.

Wilson, M. Brett. *Translating the Qur'an in an Age of Nationalism: Print Culture and Modern Islam in Turkey*. London: Institute of Ismaili Studies, 2014.

Zachs, Fruma. "Mīkhaʾīl Mishāqa: The First Historian of Modern Syria." *British Journal of Middle Eastern Studies* 28, no. 1 (2001): 67–87.

———. "From the Mission to the Missionary: The Bliss Family and the Syrian Protestant College (1866–1920)." *Die Welt Des Islams* 45, no. 2 (2001): 145–73.

———. "Toward a Proto-Nationalist Concept of Syria? Revisiting the American Presbyterian Missionaries in the Nineteenth-Century Levant." *Die Welt des Islams* 41, no. 2 (2001): 145–73.

———. *The Making of a Syrian Identity: Intellectuals and Merchants in Nineteenth Century Beirut*. Leiden: Brill, 2005.

Zachs, Fruma, and Sharon Halevi. "Asma (1873): The Early Arabic Novel as a Social Compass." *Studies in the Novel* 39, no. 4 (2007): 416–30.

———. "From difāʿ al-nisāʾ to masʾalat al-nisāʾ in Greater Syria: Readers and Writers Debate Women and their Rights, 1858–1900." *International Journal of Middle East Studies* 41, no. 4 (2009): 615–33.

Zaka, Samy F. "Education and Civilization in the Third Republic: The University Saint-Joseph, 1875–1914." PhD diss., University of Notre Dame, 2006.

Zeuge-Buberl, Uta. "Misinterpretations of a Missionary Policy? The American Syria Mission's Conflict with Buṭrus al-Bustānī and Yuḥannā Wurtabāt." *Theological Review* 36 (2015): 23–43.

Zoss, Emily. "An Ottoman View of the World: The *Kitab Cihannūma* and Its Cartographic Contexts." In Gruber, *Islamic Manuscript Tradition*, 195–219.

# Index

*Italicized page numbers refer to figures*


ʿAbay (Mount Lebanon) 24, 31, 37, 90
Abbott, Peter 60
ʿAbdul-Azīz (sultan) 127–28
ʿAbdul Ḥamīd II (sultan) 26
ʿAbidīn, Mirza Zayn al- 110
Abkariyyūs, Iskandar 97, 120
*ahl al-dhimma* 19
*ahl al-kitāb* 19, 19n14
Aleppo (city) 21, 29, 64n4, 77n66, 123
Alexandria (city) 1, 33n100, 132
ʿAli, Muhammad (viceroy) 23, 28
American Arabic (typeface)
  characteristics of 69–73, *72*, 113–14
  popularity of 92–93, 99, 101, 111–12, 129, 131
  problems with 114–15, *115* (*see also* Watts typeface, Richard)
  production of 61n92, 62n93, 69, 71, 74 (*see also* Tauchnitz type foundry, Karl)
  regional presses, use at 9, 117–22
American-Arab relations (modern) 16
American Bible Society (ABS) 34, 89n130, 92, 113
American Board of Commissioners for Foreign Missions (ABCFM)
  establishment of 15–16, 18–19
  funding, policies on 19, 34, 73, 85, 94n13, 96, 112
  press activity, policies on 17, 86–88, 90, 93–95, 98 (*see also* Anderson, Rufus)
  presses 2, 24, 68, 110 (*see also specific presses*)
  proselytizing, views on 63, 67, 81, 87
  Prudential Committee 85, 89, 92
  publications 59n69, 67 (*see also* publications, American Press)
  stations (or missions)
    Beirut station (*see* Syria Mission, American)
    Izmir station 68, 70–71
    Malta station 69, 85
    Mosul station 89n131, 112
    Sri Lanka (Ceylon) station 85
    *See also specific missions*
American civil war 24n44, 94n13
American imperialism 14
American Press (Beirut)
  book binding at 51–52, 85–86, 119, 122
  catalogs 112
  Catholic presses, competition with 77–81 (*see also* Franciscan press; Jesuit press)
  conventions, visual 17, 55, 64, 66–69, 71, 75, 91–93, 101–3, 121, 129–30 (*see also specific conventions*)
  employees 29–38, 49, 63, 75, 85, 94, 97, 101–2, 113–14 (*see also individual employees*)
  equipment 29–30, 79, 92, 110–11
  evangelical message 37, 57–59, 88
  output 85–87, 92
  policies, changes in 81, 84–86, 90, 94–99 (*see also under* Anderson, Rufus)
  publications (*see* publications, American Press)
  sales, book 37n13, 73, 74n50, 89–90
  scribal economy and 34–38, 55, 63 (*see also under* Arabic printing)
  secular publishing at 34, 87, 92–93, 96, 99, 115, 122–25 (*see also* job works, American Press)
  significance, regional 18–19, 24, 91, 99
  Syria Mission, extension of 2–3, 5
  typefaces used (*see* American Arabic; Watts typeface, Richard)
American Tract Society (ATS) 33n104, 34, 58, 64n3, 73
American University of Beirut (AUB) 2, 126n144
  *See also* Syrian Protestant College
Anderson, Rufus
  ABCFM missions, views on 81, 84–85, 89, 90, 94–95
  Arabic language, views on 75n56
  Arabic printing, views on 73
  Armenian mission, views on 68n21
  Bustānī, correspondence with al- 125
  *See also* American Board of Commissioners for Foreign Missions
Antonius, George 3
Arab heritage 5, 122–24, 128, 131–32
  *See also* Arab identity; nationalism; Syrian identity
Arabic language
  *al-fuṣḥa* 28, 34
  knowledge of, missionary 32, 58, 75, 75n56, 123
  national identity and 128 (*see also* Arab heritage; Arab identity; nationalism)
  printing, problems with 112–13 (*see also* Arabic printing)
Arabic printing
  colophons in 9, 49, 51 (*see also under* manuscripts)
  commodification of 46
  conventions of 2, 10, 25, 38–39, 101–2, 107–8 (*see also individual conventions*)
  delay of 25–27
  European, views on 17, 20, 26, 30, 81, 87, 111
  footnotes and marginal glosses in 107–8, 110, 115, 117, 131
  impact of (*see under* Arab press)
  limitations of 69–70, 110–14
  monastic communities and 25 (*see also specific presses*)
  pagination in 49–52, 64, 75, 100, 117
  readership and (*see* Ottoman readership)
  scribal practices and 4–6, 8, 10–12, 25, 35–36, 45, 52–55, 64, 100–101, 110, 115–17 (*see also* manuscripts)
  studies on 4, 6–9, 11–12, 25–26, 43–44
  title pages in 9, 45–47, 49, 51, 103
  vocalization marks in 27, 71, 113 (*see also* vocalization marks)
  Western conventions in 35, 47, 49, 52, 55–56, 103, 108, 129 (*see also specific conventions*)
Arab identity 127–29
  *See also* Arab heritage; nationalism; Syrian identity
Arab intellectuals 1–2, 132
  print culture and 2n3, 5, 17, 31, 29, 34–35, 92–93, 129
  *See also names of individuals*

Arab-Israeli conflict 4
Arab press, the
  publishing industry of (*see specific presses*)
  readership (*see* Ottoman readership)
  "revolution" of, technological 4n12, 5
  social impact of 3, 5–6, 7, 10–11
  studies on 1, 3–4, 6–9, 111
  *See also* Arabic printing
archives, missionary 2, 15
Armenian Orthodox communities 19, 21, 24, 28, 30
Armenian printing 24, 28, 68
Asīr (al-Husaynī), Yūsuf al- 31, 89, 119n107, 127
ʿAynṭūra (Mount Lebanon) 21
ʿAyn Warqa, seminary in 31
Azhar, al- 31, 89

Badger, George 62, 70, 73–74
Bagdadi, Nadia al- 5
Barthes, Roland 107–8
*basmala*
  Christian 42, 55, 64, 123
  Islamic 39–40, 124
  *tughrā*ʾ 115, 117–19, 121
Beirut (city)
  Arabic publishing in 1, 5, 16–17, 103, 111n72, 114, 121, 131–32 (*see also specific presses*)
  Arab intellectuals in 37, 92, 102, 119, 129 (*see also names of individuals*)
  battles in 61, 63, 67 (*see also* Ottoman wars)
  merchant city of 1, 23, 90
  migrations to 31
  missionary presence in (*see specific missions*)
Benjamin, Walter 12
Bey, Osman Zeki 26
Bible, Arabic (European) 21, 59–60, 78, 80
Bible, Arabic (Protestant American)
  conventions of 51, 95, 131–32
  funding for 92
  significance of 73n41, 94
  translation of 31–32, 65, 86, 89, 97
  vocalization marks in 113–14
*bīblīshiyyūn* 60, 75
*bidʿa* 26
*Bilād al-Shām* 23
Bird, Isaac 18, 58n62, 60, 65n6, 71n33, 77n61, 97n38, 137
Bītrū, ʿĪsā 42, 57n57
Black, James 126n144
book binding 2, 10, 12, 45, 52
book production
  *See* Arabic printing; manuscripts
book studies 6–10
Bou Ali, Nadia 126, 128
British and Foreign Bible Society (BFBS) 32, 36, 58–60
British missions 18
  *See also* Church Missionary Society
Būlāq press (Cairo) 1, 28–29, 38, 54nn47–48
Bunyan, John 66, 85–86
Bustānī, Buṭrus al-
  conversion (to Protestantism) 31, 124
  *Dīwān* (al-Mutanabbī) 115–18, *116*, *119*, 123
  interpreter, work as 31, 125–26
  *Khuṭba fī ādāb* (on Arab customs) 99–100, 127, *103–4*
  *Kitāb dalīl al-ṣawāb* (arithmetic) 32–33
  *Kitāb misbāḥ* (grammar) 101, *102*, 114, *115*, 124
  Maṭbaʿat al-Maʿārif 117
  missionaries, relation with 125–27
  *Nafīr sūriyya* (Clarion of Syria) 126, 128
  ordainment of 31, 125
  political views of 123, 126–29, 132
  publications by 2, 5, 30, 34, 73n45, 87, 92–93, 96–99 (*see also* publications, American Press)
  *Qiṣṣat asʿad* (Asʿad al-Shidyāq) 97–98, 100, 125
  Syria Mission, employment with 32, 34, 112
  Syrian Society, chair of 123
Busṭrus, Salīm 97, 98n44

Cairo (city)
  Azhar, al- 89
  book production in 28–29, 33n100, 132
  missions in 77n66
  presses in 1, 29, 54n48, 55, 107, 111, 116
  *See also* Būlāq press (Cairo)
calligraphy, Arabic
  conventions of 12, 26–28, 69, 73, 80n86, 81, 110
  practices, regional 61, 75
  printing and 41–42, 52, 55, 64, 114 (see also *tughrā*ʾ)
  scripts 40, 69–70
Carruthers, Jo 66–67
catechisms 25, 80, 81n89, 86n107, 90
  *See also* Watt, Isaac
Catholicism 19, 65, 78, 80 (*see also specific communities and missions*)
Catholic missions
  competition amongst 16, 19, 77
  Ottoman Empire, in the 20, 79
  *See also specific missions*
Chartier, Roger 8
Christian communities
  *See specific communities*
Chrysostom, John, Homilies (Arabic) 42, *45*, 59
Church Missionary Society (CMS) 18
  publications 36 (*see also* CMS press)
  proselytizing practices 56
Çinar, Alev 13, 13n65
"clash of civilizations" 16
CMS press (Malta)
  conventions 9n38, 32n95, 34n46, 38, 55–56
  employees 74
  publications 24, 36, 46, *56*, 57–58, 65n6, 97n35, 97n38, 124
  typeface 69n26
codicology 12
colonial presses 4, 8
Constantinople (city)
  *See* Istanbul (city)
Coptic communities (Egypt) 77
Couvent Saint-Sauveur (Sidon) 40
Cox, Jeffrey 15, 15n78
Cuche, Philippe 81
cultural imperialism 14–15

Dabbās III, Athanasius al- (patriarch) 29
Dagher, Charbel 20
Damascus (city) 20–23, 77, 89, 95
Dār al-Ṭibāʿa (Cairo) 107, 116–18
Dayr al-Qamar (Mount Lebanon) 75
Deeb, Lara 13n60
Defoe, Daniel 27n35
Dirlik, Arif 14
Dominican mission (Mosul) 112
Drucker, Johanna 9–10

Druze communities
 Maronites, conflicts with 20, 77, 95
 Ottoman Syria, residing in 20, 21, 67–68, 75
 Protestantism, conversions to 61
Dunch, Ryan 14n74
Dyrness, William 66

Eddy, William 95n20
Eisenstein, Elizabeth 7–8, 46n34
electrotyping, Arabic 92, 97n42, 112n81, 113–14
English (British) identity 66–67
English language
 instruction (at mission schools) 85
 translations 32–33, 62, 97n8
ephemera 42–43, 49, 99, 116
Eurocentrism 6, 12
European printing
 examples of 26–28
 incunabula 39, 49
 presses 1, 30, 46–47, 81
 studies on 6–7, 26

Farḥāt, Jirmānūs (patriarch) 114, 123–24
finis 51
firmans, Ottoman 60, 78, 96
Fisk, Pliny 18
fleurons (in print) 38, 103, 121
Flood, Finbarr 10
footnotes 108, 115 (*see also* marginal glosses)
Franciscan mission (Jerusalem) 77
 press *23*, 29, 81, 107
French Revolution 87, 132

Gacek, Adam 38nn17–18, 107n59
Gallaudet, Thomas
 *Child's Book on the Soul* 33
Ghazīr (Mount Lebanon) 78
Ghoṣn, Ḥanna 80–81
Glass, Dagmar 9, 93, 111n72
Goodell, William 18, 59
Graves, Margaret 10–11
Greek Catholic (Melkite) communities
 Ottoman Syria, residing in 19, 21
 Patriarch of 78
 presses of 25, 52, 70 (*see also* Shuwayr, press al-)
 Protestant missionaries and 36, 59, 61
 scholars from 30–31, 57n57, 119
Greek Orthodox communities
 Catholics, views of 78–79
 Ḥāṣbayya, conflicts in 76–77
 Ottoman Syria, residing in 19, 21
 Patriarch of 29
 presses of 117
 Protestant missionaries and 36, 59–61
 scholars from 30–31, 65, 88, 99, 111, 127
Greek printing 24, 35, 73, 75, 78

Ḥaddād, Tānnūs al-
 Arabic tutor, role as 62
 school in ʿAynṭūra 21
 Syria Mission, employment at 30–31, 32n90, 63
 translations by 33
Hallock, Homan 70–71, 74
Hanna, Nelly 28
Ḥāṣbayya (Mount Lebanon) 76–77
hegemony 23, 95
Hirschler, Konrad 35n4, 117n102
Hitti, Philip 3
Homes, Henry 43n28
Hourani, Albert 3
Howsam, Leslie 6
Hurter, George 69, 73–75

Ibrāhīm Pasha 23
*imtiyāzāt* 77
Incunabula 39, 46, 49, 108n61
Issa, Rana 113n91, 128n156
Istanbul (city)
 ABCFM mission in 68, 70
 Greek Orthodox church in 19
 Jesuits in 77n66
 presses in 11, 28, 54
Izmir (city) 24n42, 62n93, 69n24, 71n35, 74, 77n66
Izmir press (ABCFM) 24, 68, 70–71

Jerusalem
 missions in 18–19, 20, 33, 70, 77
 presses in 29, 81
Jessup, Henry 89, 112, 113, 124n136
Jesuit mission (Beirut)
 Ottoman region presence in 21n29, 77–78
 press (*see* Jesuit press)
 Protestants, competition with 79
 schools 21
Jesuit press (Beirut)
 employees of 33n100, 121
 establishment of 29
 Protestants, competition with 79–81
 publications 79–81, *82*, *84*, 90, 103, 107
 typefaces of 112, 114–15
Jewish communities
 missions to 18–19, 33, 64n4
 Mount Lebanon, residing in 1, 21
 presses of 28, 35, 70
*jizya* 19, 77n60
job works, American Press 92, 96–101, 122, 127n145, 129, 135–38
Johns, Adrian 8
Johnson, John 47–49, *48*

Karāmī, Buṭrus *39*, 119, *120–21*
*karshūnī* 29
Kempis, Thomas à 79–80
Kfarshīmā (Mount Lebanon) 31
Khalaf, Samir 14n69, 111n73
Khalīl, al-Ashraf (sultan) 119
Khayyāṭ, Antūniyyū al-
 employment of 30, 62–63
 translations by 33–34
Khūrī, Bishāra al- 88n126
Khūrī, Khalīl al- 111–12, 117–18
"Kingdom of Christ" 88
King, Jonas 18, 65, 137

Laurie, Thomas 33n99
*lawḥa* 41
Lazarist mission 77
Lebanon (present-day) 2, 13, 14n69, 131–32
 *See also* Mount Lebanon; Ottoman Syria
letterpress printing
 presses and publications 80n82, 81, 102–3, 107 (*see also specific presses*)
 studies on 12
 techniques of 26, 30, 51, 55, 79, 109–10
 *See also* Arabic printing
lexigraphy 131
lithography
 presses and publications 30, 79, 80–81, 107–10 (*see also specific presses*)
 studies on 9, 12
 techniques of 55, 110
 *See also* Arabic printing
London Jews Society 33, 64n4

MacKenzie, D.F. 8
Madrasa al-Waṭaniyya, al- 126
Maḥmūd II (sultan) 40–41

Makdisi, Ussama 14–15, 16n79, 125, 128n155
Malta 24, 31, 32, 73, 74
Malta press (ABCFM) 24, 58n69, 69, 71
manuscripts
  colophons in 45–46, 49, 51, 54
  conventions of 12, 38, 42, 49, 52, 54–55, 75, 100–101, 107 (*see also specific conventions*)
  mass-produced 27–28
  printing practices and (*see under* Arabic printing)
  production of 1–2, 4–6, 11, 16, 27–28, 34 (*see also* workshops, manuscript)
  studies on Islamic 10–13
  title pages in 46
  *ʿunwāns* in 38n17, 43, 45, 117
*Maqāmāt al-Ḥarīrī* 107, *108–9*, 109, 116–17, 123 (*see also under specific presses*)
Mār Anṭūniyyūs press (Quzḥāyya) 29
marginal glosses (notes) 107–8, 110–11, 117, 131
Maronite communities
  Druze, conflicts with 20, 77, 95
  Ottoman Syria, residing in 19, 68, 75
  patriarchs of 21, 60, 78, 114, 123
  presses of 60, 80n84
  Protestant missionaries and 21, 23, 36, 59–61, 78
  scholars from 97, 124–25 (*see also names of individuals*)
  schools of 31
  Syria Mission employees from 30, 88n126 (*see also names of individuals*)
Maronite-Druze war (1845)
  *See under* Mount Lebanon; Ottoman wars
Maronite-Druze war (1860)
  *See under* Mount Lebanon; Ottoman wars
Marzolph, Ulrich 9
Maṭbaʿa al-Amrikāniyya, al- (Beirut)
  *See* American Press
Maṭbaʿa al-Sūriyya, al- 117–18
Maṭbaʿa al-Waṭaniyya, al- 120–21
Maṭbaʿat al-Maʿārif 117, 119
McKitterick, David 26, 39, 49
*milal* 19–20, 96n23
Mirza, ʿAbbās 107
Mishāqa, Mikhāʾīl 64–65
missionary studies 12–14
modernity
  aesthetics of 48, 116, 122, 127–31
  Arabic printing and 4, 7, 12
  Arab views on 9, 108, 128
  definitions of 3n8, 5, 12–13
  *See also* modernization reforms, Ottoman
modernization reforms, Ottoman 3, 20, 23, 35–36
  *See also* modernity; Tanzimat
monastic presses (Syria) 25, 29
  *See also specific presses*
Mount Lebanon
  communities of 21, 59, 61, 75 (*see also individual communities*)
  history of 97, 124–25
  missions in (*see specific missions*)
  protectorate of 1, 19–20, 22, 131–32
  ruling dynasties of 19, 21, 31
  silk industry of 23, 78n69
  wars 20, 67–68, 77, 95, 111n75, 131
moveable type 109–10
Mudawwar, Mikhāʾīl al- 117
Mudawwar, Nakhla al- 99
*muqāṭaʿjī* 95
*muṣaḥḥiḥ* 34
Muslim communities
  education and 35–36
  Ottoman Syria, residing in 1, 19–21, 95
  presses of 8, 11, 15, 25–26, 28, 52, 55, 93, 123, 129 (*see also specific presses*)
  readership of 42, 56, 113, 124n126, 124, 128
  scholars from 29, 31, 89, 119n107, 122–24, 129
  Syria Mission, relations with 18, 30, 61
Mutanabbī, Aḥmad ibn al-Ḥusayn al-
  printed editions of, regional 115–18, *116*, *118–19*, 123
Müteferrika press, İbrahim (Istanbul) 11, 28, 54

*nahḍa, al-*
  Arabic printing and 1–7, 34 (*see also* Arabic printing)
  debates on gender and 5
  dual facets of 3
  modernization and 12–13, 160n128, 131–32 (*see also* modernity)
  nationalism and 4, 7 (*see also* Arab identity; nationalism; Syrian identity)
  publications of 129 (*see also under names of individuals*)
  scholars of 31, 38, 122–23, 130 (*see also names of individuals*)
  studies on 116
Najjār, Ibrāhīm ibn Khalīl al- 102, *107*
Naṣīr al-Dīn Haydar press (Lucknow) 109
*nassākh* 34
nationalism 1–4, 6, 123, 126n140, 126–30
  *See also* Arab heritage; Arab identity; Syrian identity
Near East School of Theology (NEST) 36
Nevins, William 64, 85–86
newspapers 132
  *Ḥadīqat al-akhbār* 111–12, 117–18
Nicolayson, John 33

Ottoman readership 1, 26, 36–37, 44–45, 57, 63, 67, 75, 87, 89–92, 107n58, 124, 128–29, 132
Ottoman Syria
  Egyptian occupation of 23–24, 68, 75n57
  missionary activity in 14, 18, 67, 77n64
  presses in 29 (*see also specific presses*)
  provinces of 1, 20–23, 22, 131
  readership of 36 (*see also* Ottoman readership)
  religious landscape of 75
  resident communities of 2, 19–20, 35, 95 (*see also specific communities*)
  wars (*see under* Mount Lebanon; Ottoman wars)
Ottoman wars 2–3, 23–24, 68, 95–96

Pact of ʿUmar 19–20
Palestine 18–19
pamphlets 16–17, 43n29, 44, 47, 49, 99, 116, 119–21, 126, 132
pan-Arabism 3
Parsons, Levi 18
Persian printing 28–29, 109–10
postcolonial studies 8, 14–15
Presbyterian Historical Society (PHS) 2
“Protestant aesthetic” 17, 65–67, 91, 131
  *See also* publications, American Press

Protestant communities
(Ottoman) 14, 21–22, 77, 95, 126
present-day 131
*See also names of individuals*
Protestantism
conversions to 21, 31, 65, 77, 89, 124 (*see also specific communities*)
ideologies of 16, 34, 66, 126 (*see also under* Syria Mission, American)
literature related to 18, 36, 67, 98 (*see also* publications, American Press)
Syrian communities on, views of 59 (*see also under specific communities*)
publications, American Press (Beirut)
arithmetic 2, 32, 59, 87, 90, 98
catechisms 25n47, 37 (*see also* catechisms)
children's books 18, 33, 37 (*see also individual authors*)
conventions, design (*see individual conventions*)
evangelical literature 33, 57–59 (*see also individual books and authors*)
geography 59, 90
*ʿIlāj mufīd* (on cholera) 42–43, 44n30, 49, *46*, *50*, 87, 122
*Kitāb al-ājurrūmiyya* (Arabic grammar) *72*, 90, 99, 100
*Kitāb al-bāb* (on the soul) *65*, 73n45, *76*, 98n48, 99
*Kitāb al-zabūr al-ilāhī* (Psalter) *51*
*Kitāb siyāḥat* (Pilgrim's Progress) 32n98, 66, 85–86
list of publications 135–38
morality literature 42, 58–59, 79–80 (*see also publications under* Whiting, George)
*Qaṭf maqālāt* (Homilies) 42, *45*, 59, 80
*Qiṣṣat ālām* (Passion of Christ) 73, 89n131
science 2
spelling cards 30, 74, 110
*Waʿẓ al-masīḥ* (Christ's sermon) 57, 59, 59n70, 68n17
wisdom literature 57, 59
*See also under individual authors*
public sphere 3, 35n4, 132

Qajar presses 28–29
publications of 9, 80n86, 108–9
Tabriz, in 55, 107, *109*, 109–11
technology and 30, 110
Tehran, in 109
Qur'an
conventions of 39–40, 73, 113
lithographed editions of 109–10
phrases from 41, 123–24
production, manuscript and printed 25–27, 51n41

Rāqim, Musṭafa 40–41
Reynault, Chevalier 78
Robinson, Edward 74
Roper, Geoffrey
American Arabic typeface, studies on 71n39, 93
CMS press, studies on 46n34, 57n58, 69n26,
printing, studies on Arabic 8, 9n38

Said, Edward 14
Sajdi, Dana 5, 28, 124n124
Salafi movement 20
Sarkīs, Amīn 119, *120–21*
Sarkīs, Ibrāhīm 31, 97
Sarkīs, Khalīl 119, *120–21*
Sarkīs, Shahīn 97n42
*sarlawḥ* (or headpiece)
manuscripts, found in 38–39
printed 42–45, 99–101, 52, 54–55, 71, 107, 117, 121
Sayyid, Jihān al- 9
Scheid, Kirsten 13
sectarianism 75, 95, 126
secular thought 1, 3–4, 13, 17, 67, 127–28, 132
Selīm III (sultan) 28
seminaries 1, 25, 36, 39–41, 51n41, 124
Shalfūn, Yūsuf 119–20
Shaykhū, Lūwīs 80nn81–82, 80n112, 112
Shidyāq, Asʿad al- 21, 97–98, 125
Shidyāq, Fāris al- 8, 31, 57n56
Shidyāq, Tannūs al- 97–98, 124–25
Shihāb, Bashīr II (emir) 20–21, 31n84, 68n15, 119
Shihābī, Ḥaydar Aḥmad al- (emir) 19–20
Shuwayr press, al- (Khinshāra) 25
conventions of 41, 52, 55
publications of 29, *53*, 55, 90n136
type foundry 115
Sidon (city) 21, 23, 40, 78, 94n14, 95, 131
Smith, Azariah 87n116
Smith, Eli
Arabic, knowledge of 32, 58, 61
Arabic typography, work on 69–70, 71n33, 71n35, 93, 111–14, 117, 131 (*see also* American Arabic)
Bible, work on Arabic 65n7, 86, 94 (*see also* Bible, Arabic)
books, collection of 47n54, 52n45
converts, views on local 77
health of 50n74, 62, 74, 86, 89, 94–95
Muslims, views on 61
Ottoman wars, views on 24n42
Press editor, role as 31, 33, 58, 75, 85, 87–88, 90, 110, 125, 127
publications by *65*, *76*, 98 (*see also* publications, American Press)
radical thought, views on 87
Stanhope press 25–26
Sublime Porte 26, 77, 96n23
*See also* Ottoman Empire
Sulaymān Pasha (viceroy) 23
Syriac language 24, 29, 59n69, 110
Syria Mission, American
book depot 89, 90, 98
Catholic missions, competition with 67, 77–80, 91 (*see also under specific missions*)
dissolution of 24
Druze, views on 61, 75
Ḥāṣbayya, Protestants in 76–77
ideologies of 16, 89, 93, 126
local communities, relations with 15–16, 19, 21–22, 36, 74, 89 (*see also under specific communities*)
missionaries (*see names of individual missionaries*)
morality, views on 42, 58–61
Muslims, views on 18, 61, 113, 129n126 (*see also under* Muslim communities)
Ottoman Syria, establishment in 2, 16, 19, 21, 24, 38
Papacy, criticism of 21, 59n73, 61, 64–65, 79 (see also Mishāqa, Mikhāʾīl; Nevins, William)
policies, changes in 61, 63, 67–68, 81–89, 91, 94 (*see also under* Anderson, Rufus)
press (*see* American Press)
proselytizing practices of 15, 42, 59–63, 78, 91–95, 99
protection, consular 19n12, 21n26, 24, 96n23
publications (*see* publications, American Press; Bible, Arabic)

schools of 84n93, 85, 87, 88, 90n136, 90, 96, 98, 110, 124, 130
seminary of 36n10, 37–38, 84–85, 87–88, 88n126, 90
Syrian Christians, relations with 60, 74, 77, 91 (*see also specific communities*)
Syrian employees, views of 88–89 (*see also under names of individuals*)
transfer (1870) 24n44
university of (*see* American University of Beirut; Syrian Protestant College)
*See also* American Board of Commissioners for Foreign Missions
Syria Mission press
*See* American Press
Syrian identity 2, 6, 93, 126–32
Syrian Protestant College (SPC) 126, 126nn143–44, 130
Syrian Society for the Study of the Sciences and Arts (1847–1852) 97, 117n104
Syrian Society of Knowledge for the Arts and Sciences (1868–1879) 123

Tanzimat (orderings) 3, 95, 127, 131–32
Tauchnitz type foundry, Karl 69, 71, 71n35, 74
Thomson, William 32, 74n50, 136
Thorn, Robert 62, 73–74
Tibawi, A.L.
Bustānī, al-, views on 117, 124nn124–25, 125, 126n137, 126n140
Syria Mission, views on 19–21
translations, Arabic 32–33, 58, 62, 90, 92, 94, 107, 123
Tripoli (city) 21, 77n66, 124n127, 131
*tughrā'*
calligraphy, found in 40–41
print, seen in *41*, 42, 115–22, 128–29
Turkish printing 24, 68
*See also* Müteferrika press, İbrahim
Tūwaynī, Fāris al- 36
typecasting 69, 114–15, 122–23
type foundries (Ottoman) 1, 26, 114, 122–23
typesetting 81, 97, 110, 114
typography, Arabic 9, 12, 26, 111
*See also* American Arabic; Watts typeface, Richard

'ulama' 25–28
*'unwān*
manuscripts, found in 38, 38n18, 45
print, seen in 42–43, 51, 54–55, 100, 115–7, 123
urbanization 1, 3

Van Dyck, Cornelius
Bible, work on Arabic 86n111, 94, 95n16, 97n42, 98, 114n92, 131
employees, views on 89, 127
missionary work of
Press editor, role as 85, 88, 127
publications by 90n139, 123n119
villages, Mount Lebanon
*See specific villages*
visual literacy 9–10
vocalization marks 27, 77, 81, 89, 110, 112–14

Watenpaugh, Keith 3n8
Watt, Isaac 37
Watts typeface, Richard 55, *70*, 69–71, 113, 115
Wells press 30, 30n74
Westernization 3, 3n6
Whiting, George 32–33, 77n61
*Kitāb fī al-imtinā'* (on temperance) *43–44*, *50*, *54*
*Kitāb irshād* (on self-examination) *122*
publications by 42, 49, 52, 59, 119
translations by 86n102, 86n104
Yājizī, criticism of al- 33n99, 88
workshops, manuscript 1, 25, 35–36, 39–40, 101, 110, 124

Yāzijī, Ḥabīb al- 121
Yājizī, Ibrāhīm al- 33n100, 112n80, 121
Yājizī, Nāṣīf al-
*Ba'ḍ mazāmīr* (hymnal) 32, 37, 57
*Kitāb faṣl al-khiṭāb* (Arabic grammar, 1836) 32, 37–40, *39–41*, 42, *47*, 47, 49, 51, 56, 57, *70*
*Kitāb faṣl al-khiṭāb* (Arabic grammar, 1854) 64, *66*
*Kitāb majma' al-baḥrayn* (Maqāmāt) 96–99, *100*, 101, 107–8, 115–16, 122–23
*Majmū' al-adab* (anthology) 32, 88, 123n120
*Nabdha* (poems) 99, *101*, *105*, 119n107, 123n120
political views of 125, 128
publications by 2, 5, 14, 30, 38, 88, 90n136, 92–93, 96, 98–99, 107, 124, 129, 132 (*see also specific publications*)
Syria Mission, employment with 30–34, 62–63, 87–89, 96, 125, 127–28
translation, Arabic Bible (*see also* Bible, Arabic)
Yājizī, Warda al- 33n100, 121